MARRIAGE AND DEATH NOTICES
FROM THE SOUTHERN PATRIOT, 1815-1830
Volume 1

Compiled by

Teresa E. Wilson

&

Janice L. Grimes

Southern Historical Press, Inc.
Greenville, South Carolina

Please direct all correspondence and orders to:

www.southernhistoricalpress.com
or
SOUTHERN HISTORICAL PRESS, Inc.
PO BOX 1267
Greenville, SC   29601
southernhistoricalpress@gmail.com

ISBN #0-89308-279-1

Printed in the United States of America

DEDICATED WITH LOVE TO

Harry and Nancy Wilson and Family
Perry and Virginia Lee and Family
Michael E. Grimes

INTRODUCTION

The Southern Patriot began publication in Charleston, South Carolina in 1815 and was published through 1848. This book consists of the marriage and death notices as they are found in this newspaper. Although the Southern Patriot was published in Charleston the marriage and death notices are not limited to this area, but encompass the entire United States as it was during that time period.

This volume will be an extremely useful genealogical reference not only for South Carolina but for the entire United States east of the Mississippi. The obituaries and marriage notices of this newspaper are given in great detail, often including dates of birth, parents and family names, as well as places of residence. Due to the extreme length of some of these notices we have extracted the vital information from the citations and ended the notices with "Eulogy". For those wanting the entire eulogy, the Southern Patriot may be found at the Charleston Library Society, Charleston, S.C., the South Caroliniana Library, Columbia, S.C. and other various libraries.

Our special thanks go to Laura Ann Wingo, B.S.N. and Mary A. Wilson for their typing expertise. We appreciate their many hours of hard work on this project. We would also like to thank Richard N. Cote for his advice, and acknowledge the Charleston Library Society and the South Caroliniana Library.

Theresa E. Wilson
Janice Lee Grimes
Charleston, S.C.
February 12, 1982

Issue of January 4, 1815

Married on the 29th ult., by the Rev. Christopher Gadsden, William Trescor, Esq. to Miss Caroline, daughter of Abraham Markley, Esq., all of this city.

Issue of January 6, 1815

Died - The friends and acquaintances of Robert Dewar, deceased, and the members of the Episcopal Clergy, Protestant Episcopal, Bible, Charleston Library, and Philosophical Societies are invited to attend his funeral, this afternoon, at 3 o'clock.

Departed this life on the 9th inst. at Newark in Delaware, William Henry Cosden, the youngest son of Jeremiah Cosden, Esq. of Elkton, in the 19th year of his age...(Eulogy)

Issue of January 10, 1815

Died on Friday last, at his plantation, Stono, in the 47th year of his age, Col. Joseph Fickling - His patriotism and private worth endeared him to his country and his friends - and he has left behind him the memory of his virtues.

Issue of January 19, 1815

Married last evening by Mr. Alexander Solomons, Mr. Elias Abrahams to Miss Catharine Cohen, both of this city.

Died on the 10th of January, in the 76th year of her age, Mrs. Rebecca Motte...(Eulogy)

Issue of February 11, 1815

Married on Tuesday evening last, by Rev. Dr. Hollenshead, Whitemarsh B. Seabrook, Esq. of Edisto Island, to Miss Margaret W. Hamilton, daughter of Paul Hamilton, Esq. late Secretary of the Navy.

Issue of February 18, 1815

Married on Thursday evening, by the Rev. Mr. Gadsden, Major Alexander Sevier, of the United States Marine Corps, to Miss Jane Bacot, daughter of Thomas W. Bacot, Esq. of this city.

Issue of March 1, 1815

Departed this life on the 19th instant, Mr. Zackariah Villepontoux, in the 25th year of his age. He was a dutiful son, a kind master and an affectionate friend.

Issue of March 8, 1815

Died, yesterday morning, between 9 and 10 o'clock, after a very few days illness, Robert Fulton, Esq. Mr. F. was aged about 42 years...(Eulogy)

Issue of March 13, 1815

Died - The friends and acquaintances of Mr. William Boyd, and particularly the members of the St. Andrews and Library Societies, are requested to attend his funeral this afternoon at 4 o'clock, from his residence East Bay.

Issue of March 14, 1815

Died, March 5th, 1815, at his residence on Black Swamp, South Carolina, in the sixty-second year of his age, Mr. Joseph Lawton...(Eulogy)

Issue of March 17, 1815

Died on the 9th inst., at Centre Hall, the seat of his uncle, Gov.

William, J.E. M'Iver, Esq. private Sec'ry to the Gov. in the 26th year of his age...(Eulogy)

Issue of March 20, 1815

Died - ...Mr. John E. M'Iver...(Eulogy)

Issue of March 24, 1815

Died - The friends and acquaintances, of the late Mr. Thomas Doughty, also, the members of the South Carolina Society and Bible Society, are invited to attend his funeral from his late residence No. 22 Anson Street, at 11 o'clock tomorrow morning, without further invitation.

Issue of April 1, 1815

Departed this life on the 26th inst. at his plantation, in St. Bartholomews Parish, Jacob H. Allison, Esq. in the 42nd year of his age...(Eulogy)

Issue of April 8, 1815

Died in September last, at Constantinople, of the plague, Solomon Lipman Begember, supposed to be one of the most wealthy Jews in the Turkish dominions...(Eulogy)

Issue of April 15, 1815

Died, recently, in Pennsylvania, Mr. Conrad Hawk, aged 97...(Eulogy)
Died near Moscow, M. Baleschoff, aged 113...(Eulogy)

Issue of April 19, 1815

Died - Amongst the last news from Philadelphia, we notice the death of Mr. Gerry, Vice-President of the United States of America...
Died - On the 5th instant, Richard Soderstrom, Esq. his Swedish Majesty's Consul General to the United States of America, aged 72, after 32 years residence in this country. His remains were intered in the burial ground of the Swedish church in this city, on the 7th inst.

Issue of April 20, 1815

Died suddenly on the 1st inst, Mr. John Lequeux, in the 42nd year of his age. He has left an affectionate wife, two children, and two brothers and a sister, to lament a loss, to them so irreparable.

Issue of April 29, 1815

Married on Tuesday evening last, by the Rev. Dr. Furman, John Campbell Smith, Esq. to Miss Catherine P. Moles of this city.
Died, yesterday morning, at 6 o'clock of a gradual decay, the lovely, and much lamented Lady Liberty, in the 39th year of her age...(Eulogy)

Issue of May 1, 1815

Died - The friends and acquaintances of Mr. Thomas Lynch, Bricklayer deceased, are invited to attend his funeral at 9 o'clock tomorrow morning, from his house, West Street.

Issue of May 6, 1815

Died - The friends and acquaintances of Messrs. Lewis and Augustus de Villers and Clementine de Villers, are requested to attend the funeral of Mr. Augustus de Villers, this afternoon, at half after 4 o'clock, from Broad Street, one door from King Street - without further notice.

Issue of May 8, 1815

Died - The friends and acquaintances of Doctor David Ramsey, are invited to attend his funeral tomorrow morning, at ten o'clock, from his late residence on Broad Street.

Issue of May 15, 1815

Died - The friends and acquaintances of Mr. and Mrs. Vieusse and Mr. Tastet, are invited to attend the funeral of Mr. Benoit Vieusse, from his late residence No. 317 King Street tomorrow morning at 8 o'clock.

Issue of May 20, 1815

Died, at Providence, R. I. on the 8th inst. in the 76th year of his age, the Hon. Jabez, L.L.D., Chancellor of Brown University in that state.

Issue of May 22, 1815

Died - The friends and acquaintances of Mr. and Mrs. William Pritchard, Jun. are invited to attend the funeral of Mrs. Pritchard, without further invitation, from her late residence, No. 2 Anson Street, this afternoon, at half past 4 o'clock.

Issue of May 24, 1815

Died - A man named William Fiddler, by trade a hatter, dropped down dead this morning on Elliot Street.

Issue of May 31, 1815

Married, on Wednesday, the 17th inst. by the Rev. Mr. Roberts, John Waties, Esq. Attorney at Law, to Miss Henrietta Bonneau Glover, daughter of the late Moses Glover, Esq. of Charleston.

Married, last evening by the Rev. Dr. Hollinshead, W. B. Tucker, Esq. to Miss Jane B. Tew, both of this city.

Issue of June 7, 1815

Died, on this 19th ult. at Pineville, in St. Stephen's Parish, where she had gone on a visit, Mrs. Sarah Darrell, widow of the late Colonel Edward Darrell of this city, in the 46th year of her age...(Eulogy)

Issue of June 12, 1815

Died - Daniel Dewey, Esq. is no more. He died at his seat in Williamstown, Berkshire County, (Ms.) on Friday morning, 26th ult. aged 48 years... (Eulogy)

Issue of July 6, 1815

Died, at Salem, (Mass.) on Friday evening June 17, Captain George Crowninshield, aged 81...(Eulogy)

Issue of July 8, 1815

Died - It is with much regret we mention, that Capt. Hall, of the ship America, from Savannah, died yesterday morning, at the quarantine hospital, Staton Island.

Married on the 4th instant, by the Rev. Dr. Buchan, Alexander Mathison, Esq. merchant, to Miss Eliza Pratt, daughter of Capt. John Pratt, of this city.

Issue of July 20, 1815

Married at New York, on the 12th inst. in Grace Church, by the Rev. Dr. Bowen, John Wells, Esq. to Miss Sabina Elliott Huger, daughter of the late Daniel Huger, Esq. of Charleston, S.C.

Issue of July 28, 1815

Departed this life, on Friday, the 14th inst. after a long and painful illness, which she bore with exemplary fortitude, Mrs. Susannah Smyth, wife of Mr. John Smyth, of this city, in the 72nd year of her age...

Issue of August 4, 1815

Died - An interesting child, Miss Ann Atkins, about 10 years of age, was unfortunately drowned last evening, while bathing, at Sullivan's Island. Her body was found this morning.

Issue of August 15, 1815

Died - Mr. Bayard is Dead! This illustrious man, fell victim to disease on the evening of the 7th inst...(Eulogy)

Died, at Philadelphia, on the 6th inst. John Smith, Esq. Post Captain in the U. S. Navy.

Issue of August 16, 1815

Died - The friends and acquaintances of Mr. James Grady, are invited to attend his funeral, from his late residence No. 57 Church Street, tomorrow morning at 6 o'clock.

Issue of August 18, 1815

Died - The friends and acquaintances of Captain Joseph Quiney, are invited to attend the funeral of his daughter, this afternoon at 4 o'clock from his residence, No. 6 Pickney Street, without further invitation.

Issue of August 22, 1815

Died, on the 26th ult. Capt. Francis Peart, of Woodford County, Kentucky...(Eulogy)

Died - The friends and acquaintances of Mr. and Mrs. Archibald S. Ball, are invited to attend the funeral of Mr. Archibald S. Ball, from his late residence corner of Montagu and Coming Streets, tomorrow morning at 7 o'clock.

Issue of September 4, 1815

Died on Saturday the 2nd inst. in the 56th year of his age, Thomas Pickney, Jun. Esq. after a short but severe illness, which he bore with the patience becoming a Christian.

Issue of September 11, 1815

Died - With deep regret, we record the death of John C. Gardner, Esq. late Merchant of this city; occasioned by his accidentally falling overboard, from a Packet Sloop, on his passage from New York to Newport. Every attempt to save this unfortunate gentleman proved abortive, and he was buried in a watery grave. Mr. G. was aged 32 years - a native of Newport, (R. I.) but a resident of this city for upwards of 12 years...

Issue of September 13, 1815

Departed this transitory life on the morning of the 10th inst. Benjamin David Harvey Thomson, adopted son of Capt. James and Mary C. Thomson, after a distressing illness of six weeks, aged 8 months and 14 days...

Issue of September 15, 1815

Died at St. James Santee, on Friday the 9th inst. after a lingering illness, Mrs. Esther Gaillard, wife of Capt. William Gaillard in the 29th year of her age...(Eulogy)

Issue of September 16, 1815

Died in Savannah on the 12th inst. Mr. Samuel M'Millan, in the 21st
year of his age, after an illness of nine days...(Eulogy)

Issue of September 18, 1815

Departed this life, on the 6th inst. at Smithville, N. C. after a long
but painful illness, which he bore with resignation to the will of his divine
Master, the Rev. Joseph Warren, rector of St. Thomas' Parish, in this
state, in the 50th year of his age; a man eminent for his piety and charity.

Issue of September 20, 1815

Died - The friends and acquaintances of Mr. George Reiley are respectfully invited to attend his funeral this afternoon at 4 o'clock, from his
late residence No. 18, Queen Street.

Issue of September 29, 1815

Died, on the 12th inst, in St. Paul's Parish, in the 65th year of her
age, Mrs. Sarah Bennett, relict of the late Capt. Peter Bennett.

Issue of September 30, 1815

Died, at Pass Christian, New Orleans, on the 8th, August, Major William
Butler, of the 3rd Regiment United States Infantry.

Issue of October 7, 1815

Married on the 28th ult. at Philadelphia, Dr. Abraham DeLeon of Charleston, (S.C.) to Miss Isabel Nones, daughter of Benjamin Nones, Esq. of
Philadelphia.

Issue of October 13, 1815

Died - ...Capt. John J. Goodwyn...He died on the 3rd instant, in the
26th year of his age...(Eulogy)

Issue of October 17, 1815

Died, at Wilmington, (N.C.) on the 6th inst. William S. Hasell, Esq.
Editor and Proprietor of the Wilmington Gazette; aged 35 years.

Issue of October 19, 1815

Married, yesterday, the 18th inst. by the Rev. Mr. Alexander Solomons,
Mr. Hart Solomons to Miss Rebecca Cohen, daughter of Mr. Abraham Cohen,
Merchant, deceased, both of this city.

Issue of October 24, 1815

Departed this life, on the 19th inst. Christopher Green, Jun. Esq. of
Warwick, R. I. aged 30 years...(Eulogy)

Issue of October 29, 1815

Died on the 6th inst. in Edgefield District, Benjamin Busby, a native
of Maryland, aged 116 years; he resided in this state 70 years, was perfectly
healthy until a few days before his death.

Died, a N. York, on Wednesday morning last, 18th inst. after a lingering illness, Maj. Thomas Chrystie of the U. S. Army. He was the brother
of the late gallant Col. John Chrystie of the 23rd infantry; both sons of
Col. John Chrystie, a revolutionary officer of Pennsylvania.

Issue of November 6, 1815

Died - The friends and acquaintances of Mr. John Owen, and the members

of the Charleston Library Society, particularly, are invited to attend his
funeral tomorrow morning, at half past 8 o'clock, from his late residence,
No. 25, Tradd Street.

Issue of November 7, 1815

Married, on Wednesday last, by Mr. A. Alexander, Sen., Mr. Solomon
Moses, Jun. to Miss Isabel LaMyers, daughter of the late Samuel Myers of
this city.

Issue of November 11, 1815

Married, on Thursday evening last, by the Rev. Dr. Leland, Mr. Robert
M'Venning to Miss Eliza Whilden, both of Christ Church Parish.

Issue of November 21, 1815

Departed this life, on the 20th inst. Miss Martha C. Darby, daughter of
Robert A. and Mary S. Darby, aged 3 years, 4 months and 15 days.

Issue of November 22, 1815

Departed this life, on Sunday the 19th inst., aged 68 years, Mrs.
Judith Lyon, consort of Mr. Mordecai Lyon, for many years a respectable
inhabitant of this city...

Issue of November 24, 1815

Died - The friends and acquaintances of Mr. John Cunningham, are invited to attend his funeral at 9 o'clock tomorrow morning, from his late
residence, Mazyckborough.

Issue of November 29, 1815

Died, on Friday last, after a lingering illness, which she bore with
virtuous fortitude, Mrs. Judith Solomons, aged 56 years - relict of the
late Mr. J. Solomons, of this city.

Issue of December 2, 1815

Married, on Wednesday, the 29th ult. by the Rev. Mr. G. Frost, Dr.
James B. Hill, of the U. S. Army, to Miss Maria Elizabeth Wyatt, youngest
daughter of Peter Wyatt, Esq. of this city.

Issue of December 27, 1815

Married, on Thursday evening last, by the Right Rev. Dr. Dehon, Mr.
Benjamin J. Smith, to Miss Sarah Smith, both of this city.
Died, on the 15th inst. in St. John's Parish, Mrs. Joannah Sherbourne,
aged 65 years.
Died at Columbia, on the 17th inst. after a few days illness, Col.
Nathan Huggins, State Senator from the election District of Winyaw.
Died, at New Orleans, the last of October in the 23rd years of his age,
Midshipman George Baker, of the U. States Navy.

Issue of December 28, 1815

Married, on Tuesday evening last, by the Rev. Dr. Brom, Mr. Joseph
Jahan, to Mrs. Marie Panpalon, both of this city.

Issue of January 12, 1816

Married, last evening, by the Rev. Dr. Flinn, Joseph Lloyd, Jun. Esq.
to Miss Harriet Nell, daughter of Jesse Nell, Esq. of this city.

Issue of January 13, 1816

Departed this life, on the 15th Dec. at his seat in St. Matthew's

Parish, Col. Francis Bremar, in the 66th year of his age...(Eulogy)

Issue of January 19, 1816

Died on the 1st instant at his residence in Newberry District, Capt. John Henderson, in the 50th year of his age...

Issue of January 25, 1816

Married, at Mount Pleasant, on Tuesday evening last by the Rev. Dr. Leland, the Rev. John Bachman, to Miss Harriet Martin.

Issue of January 26, 1816

Married, on Tuesday evening last, by the Rev. Dr. Furman, Mr. George Thompson, to Miss Ann Margaret Threadcraft; both of this city.

Died at the Euhaws, on the 21st inst. Mrs. Susan F. Houseal, the amiable consort of Dr. John G. Houseal, after a painful illness of 15 days.

Died, Amelia-Island, on the 6th inst. William Muir, Esq. Merchant of this place, in the 48th year of his age...(Eulogy)

Died, at Amelia-Island, on the 28th ult., John M'Clure, Esq. late of the house of Alexander & John M'Clure, of this city...(Eulogy)

Issue of January 27, 1816

Died, on Thursday evening, in the 85th year of his age, Colonel John Mitchell, for many years a Notary Public and Magistrate of this city.

Issue of January 31, 1816

Died - The friends and acquaintances of the late Catharine Gruber, are respectfully invited to attend her funeral, this afternoon, at 3 o'clock, from No. 73, Wentworth Street.

Died, on Edisto Island, on the 24th December, 1815, Miss Caroline Matilda Whaley, aged 5 years and 8 months, eldest daughter of Mr. J. Whaley.

Issue of February 7, 1816

Died in Havanna, on the 7th ult. Capt. Nathaniel Bingley, in the 40th year of his age; a native of Virginia, but many years a resident of this city...

Issue of February 8, 1816

Died, on the 18th ult. at his father's seat, in Bedford, Virginia, Major John Reid, of the United States Army...

Issue of February 10, 1816

Died - On the 18th Jan. departed this life, at his father's seat, in Bedford, (Va.) Major John Reid...(Eulogy)

Issue of February 14, 1816

Married, on Sunday evening last, by the Right Rev. Dr. Dehon, Josias James DuPre, Esq. merchant, to Miss Julianna Smith, both of this city.

Issue of February 15, 1816

Departed this life, on the morning of the 3rd instant at St. Helena, in this state, Mrs. Sarah Jenkins, wife of Col. John Jenkins, in the 38th year of her age...(Eulogy)

Issue of February 19, 1816

Married, on Wednesday evening last, by Mr. E. de la Motte, Mr. Jacob Cohen, of Georgetown, S. C. to Miss Rachel Lopez, of this city.

Issue of February 21, 1816

Died — The friends and acquaintances of the late Mrs. Sarah Faesch, are requested to attend her funeral, tomorrow afternoon, at 3 o'clock, from her late residence No. 344 King Street.

Issue of February 23, 1816

Died, in Lancaster District, near M'Clenahan Ferry, on the 7th inst., C. H. Jonston, wife of Andrew Jonston, of that district, and daughter of Joseph Lee, deceased.

Issue of March 2, 1816

Married, on Thursday morning, 29th ult. by the Rev. Dr. Hollinshead, the Rev. William States Lee, of St. George's Parish to Miss Mary C. Villepontoux, of this city.

Issue of March 4, 1816

Died — The Members of the Fellowship and South-Carolina Societies, as well as the relatives and acquaintances of Mr. George Dener, deceased, are invited to attend his funeral tomorrow afternoon at 4 o'clock, from his late residence, No.--, George Street opposite the College.

Issue of March 5, 1816

Departed this life on Wednesday the 14th inst. Doctor Daniel Doyley, aged 31 years. He left his native land, South Carolina...

Issue of March 7, 1816

Departed this life, last evening, Mr. John Leigh Waring, of the Theatre. - His friends and acquaintances are requested to attend his funeral tomorrow morning, at 9 o'clock, from his late residence, No. 26 Mazyck Street.

Issue of March 8, 1816

Died on Tuesday evening the 27th inst. at his residence at Greenwich, in the 68th year of his age, the Right Rev. Benjamin Moore, D.D.

Issue of March 11, 1816

Married, on Thursday last, by the Rev. Dr. Palmer, John Cart, Jun. Esq. to Miss Elizabeth C. Guerin.

Issue of March 12, 1816

Died on the 4th inst. at his late residence in St. Mathew's Parish, in the 63rd year of his age, the Rev. Mr. James O'Farrell, a native of Ireland.

Issue of March 13, 1816

Married, on Saturday evening last, by the Right Rev. Dr. Dehon, Captain Samuel Alexander to Miss Maria Burger, both of this city.

Issue of March 14, 1816

Died — The friends and acquaintances of Mrs. Lee and Miss Regina Alison, are invited to attend the funeral of Miss Alison, from the residence of her mother, No. 43 Broad Street, at 11 o'clock tomorrow morning.

Issue of March 15, 1816

Died — The friends and acquaintances of Mr. William Burger, are invited to attend his funeral, from his late residence, No. 120 Broad Street this afternoon, at 4 o'clock.

Issue of March 16, 1816

Married, on Thursday evening last, by the Rev. Mr. Frost, Thomas W. Bacot, Junior, Esq. to Miss Harriet S. Wainwright, youngest daughter of the late Richard Wainwright, Esq. deceased.

Issue of March 21, 1816

Died, at his residence near Cambridge, on the 7th inst. of the prevailing epidemic, Major Thomas Butler, in the 53rd year of his age...(Eulogy)

Departed this life, on Friday, the 15th after an illness of five days, Mr. William Burger, second son of the late David Burger of this city, aged 30 years, 11 months and 12 days.

Issue of March 22, 1816

Married, last evening, by the Rev. Mr. Palmer, Elias Simmons Bennett, Esquire, to Miss Mary W. Stiles, both of this city.

Issue of March 23, 1816

Married, on Tuesday evening, the 29th inst. by the Rev. Mr. Frost, Dr. John S. Trescot, to Miss Caroline C. Carrere.

Departed this life, on the 13th of Feb. last, on John's Island, in the 44th year of his age. Mr. Henry Fickling. He was a native of Wadmelaw Island...(Eulogy)

Issue of March 27, 1816

Departed this life, on the 18th inst. at Mount-Hope, Williamsburgh District, of the dreadfull epidemic that has for three months past prevailed there, Mrs. Martha Mary M'Donald, aged 40 years and 8 months.

Issue of March 28, 1816

Married, last evening, by the Rev. Mr. Lee, Captain William Bonner, of Abbeville, to Miss Ann Joell, daughter of Thomas Joell, Esq. of St. Thomas Parish.

Issue of April 2, 1816

Departed this life, on the 26th ult. William Harlleston, Esq. aged 59 years.

Died, in this city, at the house of Mrs. Russell, of a consumption, Mr. John Patterson, merchant, of Kingston (upper-Canada).

Died - The friends and acquaintances of Henry Smerdon, are invited to attend his funeral this afternoon, at 4 o'clock, from his late residence, No. 22 Tradd Street.

Issue of April 6, 1816

Departed this life, on the 30th ult. at the Plantation of Mrs. Eliza Fickling, on Stono, in the Parish of St. Paul, Mr. Samuel Fickling, in the 90th year of his age, an old and respectable inhabitant of this state...

Died, in Pendleton district, on the 15th ult. Mr. Alexander Moore; his death was occasioned by a fall from his horse. And on the 20th ult. his brother, Mr. Newman Moore, after a short illness - both native of Ireland, but for several years residents in that district.

Died...on Monday last Col. Joshua Baker was in perfect health; on Thursday following he departed...he was in his 54th year.

Issue of April 11, 1816

Departed this transitory life, on the 2d instant, after a short but painful illness, which she bore with Christian fortitude, Miss Rebecca C. Geyer, second daughter of Mrs. John Geyer, of this city, in the 22d year of her age...(Eulogy)

Issue of April 12, 1816

Married, at Havre-de-Grace, on the 31st ult. by the Rev. Mr. Stevens, Captain John D. Henley, of the Navy, to Miss Eliza Denison, of that place.

Issue of April 18, 1816

Died - The friends and acquaintances of Mrs. Sarah Ball, widow of Thomas Ball, deceased, are invited to attend her funeral, from her late residence on Church Street - continued, this afternoon, at 4 o'clock precisely, without a more particular invitation.

Issue of April 19, 1816

Died, on the 3d inst. Mrs. Rebecca Mills, in the 63rd year of her age...

Issue of April 24, 1816

Died, in this city, on the 15th Mrs. Margaret Keith, wife of Sylvanus Keith, in the 42nd year of her age...

Issue of May 7, 1816

Died, at Providence (R.I.) on the 23d ult. soon after his arrival from this city. Mr. Robert H. Bruce, in the 23d year of his age.

Issue of May 13, 1816

Died - The relatives and acquaintances of Mrs. Catherine Fuller, are requested to attend her funeral, at the house of Mrs. Ann Miles, Legare Street, at half past 7 o'clock tomorrow morning, without further invitation.

Issue of May 14, 1816

Died - The friends and acquaintances of Mr. John Mauger, are invited to attend his funeral, tomorrow morning, at 8 o'clock, from his late residence, No. 41, East Bay.

Died - The friends and acquaintances of Mrs. Rebecca Neall are invited to attend her funeral this afternoon, from No. 378 King Street, without further invitation.

Issue of May 20, 1816

Died - The friends and acquaintances of Mr. Thomas Flinn, a native of Ireland, are requested to attend his funeral from his late residence, corner of Queen and Friend Streets, at half-past five o'clock this evening.

Issue of May 25, 1816

Died - The friends and acquaintances of Robert Rowland, Esqr. are invited to attend his funeral at 5 o'clock, tomorrow afternoon, from his late residence on Meeting Street.

Issue of May 28, 1816

Died lately at Fort Johnson, (S.C.) Capt. Andrew Couis Madison, of the 4th Regt. U. S. Infantry. He was a native of Virginia...

Issue of May 30, 1816

Died, at Boston, on the 18th inst. Abijah Adams, Esq. senior, Editor of the Chronicle, aged 62 years.

Issue of May 31, 1816

Married, at Jamesville, Sumpter District, on Tuesday evening, the 7th instant, by the Rev. Dr. Gadsden, John Cantey, Esq. to Miss Emma Richardson, daughter of the late John P. Richardson, Esqr.

Issue of June 1, 1816

Departed this life on 22d ult., 1816, in Camden, Capt. Issac Dubose, in the 63d year of his age, a worthy and respected officer of the Revolution... (Eulogy)

Issue of June 6, 1816

Married last evening by the Rev. Mr. Motta, Mr. M. M. Russell, of Savannah, to Miss Judith Tobias, of this city.

Issue of June 8, 1816

Died - The friends and acquaintances of Edward H. Edwards, and also of Mrs. Mary Elliott, and Benjamin Elliott, are requested to attend, without further invitation, the funeral of Mrs. Mary O. Edwards, from her late residence, No. 11, Legare Street, at 7 o'clock, tomorrow morning.

Issue of June 10, 1816

Died, on Friday last, Mrs. Mary Odingsell Edwards, consort of Edward H. Edwards, Esqr. and second daughter of the late T. O. Elliott, Esqr. and Mrs. Mary Elliott...(Eulogy)

Issue of June 17, 1816

Died, on Friday last, the 14th inst. Thomas Somar Sall, Esq. aged 48 years.

Issue of June 19, 1816

Died, at Pineville, St. Stephen's, on the morning of the 12th June, Mrs. Catharine Ravenel, wife of Henry Ravenel, and eldest daughter of O. G. Stevens aged 24 years...

Issue of June 22, 1816

Died - The friends and acquaintances of Miss Angelina Ball, are invited to attend her funeral, this afternoon, from No. 168 East Bay, at 5 o'clock.

Issue of July 3, 1816

Died, at Beaufort, on Sunday last, 30th ult. the Hon. Paul Hamilton, late Secretary of the Navy of the United States.

Died, in Columbia (S.C.) on Wednesday morning last, Mrs. Sarah Faust, wife of Mr. David Faust, Printer...

Issue of July 6, 1816

Married, in Prince William's Parish, on the 3d inst. by the Rev. Mr. Parks, John Lingard Hunter, Attorney at Law, of Charleston, to Miss Sarah Elizabeth Bowler, of the former place, daughter of James Henry Bowler, Esq. deceased.

Issue of July 8, 1816

Died, at the residence of Doctor Hamilton, in Prince William's Parish, on Sunday evening, the 30th ult. Paul Hamilton, late Secretary of the Navy of the United States...(Eulogy)

Issue of July 10, 1816

Died - The friends and acquaintances of the late Washington Gibbs are requested, without further invitation, to attend his funeral tomorrow morning at nine o'clock, at No. 5, Orange Street.

Issue of July 12, 1816

Died, on the morning of the 10th inst. Mr. Washington Gibbes, second son of William H. Gibbes, Esq. in the 22d year of his age.

Died, at New York 2d inst. of a lingering illness, in the 71st year of his age, and 50th of his ministry, the Rev. Gershom Seixas, of the Jewish Congregation of that city.

Issue of July 13, 1816

Married, on Thursday evening last, by the Rev. Mr. Palmer, Mr. John W. Todd, of the U. S. Navy, to Miss Sarah Ball, daughter of the late Thomas Ball, Esq. all of this city.

Issue of July 15, 1816

Died - The friends and acquaintances of Mr. A. Kerr, are invited to attend the funeral of Miss Mary-Ann Kerr, this evening, at 6 o'clock, from No. 112, Church Street.

Issue of July 25, 1816

Departed this life, on the 22d in the 44th year of his age, the Reverend Thomas H. Price, pastor of the Presbyterian Church, of James Island... (Eulogy)

Issue of July 28, 1816

Died - A young man named Peter Williams, clerk in a grocery store in this city, was unfortunately drowned last evening while bathing at Bennett's Bridge...

Issue of July 29, 1816

Died, Saturday the 27th inst. Mr. John C. Folker, aged 64 years.

Issue of July 30, 1816

Departed this life, on Saturday last, the 27th inst. Capt. George Cross.

Issue of July 31, 1816

Died, on Saturday last the 27th inst. Mrs. Mary Warley, consort of Dr. W. Warley, aged 23 years...

Departed this life on the 23d instant, Mr. Thomas Dempsey, in the 29th year of his age.

Issue of August 10, 1816

Married, on Thursday evening, by the Rev. Dr. Palmer, Mr. Jacob P. N. Green, to Miss Mary Munro, of this city.

Died - The friends and acquaintances, of the late Mr. James Whyte, are requested to attend his funeral, from his late residence No. 74 East-Bay, this evening, at 3 o'clock.

Issue of August 14, 1816

Died, at Nassau, on the 18th ult. where he had gone for the benefit of his health, Mr. John Gilbert Chambers, in the 21st year of his age, a native of this city...

Issue of August 23, 1816

Married, at Baltimore, on the 14th inst. by the Rev. Mr. Cohen, Mr. Henry M. Russell, of that place, to Miss Rinah Tobias, of Charleston, S.C.

Issue of August 26, 1816

Died - The friends and acquaintances (and particularly the members of the two Marine Societies) are requested to attend the funeral of Captain Graeves, late of the brig Hibernia, this afternoon, at 5 o'clock from the house of Mr. Harth, No. 2, Gibbs Street.

Issue of August 27, 1816

Died - The friends and acquaintances of Mr. Thomas R. Shepheard, and the Members of the Fellowship and Neck Societies, are invited to attend his funeral, from his late residence on King Street Road, at 5 o'clock this afternoon.

Issue of August 29, 1816

Departed this life on the 25th inst. Captain Thomas Graeves, in the 24th year of his age...(Eulogy)

Died, lately in New York, the Rev. Gershom Mendes Seixas, late minister of the Hebrew Congregation in that city, in the 71st year of his age... (Eulogy)

Issue of August 31, 1816

Died, on the 29th inst. at Islington, Mr. Joseph Dickinson, house carpenter, of this city, aged 46 years.

Issue of September 2, 1816

Died - The friends and acquaintances of Mr. John Egleston, are respectfully invited to attend the funeral of his niece, Miss Mary Egleston, this afternoon, at 4 o'clock, from his dwelling East-Bay.

Issue of September 3, 1816

Departed this life, on the 31st day of August last, in the forty fourth year of her age, after a long and painful illness, Hester Rose Drayton, consort to the honorable Judge Drayton...(Eulogy)

Issue of September 4, 1816

Died - The friends and acquaintances of the late Mrs. Ann Bowles are requested to attend her funeral from Mr. A. Jones residence, No. 357 King Street, between Broad and Tradd Street, at 4 o'clock, tomorrow afternoon.

Issue of September 5, 1816

Married, on Wednesday evening by the Rev. Mr. Bachman, Mr. George Christopher Happoidt, to Mrs. Elizabeth Prauninger.

Died - The friends and acquaintances of the late Mrs. Ann Bowles are requested to attend her funeral from Mr. A. Jones residence, No. 357 King Street, between Broad and Tradd Street, at 4 o'clock, tomorrow afternoon.

Issue of September 7, 1816

Died - The friends and acquaintances of the late Robert Aitchison, are invited to attend his funeral from the house of Mrs. Cameron, East-Bay, opposite Tradd-Street, this afternoon, at 4 o'clock.

Issue of September 13, 1816

Died - The friends and acquaintances of Capt. Francis Saltus, are invited to attend the funeral of his son Thomas C. Saltus, at 5 o'clock, this afternoon, from his house on King Street, near South Bay.

Issue of September 16, 1816

Died - The friends and acquaintances of the late Mrs. Mary C. Dupont, are invited to attend her funeral from Mr. Manson's, opposite the Church in Cumberland Street, tomorrow morning, at 9 o'clock precisely.

Issue of September 19, 1816

Died – The friends and acquaintances of the late Mr. Lewis Bryer, Printer, are particularly requested to attend his funeral this afternoon, precisely at 4 o'clock, from the house of Mr. Richard Walker, No. 6, Boundary Street.

Issue of September 21, 1816

Died – The friends and acquaintances of Mr. and Mrs. Kohler, are invited to attend the funeral of his mother, from his residence in King Street, tomorrow afternoon, at half past 3 o'clock.

Issue of September 28, 1816

Departed this life in Barnwell District, on the 1st inst., Mrs. Elizabeth Juhan, consort of Col. Alexander Juhan, and daughter of the late Daniel Rourdeaux, Esq...(Eulogy)

Issue of October 1, 1816

Died – The friends and acquaintances of Messrs. George and John Rosen are invited to attend the funeral of their brother William, this afternoon at 4 o'clock, from the house of Mrs. Wooddruft, Vanderhorst's Range.

Issue of October 2, 1816

Died, at New York, on the 19th ult. Colonel John Ward of this city...

Issue of October 4, 1816

Died – The friends and acquaintances of Mr. T. W. Rawlinson, are respectfully requested to attend his funeral, without further invitation, at 9 o'clock tomorrow morning, from his late residence, at Mr. Camorin's, East Bay.

Issue of October 9, 1816

Died, at sea, on the 22d July last, Burridge Purvis, Esq. in the 46th year of his age, a native of Scotland, and for many years a respectable inhabitant of Columbia, (S.C.)...(Eulogy)

Issue of October 21, 1816

Married, on Saturday evening last, by the Rev. Dr. Leland, Mr. William Givan Steele, to Miss Eliza Hedley, eldest daughter of the Rev. John Hedley, all of this place.

Issue of October 29, 1816

Died –...Mr. Samuel Robertson, late merchant of this city, who departed this scene of his active and useful career, on the 22d inst. in the 44th year of his age...(Eulogy)

Issue of October 30, 1816

Died –...George Madison, governor of this State. He died on Monday last, at Baris Bourbon county...

Died on the 22d inst. Mr. George W. Thwing, a native of Cambridge, Massachusetts, aged 18 years and 7 months...(Eulogy)

Issue of November 2, 1816

Married, in Summerville on Thursday evening last, by the Rev. Mr. States Lee, Mr. Benjamin Singellton, merchant of this city to Mrs.

Elizabeth Ladson, of St. Paul's Parish.

Issue of November 6, 1816

Died, yesterday in Christ Church Parish, Mr. Thomas Hinds, a gentleman whose benevolence of heart and social manners endeared him to all who knew him.

Died, on the 26th ult. at Farmsville (Va.) Mr. Washington Potter, merchant of this city, universally esteemed and respected.

Issue of November 14, 1816

Died - The friends and acquaintances of Mr. and Mrs. Hardy, (lately arrived here from Boston) of Robinson & Patton, and D. Crocker & Co. are invited to attend the funeral of Mr. Hardy precisely at 10 o'clock tomorrow morning, from Mrs. Steedman's, Pinckney Street.

Issue of November 19, 1816

Died - The friends and acquaintances of William B. and Mrs. Jane Minott are invited to attend the funeral of Mrs. Minott tomorrow afternoon at 3 o'clock, from her late residence No. 4, Gibbes Street.

Issue of November 25, 1816

Died, on the 21st instant, at Wilmington, (N.C.) Mrs. Esther Lazarus, in the 33rd year of her age, the amiable wife of Aron Lazarus, Esq. merchant of that city...(Eulogy)

Died, on the 6th instant, at Pittsburgh, Pennsylvania, Richard M'Cormick Esq. late of this city. Attorney at Law; in the 34th year of his age... (Eulogy)

Issue of November 28, 1816

Died -...Mr. John Samuel Courtney who departed this life on the morning of the 24th inst. in the 20th year of his age...(Eulogy)

Issue of November 30, 1816

Married, on Thursday evening, by the Rev. Mr. Frost, Mr. John Camidge Burr, to Mrs. Lydia Pritchard; all of this city.

Issue of December 6, 1816

Married, on Thursday evening last, by the Rev. William Percy, D.D., Mr. James Wilkie to Miss Sarah De St. Julian Mazyck, daughter of the late Capt. Daniel De St. Mazyck.

Issue of December 11, 1816

Died, at Liverpool, on Saturday the 12th October the Rev. Jacob Samuel...

Issue of December 13, 1816

Died, at Savannah on the 4th inst. Captain George Haig, late of the U.S. Light Dragoons.

Issue of December 19, 1816

Married, last evening by the Rev. Dr. Leland, Mr. James T.W. Holmes to Miss Caroline Rivers both of this place.

Issue of December 21, 1816

Died, on Thursday morning last, the 19th inst. Mrs. Sarah Sarzedas, wife of David Sarzedas in the 49th year of her age...

Issue of December 24, 1816

Died, on the 4th instant, Miss Elizabeth Steel aged 27 years, a native of Ireland...

Issue of December 30, 1816

Married, on Thursday evening last by the Rev. Mr. Dalcho, William A. Wayne, Esq. to Miss Elizabeth F. Waring, daughter of the late Thomas Waring, Esq. of Pine Hill.

Issue of December 31, 1816

Died, at his Plantation in St. Stephen's Parish after a short illness, Captain John Palmer, aged 67 years and 8 months.

Issue of January 8, 1817

Died, yesterday evening, of a pulmonary complaint, Mrs. Moore, (formerly Mrs. Woodham of the Theatre)...

Issue of January 16, 1817

Died, in this city, on the 7th inst. in the 35th year of her age, Mrs. Mary Moore, wife of Col. Abraham Moore, of Massachusetts...(Eulogy)

Issue of January 20, 1817

Died, on Saturday evening last, Mr. James Elsinore, aged 31 years, a native of this city. A gentleman whose amiable and cheerful manners, endeared him to all his acquaintances.

Issue of January 21, 1817

Died, at his residence at Hamilton College in Albany, after a short but severe attack of a fever, the Rev. Dr. Backus, President of that institution...(Eulogy)

Died, at New-Haven, Conn. on Saturday the 11th inst. the Rev. Dr. Timothy Dwight, in the 65th year of his age, President of Yale College...

Issue of January 24, 1817

Died, on the 22d inst. Miss Mary Eliza Glenn, only daughter of Mrs. Margaret Glenn, just entering the 19th year of her age...(Eulogy)

Died, on the eleventh of January, after a short but severe illness Miss Isabella Reid, daughter of the late George Reid, Esq. in the twenty second year of her age...(Eulogy)

Died-The friends and acquaintances of the late Mrs. Eliza Vincent, are invited to attend her funeral from No. 3, Tradd Street, at 4 o'clock, this afternoon.

Issue of January 25, 1817

Died - At 2 o'clock on Thursday morning, at his house in Philadelphia, Alexander James Dallas...(Eulogy)

Issue of January 27, 1817

Died - The friends and acquaintances of the Rev. Dr. Hollinshead, are requested to attend his funeral tomorrow forenoon at 11 o'clock, from his late residence, No. 9 Maiden Lane.

Issue of January 29, 1817

Died - The friends and acquaintances of Mr. Peter Ayrault, are requested to attend his funeral tomorrow afternoon, at 3 o'clock, from Capt. Pains, No. 12 Hasell Street.

Issue of February 5, 1817

Died – The friends and acquaintances of the late Mrs. Mary Jones and of Henry John Jones, are requested to attend the funeral of Mrs. Jones, from her late residence, at the upper end of Tradd Street, at half past 3 o'clock tomorrow afternoon, without further invitation.

Issue of February 11, 1817

Died – The friends and acquaintances of the late Mr. James Robinson, are requested to attend his funeral from his late residence, No. 71 Market Street, this afternoon, at half past 3 o'clock, without further invitation.

Issue of February 20, 1817

Died – The friends and acquaintances of the late Nicholas Poulnot, also the members of the Mechanic Society, French Society, and the Masonic Brethren, are particularly invited by his children and son-in-law, to attend his funeral, from his late residence, No. 39 Meeting Street, this afternoon at half past 4 o'clock.

Issue of February 25, 1817

On Sunday last was married, Mr. Holman, Manager of the Charleston Theatre, to Miss Latimer – the marriage was solemnized by the Rev. Mr. Gadsden, at Mr. Holman's house in Broad Street.

Died – The friends and acquaintances of the late Samuel K. Whiting, Esq. a native of Massachusetts, and a member of the Bar of that State, are respectfully invited to attend his funeral tomorrow morning, precisely at 9 o'clock, from Mrs. Smerdon's, No. 54, Church Street, without a more particular invitation.

Issue of February 27, 1817

Died – The friends and acquaintances of Mr. Patrick Cassin, are invited to attend his funeral tomorrow morning at 8 o'clock, from his late residence corner of Pinckney and East Bay Streets, without further notice.

Issue of March 3, 1817

Married, on the 25th ult. at St. Paul's Church, by the Rev. Mr. Campbell, Edward Blake, Esq. to Miss Catharine L. Deveaux – both of this city.

Issue of March 6, 1817

Married, on Tuesday evening last, by the Rev. Dr. Gallagher, Mr. Francis Giraud to Miss Adelle Fayolle, both of this city.

Issue of March 10, 1817

Married on Thursday evening last, by the Rev. Dr. Gadsden, Col. Wade Hampton, of Columbia to Miss Ann Fitzsimons, of this city.

Issue of March 13, 1817

Died, at St. Simon's Island, at the residence of C. S. Wylly, Esqr. on Wednesday, the 5th inst. Dr. George V. Proctor, health-officer of the port of Savannah, age 35 years, a native of South Carolina...

Issue of March 19, 1817

Died – The friends and acquaintances of the late Mr. James Gordon are invited to attend his funeral tomorrow afternoon at half past 3 o'clock, from his late residence, No. 43 Bay.

Issue of March 21, 1817

Died - The friends and acquaintances of Leiutenant Joseph P. Prince, and the late Mrs. Eliza Prince, are invited to attend her funeral, at 10 o'clock tomorrow morning, from her father's, Nathaniel Cadworth, No. 9, Bull Street, without further invitation.

Issue of March 25, 1817

Departed this life on Friday the 21st inst. Mrs. Elizabeth Prince in the 38th year of her age...(Eulogy)

Issue of March 26, 1817

Died, at Okatee, Beaufort District, on the 7th inst. after a few days illness, William Norton, Esq. in the 71st year of his age...(Eulogy)

Issue of March 28, 1817

Died in Philadelphia on the 20th inst. in the 47th year of his age, the Rev. Emanuel Nunes Carvalho, formerly Pastor of the Hebrew Congregation in this city...(Eulogy)

Issue of April 5, 1817

Died - The friends and acquaintances of Mr. Palmer, (late of the U.S. Navy) and the officers of the Army and Navy, are invited to attend his funeral from Mrs. Milbury's, No. 14 Queen Street tomorrow afternoon at 4 o'clock, P.M. Masters of vessels, are requested to hoist their colours half mast.

Issue of April 9, 1817

Died, on the 21st ult. after a lingering illness of twelve years, Mrs. Elizabeth Barton, aged 58 years and 5 months.

Issue of April 10, 1817

Died - The friends and acquaintances of Mr. and Mrs. Henrickson, are requested to attend the funeral of the latter, from her late residence, Hampstead, tomorrow morning at 8 o'clock.

Issue of April 11, 1817

Married, on Thursday evening last, by the Rev. Dr. Gadsden, Major G. H. Manigault, of the U. S. Army to Miss Ann Heyward, all of this city.

Issue of April 14, 1817

＊Died - The friends and acquaintances of the late Mrs. Mary George are respectfully requested to attend her funeral, at No. 40 Market Street, tomorrow (Tuesday) at 4 o'clock in the afternoon.

Issue of April 15, 1817

Died - The friends and acquaintances of Mr. George Chapman deceased, are requested to attend his funeral from the Carolina Coffee House, Tradd Street, this afternoon, at 5 o'clock, without further invitation.

Issue of April 17, 1817

Died, at his residence in Anson Street, on the 25th ult. Mr. Issac Neufville, of this city, in the 50th year of his age...(Eulogy)

Issue of April 19, 1817

Married, at Mt. Pleasant, on Tuesday the 15th inst. by the Rev. Thomas Frost, Charles Wm. D'Oyley, Esq. of Charleston, to Miss Sarah Eliza Baker of St. Bartholomew's Parish.

Issue of April 22, 1817

Married, at Pooshe, St. John's (Berkley) by the Rev. Mr. Snowden, on the evening of the 17th inst. Daniel Broughton, Esq. to Miss Mary Martha Ravenel, daughter of Paul de St. Julien Ravenel, Esq. all of said parish.

Issue of April 23, 1817

Departed this terrestial abode in confidence of a blessed immortality, on the 14th inst. Mrs. Mary George, at the advanced age of 86 years and 6 months...

Issue of April 24, 1817

Died, on Monday the 21st inst. at the house of the Rev. A. Fowler, in the 21st year of his age, Mr. William R. Jennings, late of New York... (Eulogy)

Issue of April 29, 1817

Died - The friends and acquaintances of the late Jeremiah Shrewsbury, deceased, likewise the members of the Mechanic and Hibernian Societies are particularly requested to attend his funeral from his late residence, No. 13 Guignard Street this afternoon, at 4 o'clock.

Issue of April 30, 1817

Married last evening, by the Rev. Dr. Gadsden, Doctor Alexander Hume, to Miss Mary Gadsden Morris, daughter of Thomas Morris, Esq.

Issue of May 3, 1817

Married, in Jacksonborough, on Monday evening last, by the Rev. Mr. Floyd, Dennis O'Driscol, Esq. of Charleston to Miss Harriet Y. Evans, of the former place.

Died, in Orangeburgh, on the 23rd ult. after a distressing illness of a few days, Alexander Jones, son of Samuel P. Jones, Esq. aged 15 years and 9 months...(Eulogy)

Issue of May 8, 1817

Died - The friends and acquaintances of Mrs. Susanna Cantey, are requested to attend her funeral this afternoon, at 4 o'clock at the house of Mr. John Schutz, south end of Church Street.

Issue of May 10, 1817

Died - The friends and acquaintances of Mr. James M. Elford, teacher of Navigation and of the late Mrs. Margaret C. Elford, are invited to attend her funeral tomorrow evening at 4 o'clock from her late residence, No. 70 East Bay. Masters of vessels are also invited to attend.

Issue of May 12, 1817

Died - The friends and acquaintances of the late Mr. Robert Bell, are respectfully requested to attend his funeral without further invitation tomorrow morning, at 9 o'clock, from the house of Thomas Johnston, King Street road.

Issue of May 17, 1817

Died, on the 14th ult. at his residence on Little River, in Abbeville District, S.C. of a tedious and painful illness, which he endured with extraordinary Christian patience, Col. Joseph Calhoun, in the 67th year of his age...(Eulogy)

Issue of May 20, 1817

Married, in St. James' Parish, Santee on Thursday evening last, by the Rev. Mr. Fraser, James J. R. White, Esq. of Charleston, to Miss Mary E. Dupre of the former place.

Issue of May 26, 1817

Died, on the 9th inst. of a consumption, Mrs. Margaret Charlotte Elford, (consort of James M. Elford, teacher of navigation in this city) aged 43 years, 4 months and 20 days...(Eulogy)

Died - The friends and acquaintances of Mr. James R. Harvey, late of Boston, are requested to attend his funeral, without further invitation, this afternoon, at 5 o'clock, from the house of Mrs. Flagg, No. 349 King Street.

Issue of May 29, 1817

Died, on the 26th inst. in the 22d year of his age, Mr. James Rogers Harvey a native of Boston, Massachusetts...(Eulogy)

Issue of June 3, 1817

Died - The friends and acquaintances of Messrs. Jacob Sass and John E. Schirmer, are requested to attend the funeral of Mrs. Margaret H. Schirmer, this afternoon at 5 o'clock, from No. 100 Queen Street.

Issue of June 4, 1817

Died - The friends and acquaintances of Mrs. Elizabeth Poyas, widow of the late John Lewis Poyas, are invited to attend her funeral this afternoon, precisely at 5 o'clock, from the house of William B. Wilkie, No. 38, Market Street near King Street.

Issue of June 7, 1817

Died, at Camden, on Monday the 26th inst. Harriot Lee, youngest daughter of Francis S. Lee of that place.

Issue of June 11, 1817

Died, at Boston, on the 30th ult. Mr. William Burdick, late editor of the Boston Evening Gazette.

Died - The friends and acquaintances of Mr. John Ross, and Mrs. Jane Hunter, are invited to attend the funeral of Mrs. Ross this afternoon, at 4 o'clock, from the residence of Mr. Ross, No. 2, Church Street continued.

Issue of June 12, 1817

* Died - The friends and acquaintances and the Members of the Mechanic Society are invited to attend the funeral of Mr. Thomas Jandrell, this afternoon, at 4 o'clock from his late residence, No. 129 East Bay, without further notice.

Issue of June 17, 1817

Died, in this city, on the 7th ult. Mrs. Susanna Canty, relict of the late John Canty, Esqr. of St. Mathews Parish, in the 73d year of her age...(Eulogy)

Issue of June 19, 1817

Married, on the evening of the 11th inst. in St. Peters Parish, Beaufort District, by the Rev. Joseph Lowry, Mr. James Lowry, originally of Fairfield District, to Miss Sarah Robert, of the above Parish.

Issue of June 24, 1817

Married, at Pineville, on Tuesday the 17th inst. by the Rev. Mr. Snowden, Charles Sinker, Esq. to Miss Elizabeth Peyre, eldest daughter of Francis Peyre, Esq.

Issue of June 26, 1817

Died - The friends and acquaintances of Captain James Levin, are invited to attend his funeral at 4 o'clock this afternoon, from his late residence, No. 53 Anson Street.

Issue of June 27, 1817

Died, suddenly, on the 25th inst., Mr. James Levens, aged about 35, for many years a respectable and skillful Branch Pilot in our Harbour...(Eulogy)

Issue of July 3, 1817

Died, at Middletown, in Kentucky, on the 7th instant, Gen. Samuel Dirickson, aged about 53 years, a venerable revolutionary whig. He had lived in Kentucky but a few years, having removed thither from Delaware of which state he was a native.

Issue of July 11, 1817

Died - The friends and acquaintances of Mr. Jacob Eckhard, Jun. are invited to attend the funeral of Mrs. Elizabeth Eckhard, this afternoon, at 4 o'clock, from her late residence, No. 30, Coming Street, without further invitation.

Issue of July 14, 1817

Died - The friends and acquaintances of Mr. George E. and Mrs. Elizabeth Hahnbaum, and of the late Mrs. Mary Switzer, are requested to attend the funeral of the latter tomorrow afternoon, at 4 o'clock, from the residence of her son, Mr. G. E. Hahnbaum, No. 175 King Street opposite Black-Bird Alley.

Issue of July 15, 1817

Died - The friends and acquaintances of Mr. George E. and Mrs. Elizabeth Hahnbaum, and of the late Mrs. Mary Switzer, are requested to attend the funeral of the latter tomorrow afternoon, at 4 o'clock, from the residence of her son, Mr. G. E. Hahnbaum, No. 175 King Street opposite Black-Bird Alley.

Issue of July 18, 1817

Died - The friends and acquaintances of the late Mr. Joseph Lloyd, Sen. are invited to attend his funeral this afternoon, from his late residence, No. 55 King Street.

Issue of July 21, 1817

Died - The friends and acquaintances and members of the fellowship and Marine Societies, are invited to attend the funeral of Captain William Laidler, from his late residence in Blackbird Alley, at 4 o'clock this afternoon.

Issue of July 23, 1817

Died - Called suddenly from time to eternity on Friday last, in the 14th year of her age, Harriet Amanda, third daughter of James M. Ward, Esq. ...(Eulogy)

Issue of July 24, 1817

Died, at New York, on the 11th inst. Mr. Moses Mendes Salxas, aged 67 years.

Issue of July 28, 1817

Died - The friends and acquaintances of the Rev. Andrew Fowler, are respectfully invited to attend the funeral of his late wife, Mrs. Mary Fowler, from his residence, No. 147, Church Street continued, this evening, at 4 o'clock.

Issue of July 29, 1817

Departed this life, on the 24th inst. in the 57th year of his age, after a long and painful illness of nine weeks, Mr. James Browne, a native of England, but for forty years past a respectable resident of this place.

Died, in this city, on Saturday, the 27th inst. after a short illness, Mr. Phineas Ward, aged 25 years, son of Captain James T. Ward, of Middletown, (Con.)

Died - The friends and acquaintances of the late Mr. Lewis M'Coy, are particularly invited to attend his funeral this afternoon, at 5 o'clock, at his residence, Franklin Hotel, East Bay.

Issue of July 31, 1817

Died, in Brunswick, on the 24th inst. Alexander M'Auld, aged about 27 years and 8 months, a native of North Carolina.

Issue of August 1, 1817

Married, in Robertville, St. Peter's Parish, Beaufort District, on Tuesday evening, 22d July, by the Rev. Hezekiah Boyd, Mr. James B. Jaudon to Miss Rachel E. Polhill.

Departed this life, on the 26th instant, Mr. Peter Wartenburg, aged 40 years and 9 months, a native of Germany, but a resident of Charleston 14 years...(Eulogy)

Died - The friends and acquaintances, also the members of the Fellowship Society, are requested to attend the funeral of the late Sir William Porter, from the house of Captain Brooks, corner of Queen and Archdale Streets, at 5 o'clock this afternoon, without further invitation.

Issue of August 5, 1817

Died - The friends and acquaintances of the late Mr. J. C. Waldo, are requested to attend his funeral this afternoon, at 5 o'clock from his late residence, No. 1 Gillon Street, without further invitation.

Issue of August 6, 1817

Died, in East Greenwich, R. I. on the 21st ult. Mrs. Mary M. Greene, in the 43d year of her age; wife of the Hon. Ray Greene, and daughter of George Flagg, Esq. of this city.

Died - The friends and acquaintances of Mr. and Mrs. Duncan, are invited to attend the funeral of Mr. Alexander Duncan, from his late residence Berresford Street, tomorrow morning, at 8 o'clock.

Issue of August 7, 1817

Died - The congregation of the Protestant Episcopal Churches, particularly that of St. Michael's, the Clergy of the city, and generally the friends and acquaintances, of the late Right Reverend Bishop Dehon, D.D. Bishop of the Protestant Episcopal Church, in the Diocese of South Carolina; are invited to attend his funeral tomorrow morning, at 8 o'clock, from his residence in Mazychborough.

Issue of August 8, 1817

Died - The Right Reverend Bishop Dehon who died on Wednesday evening...
(Eulogy)

Died - The friends and acquaintances of the late Mr. William Girty, are
invited to attend his funeral this evening, at 5 o'clock, from his late
residence in Tradd Street, two doors east of the Carolina Coffee House.

Issue of August 9, 1817

Died - The death of a good man is a public calamity...It is principally
in this point of view, that I lament the death of our beloved minister,
the Right Reverend Bishop Dehon, and in expressing the feelings of my own
bosom I feel a consciousness, that I express at the same time those of the
public...(Eulogy)

Died - The friends and acquaintances of Dennis Macnamara, are invited
to attend his funeral this afternoon, at 4 o'clock, from his late residence
Tradd Street, three doors from the Bay, without further invitation.

Issue of August 11, 1817

Died, on Wednesday the 6th inst. the Rev. Theodore Dehon, Bishop of the
Episcopal Diocese of South Carolina...(Eulogy)

Issue of August 12, 1817

Died - The friends and acquaintances of the late Mr. John Ward, are
requested to attend his funeral this afternoon, at 5 o'clock, at his late
residence, No. 60 Meeting Street, corner of Halback's Alley.

Issue of August 14, 1817

Died - The relatives, friends, and acquaintances of William H. Wilson
and Mrs. Mary E. Wilson, are invited to attend the funeral of their deceased
son Thomas Doughty Wilson, without further invitation, from the dwelling
of his Grandfather, Jeremiah Condy, No. 99 Meeting Street, near the Circular
Church, at 8 o'clock tomorrow morning.

Issue of August 16, 1817

Died - The friends and acquaintances of William M'Elmoyle, are requested
to attend the funeral of his brother James, from his late residence No. 24
King Street, without further invitation. tomorrow morning, at 8 o'clock.

Issue of August 18, 1817

Died, in Beaufort, the 2nd instant, Capt. Issac Grimball Jenkins.

Issue of August 19, 1817

Died - ...The above reflections were excited by the much lamented death
of Captain Isaac G. Jenkins, who departed this life a few days ago at Beaufort, in the full vigor and pride of manhood...(Eulogy)

Issue of August 20, 1817

Died - On Sunday evening last, Mr. William Lee, of this city, had his
third son cut off by one of those accidents, which are as unexpected as
they are awful...(Eulogy)

Issue of August 21, 1817

Died - The friends and acquaintances of the late Mr. Robert H. Kirk,
his brother Mr. Alexander Kirk, and Mr. Henry Bryce, are requested to
attend the funeral of Mr. R. H. Kirk, from No. 16, Lawrence Street, at 4
o'clock precisely, this afternoon, without further invitation.

Died - The friends and acquaintances of Sebastian Spencer, are invited to attend his funeral this afternoon, at five o'clock, from the residence of Mrs. C. Ehney, No. 39 Coming Street.

Died, in the state of Georgia, on the 18th inst. Mr. Dennis O'Driscoll, son of Dr. O'Driscoll, of this place, in the 24th year of his age...(Eulogy)

Issue of August 26, 1817

Died, on the 18th inst. at the residence of Mrs. Hugh Rutledge, High Hills of Santee, Miss Sarah Hyrne Simons, second daughter of Major James Simons, deceased; lamented by numerous relatives and friends.

Died - The friends and acquaintances of Lieut. Thomas W. Legg, of the United States Marines, are requested to attend his funeral from his mother's house, No. 139, Wentworth Street, tomorrow morning, at 9 o'clock.

Issue of August 27, 1817

Died - ...The venerable General Pickens in no more! He closed his useful and honourable life on the 11th inst. at Tumassee, in Pendleton District, full of years and respect...(Eulogy)

Died - The friends and acquaintances of Mr. and Mrs. Higham, and Mr. and Mrs. Kershaw, are requested to attend the funeral of Charles Higham, from his father's residence, No. 48, Church Street, at 5 o'clock this afternoon, without further invitation.

Issue of August 28, 1817

Died, at Beaufort, S. C. on the 18th inst. William Colman Esq. a native of Boston, (Mass.)

Issue of August 29, 1817

Departed this life, in the District of Williamsburgh, on Wednesday night the 20th inst. of a Typhus Fever, of twenty days continuance, John Milton Wetherspoon, son of Gavin Wetherspoon, Esq. in the 21st year of his age... (Eulogy)

Issue of August 30, 1817

Died - The friends and acquaintances of the late Mr. George Girty, and particularly the Members of the Hibernian Society, are invited to attend his funeral tomorrow morning, at 8 o'clock, from Mr. Piegne's, in Berresford Street.

Issue of September 1, 1817

Died - The friends and acquaintances of Captain Henry Leslie, Mrs. Leslie and E. Bingley are requested to attend the funeral of Miss Francis Wood, this afternoon, at 4 o'clock, from Captain Leslie's House, No. 69 Anson Street.

Died - The friends and acquaintances of Mr. Addison Melvin, (of the Firm of Butler, Melvin & Co.) are requested to attend his funeral, from the House of Mrs. Smerdon, No. 54 Church Street this afternoon at 5 o'clock, without a more particular invitation.

Issue of September 2, 1817

Departed this transitory life, on the night of the 30th of August last, Marc Bein Amie Dastas, aged 18 years and 6 months, a native of this city... (Eulogy)

Departed this life, on the 20th ult. after a few days painful illness, which was sustained with resignation, Mr. John Parrish, about two years resident in this city, a worthy member of society-a native of North Carolina, aged 22 years and 6 months...(Eulogy)

Departed this life on the 29th ult. after a few days painfull illness, which was sustained with resignation, Mr. Daniel Parker, many years resident in this city, and a worthy member of society-a native of Boston, (Mass.)

aged about 31 years...(Eulogy)

Died, on Monday morning, of the prevailing fever, in the 28th year of
his age, Mr. Addison Melvin, of the firm of Butler, Melvin & Co. a native of
Massachusetts...(Eulogy)

Died, at Rockaway, (New York) on Saturday night, the 23rd ult. Mr.
Holman, Tragedian, late Manager of the Charleston Theatre.

Issue of September 3, 1817

Died - The friends and acquaintances of Thomas Hewitt and Mrs. Hewitt,
and Miss Ann Moles, are invited to attend the funeral of Miss Ann Moles, from
Thomas Hewitt's House tomorrow morning, at 7 o'clock precisely, No. 209 King
Street.

Issue of September 4, 1817

Died, at the Watering Place, Rockaway, Long Island, on Sunday morning,
the 24th of August instant, Joseph George Holman, Esq. in the 53d year of
his age...(Eulogy)

Issue of September 6, 1817

Married, on Sullivan's Island, on Thursday the 4th instant, by the Rev.
Mr. Gadsden, Maurice Simons, Jun. Esq. of the Daniel's Island, to Miss Eliza
Capers, youngest daughter of the late Major Gabriel Capers, of Christ Church
Parish.

Issue of September 9, 1817

Died, on the 3d inst. after a long and painful illness, deeply lamented
by a large circle of relations and friends, Mrs. Eliza White, wife of John
B. White, Esq....(Eulogy)

Died, in this city, on the 29th ult. of the prevailing fever, Mr.
Henry Childs, a native of Buck's County, (Penn.) He resided here nearly
two years in which time he formed a large and respectable acquaintance,
who sincerely lament his loss.

Died, on Sunday morning, after an illness of 5 days, Miss Martha Elizabeth Bounetheau, aged 8 years, 6 months and 18 days; second daughter of Mr.
Edward Weyman Bounetheau.

Died, suddenly at Haddrill's Point, on Friday, the 5th inst. Mr. Henry
Hunt, a native of New Orleans; his death is supposed to have been occasioned
by a fall.

Issue of September 10, 1817

Died on the 4th instant, in the fifteenth year of her age, after an illness of five days, Miss Ann S. Nichols, a native of Vermont...(Eulogy)

Died, on Sullivan's Island, on the 2d inst. of the prevailing fever,
Mr. Josiah Cross, aged 28 years, a native of Massachusetts.

Died, on Saturday morning, after three days illness with the yellow
fever, Master Edwin C. Folker, son of Mr. Joseph Folker.

Died, in Middletown (Conn.) on the 23d ult. of the typhus fever, the
Hon. Henry D. Ward, of Columbia, (S.C.) late a Senator in the Legislature
of this State, and a native of Shrewsbury, in that state.

Died - We have the melancholy duty to perform, of announcing the death
of Major General Andrew Pickens, one of the most distinguished revolutionary
characters. He departed this life on the 11th inst. at his seat at
Tomassee...(Eulogy)

Died - The friends and acquaintances of Mr. Charles Graves and of his
son, Charles Graves, Jun. are invited to attend the funeral of the latter,
from the house of his father, No. 54 Tradd Street, at 4 o'clock this afternoon.

Issue of September 15, 1817

Died, on the 11th inst. at the house of his afflicted parents in Archdale Street, in the twenty-first year of his age, Isaac Mazych, the third son of William Mazyck, of this city.

Died - The friends and acquaintances of James, Sen. and Elizabeth Badger, are requested to attend the funeral of James Badger, Sen. from his late residence next to the Independent Church, Archdale Street, tomorrow morning, at 8 o'clock, without further invitation.

Issue of September 16, 1817

Died - The relatives and friends of Mr. Adam and Mrs. Mary Ker, are requested to attend the funeral of the latter, at 5 o'clock this afternoon, from her late residence No, 386 King Street, without further invitation.

Issue of September 17, 1817

...(Died) Mr. Dearborn Dow, a native of Massachusetts, District of Maine, - but for the last nine months a resident of this city...in the 26th year of his age...(Eulogy)

Died - The friends and acquaintances of Mr. John Walton, and the Members of the Fellowship Society, are invited to attend his funeral, from his late residence, No. 213 King Street, tomorrow morning, at 8 o'clock.

Issue of September 18, 1817

Married on Sunday, 7th inst. by the Reverend Mr. Mathews, Col. John Jenkins, of St. Helena, to Mrs. Elizabeth Mary-Ann Girardeau, of Bartholomew's, daughter of the late Capt. John C. Field.

Died on the 13th inst. in the thirteenth year of her age, of the prevailing fever, Miss Mary Gould Smith, a native of England, but for many years a resident of New York...(Eulogy)

Died at Beaufort, (S.C.) on the 13th inst. of the prevailing fever of that place, Mr. John B. Hart, a native of Portsmouth, (Eng.) aged 20 years...(Eulogy)

Issue of September 22, 1817

Died, on the 13th inst. of the prevailing fever, in the 6th year of her age, Sarah Annabella Withers Read, only daughter of J. H. Read, Esq....(Eulogy)

Died - The friends and acquaintances of Dr. James MacBride, are invited to attend his funeral from his late residence No. 15, Laurens Street, this afternoon, at 5 o'clock.

Issue of September 23, 1817

* Died - The friends and acquaintances of Mr. and Mrs. Philip Ling, are invited to attend the funeral of their son, Philip, from their residence, No. 11 Guignard Street, tomorrow morning, at 7 o'clock.

Issue of September 25, 1817

Married, on the 24th of July last, by the Rev. Benjamin Tauant, Mr. Samuel Richenbaker, of Orangeburgh, to the aimiable and accomplished Mrs. Juliana Simons, daughter of Mr. Benjamin Jewel formerly Merchant of this city.

Issue of September 27, 1817

(Died) On the 17th inst. after a short illness, Mr. John Walton, late Treasurer of the Lower Division of this state...(Eulogy)

(Died) On the evening of the 6th inst. in the 50th year of her age, after a distressing illness protracted to a considerable length, Miss Sarah Cornelia Tebout.

Issue of September 27, 1817

(Died) On the 8th inst. after an illness of five days, of the prevailing fever, in the 21st year of his age, Mr. Christian H. Schwartz, a native of Bremen.

(Died) On the evening of the 14th inst. of the prevailing fever, Mr. Andrew Bare, aged 37 years.

(Died) On the 17th inst. in the village of Cannonsborough, adjoining Charleston, of a nervous fever, after ten days illness, Daniel Webb Logan, the youngest child of Mr. Wm. Logan, of that place.

(Died) On the 20th inst. after an illness of five days, of the prevailing fever, in the 23d year of his age, Mr. Richard Tunis, a native of Philadelphia, and partner in the house of Coates, West & Tunis, of this place.

(Died) On the 21st inst. of the prevailing fever, Elizabeth L. Hutchinson, aged 3 years and 10 months; only daughter of the late Legar Hutchinson, Esq.

(Died) On the 21st inst. of the prevailing disease of our city, Wiley Gresham, Esq. in the 24th year of his age.

(Died) On the 21st inst. in this city, Thomas Mellichamp. Esq. of St. Paul's Parish, eldest son of Saint Lo Mellichamp, Esq. of the same place.

(Died) On the 24th inst. of the prevailing fever, Elizabeth Ann Browne, aged 5 years, only daughter of the late James Browne, Esq.

Issue of September 29, 1817

Died, on Monday, the 22d inst. at the house of his disconsolate parents, in the 15th year of his age, Paul Mazyck, Jun. the youngest son of William Mazyck, of this city.

Died - The friends and acquaintances of Mr. Samuel Corrie and of Mr. John Smith, are requested to attend the funeral of Mr. John Smith, this afternoon, at half past four o'clock, from his late residence, No. 109 Broad Street.

Died - The friends and acquaintances of Mr. F. A. Falcke are requested to attend his funeral this afternoon, at 4 o'clock, from his residence, No. 262, King Street.

Issue of September 30, 1817

Married at Grace Church, New York, on Saturday evening, by the Rev. Dr. Bowen, Mr. Henry Brevcort, Jun. to Miss Laura Elizabeth Carson, daughter of the late James Carson, Esq. of this city.

Died, on the 26th of this month, of the prevailing fever, Mr. Mordecai Hyams, aged 30 years, a native of England...(Eulogy)

Died, on the 23d instant after a short illness, William Trescott, Esq. in the 34th year of his age...(Eulogy)

Died - The friends and acquaintances of Thomas and Mary Raine, are invited to attend the funeral of their son, tomorrow morning at 8 o'clock, from their residence in Meeting Street Road.

Died - The friends and acquaintances and the Members of the Hibernian Society, are invited to attend the funeral of Mr. William Pritchard, Jun. this afternoon at 4 o'clock from his late residence No. 2 Anson Street.

Died - The Members of the Hibernian Society are invited to attend the funeral of Mr. William Pritchard, Jun. this afternoon at 4 o'clock, from his late residence No. 2, Anson Street.

Issue of October 1, 1817

Departed this life on the 20th ult. after an illness of 10 days, Mrs. Eliza L. Brailsford, wife of Captain Robert Brailsford, of Clarendon County, Sumter District.

Died, on the 18th ult. in the 5th year of his age, of the prevailing fever, William Lothrop Price, eldest son of William Price, Esq.

Died, on Sullivan's Island, on the 26th ult. at the house of Mr. Peter Jones, after 5 days illness, of the prevailing fever, Edgar S. Jones, son of Ira Jones of Philadelphia.

Died, on Wednesday, the 10th ult. at the house of Mr. Benjamin Dupre, near Pendleton, S.C. Mr. Benjamin Hawes, of this city, aged 29 years.

Issue of October 2, 1817

The death of Dr. James MacBride, was an event, which could not fail to excite in the community very general and deep regret...(Eulogy)

Issue of October 3, 1817

Died, in Savannah, on the 24th ult. after a fortnight illness, Mr. John Lanergan, aged 26 years, a native of Ireland, and a resident in the United States eighteen years—he has left an affectionate brother and sister to mourn his loss.

Died - It is our painful duty to announce the death of Mrs. Susannah Elsworth, wife of Theophilus Elsworth, Esq. of this city, who departed this life on Saturday, the 21st day of September, aged 59 years and 4 months.

Died - The friends and acquaintances of Thomas and Margaret Addison Ham, are requested to attend the funeral of their son George, tomorrow morning, at 9 o'clock, from their residence in Hampstead.

Died - The friends and acquaintances of Mr. John Russell, dec. and the Members of the Fellowship Society, are invited to attend his funeral from his late residence in Bank Square, at 4 o'clock this afternoon.

Issue of October 6, 1817

Died, on the 30th ult. of a nervous fever, at the residence of Jonathan Lucas, Jun. Esq. Cannonsborough, Mr. Joseph Butler, Engineer, aged 26 years, a native of England.

Departed this transitory life on the 2d inst. after a short illness of three days, Mary Neilson Bell, aged nine years, ten months, and six days, eldest child of Alexander N. Bell.

Issue of October 7, 1817

Departed this life, on the 12th ult. of the prevailing fever, Mr. David Cochran, a native of New Hampshire, but for the last seven years a resident of this place...(Eulogy)

Died, on the 30th ult. after a short but painful illness, which he bore with Christian Fortitude to his timely end, Mr. Joseph Addison, of St. Thomas' Parish, in the 47th year of his age...(Eulogy)

Died, at Haddrill's Point, on the 29th ult. after a severe illness of six days, Miss Ann Ives, a native of Willingford, (Conn.) aged 23 years.

Died, on the 3d October, Catherine Votee, eldest daughter of Captain Charles Votee, of New York, aged 5 years and 1 month, after an illness of two days.

Died, in this city, on the 30th ult. aged about 23 years, Mr. Alexander M'Innes, a native of Richmond County (N.C.)

Died, at Beaufort, (S.C.) on the 28th ult. Miss Lydia Turner, a native of Norwich (England) but many years a resident of this country.

Died, at Beaufort, (S.C.) on the 30th ult. Master Daniel Bythewood, aged about 11 years, son of Captain Daniel Bythewood.

Died, on the night of the 22d ult. at the plantation of Captain William Humphrey's, near Jamesville, Sumter District, (S.C.) Captain Francis Noble, late from Boston, (Mass.) after an illness of six weeks, which he bore with Christian Fortitude.

Died, at Pendleton, (S.C.) on Monday the 22d ult. Mr. William Scott, formerly of this city, aged 32 years.

Died, at Columbia, (S.C.) on the 27th ult. Mr. William Chapman, of that place, coach maker, aged 28 years.

Died, at Columbia, (S.C.) on the 28th ult. after a few days illness, aged 26 years, Mr. Jacob Daten, carpenter or a sailor, he was a native of New York, and had been but a few days from Charleston.

Issue of October 8, 1817

Died - The friends and acquaintances of the Rev. Urban Cooper, and the Ministers of all Denominations, are invited to attend his funeral, from his residence, No. - King Street, four doors above the Inspection, tomorrow morning, at eight o'clock.

Died - The relations, friends and acquaintances of Mrs. Ann Langstaff, are requested to attend the funeral of her son Henry Howard Langstaff, from his late residence, No. 153 Church Street continued, at 5 o'clock this afternoon, without further invitation.

Issue of October 10, 1817

Married, in Cambridge (Mass.) on the 24th ult. Lieut. Edward R. Shubrick, of the United States Navy, to Miss Esther Blain, both of this city.

Died, on the 3d instant, of the prevailing fever, after an illness of 8 days Miss Angelina Mary Eliza Heath, in the sixth year of her age... (Eulogy)

Died, at Augusta, (Ga.) on the 29th ult. Kenneth M'Kenzie, Captain of Artillery, in the United States' service, stationed near that place. His remains were interred with Military and Masonic honour.

Issue of October 11, 1817

Died ...Rev. Urban Cooper...(Eulogy)

Died, on the 8th inst. of a bilious fever, in the 18th year of his age, Mr. Henry H. Langstaff...(Eulogy)

Died, in Savannah, on the 7th instant Michael Keating, a native of Ireland, but for many years a resident of this city, and lately a lieutenant in the Patriot service.

Died, at Savannah, on the 9th inst. after a short illness, Mr. Thomas Kelly, a native of Dublin, Ireland, aged 27 years.

Died, at Edgefield Court House, (S.C.) on the 22d September, Master James Fox Bacon, son of Edmund Bacon, Esq. of that place.

Died, at his residence near M'Cord's Ferry, (S.C.) on the 30th ult. in the 75th year of his age, Captain Richard Brown. He died respected by a numerous acquaintance and justly lamented by an affectionate family.

Issue of October 13, 1817

Died - The friends and acquaintances of Henry Hyrne Basquen and Samuel Yates, are invited to attend the funeral of the former, from the House of S. Yates, No. 48, Bay, at half past 4 o'clock this afternoon.

Issue of October 16, 1817

Died - The friends and acquaintances of Richard and John Fair and particularly the members of the Hibernian Society are requested to attend the funeral of Richard Fair, from his late residence, No. 170 King Street, tomorrow morning, at 8 o'clock.

Issue of October 17, 1817

Died - The friends and acquaintances of the late Peter Thomas Ryan, are invited to attend his funeral tomorrow morning, at 8 o'clock from his late residence, No. 24, Anson Street, without further invitation.

Died - The members of the Hibernian Society are invited to attend the funeral of the late Mr. Peter Thomas Ryan, from the house of Mr. Ed Mortimer, No. 24, Anson Street, tomorrow morning, at 9 o'clock.

Issue of October 18, 1817

Died - The friends and acquaintances of James S. Neilson, Esqr. and particularly the members of the Bar, are requested to attend his funeral this afternoon, at 4 o'clock, from his late residence, Dr. Uimos, Queen St.

Issue of October 21, 1817

Married, in Liverpool, (Eng.) J. G. Levy, Esq. of this city, to Miss Fanny Yates.

Died on the 15th inst. Master Oliver Utt, aged 13 years and 6 months... (Eulogy)

Issue of October 22, 1817

Died, on the 14th inst. after a lingering illness, William Mathewes, Sen. Esq. in the 62nd year of his age...(Eulogy)

Died, at his residence on the Pee Dee, on Thursday morning last, Major Richard Godfrey, one of the oldest and most respectable planters of Marion District.

Died, at Camden, on Friday the 3d inst. Miss Mary Lee, daughter of Francis Lee, Esq. of that place - ...in her eight year...(Eulogy)

Issue of October 23, 1817

Departed this life, on the 5th instant, at his father's residence in Marlborough District, after an illness of three days, in the 19th year of his age, Mr. Lewis Pledger, much and universally regretted by all who knew him...(Eulogy)

Issue of October 24, 1817

Married, last evening at St. Michael's Church by the Rev. Dr. Dalcho, Elias Horry, Esq. late Intendant of this city, to Miss Mary Rutledge Shubrick, of Belvedere.

Died, on the 21st inst. of the prevailing fever, Mrs. Catherine Rosenbaum, in the 24th year of her age. Her friends sincerely lament her loss.

Issue of October 27, 1817

Departed this life, on the 17th inst. after an illness of short but painful duration, Mr. Peter Thomas Ryan, eldest son of Peter S. Ryan, Esq. late of this city.

Died, on Thursday last, after a long experience of that never failing disease of death, the consumption, Mrs. Susan Munnerlyn, consort of Mr. Charles Munnerlyn, of Waccamaw.

Issue of October 28, 1817

Died, at Dickson's Island, on the 21st inst. after a few days illness, Mrs. Susanna Rivers, consort of Francis Rivers...(Eulogy)

Died, at the quarantine hospital, New York, on the morning of the 19th inst. Captain Richard Week, Jun. aged about 24 years, late master of the sloop Victor, from this port.

Issue of November 1, 1817

Married, at Western, (Mass.) on the 19th inst. Mr. Baxter O. Mynott, of Charleston, (S.C.) Merchant, to Miss Mary Hodges, daughter of Daniel Hodges, Esq. of the former place.

Died at Savannah, on the 25th instant, in the poor house, Mrs. Elizabeth Price, a native of New York, aged 104. She had been an inmate of that receptacle for the indigents since February, 1811; since which time it is believed she has not been out of its precincts.

Issue of November 3, 1817

Died at Walterborough, on the 22d inst. after a few days illness Miss Cornilia M'Pherson Ford...in the 11th year of her age.

Died, on Friday morning last, at Cordsville, St. John's Berkely, Dr. James Ravenel...(Eulogy)

Issue of November 3, 1817

Died - The friends and acquaintances of Mr. and Mrs. Calder, of Mr.
Charles Banks, also those of Mr. John Graham, are particularly invited to
attend the funeral of the latter, late of the firm of Graham & Banks, precisely at 4 o'clock this afternoon from Mr. Alexander Calder's, Broad Street.

Issue of November 4, 1817

Died, at Savannah, on the 1st inst. after a short and painful illness,
in the 25th year of his age Mordecai M. Sheftall, son of Dr. Moses Sheftall.

Issue of November 5, 1817

Died, on the morning of the 3d inst. after a few days illness, of the
yellow fever, Mr. John Graham, a native of Glasglow, Scotland.
Died, on the 20th September, William Monroe, aged 21 years. On the
26th Sept. William Monroe, aged 50 years. On the 27th Sept. Richard Monroe,
aged 18 years. On the 4th Oct. Barbara Monroe aged 53 years. On the 6th
Oct. Eliza Monroe aged 14 years and 7 months; and on the 18th Oct. Martha
Monroe, aged 16 years. All natives of Ireland, and of one family...(Eulogy)
(Died) ...Miss Sarah Elizabeth Phipps, who was taken from the sublunary
to the celestial world, on the 29th ult. in the 17th year of her age...
(Eulogy)

Issue of November 6, 1817

Married on Tuesday evening last, by the Reverend Dr. Gallagher, Arnold
Remoussin, Esq. to Miss Ellen Lynah, eldest daughter of Edward Lynah, Esq.
Died - Colonel Alexander Colclough is dead...This worthy old gentleman
departed this life the 14th of October...(Eulogy)
Died, in this city, on Wednesday, 29th ult. John Ball, Esq. of St.
John's Berkley.

Issue of November 7, 1817

Died, on Wednesday the 29th Oct. John Ball. Esq. of St. John's Berkley
...(Eulogy)

Issue of November 8, 1817

Married, on Monday 29th September last, by the Rev. Mr. Galuchat, Mr.
Robert A. Paisley, to Miss Charlotte J. Will, all of this city.

Issue of November 12, 1817

Married, on the 28th October, by the Rev. Mr. Carr, at the residence of
Stephen Girard, Esq. Philadelphia, General Henry Lallemand to Miss Harriot
Girard, neice of Stephen Girard. Esq. There were present Messrs. Ote de
Survilliers, Marshall de Grouchy and son, Generals Vandamme and Charles
Lallemand, Sen. and a large company of the friends of the happy couple.

Issue of November 13, 1817

Died - The friends and acquaintances of Doctor Galagher and Mrs.
Frances Galagher, are respectfully invited to attend the funeral of the
latter, at her residence No. 14, Magazine Street, this afternoon at 4
o'clock.

Issue of November 15, 1817

Married, on Wednesday evening 12th inst in St. Philips Church, by the
Rev. Christopher E. Gadsden, D. D. the Rev. Albert A. Muller, to Miss
Frances Maria Rivers, of this city.

Issue of November 17, 1817

Married, on Wednesday evening last, Dr. Abraham Sheftall, son of the late Levi Sheftall, Esq. of Savannah to Miss Sarah De La Motta, eldest daughter of Mr. E. De La Motta of this city.

Died suddenly, at his plantation in St. Paul's Parish, on Saturday last, Col. William Hayne, in the 53d year of his age...(Eulogy)

Issue of November 18, 1817

Died - The friends and acquaintances of the late Mr. Elisha Hamlin, are invited to attend his funeral this afternoon, at 3 o'clock, from the corner of John and King Streets continued.

Issue of November 25, 1817

Died - The friends and acquaintances of the late Mr. William Grogen, are invited to attend his funeral, from his late residence at Jehu Jones, Broad Street, tomorrow afternoon, at 4 o'clock precisely.

Issue of November 26, 1817

Married, last evening, by the Rev. Dr. Gadsden, Edward P. Simons, Esq. to Miss Catherine Paterson, youngest daughter of Hugh Paterson, Esq. all of this place.

Died at Savannah, on the 22d ult. Mr. Nathan Hersey, a native of (Mass.) aged 26 years.

Died on the 21st inst. Miss Eliza C. Bolles, daughter of Rob T. Bolles, aged 21.

Issue of November 27, 1817

Died, in Fayetteville on the 13th instant, the Hon. Alexander M'Millan, Attorney at Law, and member elect to congress from that district.

Died - The friends and acquaintances of the late Thos. Loughton Smith, Esq. and particularly the Members of the Bar, and of the South Carolina Society, are invited to attend his funeral, this afternoon, at half past three o'clock, from Mrs. William Loughton Smith's residence, No. 100 East Bay.

Died - The Members of the '76 Association are requested to attend the funeral of the late Thomas Loughton Smith, Esq. from the late residence of his father, corner of East Bay and Amen.-Street this afternoon, at half past 3 o'clock.

Issue of November 28, 1817

Died - The friends and acquaintances of Mr. and Mrs. Hamilton, are invited to attend the funeral of the former, from his late residence, corner of Meeting and Queen Streets, this afternoon at 3 o'clock.

Died - The friends and acquaintances, of Mrs. Ann Ross, are requested to attend her funeral tomorrow afternoon, at 4 o'clock, from her late residence, corner of Ellery and Anson Street.

Issue of November 29, 1817

(Died)...Master Charles Samuel Faber, the eldest son of Mr. Christian Henry Faber, who died on the 18th inst. after a very painful illness of 22 days duration...in the 10th year of his age...(Eulogy)

Issue of December 2, 1817

Died - It becomes the duty of a friend to announce the death of Elisha Hamlin, who was summond to the world of spiritis on the 18th ult....(Eulogy)

Issue of December 3, 1817

Died, on the 26th ult. of the prevailing fever, Mr. John Brown, a native of Portglenone...He was only twenty one years old...(Eulogy)

Died, on Friday morning, the 24th Oct. at 2 o'clock, Col. Nathaniel Ramsey of Baltimore...(Eulogy)

Issue of December 4, 1817

Married, on Tuesday evening last, by the Rev. Dr. Flinn, Mr. Samuel J. Murray, of Statesburg, to Miss Sarah Lang Robinson, of this city.

Issue of December 5, 1817

Departed this life, on the morning of the 26th November in the 33d year of her age, Mrs. Charlotte A. Wilson, consort of John L. Wilson, Esq. of this city....(Eulogy)

Issue of December 6, 1817

Died, at Pine Ridge, St. John's Berkley, on the 23d ult. Mrs. Agnes Haig, wife of Dr. Maham Haig, and daughter of Alexander Ritchie, Esq. of Glasgow.

Issue of December 9, 1817

-Departed this life after a lingering illness, Mrs. Sarah Saltus, aged 60 years...(Eulogy)

Issue of December 10, 1817

Departed...Mr. John Fabian, in the 63d year of his age...(Eulogy)

Issue of December 12, 1817

Married, on Wednesday evening, the 10th inst. by the Rev. Dr. Flinn, Mr. S. H. Skinner, one of the Editors of the City Gazette, to Miss Annette Haines of New York.

Issue of December 16, 1817

Died, on Saturday the 13th inst. after a lingering illness, Charles Elliott, Esq. aged 29...(Eulogy)

Issue of December 18, 1817

Died, on the 9th inst. Mrs. Ann Neufville, Sen. of this city, in the 75th year of her age...(Eulogy)

Died — The friends and acquaintances of Miss Mary Cropton and of Mr. and Mrs. Herior and Mrs. Weyman, are requested to attend the funeral of the former, from the house of Mrs. Weyman, Meeting Street Road, at half past 10 o'clock tomorrow morning.

Issue of December 23, 1817

Died, on the 18th inst. much regretted by her friends and acquaintances Miss Mary Cropton, a native of Norfolk, in England, and twenty years a resident in this country.

Issue of December 27, 1817

Married, on Thursday evening, by the Rev. Mr. Palmer, Mr. Nathaniel Cooper, to Miss Mary Revell, both of this city.

Issue of January 2, 1818

Married on Wednesday last, Mr. Benjamin Moise, to Miss Rebecca Levy, both of this city.

Married on Tuesday evening last, by the Rev. Dr. Flinn, Mr. Lewis Rechon, to Miss Jane Ingram, both of this city.

Issue of January 3, 1818

Died on the 22d of December last, after a long lingering of consumption, in the 43d year of his age, Mr. Hart Soloman a native of Germany, and for many years a resident of this city. Who has left a disconsolate widow and a numerous circle of friends to lament this irreparable loss.

Issue of January 8, 1818

Died - The friends and acquaintances of Mr. and Mrs. Richard M'Millan, of Mr. John R. M'Millan, and the members of the Charleston Bar, are invited to attend the funeral of the latter at his residence, No. 212 King Street, tomorrow morning, at nine o'clock without further invitation.

Issue of January 9, 1818

Married, on Wedneseay evening last, by the Rev. Mr. Galvehat, Mr. John Adams Bennett, to Miss Eliza Shilback, both of this city.

Issue of January 10, 1818

Departed this life, on the 4th inst. in the 38th year of her age, Mrs. Mary P. Peyre, consort of Francis Peyre, Esq. of St. Stephen's Parish... (Eulogy)

Died, at Georgetown, on Saturday last, Dr. Joseph Blyth, aged 65 years.

Issue of January 12, 1818

Married on Thursday evening last, by the Rev. Dr. Bowen, Robert Brodie, Esq. to Miss Sarah Harriet Waring, only daughter of Daniel Waring, Esq. deceased - all of this city.

Issue of January 14, 1818

Died, on the 7th instant, at his residence on the Santee Canal, George B. Artope, Esq. superintendent of the Canal.

Died, at his residence in Christ Church Parish on the 7th inst. Thomas Hamlin, Esq. in the sixty third year of his age, of a cancer, with which he has been afflicted for several years...(Eulogy)

Died - In reflecting on the decease of Mrs. Mary P. Peyre, the consort of Francis Peyre, Esq. who departed this life, in St. Stephen's Parish, on the 4th inst....(Eulogy)

Died - The friends and acquaintances of Mr. and Mrs. Dulles and of Mr. and Mrs. Cheves, are respectfully invited to attend the funeral of Mr. Dulles, without further invitation, from the house of Mr. Chever, No. 41, Society-Street, tomorrow the 15th inst. at 9 o'clock in the morning.

Issue of January 16, 1818

Died, at Grenwich, Captain N. Portlock, of the Royal Navy. He accompanied Captain Cooke round the world; and subsequently performed two other similar voyages, in conjunction with Captain Dixon.

Issue of January 19, 1818

Departed this life, on the 13th instant, in the 54th year of his age, Joseph Dulles, Esq. formerly a respectable merchant of this city, and for some years past a resident of Philadelphia...(Eulogy)

Issue of January 21, 1818

Died - The friends and acquaintances of Mrs. Catherine Weyman and Mr. Samuel Gale, are requested to attend the funeral of the latter, tomorrow afternoon, at 3 o'clock from the residence of Mrs. C. Weyman, corner of Reid and Meeting-Street.

Issue of January 26, 1818

Died on the 7th inst. Mr. John R. M'Millan, of this city, in the 26th year of his age...(Eulogy)

Issue of January 28, 1818

(Died)...Captain James Davis, of Santee was taken from us in the 71st year of his age. He has left a son and four grandchildren, with other relations, besides a numerous train of friends, to lament his death.

Died, at Philadelphia, on Friday, 16th inst. Mrs. Barbara Harriet Fennell, widow of the late celebrated tragedian, scholar and polite gentleman, James Fennell...

Issue of January 30, 1818

Married on Thursday evening the 8th instant, by the Rev. John Couser, Thomas Witherspoon, Esq. of Williamsburg District, to Mrs. Mary Dick of Salem, Sumter District.

Died, at Georgetowne, (S.C.) on Monday morning last, Francis Withers, Jun. Esq. eldest son of Mr. Robert F. Withers....(Eulogy)

Died, on the 12th inst. at Utica, in the state of New York, Col. Benjamin Walker, aid-de-camp and friend of Baron Steuben and of General Washington...(Eulogy)

Issue of January 31, 1818

Died - The friends and acquaintances of Mr. Charles P. Smith are requested to attend his funeral from his father's residence, No. 14 Champney-Street, at half past 8 o'clock, tomorrow morning,

Issue of February 2, 1818

Died - The friends and acquaintances of the late Miss Ann L. Smith are requested to attend her funeral this afternoon, at 3 o'clock, from Mrs. Cansler's No. 102 King-Street.

Issue of February 11, 1818

Married in Stateburg, on the 29th of January, by the Rev. Christian Hanckel, Dr. William W. Anderson, to Miss Mary M'Kenzie, both of that place.

Married at the High Hills of Santee, the 3d instant, by the Rev. Christian Hanckel, Dr. Xenophon J. Bracey, to Miss Charlotte A. Waties, daughter of the Hon. Thomas Waties, all of that place.

Issue of February 13, 1818

Died, on the 28th ult. after a lingering illness, which he bore with the firmness of a man, Mr. Charles R. Smith, in the 22d year of his age...(Eulogy)

Issue of February 16, 1818

Died, at Beaufort, South-Carolina, on the 6th instant, in the year of his age, Master John B. Woodward, only son of Mrs. Esther S. Woodward, of Charleston.

Issue of February 23, 1818

Died, at Opelousas, Louisiana, on the 8th inst. Colonel William Lyons, in the 63d year of his age. He was a native of South Carolina...(Eulogy)

Issue of February 26, 1818

Died, on the 18th instant, near Orangeburg-Mr. Alexander Christie, Jun., aged 30 years.

Issue of February 28, 1818

Married, on Wednesday last, the 25th inst. by the Rev. Dr. Gadsden, Edward H. Edwards, Esq. to Miss Frances Brewton Elliott.

Issue of March 2, 1818

Died - The relatives, friends and acquaintances of the late Mrs. Ann Darrell, and the Rev. Clergy are invited to her funeral on tomorrow afternoon, at 3 o'clock, from her late residence at the corner of Anson and George-Streets without a more particular invitation.

Issue of March 6, 1818

Died, on the 20th instant, at his residence in Yorktown, New York, John Paviding...

Died - The friends and acquaintances of the late Mr. Joseph R. M'Cay, and of T. W. Bacot and Henry H. Bacot, and the Members of the Hibernian Society, are invited to attend the funeral of Mr. M'Cay from his late residence, No. 136 Church-Street, at 4 o'clock this afternoon.

Issue of March 10, 1818

Died, at Augusta, (Geo) in June last, John M. Castens, a native of Bremes, Germany.

Issue of March 11, 1818

Died, at Havana, on the 26th ult. where he had gone for the benefit of his health, Mr. James Roddey, merchant of this city...

Issue of March 12, 1818

Married last evening, by the Rev. Mr. Gadsden, Mr. Simeon Theus, Jun. to Miss Susan Boswell Bentham, both of this city.

Died, on the 2nd inst. in the 34th year of his age, William Stephen Bull Esq....

Issue of March 16, 1818

Married on Wednesday last, by the Rev. Mr. Matthews, Doctor Joseph Lee, to Miss Mary F. Jenkins, daughter of Col. John Jenkins of St. Helena.

Issue of March 17, 1818

Died, at Detroit, on the 12th ult. Captain Thomas Hammond, a patriot and soldier....

Departed this life, at Union Hill, his seat in Washington county, on Sunday morning, the first inst. General Jared Irwin, in the sixty-eighth year of his age. He was born in Mecklenburg.

Issue of March 19, 1818

Died, on the 10th instant, of a severely painful and afficting illness, of eleven months continuance, Mrs. Christiana Harris, consort of Tucker Harris, M.D. in the sixty-eighth year of her age....

Died, suddenly, on the 10th inst. at Washington, in the 55th year of his age, Col. Robert Gardner, late Commissary of Prisoners for the United States, in Canada.

Died, at his seat at Locust Grove, near Lousiville, (Ky) on the 13th ult. the illustrious Gen. George Rogers Clark, who has received the appellation of the Father of the Western Country, in the 66th year of his age.

Departed this life, at New-Orleans, on the 16th of September, 1817, Doctor William Hudgens, a native of North-Carolina, of the prevailing Yellow Fever.

Issue of March 21, 1818

Married, on Wednesday evening last, Levi S. D'Lyon, Esq. of Savannah, Attorney at Law to Miss Leonore De La Motta, daughter of the late Mr. Isaac De La Motta, of this city.

Issue of March 24, 1818

Died, on the morning of the 15th inst. in the 37th year of her age, Mrs. Ann Maria Bounetheau...(Eulogy)

Died - The friends and acquaintances of the Rev. Dr. Gallagher, and the late Mrs. Jordon, are requested to attend the funeral of the latter tomorrow afternoon, at 4 o'clock, from the New Bridge.

Issue of March 28, 1818

Died - The friends and acquaintances of the late Mr. Henry P. Wesner are requested to attend his funeral tomorrow at 9 o'clock a.m. from Mr. S. Seyle's, No. 289 King-Street.

Issue of April 3, 1818

Died - The friends and acquaintances of Daniel Latham and Family, and of Dr. Richard L. Latham are invited, without further or more particular invitation, to attend the funeral of the latter tomorrow afternoon, at 3 o'clock, from his late residence, No. 4, Hazell-Street.

Issue of April 4, 1818

Died at Fayetteville, on the 30th March, William Barry Grove, Esq. formerly a Member of Congress, and the late President of the United States Branch Bank of that place...(Eulogy)

Issue of April 7, 1818

Married, on the 26th ult. by the Rev. Mr. Galluchat, Mr. Thomas Loney, to Mrs. Sarah A. Forno.

Departed this life, on the 3d inst. Dr. Richard L. Latham in the 26th year of his age...(Eulogy)

Issue of April 15, 1818

...Died, Mr. Joseph M'Cants, of St. Bartholomew's, resigned his spirit into the hands of his who gave it, on the 29th ult. aged 58 years...(Eulogy)

Issue of April 16, 1818

Died, on the 13th inst. in the 72d year of his age, William Doughty, Esq. of this city...(Eulogy)

Issue of April 17, 1818

Died, on the 21st ult. in the 77th year of his age, Mr. William Johnson, a native of New York, but for more than half a century one of the most useful and respectable of the inhabitants of Charleston...(Eulogy)

Issue of April 22, 1818

Married, at Laurium, (S.C.) on the 16th inst. by the Rev. Dr. Bowen, S. Colleton Graves, to Susan, youngest daughter of the late General M'Pherson.

Died - The friends and acquaintances of Mr. John M'Loll and of Mrs. Mary M'Loll, are particularly invited to attend the funeral of the latter, from her late place of residence, No. 216, Meeting-Street, this afternoon, at 5 o'clock, without a more particular invitation.

Issue of April 25, 1818

Died, in Providence, R.I., on the 21st ult. Mrs. Eve Olney Pearce, the worthy consort of Reuben Pearce, Esq. in the 56th year of her age.

Died - The friends and acquaintances of Miss Mary B. Johnson, are invited to attend her funeral, from her late residence, No. 26, Guignard-Street, at 5 o'clock tomorrow afternoon.

Issue of April 28, 1818

...Died Mrs. Mary M'Call, who in the fullhope of a joyful immortality, died in the 34th year of her age on the 22d inst....(Eulogy)

Issue of April 29, 1818

Died, at Orangeburg, (S.C.) at the house of Mrs. Cleckley, about the 1st March last, Dr. Abraham Andrus, aged from 40 to 45 years. Dr. Andrus, (it is believed) was a native of Fairfield County, Connecticut,...(Eulogy)

Issue of May 1, 1818

Departed this life, at Savannah, on Thursday night last, the 23d ult. in the 59th year of his age, Isaac Fell, Esquir, a native of Lancaster, (England)...(Eulogy)

Issue of May 4, 1818

...death of Colonel George Armistead, the gallent defender of Fort M'Henry on the melancholy occasion, the recollection of the ever memorable 14th September...(Eulogy)

Issue of May 6, 1818

Married, in St. Andrew's Parish, on Monday last, by the Rev. Mr. Fowler, Mr. Randal Robinson to Miss Eleanor M. Magwood, second daughter of Simon Magwood, Esq.

Died - The friends and acquaintances of the late Mrs. Lydia Conyers, are invited to attend her funeral this afternoon at 4 o'clock, from her late residence No. 29, Picnkney-Street.

Issue of May 8, 1818

Married, on Sunday, the 3d inst. by the Rev. Mr. Lee, Mr. George Petrie, Jun. to Mrs. Dorthe Bulfinch, both of St. George Parish.

Died, in St. Paul's Parish, on the 21st ult. in consequence of a fall from his sulkey, Robert Mackewn Haig, M.D. in the 41st year of his age... (Eulogy)

Issue of May 14, 1818

Married, on Tuesday evening last, by the Rev. Dr. Percy, Mr. James G. Bowles, to Mrs. Ann Bates, both of this city.

Issue of May 16, 1818

Married, on Thursday evening, by the Rev. Mr. Henry, Henry P. Taylor, Esq. of Columbia, to Miss Ann T. Trezevant, of this city.

Issue of May 19, 1818

Died - The friends and acquaintances of Mr. John Anthony, together those of Mrs. Anthony, are invited to attend the funeral of Mr. John Anthony, tomorrow afternoon, at 4 o'clock, from his late residence over Cannon's Bridge, next door to the Hon. Judge Johnson.

Issue of May 21, 1818

Married, in Chester District, on the 12th instant, Col. James Moorman, of Union District, to Miss Mary M'Daniel, of the former place.

Issue of May 21, 1818

Married, at Augusta, Geo. on the 15th inst. Mr. Sebastian Aimar, of this city, to Miss Ardale Manard, of the former place.

Died...among the victims of the recent accident in Wando river, was Mr. Charles Bridge, of Beverly, Massachusetts...(Eulogy)

Issue of May 22, 1818

Died, at Bordeaux, on the 6th March last, in the fifty-eighth year of his age, after a long and severe sickness, Mr. Thomas Tunno, many years settled in this city...

Issue of May 26, 1818

Married, on Sunday evening, 24th inst. Mr. Moses Joseph, of Amsterdam, to Miss Abigail Audler, of this city.

Married, on Thursday evening last, by the Rev. Dr. Flinn, Mr. James S. Galbrieth, to Miss Mary E. Martin, eldest daughter of Charles Martin deceased, both of this city.

Issue of May 27, 1818

Departed this transitory life, on Sunday, the 16th inst. by the upsetting of a boat in Wando River opposite Cat Island...Captain Joseph Quinby, a native of Newberryport, (Mass.) but for about 30 years a respectable and worthy inhabitant of this city...(Eulogy)

Issue of May 28, 1818

Died - The relatives, friends and acquaintances of the late James Wilkie and of Mrs. Wilkie, are requested to attend his funeral this afternoon, at 5 o'clock, from the house of his brother W. B. Wilkie, No. 38, Market-Street, without a more particular invitation.

Issue of June 3, 1818

Died, in Savannah, on the 15th inst. after a few hours of the most agonizing illness, Mrs. Mary Davant, wife of James Davant, Esq. in the 28th year of her age...(Eulogy)

Issue of June 8, 1818

...the late Mrs. Mary D. Logan, (wife of Wm. Logan, Esq. of this city) who died on the morning of the 5th inst. aged 39 years, 10 months, and 27 days...(Eulogy)

Issue of June 9, 1818

Died, aged 62, at Kalorama, near Washington City, on the 30th May, Mrs. Ruth Barlow relict of the late Joel Barlow, Esq. envoy extraordinary and minister plentipotentiary of the U. States at the court of France...(Eulogy)

Issue of June 11, 1818

Married, on Sunday evening, by the Rev. Mr. Galluchat, Mr. P. Kilkelly, to Miss Mary Gray, both of this city.

Issue of June 12, 1818

Married, on the 4th instant, by Mr. Brantly, John Porteous, Esq. to Miss Mary Fuller, eldest daughter of Thomas Fuller, Esq., all of Beaufort, (S.C.)

Issue of June 13, 1818

Died – The friends and acquaintances of the late Mr. Augustus W. Wright, of New-York, and those of Mr. M. Megrath and Mr. James D. Stagg, are invited to attend the funeral of the former, from Mrs. Smerdon's, No. 54, Church-Street, this afternoon at 5 o'clock.

Issue of June 18, 1818

Married on the 16th inst. by the Rev. Mr. Fowler, Whitfield Brooks, Esq. of Edgefield District, to Miss Mary P. Carroll, eldest daughter of James P. Carroll, Esq. of St. Paul's Parish.

Issue of June 25, 1818

Married, on Thursday evening last, the 18th inst. by the Rev. Mr. Bachman, Mr. Joseph Jones, to Miss Elizabeth J. Brower, both of this city.

Issue of July 2, 1818

Married, in this city, on Thursday, the 21st of May last, by the Rev. Mr. Galluchat, Mr. Francis Bready, of New-York, to Mrs. Margaret Caffily, of this city.

Issue of July 6, 1818

Died – The friends and acquaintances of Mr. Frederick Wesner, are invited to attend the funeral of his daughter this afternoon, at 5 o'clock from the corner of Queen and Mazych Streets.

Issue of July 8, 1818

Died – The friends and acquaintances of Thomas A. Vardell, and Mrs. John Ruberry, are invited to attend the funeral of the latter from her late residence, Green-Street, near the College, this afternoon at half past four o'clock.

Issue of July 16, 1818

Died, lately, at his seat in Rutherfor County, (Tenn.) Gen. Thomas Washington, aged 55 years...(Eulogy)

Died – On Tuesday, the 22d of June, departed this life, at his seat in Charlotte county, Va., Paul Carrington, Esq. in the eighty-sixth year of his age.

Issue of July 18, 1818

Married in Savannah, (Geo.) on the 15th inst. Mr. Levy Hart, to Miss Abigail Minis Sheftall, youngest daughter of the late Levy Sheftall, Esq. of that place.

Issue of July 20, 1818

Died, in this city, on the 18th inst. Thomas Mathews, Esq. in the 55th year of his age.

Issue of July 22, 1818

Died, on Edings'Bay, on the night of the 18th inst. in the 48th year of his age, Joseph James Murray, full of the faith and hope of the gospel, and much regretted by a numerous circle of relations and acquaintances.

Issue of July 28, 1818

Married, at Thea-catch-Kah, near Fort Mitchel (Creek Nation) on the 14th ultimo, William S. Mitchel, Esq. assistant Indian Agent, to Miss Jenney, eldest daughter of the celebrated Creek Warrior, General William M'Intosh.

Issue of July 28, 1818

Died, at Havana on the 12th inst. of the Yellow Fever, Mr. John Ross, of Shetland and on the same day, Dr. Christie, of Glasgow.

Issue of July 31, 1818

Died - The friends and acquaintances of Lewis Cameron, are requested to attend his funeral this afternoon, at five o'clock, from the corner of the Bay and Tradd Street.

Issue of August 3, 1818

...Dr. Ezrs Ives, the subject of this obituary, who departed this life on Saturday the 25th inst. at his house in Prince William's Parish, in the 43rd year of his age, was a native of the state of Connecticut, where he received a liberal education then obtained the degree of Doctor of Medicine ...(Eulogy)

Issue of August 5, 1818

Died, in Fairfield District, of a pulmonary disease, Mrs. Caroline L. Talley...(Eulogy)

Issue of August 6, 1818

Died on the 29th ult. in the 39th year of her age, Mrs. Harriet Smith, wife of Preess M. Smith, Esq....(Eulogy)

Died, in Savannah, on Monday evening, in consequence of a wound in the stomach, received in a duel, Mr. Aaron Mendes, a native of Charleston.

Issue of August 11, 1818

Married, at Mary-le-bone Church, London, by the Reverend the Dean of Chester, Capel Hanbury, Esq. of his Majesty's Royal Scout Regiment, youngest son of the late John Hanbury, Esquire, of Tottenham, to Ellen, only daughter of the late Wm. Franklin, Esq. formerly Governor, Captain-General and Commander in Chief of his Majesty's Province of New-Jersey, N. America, and grand daughter of the celebrated Dr. Franklin.

Issue of August 12, 1818

Died - The friends and acquaintances, of the late Mr. M. M'Farlane of Neill M'Nrill & Co. and of John Marshall, are requested to attend the funeral of the former from Mrs. Campbell's State House Square, at five o'clock this afternoon.

Issue of August 14, 1818

Died - The friends and acquaintances of the late Mrs. Abagail Muncrief are requested to attend her funeral this afternoon, at 5 o'clock, from her late residence No. 129 East-Bay.

Issue of August 17, 1818

Died - The friends and acquaintances of Dr. Thommas Denny, and the Members of the Hibernia and Medical Societies are invited to attend his funeral, from the residence of Mrs. Gowary, No. 26 Guignard-Street, at 5 o'clock, tomorrow afternoon.

Issue of August 21, 1818

Died, in Anne Arnudle County, (Md.) Priscilla Plummer, in the 97th year of her age, a Member of the Society of Friends...(Eulogy)

Died - The friends and acquaintances, of the late Mr. Paul Taylor, are invited to attend his funeral tomorrow morning, at 7 o'clock, from the House of Mr. Wm. Bell, No. -, Society Street.

Issue of August 24, 1818

Died this morning, at 7 o'clock, a poor father of a family, named Bene Marion, at his dwelling in State Street, opposite the Academy of Foreign Languages...(Eulogy)

Issue of August 26, 1818

Died, on Beach-Island, on the 15th instant Owen Fitzsimons, in the 9th year of his age, the youngest son of Christopher Fitzsimons, Esq....(Eulogy)

Issue of August 27, 1818

Died - The friends and acquaintances, the Reverend the Clergy, the officers and Members of the Protestant Episcopal Society, for the advancement of Christianity in South Carolina, are respectfully invited to attend the funeral of the late Mr. John C. Faber, Sen. from his residence No. 213, East-Bay this afternoon, at 5 o'clock.

Issue of August 28, 1818

Died, at Islington, Cannonsborough, on the 20th inst. Mr. Paul Taylor, in the 66th year of his age...(Eulogy)

Issue of September 1, 1818

Died, on Thursday the 27th ult. in the 12th year of her age, Emma, daughter of Mr. John Howard, of this city....(Eulogy)

Issue of September 5, 1818

Married, in Belfast, (Ireland) Miss Anna Maria Lynn, daughter of Robert Lynn, Sen. Esqr. of that place, to the Rev. Dr. Pea, of the Episcopal Church.

Issue of September 9, 1818

Died, at New York, on the 31st ult. Mr. G. M. Bounetheau, of this city.
Departed this life on the 14th inst. in the village of York, Edward C. M'Keluey, Esq. Attorney at Law, in the 22d year of his age. He has left a mother and four brothers to lament his loss.

Issue of September 10, 1818

Died, on Thursday, the 27th ult. at Princeton, N.J. in the 25th year of his age, the Rev. John Cruckshanks, Pastor of the Presbyterian Church on John's Island, South Carolina.
Died, on his passage from Jamaica to Liverpool M. G. Lewis, the cele-brated author, well known as Monk Lewis.
*Died, in New-York on the 11th ult. Colonel Franklin Wharton, Commandant of the United States Marine Corps.

Issue of September 11, 1818

Married, on Thursday evening the 10th inst. by the Rev. Dr. Flinn, Mr. Alexander W. Campbell, to Miss Eliza Marston, both of this city.

Issue of September 14, 1818

Died, at his farm on Laurel Hill, Somerser co. (Pa.) on Monday the 31st ult. Major-General Arthur St. Clair...(Eulogy)

Issue of September 15, 1818

Departed this life on the 25th ult. on Hilton Head, Mrs. Martha Davant, wife of John Davant, Esq. in the 37th year of her age.
Died - The relatives and friends and acquaintances of the late Mr. George Smith, are requested to attend his funeral tomorrow afternoon, at

4 o'clock, from his late residence in Anson-Street, without further invitation.

Issue of September 16, 1818

Married on Sunday evening last, by the Rev. Mr. Bachman, Mr. Augustus D. Gaffarrelly, to Miss Eliza Ann Sanders, both of this place.

Died, of the Typhus fever, on the 26th ult. at May River, the residence of William Pope, Esq. Mr. James D. Snowden, of the Firm of Wm. E. Snowden & Co. of this city...(Eulogy)

Died, in Liverpool on the 2d of August last after a short but painful illness-Captain John Safford, (a native of Ipswich in the State of Massachusetts) but for the last twenty-two years a respectable resident of this city...(Eulogy)

Issue of September 21, 1818

Died - Monday morning the 7th inst. terminated the probation of the most truly excellent and religious women, Mrs. Martha Shackelford, consort of John Shackelford, Esq. Cashier of the Branch Bank in this town, in the 58th year of her age...(Eulogy)

Issue of September 24, 1818

Died, on the 15th inst. after a short and severe illness, in the 56th year of his age George Smith, Esq....(Eulogy)

Issue of September 26, 1818

Died - The Reverend the Clergy, and the friends and acquaintances of the Reverend Dr. and Mrs. Percy, are invited to attend the funeral of the latter, from the residence of Dr. Percy, in Tradd-Street, on Monday morning, at 9 o'clock.

Died - The members of the French Protestant Church, the friends and acquaintances of Dr. P. J. Moore and of Mrs. Moore, are requested (without further invitation) to attend the funeral of the latter this afternoon, at 5 o'clock, at her late residence in King-Street.

Issue of September 28, 1818

Died - The friends and acquaintances of Mr. Marre, and the Masonic Brethren are invited to attend his funeral tomorrow morning, at ten o'clock, from Duncan's Wharf.

Married, on Saturday evening last, by the Rev. Dr. Palmer, Mr. Andrew Moffett, to Miss Anna Reid.

Issue of September 29, 1818

Departed this life, on Friday last, in the 71st year of her age, Mrs. Catherine Elliott Percy, wife of the Rev. Dr. Percy, Rector of St. Paul's Church, Radcliffeborough...(Eulogy)

Issue of October 3, 1818

Married in England, on the 13th of August, Mr. Charles Thomas Haigh, of the House of Edward & Haigh of the city, to Sarah only daughter of the Rev. John Growther, Rector of Hayfield Derbyshire.

Issue of October 6, 1818

Married on Sunday evening last, by the Rev. Mr. Muller, Mr. James Fife, to Miss Elizabeth G. Hubert, both of this city.

Issue of October 16, 1818

Married, on Wednesday evening, the 14th inst. Mr. Moses Hart, to Miss Jane Audler, both of this city.

Issue of October 16, 1818

Died - The friends and acquaintances, and particularly the Members of the Fellowship Society, are requested to attend the funeral of the late Mr. William B. Tucker at 4 o'clock this afternoon, from the residence of his brother, Mr. C. S. Tucker, No. 135 Church Street.

Issue of October 21, 1818

Died, at St. Mary's (Geo.) suddenly, on the evening of the 12th inst. James Mork, Esq. formerly of Savannah, in the 35th year of his age.

Issue of October 22, 1818

Died, on the 3d inst. Mr. Mordecai Lyon, aged 83...(Eulogy)

Issue of October 24, 1818

Died - The friends and acquaintances of the late Mr. Edward Trescot, are invited to attend his funeral at eight o'clock tomorrow morning, from the residence of Dr. John Trescot, No. 106, Tradd-Street, near Meeting-St.

Issue of November 7, 1818

Married, on Tuesday evening last, by the Rev. Mr. Palmer, Major John J. Bulow to Miss Caroline Amelia Lehre, daughter of Colonel Thomas Lehre, all of this city.

Issue of November 9, 1818

Married, on Thursday evening last, by the Rev. Dr. Gadsden, Mr. Henry Morris to Miss Melicent A. Jones, daughter of the late William Jones, Esq. of Ashepoo.

Issue of November 11, 1818

Died - The friends and acquaintances of the late Mr. Benjamin Minott, and Mr. William B. Minott, are invited to attend the funeral of the former, this afternoon at 3 o'clock, from No. 4 Gibbes-Street, without further invitation.

Died - The friends and acquaintances of the late Captain James Cooper, and those of Captain S. Hubble, are invited to attend the funeral of the former, to-morrow morning, at 8 o'clock, from his late dwelling house, on Gadsden Green, East-Bay.

Issue of November 16, 1818

Died, on Tuesday, the 10th inst. after a short and painful illness, Mr. James Minott, age 36 years a native of this city...(Eulogy)

♦Died - The friends and acquaintances of John and David Lafar, and Joseph D. Lafar, the Members of the South Carolina and Fellowship Societies, and the Members of the Charleston Ancient Battalion of Artillery, are invited to attend the funeral of the latter, from his brother's residence, No. 107 Queen-Street, to-morrow afternoon, at 3 o'clock.

Issue of November 20, 1818

Married, last evening, by the Rev. Mr. Gadsden, Mr. Adam James Browne, to Miss Laura Alvina Pinckney, daughter of the late Thomas Pinckney, Jun. Esq. deceased, all of this city.

Issue of November 21, 1818

Departed this life, on the 15th instant, after a long and painful illness, Mrs. Kester Armstrong, in the 64th year of her age, a native of London, and for the late thirty-eight years a resident of this city.

Issue of December 7, 1818

Married in this city, by the Rev. Mr. Reid, on Friday evening, the 4th inst. the Rev. Mr. John Convert, of New-York, to Mrs. Susan M'Fadden, of Salem, (S.C.)

Issue of December 14, 1818

Died, at Pittsburg about the 1st inst. Commodore Joshua Barney, in the 60th year of his age...(Eulogy)

Issue of December 16, 1818

Died - The friends and acquaintances of the late Mrs. Jane Bacot Sevier, and of her father, Thomas W. Bacot, are invited to attend the funeral of the former, from the house of the later, No. 84 Broad-Street, at 11 o'clock to-morrow morning.

Issue of December 19, 1818

Married on Thursday evening, by the Right Rev. Dr. Bowen, Dr. Isaac Motte Campbell, to Miss Anna Ramsey, eldest daughter of Dr. John Ramsey.

Died - The friends and acquaintances of Mr. William Marshall, also, the Members of the Mechanics Society, are particularly invited to attend his funeral to-morrow morning, at 11 o'clock, from the residence of Mr. J. L Pezant, No. 3, Boundary-Street.

Died - The friends and acquaintances of John Cole and Jacob Cole, are particularly requested to attend the funeral of the latter, from the residence of John W. Chitty, Sen. St. Philip-Street continued, to-morrow afternoon, at 4 o'clock, without further invitation.

Issue of December 22, 1818

Departed this life, on Tuesday, the 15th inst. Mrs. Jane Bacot Sevier, consort of Major Alexander Sevier, of Greenville, Tennessee, (late of the U.S. Marine Corps) and eldest daughter of Thomas Wright Bacot, of this city, aged 28 years and 2 months.

Died - The Reverend Clergy, and the friends and acquaintances of the late James W. Gadsden, are requested to attend his funeral from his late residence, No. 78, Queen-Street, at 9 o'clock, to-morrow morning, without a more particular invitation.

Died - The friends and acquaintances of Mrs. Mary E. Bryce, Mr. James Scot and Mr. Henry Bryce, are requested to attend the funeral of Mrs. Bryces' son, from his mothers' house, No. 16, Lauren's-Street, to-morrow morning, at 9 o'clock, without any further invitation.

Issue of December 24, 1818

Married on Wednesday evening last, by the Rev. Mr. Cohen, Col. Chapman Levy, of Camden, (S.C.) to Miss Flora Levy, of this city.

Issue of December 29, 1818

Died - The friends and acquaintances of Mr. Jonathan and Mrs. Mary Winchester, are invited to attend the funeral of the former, to-morrow afternoon at 3 o'clock, without further invitation, from his late residence corner of Cannon and Cumming-Street.

Issue of January 2, 1819

Married, on Thursday, by the Rev. Henry Gibbes, the Rev. Allston Gibbes, to Miss Sarah Chisolm, daughter of Alexander Robert Chisolm. Esq.

Issue of January 5, 1819

Died - The felatives, friends and acquaintances, and the Members of Methodist Episcopal Church, are invited to attend the funeral of Mrs. Mary

Charlotte Gibbs, from her mother's residence in State Street, tomorrow
morning, the 6th inst. at 10 o'clock, without further invitation.

Issue of January 9, 1819

Married, on Tuesday evening last, by the Rev. Dr. Gadsden, Rev. Paul T.
Gervais, to Miss Claudia G. Thayer, daughter of Mr. E. Thayer.

Issue of January 11, 1819

Died - The friends and acquaintances of John Lloyd, Jun. are invited to
attend his funeral, at his late residence No. 18, Bull Street, tomorrow
morning at 7 o'clock.

Issue of January 14, 1819

Departed this life, early on Saturday morning last, in the 74th year of
his age, Alexander Baron, M.D. a native of Scotland...(Eulogy)

Issue of January 18, 1819

Died - on Saturday morning, the 16th inst. in the 74th year of his age,
Dr. Alexander Baron, a native of Scotland...(Eulogy)

Issue of January 25, 1819

Died - The friends and acquaintances of the late Mrs. Ann Newton, and of
Mr. W. R. Minott, are invited to attend the funeral of the former, tomorrow
afternoon, at 3 o'clock, from No. 4 Gibbes Street.

Issue of January 26, 1819

Died, on Monday, the 18th inst. Henry Gaddes, Esq. aged 76 years...
(Eulogy)

Died - The friends and acquaintances of the late Mrs. Ann Newton, and of
Mr. W. R. Minott, are invited to attend the funeral of the former, this
afternoon, at 3 o'clock, from No. 14, Gibbes Street.

Issue of February 5, 1819

Died - The friends and acquaintances and the Members of the Medical
Society, are invited to attend the funeral of Dr. John Noble, from his late
residence in King Street, this afternoon, at 4 o'clock, without further
invitation.

Issue of February 6, 1819

Died, in Prince William's Parish, on the 31st ultimo, Miss Amarinthia
Perkins Lockwood, in the 24th year of her age, daughter of Joshua Lockwood,
Esq.*

Issue of February 8, 1819

Departed this life, in Christ Church Parish, on the 26th ult. Joseph
DuBose, Esq. in the 42d year of his age...(Eulogy)

Issue of February 9, 1819

Married, on Wednesday evening last, by the Rev. Mr. Galluchat, Mr. John
A. Wotton, of this city, to Miss Electa, daughter of Mr. David Granniss, of
Derby, Connecticut.

Issue of February 11, 1819

Died - The friends and acquaintances of Mr. John Johnston, are invited
to attend his funeral, without further invitation, tomorrow morning, at
9 o'clock, from the house of Mrs. Mauger, No. 99 Broad Street.

Issue of February 13, 1819

Died - The friends and acquaintances of Mr. and Mrs. Langton, are invited to attend the funeral of Mr. John Larry, from the residence of Mr. Langton, 361 King Street, this afternoon, at 4 o'clock.

Died - The friends and acquaintances, and the Northern Gentlemen at present in this city, are particularly invited to attend the funeral of Mr. James Beach, from Mrs. Blair's Boarding House, No. 25 Mazych Street, tomorrow, at 12 o'clock.

Died - The friends and acquaintances of Mr. Richard Downing Todd, are invited to attend his funeral tomorrow morning, at 12 o'clock, from his late residence No. 15, Legare Street, without further invitation.

Issue of February 17, 1819

Died, at his Plantation, in St. Paul's Parish, on the 5th inst. in the 45th year of his age, John Coburn, Esq....(Eulogy)

Issue of February 19, 1819

Married, on Tuesday evening last, by the Right Rev. Bishop Bowen, Mr. Daniel D. Bacot, to Miss Eliza M. Ferguson, daughter of the late Wm. Ferguson, Esq.

Issue of February 23, 1819

Departed this life, suddenly, on the 4th inst. of appoplexy, connected with a paralytic affect on, Doctor John Noble, a native of Abbeville District, in this state, aged about 47 years, and for the last twenty years a partitioner of medicine in this city...(Eulogy)

Issue of March 4, 1819

Married, on the 24th ult. by the Rev. Andrew Fowler, Willis J. Duncan, Esq., to Miss Ellen Barlowe Bellinger, daughter of Dr. John S. Bellinger.

Issue of March 5, 1819

Married, on Wednesday evening last, by the Rev. Mr. Cohen, Mr. Joseph Lee, Merchant, from Amsterdam, to Miss Mariam Myers, daughter of Samuel Myers, deceased, of this city.

Died, in Savannah, evening, the 20th ult., Mr. Samuel Mordica, in the 68th year of his age...(Eulogy)

Issue of March 12, 1819

Married, last evening by the Right Rev. Bishop Bowen, Sims White, Esq., to Miss Jane Purcell White, only daughter of John White, Esq.

Issue of March 20, 1819

Died - The friends and acquaintances of the late Mrs. Catherine Trescot, and of Dr. John S. Trescot, are requested to attend the funeral of the former, at her son's residence, No. 106 Tradd Street, tomorrow morning, at 8 o'clock, without further invitation.

Issue of March 23, 1819

Died - The friends and acquaintances of the Rev. Dr. Furman, and of the late Mrs. D. M. Furman, the Rev. Clergy of the city, and the Congregation of the Baptist generally, are respectfully invited to attend the funeral of Mrs. Furman, without further invitation, from her late residence No. 117, Church Street, tomorrow afternoon, at 4 o'clock.

Issue of March 25, 1819

Died, on the 24th inst. after a lingering and distressing illness, Miss Conelia Carolina M'Pherson.

Issue of March 27, 1819

Died, on the 6th inst. Mrs. Elizabeth M. Freeman, relict of the late Wm. Freeman, Esq.

Issue of April 2, 1819

Married, on the 11th inst. by the Rev. John Crawford, Mr. Benjamin Bostick, to Miss Jane A. Maner, both of Black Swamp, St. Peters.

Died - The friends and acquaintances of Mrs. Ann Mood, are requested to attend her funeral at 4 o'clock, this evening, at No. 133, Meeting Street.

Issue of April 8, 1819

Married, on Sunday evening last, at Savannah, by the Rev. Henry Kollock, Mr. Casam E. Bartlet, to Miss Sarah, only daughter of Mr. Benjamin Malhado, all of that city.

Married, at New York, by the Rev. Mr. Spring, Mr. Isaac Starr Clawson, to Mrs. Mary Sarah Holman, formerly of the Charleston, and late of the New York Theatre.

Died - The friends and acquaintances of Mr. Benjamin Crampton, late of Crampton & Johnson, are respectfully invited to attend his funeral at 5 o'clock, this afternoon, at the residence of Mrs. Blair's No. 25 Mazyck Street.

Issue of April 10, 1819

Died, on Wednesday morning the 7th inst. after a short indisposition, Miss Martha Huger, in the 54th year of her age, daughter of the late General Isaac Huger.

Issue of April 12, 1819

Died, on the 7th inst. in St. John's Parish, (Berkely) Mrs. Sarah Gaillard consort of Bartholomew Gaillard, Esq.

Issue of April 14, 1819

Married, at the High Hills of Santee, on the 6th inst. by the Rev. Parker Adams, Colonel Orlando S. Rees, to Catherine, daughter of the Honorable Thomas Waites.

Issue of April 21, 1819

Died, the 25th March, at New Orleans, Richard Claiborne, Esq. Clerk of the U.S. District Court, aged 67 years.

Died, on the 4th inst. at New York, Colonel Andrew Stocholm, aged 69 years, one of the early patriots of the revolution, and long a respectable inhabitant of that place.

Issue of April 23, 1819

Married, in this city, on Thursday evening, the 22d April, by the Rev. R. Symmes, D.D., Souverneur Morris Wilkins, Esq. of New York, to Miss Mary Somarrall Ward, eldest daughter of the late Colonel John Ward, of this city.

Died - The friends and acquaintances of Mr. John N. Strobel, are invited to attend his funeral tomorrow morning, at 8 o'clock, from his father's residence No. 33 Boundary Street.

Issue of April 29, 1819

Died, in Philadelphia, on the 9th of March, in the 26th year of his age, Mr. Charles H. Parker...(Eulogy)

Issue of April 30, 1819

Died, on the 22d inst. at Belmont, in the 33d year of his age, the Honorable Alex C. Hanson, Senator of the United States from this state.

Issue of April 30, 1819

Died, of a bullet wound, on the 10th inst. on the Florida side of St.
Mary's River, opposite Trader's Hill in this state, Lieutenant William H.
Belton...

Issue of May 3, 1819

Married, on Thursday evening the 29th ult. by the Rev. Dr. Furman, Mr.
Francis W. Saltus, (of the house of Bonnell & Saltus) to Miss Sarah W.
Grayson, of Beaufort, (S.C.)

Issue of May 6, 1819

Married, on the 4th inst. by the Rev. David Irving Campbell, William
Smith Campbell, Esq. to Miss Anna Maria Nowell, daughter of John Nowell, Esq.
all of this city.

Died - The friends and acquaintances of the late William V. Howard, and
of his brother Robert Howard, are requested to attend the funeral of the
former, this afternoon, at 4 o'clock, from his late residence, No. 103,
East Bay.

Issue of May 12, 1819

Died, on Wednesday, the 5th inst. of a pulmonary complaint, Mr. William
V. Howard, in the 32d year of his age...(Eulogy)

Died - The friends and acquaintances of Mr. John Ling and Mrs. Mary Ann
Ling, are requested to attend the funeral of the latter tomorrow forenoon, at
8 o'clock, from No. 101, East Bay Street.

Issue of May 14, 1819

Married, on the 18th of February, Captain Joel Spencer, of the U. S.
Army, to Miss Mary Boatner, of the Mississippi.

Departed this life, on the 10th inst. Mrs. Jane Dewees, consort of Wm.
Dewees, Esq. in the 58th year of her age...(Eulogy)

Issue of May 17, 1819

Died, in Portsmouth, N.H. of the dropsy, Mrs. Polly Blazdell...(Eulogy)

Married, on Thursday evening last, by the Rev. Dr. Furman, James Harvey
Merritt, Esq. to Miss Esther B. Blackwood, eldest daughter of Thomas Blackwood, Esq.

Issue of May 29, 1819

Married, in this city on the 28th inst. by the Rev. Dr. Buchan, Henry
M'Alpin, Esq. of Savannah, to Miss Helen, only daughter of Mr. Joseph M'Innis
of this city.

Issue of May 31, 1819

Died - The friends and acquaintances of Miss Louisa Jones, and Messrs.
Norman & Jones, and the Members of St. Philip's Church, are invited to
attend her funeral tomorrow morning, at 9 o'clock, from the residence of
Messrs. Norman & Jones, No. 12, Tradd Street.

Issue of June 2, 1819

Died - The friends and acquaintances of Mr. Abner Jones, are requested
to attend his funeral this afternoon, at 4 o'clock, from his late residence,
No. 357 King Street, between Broad and Tradd Streets.

Issue of June 7, 1819

Married, at Christ Church, in Savannah, on the 31st ult. by the Rev.
Mr. Cranston, Dr. William P. Marshall, of the U. S. Army, to Miss Harriet
S. Neyle, daughter of the late Wm. Neyle, Esq.

Issue of June 8, 1819

Departed this life, on Thursday the 3d inst. Mrs. Judith Minis, of
Savannah, (Geo.) aged 74...(Eulogy)

Issue of June 11, 1819

Departed this life, on Thursday afternoon, the 10th inst. after an illness of but a few days, Master Philip Levy, a son of Mr. Lyon Levy of this city. ...This opening bud had not yet reached its thirteenth summer... (Eulogy)

Issue of June 12, 1819

Died, suddenly, on the 19th of May, at St. Marks, in the Island of Cuba, after flattering prospects of recovery, the Rev. Thomas Frost, assistant Minister of St. Philip's Church.

Died — The friends and acquaintances of Mr. and Mrs. Feraud, are invited to attend the funeral of the former, at 6 o'clock, p.m. from Mr. John Caquet's, East Bay, without further invitation.

Died — The friends and acquaintances of Mr. Daniel Gabeau and Mrs. Maria S. Gabeau, are invited to attend the funeral of the latter, from her late residence, No. 39 Market Street, tomorrow morning, at six o'clock, without further invitation.

Issue of June 14, 1819

Died — The friends and acquaintances of the late Dr. James E. B. Finley, and particularly the Members of the several Societies to which he belonged, are invited to attend his funeral from his late residence No. 10, Meeting Street, tomorrow, at 12 o'clock.

Issue of Jun 17, 1819

Died — The friends and acquaintances of Mrs. David Lamb, are invited to attend her funeral, from her late residence, No. 30 East Bay, this afternoon, at 4 o'clock p.m.

Issue of June 19, 1819

Died — The friends and acquaintances of Mr. Francis Lambert are requested to attend his funeral at his house, Meeting Street Road, at 4 o'clock, tomorrow evening without further notice.

Died, in this city, on Wednesday, the 16th inst. in the 74 year of her age, Mrs. Jennet Lamb, wife of David Lamb, Esq.

Died, on the 1st inst. at his plantation, Union District, Mr. Alexander MacBeth, aged 47 years a respectable inhabitant of this state.

Issue of June 24, 1819

Died — The friends and acquaintances of Mr. John Dupont, and in particular his Masonic Brethern, and the members of the Washington Light Infantry, are requested to attend his funeral tomorrow afternoon at 5 o'clock, from his late residence No. 4 Market Street.

Issue of June 25, 1819

Died — The friends and acquaintances of the late Miss Christina Chisolm, are invited to attend her funeral tomorrow morning, at 8 o'clock, without further invitation from her father's residence, Montague Street.

Issue of July 10, 1819

Died, on the 27th of May, at Mareitta, (Ohio), Commodore Abraham Whipple — a native of Rhode Island...

Issue of July 12, 1819

Died, on the 3d inst. in the 64th year of his age, Mr. James O'Conner, senior Editor of the Norfolk Herald.

Issue of July 13, 1819

Died, on the morning of the 5th inst. in the 76th year of her age, Mrs. Joanna B. Dawson, widow of John Dawson, Esq....(Eulogy)

Issue of July 15, 1819

Died - The friends and acquaintances of Mr. and Mrs. Henry Averell are invited to attend the funeral of the former this afternoon, at five o'clock, from his late residence, No. 295, King Street.

Issue of July 17, 1819

Drowned, in James River, on the 9th instant, Lieut. John Henderson, of the United States Navy, late of Petersburg.

Issue of July 29, 1819

Married on Saturday evening, the 17th inst. by the Rev. Allen Sweat, William B. Oswald, Esq. to Miss Cecelia Chaplin, eldest daughter of the late Mr. Benjamin Chaplin, Sen. all of St. Helena.

Died, on the 21st inst. at Orangeburgh, William Hart, Esq. of the firm Hart & Hammett, merchants of this city...(Eulogy)

Died - The friends and acquaintances of Mr. William Jasper, are particularly invited to attend his funeral tomorrow morning at 9 o'clock, from his late residence, No. 351, King Street, opposite Dr. Moore, without further invitation.

Issue of July 30, 1819

Died - The friends and acquaintances of Mr. Thomas B. Wells, and Mrs. Wells, also the members of the St. Patrick Benevolent Society, are invited to attend the funeral of the former from his late residence No. 18 Archdale Street this afternoon, at 4 o'clock.

Issue of August 2, 1819

Died - The friends and acquaintances of Mr. Robert Larry, are invited to attend his funeral, this afternoon, at 4 o'clock, from the house of Mr. Langton, 361 King Street, without further invitation.

Issue of August 3, 1819

Died, in London, on the 15th May last, John Tunno, Esq. merchant.

Issue of August 6, 1819

Died, this morning, after a short illness, Master Joseph Hart, aged six years; son of Mr. S. M. Hart, of this city...

Issue of August 10, 1819

Married, on the 3d instant, by the Rev. Dr. Buchan, John Kirkpatrick, Esq. to Caroline, third daughter of Captain John Pratt, all of this city.

Married, in this city, on Sunday evening last, by the Rev. Dr. Dalcho, Mr. John Goodwin, of Boston, (Mass.) to Mrs. Elizabeth Thompson, of Fredericktown, (Maryland)

Issue of August 14, 1819

Died, last evening after an illness of three days Miss Amelia Sampson, aged 19 years...

Died - The friends and acquaintances of Mr. J. G. Happoldt and of the late Mrs. Mary E. Happoldt, are requested to attend the funeral of the latter, from the residence of Mr. Samuel Hutchins, No. 22, Hasell Street, tomorrow morning, at half past six o'clock, without further invitation.

Died - The relatives and friends of Mr. John and Mrs. Mary Ker, are requested to attend the funeral of the latter from her late residence, No. 37 Elliot Street, this afternoon, at 4 o'clock, without further invitation.

Issue of August 21, 1819

Died, at Long Branch, state of New Jersey, on the 9th of August, the Honorable John F. Grimke....in the 67th year of his age...

Issue of August 24, 1819

Died, on the 21st inst. Mrs. Mary M. I. Thomas, wife of James Thomas, Esq. Merchant of this city...(Eulogy)

Died - The friends and acquaintances of Mr. John Longsdon, and those of his brother William, are requested to attend the funeral of the former, from his late residence No. 115 Church Street, at 4 o'clock, this afternoon.

Issue of August 25, 1819

Died, on Monday last the 23d inst. after a long and painful illness of more than a year, Mr. James Mead, aged 71 years...

Issue of August 26, 1819

Died - The friends and acquaintances of Messrs. Richard and George B. Pearce, are requested to attend the funeral of their sister Miss Cynthia Pearce, this afternoon, at 4 o'clock, from her brothers' residence, No. 85, Meeting Street.

Issue of August 27, 1819

Died - The friends and acquaintances of Mr. D. W. Hall and of Mr. M. B. Latimer, and the Teachers of the Sabbath Schools, are particularly invited to attend the funeral of the latter, from the house of M. C. M'Leod, No. 5 Pinckney Street, on May's Wharf, this afternoon, at 5 o'clock.

Issue of August 30, 1819

Died on the 28th inst. after an illness of a few days, Mrs. Ann Myers, aged 24 years, daughter of Mr. Francis Daymond, of Philadelphia.

Issue of August 31, 1819

Died - The friends and acquaintances of the late Mr. Edward Henry Edwards, and those of Mr. D. C. Edwards and H. P. Dawes, are invited to attend the funeral of the former this afternoon, at 4 o'clock, from the residence of H. P. Dawes, East Bay.

Issue of September 6, 1819

Died - The friends and acquaintances of Mr. S. H. Skinner, are invited to attend the funeral of his neice, Miss Eliza Ann Oliver, from his residence No. 103 Broad Street, this afternoon, precisely at half past 4 o'clock.

Died - The friends and acquaintances of Messrs. Buxbaum and Johnson, and of Thomas Cochran are requested to attend the funeral of Mr. Johnson from his late residence, No. 101 Broad Street, this afternoon at 5 o'clock.

Issue of September 7, 1819

Died - The friends and acquaintances of Mr. John Buxbaum and Mrs. Buxbaum, and of Thomas Cochran are requested to attend the funeral of Mrs. Buxbaum from her late residence, No. 101, Broad Street, this afternoon at 5 o'clock.

Issue of September 8, 1819

Departed this life, after a short illness, at Pineridge, St. John's B. on thursday, the 2d inst. in the 23d year of her age, Mrs. Martha Rebecca Prioleau, wife of Elias Prioleau, Esq....(Eulogy)

Issue of September 8, 1819

Died, in this city, on the 1st. after an illness of six days, of the prevailing fever, Mr. James M'Illwraith, aged----years, printer.

Died - The friends and acquaintances of Captian Francis Saltus and Captain Bonnell, are requested to attend the funeral of their nephew, F. Davenport, from the house of captain Saltus, South Bay, at 5 o'clock p.m.

Issue of September 9, 1819

Died - The friends and acquaintances of Orran Burd and of Thomas Mitchell, are requested to attend the funeral of the latter from the former's residence, No.---, East Bay, at five o'clock this afternoon.

Died - The relatives and acquaintances of Mr. Robert and Mrs. Isabella Eason, are respectfully invited to attend the funeral of their son, George Griswll Eason, tomorrow morning, from his late residence Anson Street, between Hazell and Wentworth Streets, at half past 7 o'clock precisely, without further invitation.

Issue of September 10, 1819

Died, at Philadelphia, on the 1st inst. of dropsy in the chest, aged 53 years, Gen. John Rutledge, of this city.

Issue of September 11, 1819

Died - The friends and acquaintances of Tristram Tupper, are invited to attend the funeral of Mr. D. L. Potter, (of the house of Messrs. Edes & Potter, Savannah) from 240 East Bay, at five o'clock.

Issue of September 13, 1819

Died - The friends and acquaintances of Mr. Hezekiah Smith, also those of Messrs. Richard and Geo. B. Pearce, are invited to attend the funeral of the former this afternoon, at 4 o'clock, from his late residence, No. 258 King Street, without further invitation.

Died - The friends and acquaintances of Mr. William Ferrall, are invited to attend his funeral this afternoon, at half past four o'clock from Edmondston's Wharf.

Died - The friends and acquaintances of Dr. Holbrook and family, are requested without further invitation, to attend the funeral of Miss Caroline Prentiss, this afternoon, at his dwelling house, at five o'clock.

Issue of September 14, 1819

Died, at Darie, (Geo.) after an illness of five days, Mr. Isaac Sasportas, in the 26th year of his age....(Eulogy)

Departed this life at Pine Ridge, St. John's Berkley, on the 9th inst. in the 31st year of his age Elias Prioleau, Esq....(EUlogy)

Died at St. James, Goose Creek, on the 9th instant, of country fever, Mrs. Mary Ann Huff, wife of William Huff, and only daughter of Jacob and Susannah Breaker. ...had just entered her 17th year.

Issue of September 15, 1819

Died, in Pineville, on the 6th inst. in the 47th year of his age, John Palmer, Esq....(Eulogy)

Died, in this city, on the 6th instant, after an illness of 4 days of the prevailing fever, Mr. A. F. Spitz, in the 22d year of his age...(Eulogy)

Died, on the 8th inst. at Washington, after a painful and protracted illness, Robert Brent, Esq. late Paymaster General of the Army...

Issue of September 16, 1819

Died, on last Monday night, at Waccomaw, at the age of 23 years, Mrs. Sarah W. Allston, consort of Joseph W. Allston, Esq. and daughter of the late Captain David Prior.

Issue of September 17, 1819

Died - The friends and acquaintances of Andrew Moffett, and the late Alexander Moffett, are requested to attend the funeral of the latter from No. 306 King Street, precisely at 4 o'clock this afternoon.

Issue of September 22, 1819

Died - The friends and acquaintances of Messrs. John H. Benson, W. G. Benson, and John H. Benson, Jun. are requested to attend the funeral of the latter, from their residence at the corner of Broad and King Streets at 4 o'clock this afternoon.

Died - The friends and acquaintances of Mrs. Ann Langstaff, and the late Mr. John Langstaff, are invited to attend the funeral of the latter tomorrow afternoon at 4 o'clock, from his mothers residence, Boundary Street.

Issue of September 23, 1819

Died, on the 20th inst. Mr. Hugh Swinton, in the 46th year of his age.

Died, at his Plantation, (Roslin), on the 15th inst. much and justly regretted, Archibald S. Johnston, Esq. age 35 years, a native of Greenock, in Scotland...

Issue of September 24, 1819

Died, at the Lower Bluff, in M'Intosh county, (Geo.) Mr. John Blackler, aged 31 years, a native of this city, after an illness of four weeks, late teller of the Bank of Darien--he feared God, and was just to his fellow creatures.

Issue of September 28, 1819

Died, on the 10th inst. of the prevailing fever, after five days sickness, Peter Buchanan, Esq. of the house of Buchanan, Wood & Co. of this city...(Eulogy)

Died, at Blackswamp, in Beaufort District, (S.C.) on the 24th August, 1819, in the 64th year of his age, Captain William Maner, a long and respected resident of that place...(Eulogy)

Issue of October 1, 1819

(Died)...Dr. Edward D. Smith, Professor of Chemistry and Natural Philosophy in the College of South Carolina...on the 17th day of August last...(Eulogy)

Issue of October 2, 1819

Died, on the 14th ult. Captain Josias Heyward, a respectable resident of (Prince William Parish)...

Issue of October 4, 1819

Married, on Friday evening last, by the Rev. Mr. Wilson, John Balke White, Esq. to Miss Anna Rachael O'Driscol, daughter of Dr. O'Driscol, all of this city.

Died, on the 29th ult. on Sullivan's Island, of the prevailing fever, Mr. Charles Folliott, aged 24 years, a native of Wiltshire, England...(Eulogy)

Died, on the 27th ult. Philip Prioleau Gabeau, aged 13 months, the only child of Mr. Daniel Gabeau.

Died - The friends and acquaintances of Mr. and Mrs. John Skirer, and also of Miss Harriet Spinler, are requested to attend the funeral of the latter from her late residence, No. 26, Archdale Street, tomorrow morning, at 8 o'clock.

Issue of October 5, 1819

Died - The friends and acquaintances of John Myer and of his eldest son John, are invited to attend the funeral of the latter from No. 256 King Street, opposite Liberty Street, this evening, at 4 o'clock.

Issue of October 7, 1819

Died, in this city, on the 3d inst. of the prevailing fever, Mrs. Susan Rugg, aged 34 years, a native of Boston, (Mass.)...(Eulogy)

Died, lately at Kingstree, Mr. Isaac A. Cohen, aged 22 years.

Departed this life, on the 27th September, Master Edwin Grayson, aged 16 years and 2 months...(Eulogy)

Died - The friends and acquaintances of the late Mr. James Scot, and of Mr. Henry Bryce, and also the Members of the St. Anthea's Society, are respectfully invited to attend the funeral of the former, tomorrow morning, at 6 o'clock, precisely, from his late residence, No. 112 Tradd Street, near Church Street, without further invitation.

Issue of October 12, 1819

Married, at New York, on the 2d inst. at St. John's Chapel by the Rev. Dr. Brownell, W. G. Bucknor, Esq. to Miss Emma A. Bulow, daughter of Charles W. Bulow, Esq. of this city.

Issue of October 13, 1819

Died, aged nine years and four months, Robert Pringle Smith, the oldest son of Robert Smith, Esq. of this city...(Eulogy)

Issue of October 14, 1819

Died - The friends and acquaintances, and also the Members of the St. Andrew's Society, are requested to attend the funeral of Mr. James Morrison, from his late residence No. 10, Price's Alley, this afternoon, at 4 o'clock, without further invitation.

Issue of October 19, 1819

Died, in Franklin, Missouri, Dr. William Baldwin, of the United States Navy...(Eulogy)

Issue of October 21, 1819

Married, on Tuesday evening the 19th inst. by the Rev. Mr. Symes, William M'Dow, Esq. to Mrs. Susan B. Somers, both of this city.

Departed this life, at Orangeburgh, on the 5th inst. of a billious fever, after a few days illness in the ?7th year of his age...Mr. Ebenezer Bassett, a native of New Haven, (Conn.)...(Eulogy)

Departed this life, on the 7th inst. Mr. James Scot, aged 61 years and 8 months, a native of Scotland, but for 35 years a respectable inhabitant of this city...(Eulogy)

Died, at Camden, on Saturday, the 16th inst. of a short but painful illness, James, second son of James S. Murray, in the 13th year of his age ...(Eulogy)

Issue of October 23, 1819

Died, on Thursday the 14th inst. at his residence on Black River, Sumpter District, of the county fever, Mr. Samuel Montgomery...(Eulogy)

Died on the 13th inst. at his residence on Black River, Sumpter District, of the prevailing county fever, Captain Isaac Bagnal...(Eulogy)

Issue of October 26, 1819

(Died)....Colonel John D. Burgess, of Williamsburg District...(Eulogy)

Issue of October 29, 1819

(Died)...Party Republicana...(Eulogy)
Died on Sullivan's Island of a fever, on the night of the 20th inst. at the residence of Mr. Chas. Vignoles, Miss Hannah Knight, aged 22 years... (Eulogy)

Issue of October 30, 1819

Departed this life on Wednesday the 6th inst. Mrs. Jane Caldwell, aged 70 years, a native of Ireland, for many years a resident in Pennsylvania ...(Eulogy)
Married, at Walterborough, on Thursday evening last, by the Rev. Mr. Floyd, James Bowman, Jr. Esq. of Prince William's Parish to Miss Emily Sarah, youngest daughter of the late Major William Fraser, of Ashepoo.

Issue of November 1, 1819

The relatives and friends and Mrs. Sarah Mathews, relict of the late Hon. Judge Mathews, are invited to attend her funeral, at her late residence, on Harleston's Green, at ten o'clock tomorrow.

Issue of November 2, 1819

(Died)...Robert A. Darby, Esq. who died on Sunday, the 24th inst. after a short illness, in the 43d year of his age, at his residence on Harleston's Green...(Eulogy)

Issue of November 3, 1819

Died, at New Orleans, in the early part of September, Captain Cornelius Mansise, aged 47 years, a native of Haverhill (Mass.) and for a number of years a resident in Charleston. He has left an amiable wife and family to lament his death.

Issue of November 4, 1819

(Died)....Major-General William Fishburne. He expired yesterday morning at his summer residence in Walterborough...(Eulogy)
Died, on the 23d of October, at the interesting age of three years, Emily Bay Bellinger, youngest daughter of Dr. John S. Bellinger of Barnwell District...(Eulogy)

Issue of November 5, 1819

Died - The friends and acquaintances of Mr. Henry Bennett, and particularly the members of the Second Presbyterian Church, are requested to attend his funeral tomorrow afternoon, at 3 o'clock, from his residence in Hampstead.

Issue of November 6, 1819

Married, on Tuesday last, by the Rev. Mr. Leland, Mr. Jno. Fraser to Miss Bersheba Phillips, all of Christ Church Parish.

Issue of November 8, 1819

Married, on Thursday evening last, by the Right Rev. Bishop Bowen, Mr. George Trescott, to Miss Amelia Career, both of this city.
Died, at Walterborough, on the 3d instant, Major-General William Fishburne, in the 60th year of his age...(Eulogy)
Died - The friends and acquaintances of Mr. and Mrs. Thomas Napier, are requested to attend the funeral of the latter from her late residence No. 105 Broad Street, this afternoon, at 4 o'clock, without further invitation.

Issue of November 9, 1819

(Died) Mrs. Mary S. Washington Motte, the excellent consort of Abraham

Motte, Esq. of this city, died on the 1st of October, 1819, in St. Augustine
...(Eulogy)

Died - The Members of the 2d Presbyterian Church, and the friends of
Mrs. Hubble, Mrs. Mary Cooper, and Mrs. Sarah Broeske, are invited to attend
the funeral of the latter, from her late residence in St. Phillips Street,
this afternoon, at 3 o'clock.

Issue of November 13, 1819

Died, in this city, on the 29th September last, in the 25th year of his
age, Mr. Daniel M'Dowell, a native of Belfast, (Ireland)...(Eulogy)

Departed this life on Saturday evening, the 6th inst. after a long and
painful illness, which she bore with Christian fortitude, in the 60th year
of her age, Mrs. Elizabeth Horsey.

Issue of November 15, 1819

Married, in Rutherford, N.C. on the 14th September last, John Vesey,
Esq. of this city to Miss Sarah Boman; eldest daughter of the Rev. Thomas
Boman, of Rutherford.

Issue of November 18, 1819

Married, on Tuesday evening, the 16th inst. by the Right Rev. Bishop
Bowen, Lewis Trapman, Esq. late of Frankfort (Germany) to Mary Bowen,
third daughter of the late John Elias Moore, Esq. of this city.

Died, suddenly, at Northampton, (Mass.) on the 7th inst. the Honorable
Caleb Strong, late governor of that state.

Issue of November 20, 1819

Died, on Edisto River, on the 29th ultimo, Mrs. Susanna Lightsey, aged
46 years, wife of Mr. John Lightsey of said place...(Eulogy)

Issue of November 22, 1819

Died, in New York, on the 13th inst. Mr. Hopkins Robinson of the Park
Theatre in the 30th year of his age.

Issue of November 25, 1819

Died - The friends and acquaintances of Mr. William Webb, and Mr.
Thorne, are invited to attend the funeral of the former from his late
residence at Mr. Thorne's Cumberland Street, at 4 o'clock this afternoon.

Issue of November 30, 1819

Married, on the 24th inst. by the Rev. Mr. Pelxitto, Mr. Hayman Levy,
of New York, to Miss Almeria Deleon of this city.

Issue of December 1, 1819

Married, in Pineville (St. Stephen's) on the 16th ult. by the Rev.
David J. Campbell, Dr. Edwin Gaillard to Miss H. C. White.

Issue of December 2, 1819

Died - The friends and acquaintances of Miss Sarah Bird are requested
to attend her funeral from the residence of Mr. E. G. Sass No. 30 Queen
Street, at 3 o'clock, this afternoon.

Died, on Sunday evening last, after a short but painful illness of
five days, Master Daniel M. Joseph, aged 16 years; a native of London
(England)...(Eulogy)

Issue of December 3, 1819

Married, on Thursday last, the 25th inst. by the Rev. Thomas Trowell,
Mr. Shadrack Wooten, to Miss Eliza Carolina Johnston, all of St. Peters Par.

Issue of December 4, 1819

Married, on the 2d inst. by the Rev. Dalcho, Peter Parker, Esq. of Boston, to Miss Elizabeth Allston Read, daughter of Dr. William Read, of this city.

Died - The friends and acquaintances of King & Jones, and the late Capt. William Hull, are requested to attend the funeral of the latter, tomorrow, at 12 o'clock, from Mr. Floyd's boarding house, corner of Tradd Street and Bedon's Alley, without further invitation.

Issue of December 11, 1819

Married, at Statesburg, on Tuesday evening last, by the Rev. Mr. Parker Adams, Robert Bentham, Esq. of this city to Francis Caroline, daughter of William Mayrant, Esq. of the former place.

Issue of December 17, 1819

Died, on the 24th ult. in the 25th year of his age, William Webb, Esq. ...(Eulogy)

Died, on Beaver Creek, Kershaw District, on the 24th ult. Mr. Thomas D. Carnell, aged 28 years...(Eulogy)

Issue of December 20, 1819

Married, on Thursday the 9th ult. by Bishop Bowen, W. Skerving Smith to Elizabeth, daughter of Col. M'Pherson.

Issue of January 4, 1820

Married, on Sunday evening, the 12th December, at St. Mark's Church, New-York, by the Rev. Mr. Creighton, the Rev. John White Chandler, of this city, to Miss Elizabeth S. Winthrop, eldest daughter of Benjamin Winthrop, Esq. of New York.

Issue of January 6, 1820

Died - The friends and acquaintances of the late Thomas Horry, Esq. and of Elias Horry, are invited to attend the funeral of the former, from his late residence corner of Meeting-Street, near South-Bay, tomorrow afternoon, at 3 o'clock, precisely.

Issue of January 10, 1820

Married, on the 22d of December last, in St. Paul's Parish, Stono, by the Rev. Albert A. Muller, Captain Benjamin Bailey, of Edisto Island, to Mary Washington, youngest daughter of John Townsend, Esq. of the same Parish.

Departed this world, after a short illness, on Sunday, the 26th December, 1819, Mrs. Elizabeth Charlotte Mazych, relict of Alexander Mazych, Esq. aged 67 years and 8 weeks...(Eulogy)

Died, suddenly, in this city on Monday the 3d inst. in the 57th year of her age, Mrs. Mary Elliott, widow of Thomas Odingsell Elliott, and eldest daughter of the late Colonel Pinckeny.

Issue of January 11, 1820

Died, on the night of the 5th inst. Thomas Horry, Esq. an old and respectable inhabitant of this city, in the 72d year of his age.

Issue of January 13, 1820

Married, at the Elms, on the 8th inst. by the Rt. Rev. Bishop Bowen, Thomas Middleton, Esq. to Miss Maria Izard; and Joseph Heyward, Esq. to Miss Alice Izard, daughters of Henry Izard, Esq.

Maried, lately in this city, by the Rev. Mr. Muller, Mr. H. Herve, to Miss Elizabeth Harvey, both of London.

Issue of January 15, 1820

Died, in this city, on Sunday night last, the 9th inst. Mrs. Starr Barrett, after having fully completed One Hundred and Twenty Years of an active and various life...(Eulogy)

Issue of January 17, 1820

Died, on the 14th inst. Elizabeth Pinckney, aged 16 years and three months, second daughter of Roger and Susanna Hayne Pinckney.

Issue of January 18, 1820

Died - The friends and acquaintances of Henry J. Chalmers, Esq. and of his consort, Mrs. Elizabeth Chalmers, are invited to attend her funeral, from the corner of Beaufain and Cumming-Streets, tomorrow afternoon, at 3 o'clock.

Issue of January 19, 1820

Married, last evening by the Right Rev. Dr. Bowen, Robert C. Ludlow, Esq. of New York, to Mary, youngest daughter of the late William B. Peters, Esq.

Issue of January 21, 1820

Died, on the 17th instant, in the 53d year of age, Mrs. Hetty Mordecai, a native of Philadelphia, but for the last 13 years, a resident of this city...(Eulogy)

Issue of January 22, 1820

Died, at Sea, on his voyage to Barbadoes, Rear Admiral Donald Campbell, of the white Squadron, and commander of H.B.M. ships and vessels on the windward and leeward island station.

Issue of January 28, 1820

Died, on the morning of the 17th inst. in the 37 year of her age, Miss Eliza W. Jenkins, eldest daughter of the late Capt. Isaac Jenkins, of Edisto Island, greatly lamented by her relations and friends.

Issue of February 3, 1820

Died, at his residence in St. John's (Berkley) on the 30th ult. Paul D. Ravenel, Esq. in the 56th year of his age.

Issue of February 9, 1820

Died - The friends and acquaintances of John Sinclair and Wm. Sinclair are requested to attend the funeral of the former from the house of Mrs. Taylor, Guignard-Street, tomorrow morning, at 9 o'clock.

Issue of February 11, 1820

Married, on Tuesday evening the 8th instant, by the Rev. Dr. Furman, Mr. Ulysses C. Gourlay to Miss Rebecca Slowman; all of this city.

Issue of February 15, 1820

Died, of the Consumption, at Montrevil, France, on the 20th December, 1819, Mrs. Catherine Victoire Sophie Goure, aged 38 years, a native of Cruy...(Eulogy)

Issue of February 18, 1820

Died - The friends and acquaintances of Mr. and Mrs. John M. Ogier, are invited to attend the funeral of the latter, from the residence of Mr. Lewis Ogier, Anson-Street, at 10 o'clock to-morrow morning.

Issue of February 22, 1820

Died, on the night of the 17th inst. in the 25th year of her age, Mrs.
Providence Grimball Ogier, youngest daughter of Mr. John Jenkins, of Edisto
Island...(Eulogy)

Issue of February 25, 1820

...Died the Rev. Andrew Flinn D.D., Pastor of the 2d Presbyterian
Church, in this city...(Eulogy)
Died - The friends and acquaintances of the Rev. Dr. Flinn; the Rev.
the Clergy and the Members of the different Congregations, particularly
those of the Second Presbyterian Church; also the different Societies of
which he was a member, are invited to attend his funeral from his late
residence on South Bay, tomorrow afternoon, at 3 o'clock.

Issue of February 26, 1820

Married on Thursday evening last, by the Rev. Dr. Gadsden, Dr. Marcus
N. Kelly, of Cavan, (Ireland) to Miss Rebecca, daughter of Daniel O'Hara,
Esq. of this city.
Married, in Caswell county, N.C. by the Rev. Mr. Graves, Capt. William
Graves, to Miss Nancy Graves, daughter of Gen. Azarial Graves...

Issue of March 3, 1820

In Warren County, Georgia (married), Mr. Bird Perry, to Miss Rebecca
Cloud...
Married in Hamstead, (N.Y.) the Rev. William H. Heart to Miss Lydia
H. More.

Issue of March 4, 1820

Died, at Matanzas, on the 15th February in the 57th year of his age,
Mr. Joseph Durbec, a native of Marseilles, France; and a resident of this
place for twenty one years...(Eulogy)
Died - The friends and acquaintances of Mr. Anthony Gabeau, Wm. Evans
and S. Gabeau, are requested to attend the funeral of the latter, from the
residence of his father, No.--, St. Philip's Street, tomorrow morning, at
8 o'clock, without further invitation.

Issue of March 14, 1820

Died - The friends and acquaintances of Miss Angeline Gibbes, are
invited to attend her funeral to-morrow morning, at ten o'clock, from her
mother's residence, Church Street, without further invitation.

Issue of March 16, 1820

Married, on Thursday evening, 24th ultimo, by the Rev. Mr. Richard,
Avery Taylor, of James City County, but last from Richmond, Va., to Miss
Ann Elliott, of this city.

Issue of March 23, 1820

Died, at Marblehead, Captain William Crowninshield, aged 86, a native
of Marblehead.

Issue of March 30, 1820

Died - The friends and acquaintances of Mr. and Mrs. Abraham Markle are
invited to attend the funeral of the latter, this afternoon, at 4 o'clock,
from her late residence, No. 14, St. Philip's Street.

Issue of April 3, 1820

Died - The friends and acquaintances of Mr. and Mrs. Picault, are requested to attend the funeral of the former, this afternoon, at 4 o'clock, at his residence No. 215 Meeting Street.

Issue of April 4, 1820

Married on Sunday evening, 2d inst. by the Rev. Dr. Bachman, Mr. Conrad Knauff to Miss Ann Louise F. Jandrell, both of this city.

Died - The friends and acquaintances of Mr. John Thomas, are respectfully invited to attend his funeral from his late residence No. 202, Meeting-Street, at 4 o'clock this afternoon.

Issue of April 5, 1820

Died - The friends and acquaintances of Mr. William Pressly, particularly the Members of the Second Presbyterian Church, and Members of the Bible and Fellowship Societies are invited to attend his funeral to-morrow afternoon, at 4 o'clock, from his late residence corner of King and Wolf-Streets, without further invitation.

Issue of April 11, 1820

Died - The friends and acquaintances of Mr. and Mrs. Nathaniel Russell, and of Mr. Arthur Middleton; the Rev. Clergy, of all denominations, and the Members of the Bible and New England Societies are invited to attend the funeral of Mr. Nathaniel Russell, at 10 o'clock to-morrow morning.

Died - The friends and acquaintances and particularly the Members of the Methodist Episcopal Church, are invited to attend the funeral of Mr. George Airs, from his residence in Archdale-Street, opposite Parsonage-Lane, this afternoon, at 4 o'clock without further invitation.

Issue of April 13, 1820

Died - The friends and acquaintances of the Rev. Mr. Gervais and of Mrs. Gervais, are invited to attend the funeral of the latter from her late residence in Meeting-Street, to-morrow forenoon, at 10 o'clock.

Issue of April 17, 1820

Died, on the evening of the 12th inst. in the 23d year of her age, sincerely lamented by her friends, Mrs. Claudia G. Gervais, consort of the Rev. Mr. Gervais.

Issue of April 20, 1820

Died - The relatives and relations and acquaintances of Mrs. K. Darret, are requested to attend her funeral (from the House of her son-in-law, Mr. Henry Muckenfuss, Wentworth Street) tomorrow morning, at 9 o'clock.

Issue of April 24, 1820

Married, by the Rev. Mr. Bachman, Mr. Henry Parker, to Miss Henrietta Wilhelmina Wilmans, eldest daughter of Mr. August F. Wilmans, all of this city.

Issue of April 28, 1820

Died, at Bermuda, on the 18th ult. Theodore George Alexander, Esqr. Senior, Assistant Justice of the General Court...(Eulogy)

Issue of April 29, 1820

Married, in Hebron, the Rev. Lorenzo Dow, to Miss Lucy Dolbear, of Montville.

Issue of May 4, 1820

Died, on the 2d of April last, Mr. George Gardner, of Newport, Rhode-Island, aged 28 years, a resident here for the last ten years past.

Issue of May 11, 1820

Died, in this city, on the 6th inst. after a long and painful illness, Mrs. Sarah Ann Sarzedas, wife of David Sarzedas, Jr....(Eulogy)

Issue of May 16, 1820

Married, on Thursday, the 11th inst. by the Rev. Mr. Reed, Mr. Thomas Addison, merchant, to Miss Mary Palmer, all of this city.

Departed this life, on Thursday evening, the 4th inst. at the residence of General J. J. Faust, near Columbia, after a long and painful illness, Mrs. Ann L. O'Driscol, relict of the late Dr. Matthew O'Driscol, of this city.

Issue of May 17, 1820

Died, at Tangiers, (Morocco) on the 8th of March, suddenly, of a fit of apoplexy, James Simpson, Esq. Consul of the United States, for the Empire of Morocco.

Issue of May 18, 1820

Married, on Monday evening the 15th inst. by the Rev. Mr. Wilson, Henry Trescott, Esq. to Sarah, daughter of the late John M'Crady, Esq.

Issue of May 22, 1820

Married, on Thursday evening the 18th instant, by the Rev. Dr. Palmer, Mr. Oliver Crocker, of Falmouth, Mass. to Miss Ann Bunce, of this place.

Issue of May 26, 1820

Married, on Tuesday evening last, by the Rev. Mr. Boice, Stephen Thomas, Jun. Esq. to Miss Martha J. M. Malcomson, all of this city.

Issue of May 29, 1820

Married, on Thursday evening last, the 25th inst. by the Rev. Mr. Dalcho, Thomas Pinckney Alston, Esq. of Waccamaw, to Miss Jane Smith, eldest daughter of the late John R. Smith, off this city.

Died, at Marseilles, on the 24th of March last, Mr. William L. Richardson, late master of the schooner Louisa, of this port.

Issue of May 30, 1820

...Died the Reverend Andrew Flinn, D.D. the late worthy and respectable Minister of the second Presbyterian Church, in Charleston, S.C....(Eulogy)

Issue of June 5, 1820

* Died, in March last, in the Parish Aigish Fillarney, at the age of 115, Theodore O'Sullivan, the celebrated Irish Bard...(Eulogy)

Issue of June 6, 1820

Married, on Wednesday evening, the 31st ult. by the Rev. Dr. Dalcho, Col. Robert Y. Hayne, Attorney General of this State, to Miss Rebecca Brewton Alston, daughter of Col. Wm. Alston, of Waccamaw.

Departed this life on the 4th inst. in the 24th year of her age, Miss Judith Mordecai...(Eulogy)

Issue of June 7, 1820

Died - The friends and acquaintances generally (and particularly the Members of the St. Andrew's Society) of Mr. and Mrs. Marshall, are requested to attend the funeral of the former to-morrow afternoon, at half past four o'clock, from his late residence, East-Bay, Gadsden's Green, without further invitation.

Issue of June 9, 1820

Died, on Sunday night, the 4th inst. at his residence in the South-
Carolina College, Dr. Jonathan Maxcy, for sixteen years, the admired and
revered President of that Institution...(Eulogy)

Issue of June 13, 1820

Departed this life, on the 7th inst. Mr. John Marshall, Merchant of
this city, in the 31st year of his age...(Eulogy)
Died, at his residence on Edisto Island, on Thursday morning last, Mr.
Henry Calder, a native of Scotland, and for many years a respectable
Planter on that island and its vicinity.

Issue of June 14, 1820

Died - The friends and acquaintances of Mr. Edward Dowling, are invited
to attend his funeral, from his late residence in Society-Street, at 5
o'clock this afternoon, without further invitation.

Issue of June 16, 1820

Died, on Sunday, 11th inst. Mrs. Maria, wife of Doctor M. Holbrook, and
daughter of A. Prentiss, Esq. of Boston, (Mass.) in the 32d year of her
age...(Eulogy)
Died - The friends and acquaintances of Mr. James Gabeau, and particularly the Members of the South-Carolina Society, are requested to attend
his funeral this afternoon, at 4 o'clock, from his late residence No. 54,
Queen-Street, without further invitation.
Died - The friends and acquaintances of Mr. Frederick Kohler, are
requested to attend his funeral, from his late residence on King Street
Road, tomorrow evening, at 4 o'clock without further invitation.

Issue of June 17, 1820

Died - The friends and acquaintances of Mrs. Mary Hallon are invited to
attend her funeral at Mr. John Steels', near Mr. B. Carrol's, this afternoon,
at half after 5 o'clock.

Issue of June 20, 1820

Married, on Saturday evening last, by the Rev. Dr. Bachman, Mr.
Alexander Berry, to Miss Maria Marlen, both of this city.
Died, on Friday 15th instant, Octavious Crips...(Eulogy)
Died, on Thursday last, Mr. James Gabeau, of this city, aged 40 years
...(Eulogy)

Issue of June 26, 1820

Married, on Saturday evening last, by the Right Rev. Dr. Bowen, Jacob
Guerard, Esq. of Beaufort, to Miss Ann Fraser, of this city.
Died - The friends and acquaintances of Captain Robert S. Long, and
Mrs. Mary Long, together with those of Moses Andrews, are requested to
attend the funeral of Albert James Long, from his late residence No. 7,
Wall-Street, to-morrow afternoon, at 4 o'clock.

Issue of July 3, 1820

Died - The friends and acquaintances of Doctor Isaac Auld, and Mrs.
Francis Auld, are requested to attend the funeral of the latter precisely
at 5 o'clock this evening, from her late residence No. 14 St. Philip Street.

Issue of July 5, 1820

Died - The friends and acquaintances and particularly the relatives of
Mr. James and Mrs. Dorothy Eason, are requested to attend the funeral of
their sons, James and William Eason, this afternoon, at 4 o'clock, from their

residence, No. 13, Middle-Street, without further invitation.

Died, on the morning of the 4th inst. in the St. Paul's Parish, Doctor Stubbins Firth, in the 39th year of his age.

Died - The friends and acquaintances of Mr. and Mrs. Peter Wyatt, together with the Members of the St. Andrew's, and Mechanic's Societies, are invited to attend the funeral of the former, from his late residence, on Harleston's Green, this afternoon, precisely at 4 o'clock, without further invitation.

Issue of July 10, 1820

Died - The relatives and friends of Mrs. Constantia Wigfall, are invited to attend her funeral from her late residence in George-Street, this afternoon at five o'clock, without further invitation.

Issue of July 13, 1820

Died - The friends and acquaintances of Thomas Karwon, are requested to attend his funeral tomorrow morning precisely at 6 o'clock, from his late residence Hasell-Street, without further invitation.

Issue of July 14, 1820

Died, at her residence in George Street, on the evening of the 10th inst. Mrs. Constantia Wigfall, in the 78th year of her age...(Eulogy)

Departed this life on the 13th inst. in the 76th year of his age, Thomas Karwon, Esq....

Died - The friends and acquaintances of Mrs. Elizabeth You, Mr. John Clifford You, and the late Mr. Joseph Lewis, are requested to attend the funeral of the latter, this afternoon, at 4 o'clock, from the residence of Mr. John C. You, No. 32, Archdale-Street.

Issue of July 20, 1820

Died - The friends and acquaintances of the late Mr. Hugh Monies, are invited to attend his funeral, from the residence of Mrs. Munroe, No. 36 Church-Street, this afternoon, at 4 o'clock, without further invitation.

Issue of July 29, 1820

Died, on the 26th inst. John Champneys, Esq. in the 77th year of his age.

Issue of July 31, 1820

Died - The friends and acquaintances of Mr. and Mrs. Meeds, and particularly the Members of the Fellowship Society, are requested to attend the funeral of the former from his late residence, No. 41, East-Bay, precisely at 5 o'clock, this afternoon, without further invitation.

Issue of August 1, 1820

Died, on the 19th inst. in Barnwell District, in the sixth month of his age, John Belliger Duncan, only son of Willis J. Duncan, Esquire.

Issue of August 2, 1820

Died - The friends and acquaintances of Mr. and Mrs. Wilkie, and of Mr. and Mrs. Leitch, are respectfully invited to attend the funeral of the late Mrs. Wilkie, without further invitation, from the house of Mr. Leitch No. 283 King-Street, this afternoon, precisely at 5 o'clock.

Issue of August 3, 1820

Died - The friends and acquaintances of the late Mr. James Maggregor, and of Messrs. Buchanan, Wood & Co. are requested to attend the funeral of the former, from his late residence, No. 25, East-Bay, this afternoon, at 4 o'clock.

Issue of August 5, 1820

Died - The friends and acquaintances of Mrs. Margaret Milligan, and particularly the Members of the Presbyterian Churches, are requested to attend her funeral from her late residence in Mazychborough, to-morrow morning, at 7 o'clock precisely without further invitation.

Issuu of August 7, 1820

Died, on the 1st inst. Mrs. Jame Wilkie, wife of William Wilkie, Esq. of Rantowles, in the 35th year of her age...(Eulogy)

Died - The friends and acquaintances, of Arnold Remoussin, Esq. are requested to attend his funeral, from his late residence No. 44, Beaufain-Street, to-morrow morning, at 9 o'clock.

Issue of August 9, 1820

Died, on Monday, the 7th inst. Arnold Remoussin, at the age of 37... (Eulogy)

Issue of August 10, 1820

Married, on Sunday, the 30th July, in Marion District, by the Rev. Wm. Hemmenway, Mr. Daniel D. Scott, to Miss Rebecca Sarah Cotton, only daughter of Robert Cotton, Esq. of Georgetown District.

Died - The friends and acquaintances of Mr. and Mrs. Benjamin Pepoon, and Miss Caroline D. Pepoon, are requested to attend the funeral of the latter, from the residence of Mr. D. Perkin's, No. 18, Queen-Street, this afternoon, at six o'clock, without a more particular invitation.

Died - The friends and acquaintances of Mr. A. Masselin Jurel, and of Messrs. Pitray & Uiel, are requested to the funeral of the former at 7 o'clock, tomorrow morning, without further invitation, from his late residence No. 91, East-Bay.

Died - The friends and acquaintances of Captain James Dennison, and the Members of the St. Andrew Society, are invited to attend his funeral from his late residence in Elliott-Street, at 3 o'clock tomorrow afternoon.

Issue of August 11, 1820

Died, on Sunday, the 5th inst. Mr. William Sherbourn, Professor of Music, a native of England, in the 26th year of his age.

Issue of August 12, 1820

Died, on the 8th inst. Jacob Williman, Esquire, in the 78th year of his age.

Issue of August 14, 1820

Departed this life on the 5th inst. in the 60th year of her age, Mrs. Margaret Mulligan, relict of the late Joseph Mulligan...(Eulogy)

Died, at his residence on James Island, on Saturday last, Hugh Wilson, Sen. Esq. in the 70th year of his age.

Died, on the 11th inst. in the 77th year of his age, Dr. Charles Drayton.

Issue of August 21, 1820

Died - The friends and acquaintances of Mr. James Adger, and of Mr. Robert Adger, are invited to attend the funeral of the latter, from his residence corner of Spring-Street and King-Street road, this afternoon, at 5 o'clock, without a more particular request.

Issue of August 22, 1820

Died - The friends and acquaintances of the late Col. Daniel D'Oyley, and particularly the Members of the South-Carolina Society, are requested to attend his funeral, from his late residence, No. 1, St. Philip Street, tomorrow afternoon, at 5 o'clock.

Died - The Members of the State Society of the Cincinnati, are invited to attend the funeral of their deceased brother, the late Col. Daniel D'Oyley, from his late residence No. 1, St. Philip-Street, tomorrow afternoon, at 5 o'clock.

Died - The friends and acquaintances of John W. Cole and J. W. Chitty, Sen. are requested to attend the funeral of Master Gabrial Duval Moore, this afternoon, at 4 o'clock, from the residence of J. W. Chitty, Sen. St. Philip Street continued.

Issue of August 24, 1820

Married, on Wednesday evening 23d inst. in this city, Levi S. D'Lyon, Esq. Attorney at Law, of Savannah, (Geo.) to Miss Rebecca De Lamotta, daughter of the late Isaace de Lamotta, of the former place.

Died, on the 8th inst. at Clarendon, after a short illness, much lamented, Alexander Wigfall Garden, M.D. in the 32 year of his age...(Eulogy)

Died, at Sullivan's Island, on the 23d instant, Lieut. Henry Massingbird Simons, of the United States Artillery.

Issue of August 26, 1820

Died - The friends and acquaintances of Mrs. Catherine Davis and Mrs. Jane Heyden, are requested to attend the funeral of the late Master Mathew Heyden, tomorrow morning, at 7 o'clock, from the residence of Mrs. Heyden's Hampstead.

Issue of August 29, 1820

...We have been led to these reflections by the recent death of two young ladies, Miss Maria and Miss Caroline Pepoon, who fell victims to the county fever-the former on the 28th ult. and the latter on the 10th inst. ...(Eulogy)

Died - The interesting subject of this obituary, was Margaret Hayes, eldest daughter of Wm. S. Bennett, Esq. who died on the 21st instant at the age of thirteen years and three months, after three days illness of a Bilious fever...(Eulogy)

Died, on Friday afternoon last, in the 60th year of his age, after a short but painful illness, which he bore with fortitude and resignation, Thomas Parker, Sen. Esq. late District Attorney of South Carolina.

Died, on the morning of the 20th instant, Doctor Charles Watts, a native of Virginia, but for several years a resident of this place...(Eulogy)

* Died, on Tuesday morning last, in the 39th year of his age, Mr. John T. Darrell of Bermuda, and for some years past a respectable merchant of this place...(Eulogy)

Issue of September 5, 1820

Died, on the 27th ult. John Heyward, Esq. aged 69 years and 8 months... (Eulogy)

Issue of September 6, 1820

Died, in Columbia, (S.C.) on the 31st ult. of a bilious fever, Miss Harriet Margaret Sollee, youngest daughter of the late Mr. John Sollee.

Issue of September 7, 1820

Died, at West Point, on the 28th ult. Andrew Ellicolt, Professor of Mathematics at the Military Academy, aged 67.

Issue of September 7, 1820

Died - The friends and acquaintances of Mr. and Mrs. C. D. Burns, (late of Parker's Ferry,) are respectfully invited to attend the funeral of the latter, without any further invitation, tomorrow morning, precisely at 8 o'clock, from No.---, west side of Meeting-Street, directly opposite Henrietta-Street.

Issue of September 8, 1820

Departed this life on the 31st of August, in the 23d year of his age, Dr. Edward D. C. Jenkins, a native of this place.

Issue of September 12, 1820

Died - The friends and acquaintances of Mrs. Johnson, and Miss Sarah Johnson, are requested to attend the funeral of the latter without further invitation from the N. E. corner of Guignard and Anson-Streets, this-evening, at five o'clock.

Issue of September 14, 1820

Departed this life, on the 11th inst. in the 35th year of her age, Miss Sarah Johnson, daughter of the late William Johnson...(Eulogy)
Departed this life, on the 4th inst. in the 59th year of her age, Mrs. Judith Ladson, relict of Major James Ladson...(Eulogy)
Died, on the 19th of August, at the Catawba Springs, N.C. in the 29th year of his age, Francis Reyre, Jun. of St. Stephen's Parish...(Eulogy)

Issue of September 19, 1820

Died, on the 12th instant, Miss Sarah Johnson, in the 35th year of her age...(Eulogy)

Issue of September 21, 1820

Died - The friends and acquaintances of the late John Russell, and particularly the Members of the Mechanic Society, are requested to attend his funeral, from his late residence No. 124 Wentworth-Street, tomorrow morning at 9 o'clock, without further invitation.

Issue of September 22, 1820

Died - The friends of Mrs. C. Trezvant, are requested to attend her funeral from her son's residence in Stoll's Alley, tomorrow morning, at 9 o'clock without further invitation.

Issue of September 25, 1820

Died, at her mother's residence, King-Street Road, on the 21st instant, in her 24th year, Mrs. Small, a native of Demgamron, Tyrone, Ireland.

Issue of September 26, 1820

Died, on the morning of the 22d inst. Mrs. Catherine Trezvant, relict of the deceased Mr. Theodore Trezvant, aged 84 years and 8 months.

Issue of September 28, 1820

Died, at New-Orleans, on the 25th ult. J. P. C. Sampson, Esq. Editor of the Louisiana Advertiser, and son of Counsellor Sampson, of New-York.

Issue of September 29, 1820

Died, in St. Matthews Parish, on the 8th inst. after a very few days sickness, Mrs. Rachel Richardson, in the 63d year of her age...(Eulogy)

Issue of September 30, 1820

Died, at Savannah, on the 17th instant, after a long and painful illness, Charles M. Parish, a native of Charleston, S.C. aged 24.

Issue of October 4, 1820

Died, at Fort Johnson, Charleston Harbor, on the 2d inst. of the County Fever, Doctor William Horace Buckner, post Surgeon, United States Army... (Eulogy)

Died - The friends and acquaintances of Mrs. Eliza A. Woodrouffe, are requested to attend her funeral, this afternoon, at 4 o'clock, from the residence of Mr. Geo. Perman, No. 36, Bay.

Issue of October 5, 1820

Died - The friends and acquaintances of Captain Stephen Fisher, and of John Haslett, are invited to attend the funeral of the former, at half past 4 o'clock this afternoon, from the ship Ceres, at Chisohn's lower Wharf.

Issue of October 10, 1820

Died, at Ashville, N.C. on the 26th September, in the 61st year of his age, Francis Peyre, Esq., of St. Stephen's Parish...(Eulogy)

Died, at Savannah, on Friday morning, the 6th inst. Mr. Francis A. Dillon, Deputy Post Master, and a native of that city...(Eulogy)

Died, on the 6th inst. Mr. Thomas Crapon, a native of Providence, R.I.

Died, on the 23d of September, Mr. Frederick Abel, aged 26 years.

Issue of October 11, 1820

Departed this life on the 9th inst. in the 57th year of his age William Crafts, Esquire...(Eulogy)

Departed this life, in firm assurance of a better, on Sunday morning, the 1st inst. William Gibbes Warham, in the 29th year of his age...(Eulogy)

Issue of October 20, 1820

Departed this transitory life, at Beaufort, S.C. on the 23d July last, Mr. Francis Duffy, after a short, but painful illness...(Eulogy)

Issue of October 24, 1820

Died, in the state of Alabama, on the 24th September, Mrs. Francis D. Hayne, wife of Col. Arthur P. Hayne, and daughter of Judge Duncan, of Pennsylvania...(Eulogy)

Died, on the 23d September, at his Plantation in St. James, Goose Creek, after a short illness, in the 70th year of his age, Mr. Lewis Pappenheim, a native of Germany, but for the last forty years a resident of this state.

Issue of October 31, 1820

Married, on the evening of the 26th instant by the Rev. Dr. Leland, Col. Benj. Fanuel Runt, to Miss Susan Barksdale, second daughter of William Mathewes, Esq. of St. James, Santee.

Issue of November 1, 1820

Married, last evening, by the Rev. Dr. Fenwick, Theodore Fayolle, Esq. to Miss Melanie Chissey; both of this city.

Issue of November 2, 1820

...Dr. James Brickell Hill, who departed this life on the 25th ult. at his residence in Marlborough District...(Eulogy)

Issue of November 2, 1820

Died, at Mulberry, St. John's (Berkly) on the 29th ult. Philip Alexander Broughton, son of Philip Porcher Broughton, Esq. aged three years...(Eulogy)

Issue of November 3, 1820

Married, last evening, by the Rev. Mr. Gilman, Mr. Edward Christie, to Miss Ann Caroline, eldest daughter of Mr. John William Chitty; all of this city.

Died - The friends and acquaintances of Mr. John Dill Rivers, Mrs. Jane Eliza Dill, and Mr. Joseph Taylor, are invited to attend the funeral of the former, from No. 13 Lamboll-Street, tomorrow morning, at 8 o'clock.

Issue of November 13, 1820

Died - The friends and acquaintances of Mr. and Mrs. James O'Reilly, and the Members of the St. Patrick Benevolent Society, are requested to attend the funeral of the former, tomorrow afternoon, at four o'clock, from his late residence No. 97, Church-Street, without further invitation.

Issue of November 15, 1820

Died...Mr. William Clement...(Eulogy)

Died, in New York, on the 4th inst. Mrs. Hannah R. Rivers, aged one hundred years, relict of the late Mr. J. R. Rivers...(Eulogy)

Issue of November 17, 1820

Married last evening, by the Rev. Dr. Dalcho, Mr. Joseph L. Enslow, to Charlotte, daughter of Mr. J. M. Elford, all of this city.

Married last evening, by the Rev. Mr. Gilman, Mr. James B. Bullock, Merchant, to Miss Eliza Greer Courtenay, all of this city.

Married, at Sempronious, (N.Y.) William Borter, aged 16 years, to Miss Mindwell Forbush, aged 13, after a courtship of ten evenings.

Died - The friends and acquaintances of Mr. and Mrs. Lewis Ogier, and the members of the South Carolina Society are particularly requested to attend the funeral of the former at 10 o'clock tomorrow morning, from his late residence, No. 154, East Bay, without further invitation.

Issue of November 18, 1820

Died, at Washington City, on the 11th inst. Commodore Hugh G. Campbell, one of the oldest Post Captain in the United States' Navy, and for several years commander of this station.

Issue of November 21, 1820

Married, on Monday evening last, by the Rev. Bishop Bowen, Robert S. Jenkins, Esq. of Edisto Island, to Miss Henrietta T. Calvert, of this city.

Issue of November 22, 1820

Married on Sunday evening last, by the Rev. Mr. Bachman, Dennis Vanholten, Esq. of this city, to Miss Sarah, only daughter of the late John Raoford, Jun. Esq. of St. John's, Berkley,

Issue of November 25, 1820

Departed this life, at Cannonsborough, on the 8th inst. Mrs. Catherine Simons, aged 79 years and 9 months...(Eulogy)

Issue of November 28, 1820

Married, at New York, on the 18th inst. by the Rev. Dr. Kuypers, Daniel Macaulay, Esq. merchant, of Charleston, S.C. to Miss Mary Leaycraft Henderson, daughter of the late Captain John Henderson, of New-York.

Issue of December 6, 1820

Married, last evening, by the Rev. Dr. Furman, Mr. Joseph Milligan, of this city, to Miss Elizabeth Fripp, daughter of B. Adams, Esq. of Wadmalaw.

Died - The friends and acquaintances of the late James Parsons Carroll, are invited to attend his funeral this afternoon, at four o'clock, from his late residence in Boundary-Street.

Died - The Members of the Hibernian Society are hereby requested to attend the funeral of the late Mr. James P. Carroll, this afternoon, at four o'clock, from his late residence in Boundary-Street, nearly opposite the residence of the late Wm. Holmes.

Died - The friends and acquaintances of Mr. John G. Thorne, and Mrs. Sarah Thorne are invited to attend the funeral of the former from his late residence No. 5, Cumberland Street, to-morrow afternoon, at 3 o'clock; also the Members of the Fellowship Society are particularly invited to attend.

Issue of December 8, 1820

Married, last evening, by the Rev. Mr. Bachman, Dr. John Buxbaum, to Miss Eliza Ashby Smyth, the only daughter of James Smyth, Esq. of this city, merchant, deceased.

Issue of December 23, 1820

Married, at Boston on the --- ult. Mr. John Milk to Miss Eliza Water.

Issue of December 28, 1820

Died - The friends and acquaintances and Members of the Marine Society, are requested to attend the funeral of Captain Henry Purcell, this afternoon, at 4 o'clock, from the residence of Alexander Gillon, No. 2, Wall-Street.

Issue of January 8, 1821

Died, on the 27th ult. at his Plantation in Walterborough St. John's, Charles De Tollenare, Esq. aged 91 years, a native of Nantz, and for nearly 50 years a resident in this state.

Died - The friends and acquaintances, and particularly the Members of the Methodist persuasion, are requested to attend the funeral of Mrs. Tamson Addison, relict of the late Captain John Addison, of Georgetown in Thomas Ham, in Hampstead, this afternoon, at 4 o'clock precisely.

Issue of January 10, 1821

Died - The friends and acquaintances of Dr. Rutledge, are invited to attend his funeral at 10 o'clock tomorrow morning, from his late residence, New Street.

Issue of January 13, 1821

Died - The friends and acquaintances of Mrs. Catherine Duvall, are invited to attend her funeral tomorrow afternoon, at 4 o'clock, from her late residence, No. 134 Church Street.

Issue of January 15, 1821

Departed this life, on the 13th inst. at his residence in St. John's Parish, (Berkeley) Samuel Gourdin, Esq. aged 55 years and 8 days.

Issue of January 17, 1821

Died, at Pineville, on the 3d inst. Mrs. Catherine Sinkler Gaillard, consort of Dr. Theodore S. Gaillard, and daughter of the late Francis Peyre, Esq. aged 23 years...(Eulogy)

Died at the residence of John Axson, Esq. in the parish of St. James Santee, on Friday, the 12th inst. Abraham Mechau, Esq. in the 42d year of his age...(Eulogy)

Died - The friends and acquaintances of Phillip Frazer and James S. Frazer, Printer, are requested to attend the funeral of the latter, this afternoon at four o'clock from his late residence, Magazine Street.

Issue of January 18, 1821

Married last evening by the Rev. Mr. Galluchat, Mr. Thomas Hamlin, of Christ Church Parish, to Miss Mary, eldest daughter of Mr. Philip Moore, of this city.

Married, on Thursday evening last, by the Right Rev. Dr. England, Dr. James C. W. M'Donald, to Miss Elizabeth Ryan.

Married, on Thursday evening the 28th ult. by the Rev. Mr. Fenwick, Mr. John E. M'Donnald, to Miss Mary Ann Hoey.

Issue of January 19, 1821

Died - The friends and acquaintances of the late Mr. Josiah Lovell, are requested to attend his funeral tomorrow afternoon, at 3 o'clock, from his late residence in King Street.

Issue of January 22, 1821

Died, on the evening of the 19th inst. Mrs. Miriam Hyams, the wife of Mr. Samuel Hyams, of this city. This lady was in the 42d year of her age ...(Eulogy)

Issue of January 30, 1821

Died, on the 16th inst. Mr. James S. Fraser, Printer, aged 31 years, son of Hugh Fraser, deceased, formerly of this city.

Issue of January 31, 1821

Died - The Rev. the clergy, and the friends and acquaintances of the Reverend Dr. Donald M'Leod are invited to attend his funeral to-morrow afternoon, at half after 3 o'clock from the house of Mrs. Munro, No. 36 Church Street.

Died, at New York, on Saturday the 20th instant, the Rev. Solomon Allen, in the 70th year of his age, formerly of Northampton, Mass.; father of Messrs. S. & M. Allen.

Issue of February 3, 1821

Died, at New Orleans, on the 8th Jan. last, John R. Cleary, Esq. late Shaeriff of Charleston District, in the 69th year of his age.

Died, at his residence, in Fairfield dsitrict, on the 20th December last, James Craig, Esq. in the 65th year of his age.

Issue of February 5, 1821

Died, at his seat on Bowman's Folly (Vir.) on the 15th inst. General John Cropper, in the 68th year of his age, after an illness of eleven days.

Died - The friends and acquaintances of Mr. John T. Bowles and of Mr. James G. Bowles are requested to attend the funeral of the latter from his late residence No. 2, Black Bird Alley, tomorrow afternoon at 4 o'clock.

Issue of February 7, 1821

Died, on Sunday the 28th ult. Mr. John Horry Ferguson, aged 57 years; and on the Thursday following, Mrs. Rebecca Ferguson, his relict, ceased to be among the living, in the 52d year of her age.

Issue of February 9, 1821

Died, on the 5th inst. at Ashepoo, of a Typhus Fever, Mrs. Mary

Robinson, aged 20 years; and also, an hour after, of the same disease, her youngest child.

Issue of February 12, 1821

Died - The friends and acquaintances of Mr. and Mrs. James M'Call, together with the members of the South Carolina Society, are invited to attend the funeral of the former from the residence of Mrs. Joshua Ward, Meeting Street, tomorrow morning at 9 o'clock, without further invitation.

Issue of February 13, 1821

Died - The friends and acquaintances of Mr. E. B. Gould, and G. W. Smith, are requested to attend the funeral of the latter, from the house of Mr. Gould, No. 111 Church Street tomorrow morning, at 8 o'clock, without further invitation.

Issue of February 14, 1821

(Died)....Rev. Dr. Donald M'Leod, who departed this life in this city, on the 30th ult in the 58th year of his age...(Eulogy)

Issue of February 15, 1821

Married, on the evening of the 8th inst. by the Rev. James H. Mellard, Colonel William Mellard, to Miss Mary Elizabeth Shingler, of St. James, Goose Creek Parish.

Issue of February 17, 1821

Departed this life on the 5th inst. of a pulmonary affection, which he bore with manly fortitude, Mr. James George Bowles, in the 24th year of his age...(Eulogy)

Died - The friends and acquaintances of Mrs. Rebecca Edwards are invited to attend her funeral tomorrow afternoon, at 4 o'clock, p.m. from the residence of J. B. Holmes, No. 6, Meeting Street.

Issue of February 20, 1821

Died - The friends and acquaintances of Mr. and Mrs. Graiser, are invited to attend the funeral of the latter, from her late residence corner of Archdale and Beaufain Streets, tomorrow afternoon, at 3 o'clock.

Issue of February 24, 1821

Married, on Thursday evening last, by the Rev. Dr. Furman, William E. Balley, Esq. to Miss Susan Eliza and William Royall, Jr. Esq. to Miss Mary Ann, daughters of John Riley Esq. all of Charleston.

Died - The relatives, friends and acquaintances of Mrs. Eliza D. Stowe, also those of her brother's John and Josiah Darrell, are respectfully invited to attend the funeral of the former tomorrow, at 12 o'clock, from her late residence, No. 98 Wentworth Street, without further invitation.

Issue of February 26, 1821

Died, at Norfolk on the 16th inst. Mr. David Miluado, a respectable merchant of that place.

Died - The friends and acquaintances of Major Jacob Holt, and of Mrs. Charlotte Holt, are requested to attend the funeral of the former, tomorrow, at 10 o'clock, at the residence of Mr. Belcher, No. 2 Liberty Street.

Issue of February 28, 1821

Died - The friends and acquaintances of Mrs. Esther Bellamy are invited to attend her funeral from the house of Thomas Blackwood, Pitt Street, tomorrow afternoon, at 3 o'clock.

Issue of March 1, 1821

Died - The friends and acquaintances of L. Danjou, the members of the South Carolina Society, and also those of the French Benevolent Society, are requested to attend his funeral tomorrow morning, at 9 o'clock, from his late residence corner of Church and Tradd Streets, without further invitation.

Issue of March 8, 1821

Married on Tuesday evening last, by the Right Rev. Dr. Bowen, Dr. Jacob D. Guerard, to Miss Alice Scriven, second daughter of Dr. Richard B. Scriven, all of Beaufort.

Issue of March 9, 1821

Married, last evening, by the Rev. Mr. Bachman, Mr. John A. Kelly, to Miss Anna Maria Friedle, all of this city.

Issue of March 10, 1821

Died - The relatives, friends and acquaintances of the Mr. Thomas Gadsden, are invited to attend his funeral from the house of Mr. John Horlbeck, corner of Meeting and Boundary Streets, tomorrow morning, at 9 o'clock, without further invitation.

Issue of March 14, 1821

Married, last evening, by the Rev. Mr. Galluchat, Mr. John Ralph Ham, to Miss Caroline Matilda Dickinson, all of this city.

Died, on Sunday, the 11th of February last, in the 85th year of his age, Captain John Johnson, a native of the city of New York...(Eulogy)

Departed this transitory life, on the 12th February, James M'Call, Esq. in the 75th year of his age...(Eulogy)

Died, in January last, at Wigton, (Scotland) of a rapid consumption, Mr. James W. Broadfoot, late of this city, in the 22d year of his age... (Eulogy)

Departed this life on Sunday, the 18th Feb. in the 48th year of her age, Anne Marie Graeser, consort of C. I. Graeser, of this city...(Eulogy)

Issue of March 15, 1821

Died - The friends and acquaintances of Mrs. Ann M'Cants and of Mr. and Mrs. Mellichamp, are invited to attend the funeral of the latter, from the residence of Mrs. M'Cants, No. 3, Savage Street tomorrow morning at 9 o'clock, without further invitation.

Issue of March 16, 1821

Died on Tuesday 13th inst. of a consumption, Mr. Samuel Stilwill, aged 38 years...(Eulogy)

Issue of March 20, 1821

Married, on Tuesday evening, the 8th inst. at Rumney Farm, by the Rev. Dr. Gadsden, Mr. Robert Whitfied to Miss Ann Marie, eldest daughter of Benjamin Langstaff, Esq. deceased.

Died, on the 15th February last, Mr. Joseph Nicholas Crand, at the age of 75 years...(Eulogy)

Issue of March 21, 1821

Married, on the 15th inst. by the Rev. Dr. Dalcho, Dr. John Ward M'Call to Miss Mary, eldest daughter of the late Daniel Ravenel, Esq.

Issue of March 26, 1821

Died - The friends and acquaintances of Mr. and Mrs. Nathan Foster, are

requested to attend the funeral of the former from his late residence, No. 47, Elliott Street, tomorrow afternoon, at 4 o'clock, without further invitation.
The President and members of the New England Society, are respectfully invited to attend.

Issue of March 28, 1821

Died, on the 22d instant, Mrs. Susannah Haynes Simmons, in the 62d year of her age...(Eulogy)

Issue of March 29, 1821

Departed this life on Monday, the 12th ult. Mr. Charles Frish, aged 78 years and 2 days...(Eulogy)
Died - The friends and acquaintances of Mr. and Mrs. Clayton, and of Mrs. Lafer and sons, are invited to attend the funeral of Mrs. Clayton, tomorrow afternoon, at 4 o'clock, from her late residence, No. 12, Pinckney Street.

Issue of April 2, 1821

Died, on the 11th ult. Mr. Thomas Gadsden, in the 53d year of his age.
Died - The friends and acquaintances of the late Jonathan Lucas, Sen. and those of his sons Jonathan, John, and William, are invited to attend the funeral of the former, from the residence of Jonathan Lucas, Cannonsborough, this afternoon, at 4 o'clock, without further invitation.

Issue of April 3, 1821

Died - The friends and acquaintances of Mr. and Mrs. Julius Petsch, and the officers and Members of the Fellowship Society, are invited to attend the funeral of the former, from his late residence No. 7, Liberty Street, tomorrow afternoon, at 4 o'clock, without further invitation.

Issue of April 4, 1821

Married, at Richmond, (Va.) on Wednesday, the 28th ult. by the Rev. J. H. Judah, A. Lazarus, Esq. of Wilmington, N.C. to Miss R. Mordecai, daughter of Jacob Mordecai, Esq.

Issue of April 5, 1821

Married, on Thursday evening last, at Marlborough, (S.C.) Mr. Joel Emanuel, merchant to Miss Mary Pledger, eldest daughter of Major William Pledger; all of said place.

Issue of April 6, 1821

Died, in New Haven, (Conn.) Rosalei daughter of Joseph Bennett, Esq. of this city, aged 18 months.

Issue of April 13, 1821

Married, last evening, by the Rev. Dr. Dalcho, James Creighton, Esq. of Baltimore, (Md) to Ann, daughter of the late General John M'Pherson, of this city.
Married, on the 11th inst. by the Rev. Mr. Piexotto, A. Seixas, Esq. of New York, to Miss R. M. Cardozo, daugher of David N. Cardozo, of this city.
Died, at Aberdeen, in Scotland, on the 18th Sept. last, in the 45th year of his age, James Ogilvie, the orator...(Eulogy)
Died, at Philadelphia, on the 4th instant Charles Biddle, Esq. aged 76 years.

Issue of April 14, 1821

Departed this life, on Wednesday, the 14th ult. of a protracted illness,

Mrs. Eliza Mary Mellichamp, in the 25th year of her age...(Eulogy)

Issue of April 16, 1821

Died, at Waterford, (Ireland) on the 7th Sept. last, Mr. Alexander Hammet, (brother of the late Rev. Wm. Hammet) aged 65 years; leaving a numerous and respectable circle of relatives and friends, to lament his death.

Issue of April 18, 1821

Died, at Greensburg, (Pa.) William Findley, Esq. a hero of the Revolution, and for many years a representative in Congress from the above district.

Issue of April 21, 1821

Married, on Thursday evening, the 19th inst. by the REv. Mr. Hanckel, Mr. Micah W. Jos. Jenkins, of John's Island, to Elizabeth Chaplin, eldest daughter of Wm. Reynolds, Esq. late of Wadmalaw Island, deceased.

Issue of April 26, 1821

Married, on Tuesday evening, the 24th inst. by the Rev. Allston Gibbes, Dr. Alexander Robert Chisolm, to Ellen Cecila, eldest daughter of Theodore Gaillard, Jun. all of this place.

Died, on the 20th inst. after a lingering illness...Mr. Lyon Moses, a native of Amsterdam...He was in the 72d year of his age...(Eulogy)

Died, on the 19th inst. in the 73d year of his age, James Miller, Sen. for many years a respectable merchant of this city...(Eulogy)

Issue of April 28, 1821

Married, on Thursday evening last, by the Rev. Frederick Dalcho, Symer Bonneau, Esq. to Miss Charlotte M. Ingraham, daughter of the late Nathaniel Ingraham, Esq. all of this city.

Issue of May 7, 1821

Married, on the 29th of March; at Herculaneum, Missouri, John W. Honey, Esq. to Miss Mary S. Austin, daughter of Mr. Horace Austin...

Issue of May 12, 1821

Married, on Wednesday, the 2d inst. by the Rev. Mr. Piexotto, Mr. W. H. Oppenhfim, merchant of Hamburg, to Miss Catherine Moses, eldest daughter of Joseph Moses, deceased, of this city.

Departed this life on the 4th instant Mr. Charles Bradley, Printer, aged 43 years and 6 months, a native of Ireland...(Eulogy)

Died - The friends and acquaintances of Mr. John Moncrieffe, and the officers and members of the St. Andrew's Society, are invited to attend his funeral, from his late residence, No. 13, Society Street-west side of Meeting Street.

Issue of May 17, 1821

Died, on the 12th inst. in the 72d year of his age, John Moncrieffe, Esq. a native of Perth, in Scotland...(Eulogy)

Died - The friends and acquaintances of Mr. Emanuel Dela Motta, and the members of the Hebrew Orphan Society, are requested to attend his funeral tomorrow afternoon, at 3 o'clock, from his late residence, No.-- upper end of Queen Street, without further invitation.

Issue of May 19, 1821

Departed this life, on the 15th instant Mrs. Anne Rebecca D'Oyley, relict of Colonel Daniel D'Oyley, lately deceased, in the 58th year of her age.

Issue of May 19, 1821

Died, on Thursday last, Mr. Emanuel Dela Motta, in the 61st year of his age...(Eulogy)

Issue of May 21, 1821

Died - The friends and acquaintances of Captain John Pratt and Charles Edmondston, are requested to attend the funeral of Dr. Botafeur, this afternoon, at half past 3 o'clock precisely, from Mr. Edmondston's residence, Church Street, next door to the new Baptist Church.

Issue of May 31, 1821

Married, at New York, on Sunday evening, the 20th inst. by the Rev. Mr. Piexotto, Mr. A. L. Gomez, of Wilmington, N.C. to Miss H. Hendricks, daughter of Mr. H. Hendricks, of New York.

Issue of June 1, 1821

Died - The friends and acquaintances of Mr. Ira Hunter and Mrs. Elizabeth Hunter, are respectfully invited to attend the funeral of the latter, tomorrow morning at 9 o'clock, from her former residence, No. 266 King St.

Issue of June 5, 1821

Married, on Sunday last, by the Rev. Dr. Gillman, Mr. Florence O'Sullivan to Miss Sarah Elizabeth Wilkings Lloyd; both of this city.

Issue of June 13, 1821

Married, last evening, by the Rev. Dr. Gadsden, Mr. John J. Frazer, to Miss Sarah Townsend, both of this city.

Issue of June 14, 1821

Married, last evening, by the Rev. Mr. Piexotto, Mr. Elias Levy, to Miss Rachel Moise, daughter of Cherry Moise, Esq. all of this city.

Issue of June 16, 1821

Married, on the 14th inst. by the Rev. Samuel Gilman, J. B. Whitridge, M.D. to Miss Sarah B. M'Leod, daughter of the late Rev. Donald M'Leod, D.D. of Edisto Island.

Issue of June 21, 1821

Died, after a short illness, on the morning of the 10th inst. Mrs. Lucretia Constance Radcliffe, widow of R. Radcliffe, Esq. aged 63 years... (Eulogy)

Married, at Darien, on the 15th inst. by the Rev. Walter Cranston, Daniel H. Brailsford, Esq. to Miss Jane Spalding, eldest daughter of Thomas Spalding, Esq. of that city.

Married, at Darien, on the 14th inst. by the Rev. W. Cranston, Dr. Charles Belton to Mrs. Ann H. Macomber, of that city.

Issue of June 22, 1821

Died - The friends and acquaintances of Edward and Martha Mortimer, are invited to attend the funeral of the latter, this evening, at 5 o'clock, from No. 24, Anson Street, without further invitation.

Issue of June 30, 1821

Died, of a consumption, on Saturday, the 16th inst. at the Quarantine ground of New York, the day after his arrival from Charleston, Mr. Hugh M'Doygall, of New York, aged 26 years. He has left a wife and one child to lament his loss.

Issue of July 3, 1821

Married, on Thursday evening last, by the Rev. Dr. Palmer, Thomas
Napier, Esq. to Mrs. Rebecca Stiles, daughter of the late Major Simeon Theus.

Issue of July 9, 1821

Died — The venerable Tucker Harris, M.D. died on the afternoon of the
6th inst. aged 73 years and 10 months.

Issue of July 11, 1821

Departed this life, suddenly, on Friday the 6th inst. at his residence,
in Walterborough, Colonel Richard Singleton, in the 45th year of his age...
(Eulogy)

Issue of July 14, 1821

Died, at Brainerd, (Tenn.) on the 7th June, the Rev. Samuel Worcester,
D.D. the highly respected and venerated Senior Pastor of the Tabernacle
Church and Society of Salem, Mass.

Issue of July 16, 1821

- Died, on the 30th ult. in the 16th year of her age, Miss Eliza Black,
daughter of Mr. James Black, merchant of this place. Her memory will be
long cherished by those friends who had an opportunity of knowing her worth.

Issue of July 17, 1821

Died — The friends and acquaintances of Mr. N. Raymond, and Mr. James
Stilman, are requested to attend the funeral of Alfred F. Raymond, at 5
o'clock this evening, at No. 97 East Bay.

Issue of July 19, 1821

Died, at Great Corn Island, near the Spanish Main, on the 1st of May,
aged 37 years, Captain William Wilson Mitchell...(Eulogy)
Died, at Breaver, Pennsylvania, on the 24th ult. Mrs. Bryan, consort of
John Bryan, of that county...(Eulogy)

Issue of July 26, 1821

Departed this life, in this city, on the 18th inst. in the 17th year of
his age, Alfred F. youngest son of Mr. N. Reynolds...(Eulogy)

Issue of July 27, 1821

Died, in this city on Monday, the 23d inst. in the 20th year of her
age, Mrs. Ann S. Mazych, the wife of William Mazych, Jun. and second daughter
of James Stanyarne, Esq. of Stono.

Issue of July 28, 1821

Died — The friends and acquaintances of Mr. Robert Shand, are requested
to attend the funeral of his son Alexander, from his residence No. 14
Pinckney Street, this afternoon, at 4 o'clock, without further invitation.

Issue of July 29, 1821

Died — The friends and acquaintances of Mr. and Mrs. McElmoyle, are
requested to attend the funeral of their son, at 5 o'clock this afternoon,
from their residence, corner of King and Tradd Streets, without further
invitation.

Issue of August 1, 1821

Departed this life, on Monday morning, the 30th ult. Master Philip G.
Prioleau after a short and severe illness of six days, only son of William

and Eliza M'Elmoyle, of this city, aged 5 years 8 months and 20 days.

Issue of August 2, 1821

Died - The friends and acquaintances of Mrs. A. Colzy and of her son John F. Colzy, are invited to attend the funeral of the latter from his residence No. 43 Church Street, this afternoon, at 4 o'clock.

Issue of August 4, 1821

Died, at Philadelphia, on the 29th ult. of a pulmonary disease, Hext M'Call, Esq. of this city.

Died - The friends and acquaintances of Mr. Walter Elliott, and of Mr. Henry Shields, are requested to attend the funeral of the former, tomorrow afternoon, at 5 o'clock, from his late residence, 329 King Street.

Issue of August 7, 1821

Died, on the 5th inst. Mr. Walter Elliott, a native of Roxburgh, (Scotland) in the 32d year of his age.

Died, on the 4th inst. of Typhus Fever, in the 19th year of her age, Leah, daughter of Lyon Levy, Esq....(Eulogy)

Issue of August 10, 1821

Died, in Chanba, Alabama, lately Col. John Taylor, receiver of public monies, and formerly member of Congress, from this state.

Issue of August 11, 1821

Died, in Newport, R.I. on the 22d ult. Mrs. Rutledge, wife of Mr. William Rutledge, of this city.

Issue of August 14, 1821

Died, in Saint Mathew's Parish, on the 7th inst. after a lingering illness of nearly two months, William Hampton Fludd, in the 26th year of his age, eldest son of Daniel Fludd, Esq.

Issue of August 15, 1821

(Died)...William H. Fludd, who departed this life on the 7th inst. at Santee, in the 27th year of his age...(Eulogy)

Issue of August 17, 1821

Died, at Georgetown, on Sunday evening, the 12th inst. Captain Peter Bacot, aged 70 years. Captain Bacot resided many years in Charleston, in the early part of his life...(Eulogy)

Issue of August 20, 1821

Died - The friends and acquaintances of Mrs. Sarah Vonhagon, and of her son, Mr. Henry Shoup, are respectfully invited to attend the funeral of the latter, this afternoon, at 4 o'clock, from his late residence No. 110 Wentworth Street, near Meeting Street.

Died, on Saturday, the 18th inst. Miss Ann Mary Tunno, aged 19 years, granddaughter of James Champneys.

Died, at Edisto Island, on the 13th inst. of the Typhus Fever, James McMeikan, a native of Scotland, aged about 38 years...(Eulogy)

Issue of August 23, 1821

Died - On the morning of the 13th inst. departed this life, Peter Smith, Esq. having nearly completed his 67th year...(Eulogy)

Issue of August 27, 1821

Died, on Thursday last, the 23d inst. in the vicinity of Coosawhatchie, after a short but severe illness, John F. Trezvant, Attorney at Law... (Eulogy)

Issue of August 28, 1821

Died, on Friday, the 10th inst. at his farm, on 18 mile creek, aged 85 years, Mr. Andrew Pickens, one amongst the first settlers in Pendleton District.

Issue of August 30, 1821

Died - The friends and acquaintances of Miss Mary Lee, of Thomas and William Lee, and of Robert Howard, are invited to attend the funeral of the former this afternoon at 5 o'clock, from the residence of Rob Howard, corner of Meeting and George Streets.

Issue of September 3, 1821

Died - The friends and acquaintances of Mr. and Mrs. Cleapor, and Miss Sarah Cleapor, are invited to attend the funeral of the latter, this afternoon, at 4 o'clock, from No. 24 Ellery Street.

Issue of September 5, 1821

Died, at Sumterville, (S.C.) on the 18th inst. Charles Miller, Esq. a member of the Senate of this State.

Issue of September 6, 1821

Died - The friends and acquaintances of the late Jacques Roumillat and those of the family, are requested to attend his funeral this afternoon, at 4 o'clock, from his late residence, No. 37 Meeting Street, without further invitation.

Issue of September 7, 1821

Married, at New York, on the 30th ult. by the Rev. Mr. Peixotto, Mr. Myer J. Ellis, of Charleston, (S.C.) to Miss Francis Polack, daughter of Mr. Jacob Abrahams, of that city.

Died, on the 30th ult. after a painful illness Miss Mary, third daughter of the late Colonel William Lee...(Eulogy)

Died, at Wilmington, (N.C.) of the prevailing fever on the 25th ult. Mrs. Margaret Morrison.

Died, at Wilmington, N.C. on the 29th ult. Mrs. Knight.

Died, at Wilmington, N.C. on the 30th Mr. Daniel O'Neal.

Died, at Wilmington, N.C. on the 31st Mrs. Eliza Dick.

Died, at Wilmington, N.C. on the 31st an infant child of the late Joseph Bishop.

Issue of September 10, 1821

Died - The friends and acquaintances of the late Mrs. Sarah Cromwell, and of her son, Warham Cromwell, are invited to attend her funeral this afternoon, precisely at 4 o'clock, from her house in Stoll's Alley, without further invitation.

Issue of September 14, 1821

Died, at Columbia, (S.C.) on the 30th ult. Mrs. Louisa Adeline Creyon, aged 27 years.

Died, at Columbia, (S.C.) on the 1st inst. Captain Zachariah Phillips, aged 44 years.

Died, at Columbia, (S.C.) on the 2d Mrs. Eliza De Saussure, consort of the Hon. Judge De Saussure.

Issue of September 14, 1821

Died, at Columbia, S.C. on the 31st ult. Mr. Henry Gallman,

Died Wilmington, (N.C.) on the 1st inst. Mrs. Cecelia Evirett, aged 60 years.

Died, at Wilmington, (N.C.) on the 1st inst. of the yellow fever, Mr. Edward Robeson.

Died, at Wilmington, (N.C.) on the 2d inst. Mrs. Margaret Harris, aged 20 years.

Died, at Wilmington, (N.C.) on the 5th Mrs. Hannah Conyers.

Died, at Wilmington, (N.C.) on the 6th Master David Tumen.

Died, at Wilmington, (N.C.) on the 7th Mr. Isaac Jacobs.

Died - The friends and acquaintances of Mrs. Elizabeth Elliott, are requested to attend her funeral from her late residence, the corner of King and Tradd Streets, this afternoon, at 4 o'clock.

Issue of September 21, 1821

Departed this life on Sunday morning, 29th July last, in this city, after a few weeks illness, which she bore with Christian resignation, Mrs. Elizabeth Cambridge, in the 61st year of her age, relict of the late Tobias Cambridge, Esq. formerly a respectable merchant of this place...(Eulogy)

Issue of September 24, 1821

Died, at Bennett's Point, near Ashepoo, on Saturday morning the 25th August, after an illness of five weeks, which he bore without a murmur, Samuel S. Brown of St. Bartholomew's Parish, aged 34 years and 14 days... (Eulogy)

Issue of September 27, 1821

Departed this life, on the 18th instant, Mr. Samuel M. Brailsford, in the 18th year of his life...(Eulogy)

(Died)...Mr. Henry Foster...Mr. Foster was a member of the late firm of John Brandt & Co. of the city of New Orleans and died on the 29th day of August, after an illness of nine days-which he bore with patience and resignation.

Mr. Foster was born in Charleston, and is a son of the late Mr. Thomas Foster.

Issue of September 28, 1821

Married, last evening, by the Rev. Mr. Bachman, Mr. Francis Orlando Curtis, of this city, to Miss Sarah R. C. Seabrook, second daughter of Joseph S. Seabrook, Esq. of Stono.

Departed this life, on the 12th inst. Mrs. Elizabeth Hall Condy, daughter of the late Thomas Daoughty, Esq. and consort of Jeremiah Condy, Esq. in the 50th year of her age...(Eulogy)

Died, at Columbia, on the 21st inst. Mrs. Caroline Marshall, wife of John F. Marshall.

Died, at Columbia, on the 20th, Mrs. Sarah Goodwyn wife of Major John Goodwyn.

Died, at Columbia, on the 21st Mrs. Pritchard, widow of Wm. Pritchard.

Died, at Edgefield, C. B. on the 18th, Colonel George Butler, Attorney at Law.

Died, at Wilmington last week, of the prevailing fever, Mrs. Allen, wife of James Allen, Mr. Silas Varnum, and Mrs. Calhorda, wife of J. P. Calhorda.

Issue of October 3, 1821

Died, at Camden, (S.C.) on the 20th ult. Benjamin, son of Mrs. Alford.

Died, at Camden, (S.C.) on the 19th John, son of Hugh M'Call.

Died, at Camden, (S.C.) on the 19th Peirce, son of Francis Allen.

Issue of October 3, 1821

Died, at Camden, (S.C.) on the 19th Mrs. Joanna Parker.
Died, at Camden, (S.C.) on the 22d Captain Postell McCaw.
Died, at Louisville, (Ky.) William Cochrane, Esq. Cashier of the U.S.
Bank at this place.
Died - The friends and acquaintances of Mrs. Cassin, the Mother of
Connelly Cassin, are invited to attend her funeral, from her dwelling, beyond
the Lines between the hours of 7 and 8 o'clock, tomorrow morning, without
further invitation.

Issue of October 5, 1821

Died, at North Island, near Georgetown, on the 22d September, Mrs.
Rebecca Elliott Pinckney, the affectionate consort of Henry L. Pinckney...
(Eulogy)
Died - The friends and acquaintances of Mr. and Mrs. Francis Dickenson,
are invited to attend the funeral of their daughter Susan, from their
residence, No. 71 Broad Street, this afternoon, at 4 o'clock.
Died, at Wilmington, (N.C.) last week by malignant fever, Mrs. Ann
Wingate, Master Edward Robinson, Mrs. Rebecca Murphy, Mrs. Ann Cole, Master
John Murphy, Mrs. Harris, wife of the late Peter Harris, Sen. and Master
Henry Howell.

Issue of October 8, 1821

Departed this transitory life, on Monday the 1st October Mr. John
Bounetheau Miller, aged 24 years and 9 months, youngest son of the late
Major John David Miller...(Eulogy)
Died, on the 24th Sept. last, after a painful illness of ten days,
Nathaniel Prince, in the 14th year of his age, second son of Joseph P.
Prince.

Issue of October 9, 1821

Died - The friends and acquaintances of Messrs. R. Pillot, O. Pillot,
and John Pillot, are requested to attend the funeral of the latter, from
his late residence Meeting Street Road, this afternoon, at 4 o'clock.

Issue of October 10, 1821

Departed this life, on the eve of the 26th September, 1821, Isaac M.
Goldsmith, a native of Rotterdam, in the Kingdom of Holland, in the 48th
year of his age...(Eulogy)
Died, at Abbeville, (S.C.) on the 14th ult. Elijah Gilbert, Esq. in the
29th year of his age, sincerely regretted by his relatives and friends.

Issue of October 12, 1821

Married, on Wednesday evening last, by the Rev. Dr. Gadsden, Arthur
Kiddell, Esq. to Miss Elizabeth, second daughter of Benjamin Langstaff,
Esq. deceased.
Departed this life, on Thursday, the 4th inst. Miss Susan E. Dickinson,
eldest daughter of Francis Dickinson, Esq. of this city...(Eulogy)
Departed this life, on Friday, the 5th October, Mr. Patrick Byrne, a
native of Ireland, and for many years a respectable inhabitant of this city,
aged 65 years and 4 months.

Issue of October 13, 1821

Married, on Wednesday evening last, by the Rev. Dr. Hall, Mr. Eljar
Kingman, Jun. to Miss Sophia Thompson, both of this city.

Issue of October 15, 1821

Died - The friends and acquaintances of Mrs. Catharine Austen, are
requested to attend her funeral, tomorrow morning, the 16th inst. at 8

o'clock, from her late residence, No. 117 East Bay (formerly No. 68) without further invitation.

Issue of October 19, 1821

Died, at Camden, (S.C.) on the 11th inst. the Hon. Judge Brevard, after a short illness.

Issue of October 22, 1821

Died - The friends and acquaintances of the late Mr. Jacob Williman, and Mrs. Elizabeth Schmidt, are requested to attend the funeral of Dr. Jacob Schmidt, at his mother's house, No. 9 in Montague Street, tomorrow afternoon, at 4 o'clock.

Issue of October 24, 1821

Departed this life, on the 17th inst. in the 26th year of her age of a pulmonary complaint; Miss Martha W. Dorman, after a painful and lingering illness of twelve months, which she sustained with the piety and resignation of a Christian.

Issue of October 25, 1821

Married, on Wednesday, the 24th inst. by the Rev. Mr. Bachman, Mr. Edward S. Courtenay, to Miss Elizabeth S. Wade, all of this city.

Died, at Walterborough, on the 9th inst. Miss Susan Lockwood...(Eulogy)

Died, at Savannah, on the morning of the 21st instant, Colonel Charles Fisler, aged 26 years, after an illness of a few days, which he bore with the fortitude of a soldier, and resignation of a Christian.

Died - The friends and acquaintances of Mr. Henry Delanvincendiere, are invited to attend his funeral this afternoon, at 4 o'clock, from his late residence, King Street continued.

Issue of October 26, 1821

Married, on the 3d of April last, by the Rev. Dr. Dalcho, Mr. John P. McCall, to Miss Martha Ann Lequeux, both of this city.

Issue of October 29, 1821

(Died)...Dr. Oliver Hawes...He was a native of Connecticut, but for many years a resident of this state...(Eulogy)

Issue of October 31, 1821

Died, on the 29th inst. in the 59th year of his age, Mr. William Marshall, a native of the parish of Gretna (Scotland) but for the last thirty-six years a respectable Merchant and Vendue Master of this city... - (Eulogy)

Issue of November 2, 1821

Departed this life, on the morning of Saturday, the 27th ult. in Prince William's Parish, Reading Fields, in the 70th year of his age... (Eulogy)

Issue of November 3, 1821

Married, on Thursday evening, the 1st inst. by the Rev. Mr. Bachman, Mr. Thomas Muggridge, to Miss Francis Gibbs.

Married, on Thursday evening, the 1st inst. by the Rev. Dr. Leland, Abraham Wilson, Esq. of James Island, Planter, to Miss Susan S. Clement, eldest daughter of the late William Clement, Esq. deceased, of this city.

Died, at Burlington, New Jersey, on the 24th ult. at the advanced age of 82, the Hon. Elias Boudinot, L.L.D. President of the American Bible Society, and one of the most eminent philanthropists of the age.

Issue of November 6, 1821

Died at Wansborough, (Georgia) on the 24th ult. after a short illness, Mrs. Charlotte S. Neyland, daughter of John Prioleau, deceased, of this city, in the 43d year of her age.

Issue of November 7, 1821

Died - The relations, friends and acquaintances of Miss Ann Edmonds, are requested to attend her funeral tomorrow morning, at 11 o'clock, from the residence of Mr. Josiah Smith, in Anson Street, without further invitation.

Issue of November 10, 1821

Died, at St. Bartholomew's Parish, on the 1st of October, after a short illness, which she sustained with pious resignation, Mrs. Elizabeth Young-blood, consort of Major Gen. William Youngblood...(Eulogy)

Issue of November 13, 1821

Died - The friends and acquaintances of Mr. James and Mrs. Ann Grantt, also the members of the Franklin Typographical Society, are requested to attend the funeral of the former from his late residence No. 9 Wall Street, at 3 o'clock this afternoon, without further invitation.

Issue of November 14, 1821

Died - The friends and acquaintances of M. Kelly and Mrs. S. Baker, are invited to attend her funeral at 4 o'clock, this afternoon, from No. 91 (formerly 52) East Bay.

Issue of November 16, 1821

Married, last evening by the Rev. Mr. Boies, Samuel M'Clary, Esq. to Miss Ann Long, both of this city.

Issue of November 20, 1821

Married, on Wednesday evening last, by the Rev. Mr. Piexotto, Aaron Phillips, Esq. to Miss Isabel Lazarus, daughter of Marks Lazarus, of this city.

Died, on the 11th inst. at his residence in St. Georges' Dorchester, Mr. Thomas Smith, Sen. aged 64 years and 5 months.

Issue of November 26, 1821

Died, on the 12th inst. Mr. James Grantt, for many years foreman of respectable Printing Establishments in this city...(Eulogy)

Issue of November 28, 1821

Died on Saturday the 24th inst. in this city, Miss Susan Mary, only daughter of Major Seth T. Prior, aged 13 years and 9 months.

Issue of December 1, 1821

Married, last evening, by the Rev. Dr. Dalcho, Mr. Edwin Gibbes, to Miss Caroline Sinclair Thayer, daughter of Mr. Ebenezer Thayer, all of this city.

Issue of December 5, 1821

Departed this life, on the 27th November, after a short but painful illness, which she bore with Christian fortitude, Mrs. Grace Doyle, aged 54 years, of Monk's Corner, St. John's a native of Ireland, but for many years a humane, benevolent, and respectable inhabitant of the former place.

Issue of December 6, 1821

Died - The friends and acquaintances of Mr. Anthony Gabeau and Daniel Gabeau are invited to attend the funeral of the latter from the residence of the former, tomorrow morning, at 9 o'clock, without further invitation.

Died - The friends and acquaintances of Mr. Charles Stone and Sarah Stone, are requested to attend the funeral of Mrs. Mary Tucker, from her late residence, No. 31 King Street, opposite Whim Court, at 3 o'clock tomorrow afternoon, without further invitation.

Issue of December 13, 1821

Died - The relations and friends of Mr. and Mrs. John Bryan, are invited to attend the funeral of their son, John, tomorrow morning, at half past 9 o'clock, from No. 16, Hasell Street.

Issue of December 14, 1821

Married, on Sunday evening last, by the Rev. Mr. Reid Samuel B. Northorp Esq. to Miss Ann V. Wyatt, eldest daughter of Peter Wyatt, Esq. deceased.

Issue of December 21, 1821

Died, in this city, on the 17th inst. Mr. Alexander L. McGregor, in the 39th year of his age.

Died - The friends and acquaintances of Doctor William Warley, and the Medical and Cincinatti Societies are invited to attend his funeral this afternoon, at 4 o'clock, at his late residence, Church Street.

Issue of December 24, 1821

Died, on the 4th inst. at her residence, in St. John's Parish, after a long and painful illness Mrs. Margaret Sinkler, the relict of the late James Sinkler, Esq.

Issue of January 3, 1822

Died - The friends and acquaintances of Mrs. Mary Brailsford, are invited to attend her funeral from her late residence No. 41, Tradd-Street, tomorrow afternoon, at 3 o'clock, without further invitation.

Died - The friends and acquaintances of Mrs. Sophia Chalmers, Henry J. Chalmers, and John Gebbes, are invited to attend the funeral of the former, tomorrow afternoon, at half past 3 o'clock, from her late residence in Broad Street.

Issue of January 10, 1822

Married, at St. Helena (B.D.) by the Rev. P. Mathews, on Thursday, the 3d inst. Mr. Samuel P. Chisolm to Miss Martha Chaplin.

Issue of January 11, 1822

Departed this life on the 3d inst. in the 56th year of her age, after a lingering illness, Mrs. Mary Brailsford, relict of Mr. Morton Brailsford, formerly a merchant of this city...(Eulogy)

Issue of January 16, 1822

Departed this life, on the 12th inst. in the 45th year of his age, after a long and painful illness.... Captain Joseph Hunt, a native of Boston, (Mass.) but for many years past a resident in this city...(Eulogy)

Issue of January 19, 1822

Died, on the 5th inst. at his uncle's, and near Statesburgh, Mr. Joseph Inglisby, of this city, aged 18 years.

Died, at New York, on the 10th inst. Barent Gardenier, Esq. of that city, Counsellor at Law.

Issue of January 25, 1822

Married, on the 24th inst. in this city by the Rev. Dr. Gadsden, Davison M'Dowall, Esq. of Pee Dee, S.C., to Miss Mary Moore, of this city.

Issue of January 26, 1822

Married, by the Rev. Dr. Gadsden, on the 22d inst. Joseph F. Bee, Esq. of St. Andrew's Parish, to Miss Mary S. second daughter of the late James W. Gadsden, Esq. deceased.

Died, at Pensacola, on the 15th ult. John G. Bird, Esq. United States District Attorney for the Province of East Florida.

Died - The friends and acquaintances of Mr. Charles Burger, and also those of Samuel Burger, are requested to attend the funeral of the former from his late residence at Mrs. Potter's, No. 37, East Bay, tomorrow after-noon, at 4 o'clock.

Issue of January 29, 1822

Married, on Thursday last, by the Rev. Mr. O'Hennan, Thomas Duggan, Esq. to Miss May Vernal, all of this city.

Issue of January 31, 1822

Died - The friends and acquaintances of States Gist, Esqr. deceased, and the Members of the Society of Cincinnati, and of Union Kilwinning Lodge, No. 4; are requested to attend his funeral at three o'clock, tomorrow afternoon, at the late residence of the deceased, No. 5 Meeting Street.

Issue of February 1, 1822

Died, at New York, on the 22d inst. after a lingering illness, Mr. Manuel Noah, aged 67 years.

Issue of February 5, 1822

...Mr. Charles Burger, who departed this life on the 26th ult. in the 33d year of his age, was a native, and for some time past, a respectable merchant of this city...(Eulogy)

Died, on Saturday night, the 19th inst. Col. Sampson Butler, at his residence near Edgefield Court House, aged 52 years.

Issue of February 6, 1822

Married, on Sunday evening, the 3d inst. by the Rev. Dr. Bachman, Mr. George Jacoby, native of Prussia, to Miss Elizabeth Bachman, of this city.

Issue of February 7, 1822

Departed this life, on the 21st ult. Mrs. Elizabeth M. Izard, aged 34 years and seven months, wife of Ralph Izard, Esq. of this city.

Died - The friends and acquaintances of Mr. Joseph Yates, also the officers and members of the St. Andrew's, South Carolina and Marine Societies, are respectfully invited to attend his funeral, from his late residence, Meeting Street, to-morrow afternoon, at 4 o'clock.

Issue of February 9, 1822

Married, on Thursday evening last, by the Rev. Dr. Palmer, William H. Holmes, to Miss Margaret Green, both of this city.

Issue of February 11, 1822

Married, on Wedneaday evening 6th inst. by the Rev. Mr. John Bachman, Mr. Christian G. Schnedier, to Miss Mary Ann Butler, both of this city.

Died, lately at Paris, after a few days illness the celebrated Colonel Thorton, late of Thernville Royd in the county of York, (Eng.)....(Eulogy)

Died – The friends and acquaintances of Robert Flemming, Alexander Henry and Thomas Flemming, are invited to attend the funeral of Alexander Flemming, tomorrow afternoon, at 3 o'clock, from No. 18, George Street, without further invitation.

Issue of February 12, 1822

Died – The friends and acquaintances of Mr. John Geyer, are invited to attend the funeral of his daughter Sarah Geyer, from his residence No. 16, Lynch's Lane, tomorrow morning at 9 o'clock.

Issue of February 14, 1822

Married on Monday evening last, the 11th inst. by the Rev. Mr. Boice, Mr. Moses Wood, to Miss Caroline Ann, daughter of the late John Coburn, Esqr. of St. Paul's Parish.

Issue of February 18, 1822

Departed this transitory life, on Tuesday morning, 12th inst. (after a protracted illness of many months) Miss Sarah S. Geyer, daughter of Mr. John Geyer, of this city...(Eulogy)

Issue of February 21, 1822

Died – The friends and acquaintances of Mrs. Susanna Martin, Mr. and Mrs. Thomas Martin, Mrs. Ogier, and Mrs. Berney, are requested to attend the funeral of the former, from her late residence No. 3, Middle-Street, tomorrow morning, at 9 o'clock.

Issue of February 22, 1822

Died – The friends and acquaintances of Mr. Charles Cleapor, are invited to attend his funeral tomorrow afternoon, at 3 o'clock, from his former residence No. 22, Ellery Street.

Issue of February 26, 1822

Died, at his Plantation in St. John's Berkeley, on the 10th inst. Mr. Rene Ravenel, in the 60th year of his age...(Eulogy)

Issue of February 27, 1822

Died – The friends and acquaintances of Mrs. Loyd, and of Mr. and Mrs. O'Sullivan, are requested to attend the funeral of the latter, at her late residence, No. 36 Bull Street, tomorrow the 28th inst., precisely at 10 o'clock.

Issue of February 28, 1822

Died – The friends and acquaintances of Mrs. James Hunter, and Mr. Thomas Hunter, also of Mrs. Ann Kay, are requested to attend the funeral of the former tomorrow afternoon at 4 o'clock, from her late residence Warren-Street, next to St. Paul's Church.

Issue of March 1, 1822

...death of Mr. William Patterson, Jun. who departed this life on the ?4th inst. at his place of residence, near Saltkeicher Bridge, Prince William's Parish, in the 33d year of his age...(Eulogy)

Issue of March 1, 1822

Died, at Wilmington, (N.C.) on the 21st ult. Captain Joseph Burch, for many years commander of the Revenue Cutter on this station, aged 48 years.

Issue of March 2, 1822

Died - The relatives, friends and acquaintances of Mr. and Mrs. Joseph Fordham; also of Robert Fager, are invited to attend the funeral of the late Mrs. Mary Fordham, tomorrow morning, at half past eight o'clock, from the residence of her mother, on Williams' Wharf, without further invitation.

Issue of March 4, 1822

Died, in Boston, in February last, Mr. Solon Hodges, formerly a resident of this place, aged 20 years.

Issue of March 5, 1822

Died - The officers and Members of the South Carolina, and Bible Soceities, the members of the Methodist Society, the honorable Members of the City Council of Charleston, the officers of the Marine Hospital, and the friends and acquaintances of the late Captain James George are invited to attend the funeral of the latter from his late residence No.--, East Bay Street, tomorrow afternoon, at half past 3 o'clock, without further invitation.

Issue of March 6, 1822

Died, at Savannah on the 12th ult. Mrs. Harriet Sophia Marshall, wife of Dr. Wm. P. Marshall, and daughter of the late William Neyle, Esq. of that city.
Died - The friends and particularly the masonic Bretheren of Robert Wilson, deceased are requested to attend his funeral at 3 o'clock this afternoon, from the residence of Mr. Klints, No. 10 Smith's Lane, without further invitation.

Issue of March 9, 1822

Married, on Thursday evening last, by the Rev. Mr. Bachman, Mr. Samuel Lord, to Miss Eliza Catherine Power, all of this city.
Died - The friends and acquaintances of Mrs. Hannah M'Kay and Miss Mary M'Kay, are invited to attend the funeral of the latter from the house of the Rev. Dr. Furman, No. 117 Church Street, tomorrow at half-past 12 o'clock.

Issue of March 12, 1822

...Died, on Monday, the 4th inst. Capt. James George...(Eulogy)

Issue of March 15, 1822

Married, on Wednesday evening, the 13th inst. by the Rev. A. W. Leland, Capt. John Rivers, to Miss Sarah, youngest daughter of the late Jonah Rivers all of James Island.

Issue of March 22, 1822

Died, on the 16th inst. at his residence in Lexington District, Alexander B. Stark, Esq. late a Member of the Senate of this state from said district.

Issue of March 25, 1822

Departed this life, on Tuesday, the 12th inst. of a consumption, Miss Ann Brown, eldest daughter of Mr. Samuel Scott Brown, in the 22d year of her age...(Eulogy)

Issue of March 27, 1822

Died, at New York on the 18th inst. after an illness of about 12 hours, John M. Ehrich, Esq. a native of Germany, for many years a respectable merchant in Charleston S.C. and for the last 7 years an inhabitant of New York.

Issue of March 28, 1822

Married, on Tuesday last, by the Rev. Dr. Gadsden, James F. Edwards, Esq. to Miss Harriet R. Gadsden, both of this city.

The death of Commodore John Gassin,...he expired on Sunday, the 24th inst. about 4 o'clock in the afternoon, in the 62d year of his age.

Died - The friends and acquaintances of Mr. and Mrs. William Birnie, are respectfully invited to attend the funeral of Mrs. Birnie, tomorrow afternoon, at 4 o'clock, from her late residence No. 4, Church Street continued.

Married, last evening, by the Rev. Mr. Buist, Edward C. Burch, to Miss Ann McCants Rivers, both of this city.

Issue of March 30, 1822

Died - The friends and acquaintances of the late Mr. Emanuel Jones, Sen. and the Members of the different Lodges, are invited to attend his funeral tomorrow morning, at 12 o'clock, from the upper end of Tradd-Street.

Issue of April 3, 1822

Died, in Newport, on the 24th ult. Mr. Jacob Lopez, aged 70...(Eulogy)

Died, at Camden, on the 28th March, after a lingering illness, which she sustained with Christian fortitude, Mrs. Sarah Barry Murray, wife of James Syng Murray, Esq. of that place.

Issue of April 6, 1822

Died - The friends and acquaintances of Miss Anna Maria Graeser, and Mr. C. J. G. Graeser, are respectfully invited to attend the funeral of the former, this afternoon, precisely at 4 o'clock, from her father's residence, corner Archdale and Beaufain Streets.

Issue of April 18, 1822

Married, on Tuesday evening last, by the Rev. Dr. Gadsden, Capt. Robert Coleman, to Miss Eliza Mayers, of this city.

Issue of April 20, 1822

Married, on Monday evening last, by the Rev. Mr. Hanckel, Mr. David B. LaFar, of this city, to Miss Harriet Purdy, of N. York.

Issue of April 22, 1822

Married, on Wednesday the 17th inst. by the Rev. Mr. Bachman, Mr. John Beckley, Esqr. of Barnwell, to Miss Mary Desel.

Issue of May 1, 1822

Departed this life, on the 18th ult. Mr. Richard J. Cox, of the U. S. Navy, late attached to the Norfolk station...(Eulogy)

Issue of May 3, 1822

Died - The friends and acquaintances of Mrs. Mary Ward, and Mr. and Mrs. J. Harper, are invited to attend the funeral of the former, this afternoon, at 4 o'clock, from her late residence, No. 48, State Street.

Issue of May 6, 1822

Departed this life, on the 27th ult. in the 62 year of her age...Mrs.

Ann Wainwright, relict of the late Richard Wainwright, Esq. of this city...
(Eulogy)

Died - The friends and acquaintances of Dr. John Mackey and of Mrs.
Mackey are invited to attend the funeral of the latter from No. 117, Broad
Street, this afternoon, at 4 o'clock.

Issue of May 7, 1822

Died, on Sunday evening, Abigail, wife of Dr. John Mackey, in the 57th
year of her age...(Eulogy)

Issue of May 14, 1822

Died, on the 4th day of April last, departed this life, Miss Anna
Maria Graeser, eldest daughter of Mr. C. J. Graeser, of this city...(Eulogy)

Issue of May 25, 1822

Died, in this city, on Thursday evening, the 23d inst. in the 33d year
of his age, Thomas Palmer, of St. Stephen's Parish...(Eulogy)

Issue of May 30, 1822

-Married, on Tuesday, the 21st inst. at St. Helena, William M'Kenzie
Parker, Esq. to Miss Anna Smith Coffin, daughter of the Ebenezer Coffin, Esq.

Issue of May 31, 1822

Died, on the 28th inst. after a lingering and severe illness, David
Campbell, Esq. of St. Bartholomew's Parish, in the 62d year of his age.
Died, at Portsmouth (Va.) on the 24th inst. Mr. Stephen Wilson, a
native of Charleston, S.C....(Eulogy)

Issue of June 1, 1822

Died, of the County Fever, on the 28th inst. in the 18th year of his
age, Mr. Charles Joseph Farr...(Eulogy)
Died - The friends and acquaintances of Mrs. Fourcard, and of Mrs. M.
Camp, are respectfully invited to attend the funeral of the former, from
the residence of the latter, No. 44, Hazel Street, this afternoon, at
5 o'clock, without further invitation.

Issue of June 4, 1822

Died, on the 30th ult. Mrs. Margarett Lord, after a long and painful
illness, which she bore with Christian fortitude, aged 74 years.

Issue of June 10, 1822

Died, near Salisbury, North Carolina, on the 24th ult. after a short
illness, the Hon. James Overstreet, Member of Congress from South Carolina.

Issue of June 11, 1822

DIed - The friends and acquaintances of Mr. David Lamb and of his sons
D. Lamb, Jun. and James Lamb, are invited to attend his funeral from his
late residence No. 51, East Bay, at 7 o'clock, tomorrow morning.

Issue of June 14, 1822

Died, on the 11th inst. in the 71st year of his age, David Lamb, Esq.
Merchant...(Eulogy)

Issue of June 15, 1822

Died, at N. York, 8th inst. Mr. James Murray, aged 28 years, late of
Charleston.

Issue of June 17, 1822

Died, at Philadelphia on the 8th inst. of pulmonary consumption, Mrs. Eliza Conover, late of Charleston, S.C. and formerly of Philadelphia, eldest daughter of John Dorsey, Esq. deceased.

Issue of June 21, 1822

Married, on Wednesday evening last by the Rev. Mr. Gilman, Wm. Cummens, Esq. to Miss Ann M. Otis, all of this city.

Issue of June 22, 1822

Married, on Thursday evening last, by the Rev. Dr. Bachman, Mr. Andrew A. Loavegreen, to Miss Sarah Hannah Benson.

Issue of June 24, 1822

Died - The friends and acquaintances of Mr. Wm. Ward are requested to attend his funeral, from his late residence, No. 9 Queen Street, this afternoon, precisely at half-past 4 o'clock.

Issue of June 26, 1822

Died - The friends and acquaintances of Mrs. Sarah Taylor, Mrs. Mary Taylor and Mrs. Robert ?, are requested to attend the funeral of the former this afternoon, at 4 o'clock, from her late residence, Reaper's Alley.

Issue of June 27, 1822

Died - The friends and acquaintances of Mr. and Mrs. William Disher, are invited to attend the funeral of the former from his late residence No. 51 Cumming Street, this afternoon, at 4 o'clock.

Died - The Members of the Charleston Ancient Artillery Society, are invited to attend the funeral of Mr. William Disher, from his late residence No. 51 Cumming Street, this afternoon, at 4 o'clock.

Issue of July 1, 1822

Departed this life, yesterday morning the 30th ult. in the 27th year of his age, Mr. Wall, a native of Rockbridge County Virginia...(Eulogy)

Died, on Thursday morning last, after a short but painful illness, Mr. William Disher, in the 30th year of his age...(Eulogy)

Issue of July 2, 1822

Died, on Sunday last, at the age of 76 years and 6 months, Mrs. Susannah Swinton, relict of the late Hugh Swinton, Senior.

Died, on Edisto Island, on the 10th June, Mrs. Louisa B. Whaley, in the 30th year of her age, wife of Mr. Joseph Whaley...(Eulogy)

Died - The friends and acquaintances of the late Mr. James Kay, are respectfully invited to attend his funeral, from Mr. John Lewis' residence, No. 12 Meeting Street, at 4 o'clock this afternoon, without further invitation.

Issue of July 3, 1822

Died on the 25th ult. Mrs. Sarah Taylor, in the 66th year of her age... (Eulogy)

Issue of July 5, 1822

Died, at St. Marys, (Geo) on the 28th ult. Virginia W. Paine, aged eleven months and twenty days, youngest daughter of Liut. Paine, of the U. S. Navy.

Issue of July 6, 1822

Departed this life, on Friday, the 28th June, Elizabeth Farr Ravenel, daughter of D. Ravenel, Esq. aged 6 years and 2 months.

Issue of July 8, 1822

Departed this life on Tuesday, the 2d inst. after a short illness..., Mrs. Mary Elfe, in the 60th year of her age...(Eulogy)

Issue of July 12, 1822

Departed this life, on the 30th ult. Lieutenant James Coxe, of the U.S. Navy, in the 25th year of his age, and son of Tench Coxe, Esq. of Philadelphia.

Issue of July 13, 1822

Died - The friends and acquaintances of Mr. Cornelius and Thomas Reed, are requested to attend the funeral of the former from his late residence No. 133, Church Street, at 7 o'clock tomorrow morning, without further invitation.

Issue of July 22, 1822

Died - The friends and acquaintances of Mr. and Mrs. Beekman M'Call, are requested to attend the funeral of the latter, from her late residence, corner Hasell Street and East Bay, tomorrow morning, at 7 o'clock.

Issue of July 24, 1822

Died - The relatives and friends of William H. Wilson, and Mary E. Wilson, are respectfully invited to attend the funeral of their deceased son, Condy Wilson, without further invitation, from their dwelling in Meeting STreet, No. 100, this afternoon, at 5 o'clock.

Issue of July 26, 1822

Died - The friends and acquaintances of Mr. George W. Bee, are requested to attend his funeral, tomorrow morning, at 7 o'clock, from his late residence, Friend Street.

Issue of July 27, 1822

Died - The friends and acquaintances, the members of the South Carolina and Hibernian Societies are requested (without further invitation) to attend the funeral of Colonel Charles O'Hara, from his late residence, Smith's Lane, at 12 o'clock, tomorrow.

Issue of July 29, 1822

Died - The friends and acquaintances of the late John Gyles (Mr.), and the officers and Members of the Fellowship Society, are requested to attend his funeral this afternoon, at 5 o'clock, without further invitation, from his late residence No. 198 King Street,

Issue of August 2, 1822

Died, suddenly, on the morning of the 29th ult. in the 42d year of his age, Mr. John Gyles...(Eulogy)

Issue of August 3, 1822

...Mr. John H. Rutledge, the subject of this obituary, had not quite attained the age of 22 years...(Eulogy)

Issue of August 5, 1822

Died - The friends and acquaintances of Mr. Peter Murphy, and Mrs.

Murphy, are requested to attend the funeral of the latter at 5 o'clock this afternoon, from her late residence No. 233 King Street, without further invitation.

Issue of August 6, 1822

Died, at his Plantation, near Abbeville Court House, of an inflammatory fever, on the 25th ult. Edwin Parker, youngest son of the late Thomas Parker, deceased, deservedly regretted by his numerous friends and relations.

Issue of August 7, 1822

Departed this life, on the 27th ult. Colonel Charles O'Hara, aged 50 years...(Eulogy)

Issue of August 8, 1822

Died, on Sunday, the 28th ult. Mr. John P. Randall, aged 25 years... (Eulogy)

Died - The friends and acquaintances of Mr. and Mrs. Norman, and of Thomas Jones, late of the firm of Norman & Jones, are invited to attend the funeral of the latter tomorrow morning, at 8 o'clock, from his late residence, No. 12, Tradd Street.

Issue of August 14, 1822

Died, at Leeds, England, Mr. John Bray, Comedian, for 17 years a resident of the U.S.

Issue of August 15, 1822

Died, at New York, on the 5th inst. of Yellow Fever, Mrs. Rachael Phillips, the beloved consort of Mr. N. Phillips, and daughter of the late Moses Seixas, Esq....(Eulogy)

Issue of August 26, 1822

Departed this life, on Tuesday, the 13th inst. after a long and painful illness, Mrs. Sarah Levy, aged 41 years...(Eulogy)

Issue of August 27, 1822

Died, in Walterborough, on the 23d inst. Charles Fushburn, son of the late Gen. Wm. Fishburn, in the 23d year of his age...(Eulogy)

Issue of August 28, 1822

Departed this transitory life, on the night of the 19th instant, in the ninth year of his age, Washington, youngest son of Alexander Robinson, of this city.

Died - The friends and acquaintances of the late Mrs. Luce Chissey, are invited to attend her funeral tomorrow morning, at 8 o'clock.

Issue of September 3, 1822

Died, at Lynchburg, Va. Signor Brosa, Ballet Master of the Richmond, Charleston, and Savannah Theatres.

Issue of September 4, 1822

Died, on the 1st instant, Mrs. Frances S. Pinckey, in the 79th year of her age

...death of Mr. Henry D. Zantzinger, Midshipman of the U.S.Navy... (Eulogy)

...departed this life on the 30th ult. at his residence in the County of Abington, Va., Colonel William Edmondson, in the 88th year of his age.

Issue of September 6, 1822

Died, at Staten Island, (New York) on the 25th ult....Moses Miller, Jun. Esq. in the 41st year of his age...(Eulogy)

Issue of September 9, 1822

Died, at Walterboro', on the 5th inst. after a long and distressing illness, Captain Richard Henry Fishburne, much and deservedly lamented.

Died, at the Naval Hospital in Gosport, on the 30th ult. about 4 o'clock, Mr. Edwin B. Newton...(Eulogy)

Issue of September 12, 1822

Died, at Society Hill, (S.C.) 1st inst. Dr. Enoch J. Evans.
Died, at Society Hill, (S.C.) 6th inst., John L. McCollough.
Died, at Savannah, 5th inst. John Hash.
Died, at Savannah, 9th inst. Master Joseph Milnor.

Issue of September 13, 1822

...Peter Timothy, Esq. who departed this life on the 8th inst. after a short illness of highly bilious fever, in the 29th year of his age...(Eulogy)

Died, at Cheraw, on the 25th ult. John A. Prentis, aged 24 years, a native of New England.

Died, at Cheraw on the 3d inst. Mr. Campbell, from Fayetteville.

Died, at Cheraw on the 4th inst. Dr. Thomas Jennings, of North Carolina.

Died, at Washington City, on the 5th inst. the Honorable Josiah Meigs, Commissioner of the General Land Office, aged 65 years.

Died, at Columbia, S.C. on the 31st ult. Mrs. Mourning Ferguson.

Died, at Harper's Ferry, Va. Colonel Jacint Laval, formerly of this state.

Issue of September 14, 1822

Died, at the Magazine Station, on Charleston Neck, on the 11th inst. after a illness of 5 days, Samuel Doolittle, a native of Connecticut, aged 30 years.

Issue of September 16, 1822

Died - The friends and acquaintances of the late Mr. Thomas Woolley, are requested to attend his funeral this afternoon, at 4 o'clock, from his late residence, King Street, near the Lines.

Issue of September 17, 1822

Died, at the Warm Springs, (Va.) on the 8th inst. Spencer Roane, Esq. one of the Judges of the Court of Appeals in the above state...(Eulogy)

Issue of September 18, 1822

Died - The friends and acquaintances of Mr. James L. Peigne, and of Mr. Eli Sutcliffe, are invited to assemble at the French Church, corner Queen and Church Streets, this evening, at 7 o'clock, in order to attend the funeral of Mrs. Sutcliffe.

Died - The friends and acquaintances of Miss and Mrs. Crosby, and Mr. N. Cooper, are particularly requested, without further invitation, to attend the funeral of Miss Mary Crosby, tomorrow morning, at half past 8 o'clock, from her late residence, 64 Anson Street.

Issue of September 20, 1822

Died, at Walterboro', S.C. on the 16th inst. suddenly and after a short illness, Robert Campbell, son of Archibald Campbell, aged one year and six month.

Issue of September 21, 1822

Died - The friends and acquaintances of Miss Amarinthea Elliott, are invited to attend her funeral from her late residence Legare-Street, at 7 o'clock, tomorrow morning, without further invitation.

Issue of September 23, 1822

Died, at his residence in St. Matthew's Parish, on the 14th inst. William Caldwell, Esq. in his 54th year...(Eulogy)

Issue of September 24, 1822

Died, at her residence in Legare Street, on the 20th inst. Mrs. Amarintha Elliott in the 82d year of her age...(Eulogy)

Issue of September 26, 1822

Died - The relatives, friends and acquaintances of the late Captain Joseph V. Spencer, are requested to attend the funeral of his daughter Virginia, tomorrow morning, at 10 o'clock precisely, from her late residence No. 19, Queen Street.

Issue of September 28, 1822

Died - The friends and acquaintances of the late Mr. John Wilson, and of Mrs. Mary Wilson, are particularly requested to attend his funeral from the residence of Mrs. Wilson, corner of Read and Meeting Streets, tomorrow morning, at 8 o'clock, without further invitation.

Issue of October 4, 1822

Died, on Monday night, the 23d ult. Eliza R. Bull, aged 12 years, the only daughter of the late Wm. S. Bull, Esq.

Issue of October 5, 1822

Married, on Thursday evening, the 3d inst. by the Rev. Dr. Palmer, Colonel James Ribben, to Miss Rebecca Theus, only daughter of the late B. Stiles, Esq. deceased.
Died, at Georgetown, on the 27th ult. Mr. Thomas Berry, aged 26 years.

Issue of October 9, 1822

Died, at Augusta, on the 25th ult. Joseph Cart, Esq. aged 55 years - a native of Charleston, but for many years a respectable citizen of Augusta.

Issue of October 11, 1822

, Died, at Columbia, S.C. on Friday morning last, Mrs. Maria Eliza Coleman, consort of Isaac H. Coleman, Esq. at the age of twenty years and eight months.

Issue of October 12, 1822

Died, on Monday last, the 7th inst. in the 65th year of her age... Mrs. Elizabeth Farr.
Departed this life, on Waccamaw Sea Short on the 4th inst. Mrs. Mary McDowall, consort of Davison McDowall, Esq. of Pee Dee...(Eulogy)
Died - The friends and acquaintances of M'Lauchlan M'Lean, and Mrs. Jane Welsh, are invited to attend the funeral of the former, tomorrow, at 12 o'clock, from No. 5, Legare Street.

Issue of October 15, 1822

Died - The friends and acquaintances of Mr. John Lathrop, Messrs. B. Lathrop, W. Turner, Samuel H. Lothrop. Charles Warley and Thomas Napier, are invited to attend the funeral of the former, from his late residence,

Planter's Hotel, this afternoon, at 4 o'clock.

Issue of October 16, 1822

...Departed this life, on the 18th ult. of the Bilous Fever, Miss Mary Crosby, aged 22 years...(Eulogy)

Issue of October 17, 1822

Died - The friends and acquaintances of the late Mr. L. B. DePau, are invited to attend his funeral, this afternoon, at 4 o'clock, from his late residence No. 23, Queen Street,

Died - The relations, friends and acquaintances of Mr. Thomas Ham, and of Mrs. Margaret Addison Ham, are respectfully invited to attend the funeral of the latter, from her late residence in Hampstead, tomorrow afternoon, at 4 o'clock.

Issue of October 26, 1822

Died - The friends and acquaintances of Mr. John Brown, Sen. and of Mrs. Jane Brown, are invited to attend the funeral of the former, from his late residence, corner of Berresford and Archdale Streets, tomorrow after-noon, at 4 o'clock, without further invitation.

Issue of October 28, 1822

Died - Our worthy fellow citizen Francis S. Lee, is no more. He expired on the 20th inst....(Eulogy)

Issue of October 29, 1822

Died - The friends and acquaintances of Mrs. Ann M. Chitty and J. W. Chitty, Sen. are particularly requested to attend the funeral of the former, at 4 o'clock this afternoon, from her late residence St. Philip's Street continued.

Issue of October 30, 1822

Departed this life on Saturday, the 19th inst. Eleanor, second daughter of Thomas and Mary Burnham...(Eulogy)

Issue of November 2, 1822

Died, at Lebanon, (Conn.) Miss Hepzibah Strong, aged 67 years...(Eulogy)
Died, at Philadelphia, suddenly, of the bilious cholic, on the evening of the 19th inst. Henry Drinker, Esq. Cashier of the Bank of North America.

Died - The friends and acquaintances of James William and Alexander Main, likewise the friends and acquaintances of Mr. R. A. Beaird and Mrs. Susan Beaird, are invited to attend the funeral of the latter, from her late residence No. 25 Wall Street, tomorrow, at 12 o'clock.

Died - The friends and acquaintances of Mrs. Catharine Stoll, and of her sons, James G. Stoll, and William F. Stoll, are invited to attend the funeral of the latter, from his mother's residence, No. 8 Magazine Street, tomorrow afternoon, at 4 o'clock.

Issue of November 5, 1822

Died, on the 26th ult. Mrs. Eleanor C. Chisolm, in the 25th year of her age, consort of Dr. A. R. Chisolm, and daughter of Theodore Gaillard, Jun.

Issue of November 9, 1822

...death of Mr. William Frederick Stoll, who departed this transitory life on the morning of Saturday, the 2d inst. in the 31st year of his age... (Eulogy)

Issue of November 12, 1822

Married, on Monday evening, by the Rev. Bishop England, Alexander Walter Wright, Esq. to Miss Eliza Marks, both of this city.

Issue of November 14, 1822

Died, on Thursday, the 7th inst. Mrs. Sarah Ann Nowell, the lamented consort of John L. Nowell, Esq. in the 21st year of her age.

Issue of November 16, 1822

Departed this transitory life on the 28th ult. Mrs. Ann Margaret Chitty, of this place, in the 46th year of her age...(Eulogy)

Issue of November 18, 1822

Died, suddenly, at Savannah on the 14th inst. Mr. Foster Burnett, late Merchant of this city.

Issue of November 19, 1822

Died, at Philadelphia, on the 8th inst. Mr. Jacob Phillips, aged 22 years, grandson of the late Rev. Jacob Cohen, of the years.

Issue of November 22, 1822

Died, in Green County, (A.) Joseph Noble, Esq. Attorney at Law, formerly of Abbeville, S.C.
Died, in Union District, S.C. Captain James McCulloch, aged 69 years.

Issue of November 23, 1822

Died yesterday, on Edisto Island, of Typhus Fever, Mrs. Ann N. Baynard, consort of W. G. Baynard, Esq.
Died - The friends and acquaintances of Mrs. Catharine Stoll, and of her late son, James G. Stoll, are invited to attend his funeral tomorrow afternoon, at 4 o'clock, from No. 8 Magazine Street.

Issue of November 26, 1822

Died, at Pendleton, S.C. on the 4th inst. Mrs. Margaret Hamilton, aged 40 years, wife of Major Andrew Hamilton.

Issue of November 27, 1822

Died - The friends and acquaintances of Mr. and Mrs. Wm. H. Cilliland, are requested to attend the funeral of their daughter Catherine, at four o'clock this afternoon, from their residence, corner of King and George Streets, without further invitation.
Died - The friends and acquaintances and Members of the Bar, are invited to attend the funeral of Judge Drayton, from his late residence, No. 92 Wentworth Street, tomorrow morning, at 9 o'clock, without further invitation.

Issue of November 29, 1822

Married, on Wednesday last, by the Right Rev. Bishop Bowen, Col. A. P. Hayne, to Elizabeth Laura, daughter of William Alston, Esq. of Waccamaw.

Issue of November 30, 1822

Died - The friends and acquaintances of Aeneas S. Reeves, also the members of the Cincinatti and St. Andrew's Societies, are respectfully invited, without further invitation, to attend his funeral from his late residence, Harleston Green, tomorrow morning, at 12 o'clock.

Issue of December 2, 1822

Departed this transitory life, of the Consumption, on Saturday, the 23d
ult. Mr. James Gregson Stoll, in the 29th year of his age...(Eulogy)

Issue of December 10, 1822

Died, at New York, on the 5th inst. Mr. Joseph Lopez, aged 70, formerly
of Newport, R.I.

Issue of December 11, 1822

Married, on Tuesday evening, the 10th inst. by the Rev. Dr. Gallagher,
Mr. Eugene O'Reilly, to Mrs. Caroline O'Reilly, both of this place.

Issue of December 13, 1822

Died, on board the U. S. schooner Alligator on the 20th Oct. Acting
Lieutenant David M. McRorie, of North Carolina, after 4 days illness of
Yellow Fever.
Died, in Barnwell District, on the 6th inst. Captain Bartlett Brown,
aged 68 years.

Issue of December 18, 1822

Died - The friends and acquaintances of Alexander Black, John S.
Bennett, and Cyris R. Keith, are invited to attend the funeral of the
latter, this afternoon, at 4 o'clock, from his late residence corner of
Elliot Street and Gadsden's Alley, without further invitation.

Issue of December 19, 1822

Married, at New York, on Friday evening, the 13th inst. Captain John
B. Crane, of the lineship Annetta, to Miss Eliza Montgomery.

Issue of December 21, 1822

Died - The friends and acquaintances of Mrs. Benoist and of Mr. Theodore
Sompayrac, are requested to attend the funeral of the latter, from his late
residence No. 26, Tradd Street, without further invitation, this afternoon,
at 4 o'clock.

Issue of December 24, 1822

Died, on the morning of the 21st inst. in the 65th year of his age,
Major Wilson Glover...(Eulogy)

Issue of December 28, 1822

Departed this life on the 13th inst. in the 62d year of his age,
William Smith, Esq....(Eulogy)
Died on Sunday evening, the 22d inst. after a week of severe suffering,
Josephine Christiana, eldest daughter of Joseph and Jane Woodruff, of this
city...(Eulogy)

Issue of December 30, 1822

Died - The friends and acquaintances of Mr. James Jacks, and the members
of the St. Andrews Society, are invited to attend his funeral, from his late
residence in Wraggborough, tomorrow morning, at 9 o'clock, without a more
particular invitation.

Issue of December 31, 1822

Died - The friends and acquaintances of Mr. S. G. Low, of Boston; also
of Charles Edmondston, A. S. Willington, and G. W. Prescott & Co. are
invited to attend the funeral of the former tomorrow morning, at 9 o'clock
from the Planter's Hotel, corner of Church and Queen Streets.

Issue of January 2, 1823

Married, on Tuesday evening last, by the Right Rev. Bishop Bowen John James Alexander, Esq. of this city, to Miss Eleanor Ann Kinlock, youngest daughter of the late Rev. George Heartwell Spierin, of Georgetown, South Carolina.

Issue of January 3, 1823

Married, on Wednesday evening last, by the Rev. Mr. Peixotto, Mr. N. H. Hart, to Miss Sarah, daughter of the late Joseph Moses, deceased, all of this place.

Issue of January 9, 1823

Married, on Tuesday evening last, by the Rev. Dr. Furman, John Blackwood, Esq. to Miss Caroline L. daughter of George Gibbs, ESq. of this city.

Died, at Philadelphia, on the night of the 30th ult. Mrs. John Melish, aged 52 years, well known as a distinguished Geographer.

Died - The friends and acquaintances of Mr. and Mrs. John Schroeder; and the children of the Evangelical Sunday School of the Lutheran Church of German Protestants, are invited to attend the funeral of Miss Maria Wartenberg, from her uncle's residence, corner of Philadelphia and Amen Streets, tomorrow, at 3 o'clock p.m.

Issue of January 10, 1823

Died - The friends and acquaintances of James Mair, Esq. are invited to attend his funeral tomorrow afternoon, at 3 o'clock, from his late residence, corner of Montague and Rutledge Streets, near Cannons bridge, without further invitation.

Issue of January 18, 1823

Married, on Wednesday evening the 15th inst. by the Rev. Bishop Bowen, George A. Hazelhurts, Esq. to Miss Mart Mortimer, daughter of E. Mortimer, Esq.

Died, at Havana, on the 12th inst. of the Yellow Fever, Capt. Stevens, of the ship---, of Boston, (Mass.)

Issue of January 21, 1823

Died - The friends and acquaintances of the late Mrs. Elizabeth Feish and the Congregation of the Lutheran Church, generally, are respectfully invited to attend her funeral from her late residence, No. 263 King Street, tomorrow afternoon, at 3 o'clock.

Issue of January 29, 1823

Died - The friends and acquaintances of Captain Gardner, of Baltimore, and of Capt. Noyes, are requested to attend the funeral of Mr. Oabed G. Swain, this afternoon, at 4 o'clock, from the New England Coffee House of the Bay.

Issue of January 31, 1823

Died, on the 19th inst. in the 78th year of his age, John Wilson, Esq. an old and respected inhabitant of Marlborough District...(Eulogy)

Died, near Georgetown, on Sunday last, Mrs. Sarah Thompson, consort of John Thompson aged 46 years and a few days. She has left a husband and five children.

Issue of February 1, 1823

Died - The friends and acquaintances of the late William Roach, are requested to attend his funeral, from No. 13 Society Street, tomorrow afternoon, at four o'clock.

Died – The friends and acquaintances of Mrs. Mary Preble, and Members of the German Lutheran Church, are invited to attend her funeral, without further invitation, at 4 o'clock tomorrow afternoon from her house, No. 123, Church Street.

Issue of February 4, 1823

Departed this life, on Saturday, the 1st inst. Mrs. Susannah Smilie, in the 77th year of her age...(Eulogy)

Issue of February 7, 1823

Died, at Columbia, (S.C.) on Friday last, Mr. C. E. Williamson, for a long time an inhabitant of that place.

Died, at Brunswick, (Maine) Gen. James W. Ryan, at the advanced age of 107 years...(Eulogy)

Issue of February 8, 1823

Died, on the 16th ult. at his plantation in St. Bartholomew's Parish, the Hon. James Morgan, Senator in the State Legislature, in the 43d year of his age...(Eulogy)

Died, on the 29th ultimo, at the residence of his father, in Edgefield District, aged 24 years, Mr. Lewis Elilius Delavigne, a native of the United States.

Issue of February 10, 1823

Married on Thursday the 30th of January by the Rev. Mr. Hankell, James Gregorie, Esq. to Martha, second daughter of Col. James E. M'Pherson.

Died, on Friday last, the 7th inst. Mr. William Tunno, in the 65th year of his age.

Issue of February 11, 1823

Died, at New Orleans, on the 2d ult. Gen. F. Humbert, formerly of the Army of French Republic...(Eullgy)

Died – The friends and acquaintances of Mr. and Mrs. Collier, will attend the funeral of the latter at eleven o'clock tomorrow forenoon, from her late residence No. 14 Wentworth Street.

Issue of February 12, 1823

Married, on Tuesday evening last, by the Right Rev. Bishop Bowen, George Parker, Esq. of Boston, to Anna, daughter of the late John Elias Moore, Esq. of this city.

Issue of February 14, 1823

Died, at Pendleton, (S.C.) on the 30th ult. Mrs. Mary Elizabeth Gaillard, aged 38 years, consort of Josiah D. Gailliard, Esq.

Died, at Cheraw, on the 5th inst. Mr. Donald Nicholson, Merchant.

Married, on Tuesday evening last, by the Rev. Mr. Gilman, Mr. Francis S. Yates to Miss Harriet Angerona, daughter of the late Dr. James Airs.

Married, on Thursday evening, the 13th inst. by the Rev. Mr. Buist, Mr. Hugh Rosebanks, to Miss Caroline T. Mann, both of this city.

Issue of February 15, 1823

Died – The friends and acquaintances of the late Dr. Henry Gleize, and Mrs. Susan Gleize and family, are requested to attend the funeral of the former, at 4 o'clock, tomorrow afternoon, the 16th inst. at his late residence No. 122 Meeting Street, without further invitation.

Issue of February 17, 1823

Died, at Savannah, 17th inst. after a short but severe illness, Mr. William Starr, Jr. of the firm of Hall, Hoyt, & Co.

Died — The friends and acquaintances of Mrs. Mary C. Gregorie, are requested to attend her funeral from her late residence, Anson Street, tomorrow morning, at 12 o'clock.

Issue of February 19, 1823

Died, in St. John's Parish on the 22d of January, Mrs. Edward Harleston, Jr. aged 23 years...(Eulogy)

Issue of February 21, 1823

Died, at Georgetown, on the 15th inst. Dr. George Ford, aged 47 years.
Died, at Darlington, on the 15th inst. Mr. Samuel Blackwell, aged 48 years.

Issue of February 25, 1823

Died — The friends and acquaintances of Captain John Monroe, are invited to attend his funeral tomorrow afternoon, at four o'clock, from the corner of Amen and Philadelphia Streets.

Issue of February 27, 1823

Died, on the 20th inst. George Taylor Bellinger, aged one year and two months, youngest child of Dr. J. S. Bellinger, and the only remaining one of his truly afflicted mother and grand-mother.

Departed this life at his residence, in St. John's B. on Saturday last, the 22d inst. with resignation to the Divine will, and in peace, Capt. Henry Ravenel, aged 72 years...(Eulogy)

Issue of March 1, 1823

Died, on Friday the 31st of January, Mr. William Roach, in the 65th year of his age...(Eulogy)

Married, on Thursday evening last, by the Rev. Dr. Leland, Mr. Daniel G. Joye, to Miss Elvira G., daughter of the late Peter Lewis, Esq. of North Santee, deceased.

Issue of March 5, 1823

Married last evening, by the Rev. Bishop Bowen, Robert Field Stockton, Esq. of Princeton, (N.J.) to Miss Harriett Maria Potter, daughter of John Potter, Esq. of this city.

Married on Thursday evening the 27th ult. by the Rev. Mr. Lee, Mr. Jeremiah Dickinson, to Caroline, youngest daughter of the late Stephen Shrewbury, Esq. all of this city.

Issue of March 6, 1823

Died — The friends and acquaintances of Mr. and Mrs. Jesse Nell, are invited to attend the funeral of the former, from his late residence, Rope Walk, Meeting Street, near the lines, tomorrow afternoon, at 3 o'clock.

Issue of March 7, 1823

Married, on Wednesday last, by the Rev. Mr. Piexotto, Mr. Abraham Tobias to Miss Eleanor Lopez, both of this city.

Issue of March 10, 1823

Departed this life, at Philadelphia, on Friday the 21st inst. after a short, but very severe illness, Benjamin Nones, son of Aaron B. Nones, Esq.

Issue of March 11, 1823

Departed this life on the 25th ult. Mrs. Jane L. Alston, wife of Thomas Pinckney Alston, Esq. in the 24th year of her age...(Eulogy)

Died, on the 28th ult. after a short illness, Captain Thomas Joel, aged 64 years...(Eulogy)

Issue of March 14, 1823

Died, on the 12th of Jan. last Mrs. Annette Skinner, wife of Mr. Samuel H. Skinner, aged 24 years and 10 months...(Eulogy)

Died, in Newberry District, on Friday, 21st ult. after a few days illness, Mr. Thomas Hardy, who for many years had been a highly respectable inhabitant of said district.

Died - The friends and acquaintances of Mr. John Inglesby, are invited to attend his funeral this afternoon, from his late residence, Church Street continued, at 4 o'clock.

Issue of March 18, 1823

Died - The friends and acquaintances of Captain Neil MacNeal, Masters of Vessels, the officers and members of the St. Andrew's and Hibernian Societies are requested to attend his funeral tomorrow afternoon, at three o'clock, from his late residence King Street.

Issue of March 19, 1823

Married, in Richmond township, (Pa.) on the 23d ult. Mr. Jacob Hahn, aged 17, to Miss Susan Myers, aged almost 12.

Died, at Savannah, on the 15th instant, (March, 1823) of a consumption, J. C. Mulvey, Esq. his Catholic Majesty's Vice Consul, aged 29.

Issue of March 20, 1823

Died, on the 18th inst. at her residence near Savannah, Mrs. Hanna Barbara, aged 88 years, a native of Georgian, and born in the vicinity of White Bluff.

Issue of March 29, 1823

Married, on Tuesday evening 25th inst. by the Rev. Mr. Gilman, William Stuart, Esq. of Manchester, England, to Miss Mary Gibbes Air, of this city.

Issue of April 14, 1823

Died - The friends and acquaintances of Mrs. Mary Macklish, of her daughters, and grandson, W. C. Hichborn, are invited to attend the funeral of the former (without further invitation) from her late residence No. 30 Tradd Street, tomorrow afternoon, at 4 o'clock.

Issue of April 16, 1823

Married, last evening, by the Rev. Dr. Dalcho, Doctor Edmund Ravenel, to Miss Charlotte Matilda, daughter of Timothy Ford, Esq.

Issue of April 19, 1823

Married, at Maryville Ashley River, on Thursday evening last, by the Right Rev. Nathanniel Bowen, Alexander Adams, Esq. of Edinburgh, to Mary, eldest daughter of the late A. Bethune, Esq. of this city.

Died - The friends and acquaintances of Benjamin Moodie, Esq. and the members of the Saint Andrew's and St. George's Societies, are requested to attend his funeral tomorrow afternoon, at 5 o'clock, from his late residence, No. 63 Meeting Street.

Died - The friends and acquaintances of the Rev. Joseph Brown, and Mrs. M. H. Brown, are requested to attend the funeral of their infant daughter, from the house of Mrs. E. Palmer, corner of Queen and State Streets, tomorrow, at half past 12 o'clock, without further invitation.

Issue of April 23, 1823

Died, on the 9th of March, at Litchfield, (Con.) Mr. John S. Dart, of this city, in the 23d year of his age.

Died - The friends and acquaintances of Wm. B. Walter, (a native of Boston) and lately from there, are requested to attend his funeral this afternoon, at 5 o'clock, from the Planter's Hotel.

Issue of April 24, 1823

Departed this life, on the 19th April, aged 29, Mrs. Ann Deveaux, consort of Stephen G. Deveaux, Esq. of St. John's Berkley, and daughter of the late Francis Peyre, Esqr....(Eulogy)

Issue of April 28, 1823

Died, on the 24th inst. after a short illness, Sebina E. Ramsay, aged 4 years and 11 months, daughter of David Ramsay, Esq.

Issue of May 9, 1823

Married, at Clear Spring, on Thursday, the 1st of May, by the Rev. Mr. Gilbert, Colonel H. B. Armstrong, of New York, to Miss Mary D. Simons, daughter of Major James Simons, deceased.

Issue of May 10, 1823

Married, on Thursday evening last, by the Rev. Mr. Bachman, Mr. Lorens Stoppelbein, to Miss Eliza Clarke, of this city.

Issue of May 13, 1823

Died, at his residence in St. Matthew's Parish after an illness of a few days, on the 7th inst. Robert Caldwell, in the 43d year of his age, leaving numerous friends and relations to mourn his loss. He lived respected and died lamented.

Issue of May 15, 1823

Married, at Westelo, N. Y. on the 1st inst. by the Rev. Berrian Hotchkins, Deacon Daniel Jewell, of Greenville, in his 82d year, to Mrs. Mary Allen, grandmother to the late lamented Lieut. Allen, in her 85th year...

Died - The friends and acquaintances of Mr. Robert Primerose, and the members of the South Carolina and St. Andrew's Societies, are invited to attend his funeral this afternoon, at 4 o'clock, from his late residence No. 54, Wentworth Street.

Issue of May 16, 1823

Died, in Winnsborough, (S.C.) on the 29th ult. of the Typhus Fever, after a painful and protracted illness of six weeks, Mrs. Margaret Moore, consort of Major Wm. Moore, in the 20th year of her age.

Issue of May 17, 1823

Died, on the 12th ult. Mr. Phineas W. Parker, a native of this city, but for the last 6 years a resident of Prince Williams Parish. He has left numerous friends to mourn his loss.

Issue of May 19, 1823

Died, at Richmond, on the 12th inst. John W. Green, formerly Manager of the Richmond and Southern Theatres....(Eulogy)

Issue of May 23, 1823

Died, on the 25th ult. at the house of Mr. George Summers, in Union district, Mr. Garret Hendricks, aged 107 years, one month, and eight days... (Eulogy)

Issue of June 3, 1823

Died - The relatives and friends of the late James M. Ward, are requested to attend at the Service, at the House No. 94 Tradd Street, tomorrow morning, at 7 o'clock.

Died - The Members of the Bar are invited to attend the funeral of Benjamin B. Smith, this afternoon, at 4 o'clock, from his late residence East Bay.

Died - The friends and acquaintances of Mr. John Sevrie, and of Dorothy, his late wife, are invited to attend her funeral this afternoon, at 4 o'clock, from her late residence in St. Philips Street, near St. Paul's Church.

Issue of June 6, 1823

Died, at his residence near Winsborough, on the 18th ult. James Barkley, Sen. in the 67th year of his age.

Died, at New Orleans, on the 27th Nov. 1822, in the 37th year of his age, Mr. Louis Cruchet, Ex-Chief d'Esquardron....(Eulogy)

Issue of June 9, 1823

Departed this life, on Saturday, 31st ult. at Columbia, (S.C.) after two hours indisposition, Mrs. Flora Levy, aged twenty-two years, consort of Col. Chapman Levy....(Eulogy)

Died, in Boston on the 29th ult. the Hon. John Phillips, late Mayor of the City...(Eulogy)

Died, at Nantucket, Frederick Allen, aged 13, son of David Allen, Esq. His death was occasioned by having accidentally swallowed, some months since a half of dollar.

Died - The friends and acquaintances of Mr. and Mrs. Hussey, are invited to attend the funeral of the former, from his late residence, No. 9 Stoll's Alley, at 9 o'clock tomorrow morning, 10th inst.

Died - The Members of Prudence Lodge, No. 35, and the Masonic Brethren of this city, are invited to attend the funeral of Brother Bryan Hussey, tomorrow morning, at half past 8 o'clock, from his late residence No. 5 Stoll's Alley, by order of the Worshipful Master of Lodge, No. 35.

Issue of June 10, 1823

Died, at Arkansas, on the 26th September last, Major George M'Glassin, aged 30, late of the United States Army.

Issue of June 13, 1823

Departed this life, at Kingston (Jam.) on the 4th of March last, Mr. Solomon Depass, after a tedious illness, aged 57 years.

Issue of June 21, 1823

Departed this life, on the 14th inst. Mrs. Henrietta S. Wigfall, consort of William Moore Wigfall, in the 20th year of her age...(Eulogy)

Issue of June 26, 1823

Died - The friends and acquaintances of the late Mr. William Price, are invited to attend his funeral tomorrow morning, at 8 o'clock, from No. 2 Short Street.

Died - The friends and acquaintances of the late S. C. Graves, Esq. are invited to attend his funeral at half after 4 o'clock, this afternoon, from the residence of Mrs. M'Pherson, Broad Street.

Issue of June 27, 1823

Died, on the 18th inst. in Yorkville, (S.C.) Robert McCan, Esq.

Issue of June 30, 1823

Died, on Sunday, the 24th inst. Miss Charlotte M. Huger, second daughter of Daniel Huger, Esq. in the 16th year of her age...(Eulogy)

Died, on the 15th instant, Joseph DeJongh, Esq. a native of Ostend, and for several years past a respectable inhabitant of this city.

Died, on the 21st, Ernest Augustus DeJongh, son of the late J. DeJongh, aged 6 years.

Died - The friends and acquaintances of the late John Holmes, and the members of the South Carolina Society, are respectfully invited to attend his funeral tomorrow morning, at 6 o'clock, from his late residence No. 25 Legare Street, without further invitation.

Issue of July 2, 1823

Died - The friends and acquaintances of Mr. and Miss Datty, are invited to attend the funeral of the former, from his late residence, No. 23 King Street, at 8 o'clock, tomorrow morning,

Issue of July 3, 1823

Married, on the 19th ult. at Boston, the Hon. William Crafts, of Charleston, S. C. a member of the Senate of this State, to Miss Caroline C. Holmes, of Boston.

Departed this transitory stage of existence, on Monday last, in this city, aged 37 years, John Holmes, Esq. of John's Island, Planter.

Issue of July 5, 1823

Died, at Matanzas, on the 27th ult. Mr. Christopher Fowler, Jun. a native of Newport, (R.I.)

Issue of July 9, 1823

Died, at Norfolk, on the -- inst. Mrs. Elizabeth Barron, consort of Com. James Barron, of the U. S. Navy.

Issue of July 11, 1823

Died, at Wilmington, (N.C.) on the 1st inst. in the 41st year of his age, Captain Robert Rankin, Deputy Collector of that port, and Deputy Marshal of that district.

Issue of July 14, 1823

➤ Died, on the 25th of June, William Price, Esq. in the 85th year of his age...(Eulogy)

Departed this life on the 4th inst. Miss Susan M. Day, aged 32 years... (Eulogy)

Issue of July 15, 1823

Died - The friends and acquaintances of Mr. and Mrs. Alexander Christie, and family, and the Members of the Library Society, are requested to attend the funeral of the former, from his late residence in Church Street, tomorrow forenoon, at 11 o'clock.

Issue of July 22, 1823

Died, on the 15th inst. Mr. Alexander Christie, in the 65th year of his age...(Eulogy)

Died, at Wilmington, (N.C.) on the 13th inst. Mr. John Flotard, formerly of Charleston.

Died, at Wilmington, (N.C.) on the 15th, Edmund Bridge, Jun. Esq. of Dresden, (Me.) aged 52.

Issue of August 1, 1823

Died, on the 16th ult. in the vicinity of Winnsboro, (S.C.) after a very few hours sickness, Mrs. Rebecca Johnston, wife of Mr. Samuel Johnston, in the 42d year of her age.

Died - The friends and acquaintances of Miss H. Esther Black, are requested to attend her funeral, from the House of William Bell, No. 46 Society Street, this afternoon, at half past 4 o'clock, without further invitation.

Issue of August 6, 1823

Died - The friends and acquaintances of Mr. James Houston, and the Hibernian and Mechanic Societies, are respectively invited to attend his funeral this afternoon, at five o'clock, without further notice, from his late residence No. 20, Wall Street.

Issue of August 7, 1823

Died - The friends and acquaintances of Captain James C. Martindale, are requested to attend his funeral tomorrow morning, at 7 o'clock, from his late residence King Street Road.

Issue of August 8, 1823

Died, at Ashepoo, on the 5th instant, Mrs. Charlotte C. Thackam, a native of this city, and late consort of Mr. F. P. Thackam, aged 25 years, 4 months and 23 days.

Issue of August 13, 1823

Died, in Cheraw, on the 2d inst. Capt. John M'Call, after an illness of about a week, of the utmost severity, aged about 28 years.

Issue of August 18, 1823

Died - The friends and acquaintances of the late Captain John Brown, and of Mrs. Maria Brown, are invited to attend the funeral of the former, at 4 o'clock, this afternoon, from his late residence, No. 180 East Bay, without further invitation.

Issue of August 20, 1823

Died - On the evening of Friday the 13th inst....at Irthington, near Charlisle, in the 118th year of his age. Mr. Robert Bowman...(Eulogy)

Issue of August 22, 1823

Died, at Columbia, on the 13th inst. after an illness of about nine days, Mr. George Blackburn, formerly Professor of Mathematics in the South Carolina College...(Eulogy)

Issue of August 26, 1823

Died, in Cheraw, (S.C.) on the 18th inst. Mr. Marlboro S. Hamilton, aged about 20 years, formerly of Charleston.

Issue of August 27, 1823

Died, at Savannah, on the 25th inst. Mrs. Elizabeth Fell.

Died, at Savannah, on the 25th inst. Mrs. Mary Muir.

Issue of August 27, 1823

Died, at Savannah, on the 25th inst. Mr. William Eppinger.
Died, at Savannah, on the 25th inst. Mr. Murdock McLeod.

Issue of September 5, 1823

Died, at Botetourt Springs, in Virginia, on the 18th ult. Mr. Ainsley Hall, an eminent merchant in this town, and a most valuable member of society...(Eulogy)

Issue of September 8, 1823

Died - The friends and acquaintances of Patrick O'Neill, are invited to attend the funeral of his daughter Sarah, from the residence of his brother, Edmond O'Neill, corner of Cannon and Pinckney Streets, tomorrow morning, at 8 o'clock.

Issue of September 10, 1823

Died, on the 31st ult. at Newberry Court House, after a short illness, Mrs. A. Boyce, consort of Ker Boyce, Esq. merchant of this city.

Issue of September 11, 1823

Died, on Saturday last, the 6th inst. at Sullivan's Island, after a painful illness, which she bore with Christian fortitude, Mrs. Elizabeth Mintzing, consort of Jacob F. Mintzing, Esq. and daughter of James Custer, Factor, deceased.

Issue of September 17, 1823

Died, on the 12th inst. in the 64th year of his age, at his seat near Statesburgh Cleland Kinlock, Esqr....(Eulogy)

Issue of September 18, 1823

Died, at Newberry Court House, (SC) on the 31st ult. in the 28th year of her age, Mrs. Ann Boyce, consort of our respectable fellow citizen, Ker Boyce, Esq....(Eulogy)
Died, on Sunday last, the 14th inst. Mrs. Eliza Rivers, wife of Thomas Rivers of this city...(Eulogy)
Died, on Tuesday morning, 19th inst. Miss Eliza C. Izard, third daughter of Henry Izard, Esq. after an illness of some weeks.

Issue of September 19, 1823

Died - The friends and acquaintances of Mr. and Mrs. Langton, are respectfully invited to attend the funeral of the latter this afternoon, at 4 o'clock, from her late residence corner of Wentworth and Cuming Street.

Issue of September 20, 1823

Died, in Camden, (S.C.) on the 12th inst. Mr. George DeBruhl, aged 23 years.
Died, in Camden, (S.C.) on the 13th, Mr. James Lang, and Cornelia, aged 4 years, and Margaret, aged 6 years, his daughters.
Died, in Camden, (S.C.) on the 13th, Mrs. Margaret Guppell.
Died, at Statesburg, Col. Peter Edwards.
Died, in Alabama, Dr. R. W. Carter, formerly of Camden; at the same place, Sarah Ann, his daughter.
Died, in Sumpter District, Mr. William Carter.

Issue of September 24, 1823

Died, at Bordentown, (New Jersey) on the 15th inst. of a disease of the stomach, General Henry Lallemand, formerly a distinguished officer under Bonaparte.

Issue of September 25, 1823

Died, at his residence, near Parkersburg, Va. Jacob Beeson, Esq. U. S. Attorney for the Western District of Virginia.

(Died) In New Haven, Connecticut, on the 28th of April, the Hon. Charles Chauncey, L.L.D. in the seventy sixth year of his age. He was born at Durham May 30th, O. S. 1747

Issue of September 26, 1823

Died, at Columbia, (S.C.) on the 20th inst. James Widdifield, (of Philadelphia), aged 21 years.

Died, at Columbia, (S.C.) on the 11th inst. Mrs. Mary Tidwell.

(Died) In Union District, Wm. F. Gist, eldest son of Col. Joseph Gist, aged 22 years.

(Died) In Fairfield District, on the 5th inst. Mr. Joel Ashford.

(Died) In Fairfield Dsitrict, on the 5th inst. Capt. Robert Railford Pearson, of Newberry District, aged 23.

(Died) In Fairfield District, on the 2d inst. Capt. Wm. Stanton.

(Died) In Yorkshire District, Dr. Robert L. Armstrong, aged 30 years.

Issue of September 29, 1823

Died, some time since, at his residence in Darlington District, much* regretted Col. Peter Edwards.

Issue of October 1, 1823

Died - The friends and acquaintances of the late John E. Farr, are invited to attend his funeral from his residence in Hampstead, at 8 o'clock tomorrow morning, without further invitation.

Issue of October 3, 1823

Died, at Columbia, (S.C.) on the 17th ult. Daniel Sturges, Surveyor General of Georgia.

Died, in Statesburg, 13th ult. Patrick Lyne of New York.

Died, in Pendleton District, 12th ult. Mrs. Franklin Earle, aged 33.

Died, in Upper Salem, Dr. John J. Muldrow, aged 36.

Died, in Swansboro, Samuel Knox, aged 48.

Died, in Union District, Capt. John Sanders, aged 75

Died, in York District, Mr. Wm. Thompson, aged 73.

Issue of October 6, 1823

Died, on the 1st inst. Miss Adelaide Decima Dawson, daughter of the late John Dawson, Esq. aged 18 years...(Eulogy)

Died, at Pine Ridge, in St. John's Berkley, on the 2d inst. Lawrence Monck Dawson, Esq. late of this city, aged 30 years.

Issue of October 7, 1823

Married, on Thursday evening last, by the Rev. Mr. Hanckel, Mr. Peter J. Shand, to Miss Ann W. Wright, both of this city.

Died - the friends and acquaintances of Captain Edward P. Simons, are invited to attend his funeral, from his residence in Laurens Street, tomorrow, at 10 o'clock, a.m.

Issue of October 8, 1823

Died, at his residence in Buncombe county, N.C. on the 22d ult. Dr. Benjamin Howworth, in the 52d year of his age. He has left a worth of five children to deplore his loss.

Issue of October 10, 1823

(Died)...Mrs. Margaret Seabrook, consort of Mr. Benjamin Seabrook, in the 61st year of her age...(Eulogy)

Issue of October 17, 1823

Died, on Sunday the 5th inst. in the 42d year of his age, in New York,
Mr. Cherry Moise, a native of the island of St. Domingo, but for many years
a respectable Commission Merchant of this city...(Eulogy)

Died, in Lexington District, on the 8th inst. Mr. John Rufus Baker,
aged 18 years.

Died in Lexington District on the 11th inst. Wm. Arthur, aged 30 years.

Died near Camden, on the 10th inst. Mr. Samuel Mathis, aged 63 years.

Issue of October 18, 1823

Died, in Philadelphia, on the 9th inst. Mr. Jacob J. Cohen, long a
respectable inhabitant of that city, in the 80th year of his age.

Issue of October 21, 1823

Died - The friends and acquaintances of Mrs. Mary Stone, and of her
grand daughters the Miss Kers, are requested to attend the funeral of the
former from her late residence No. 10, Pinckney Street, tomorrow afternoon,
at 3 o'clock, without further invitation.

Issue of October 22, 1823

Departed this life, on the 16th inst. at Columbia, Mrs. Octavia T.
Davie, wife of F. W. Davie, Esq. and daughter of the Hon. Judge DeSaussure.

Issue of October 28, 1823

Died, in this city, on the 5th inst. Mr. Geo. J. Howell, a native of
Philadelphia.

Died, at Kingstree, Williamsburg District, a short time since, Doctor
George Erving formerly of Cheraw, S.C. aged about 34 years.

Issue of October 29, 1823

Died, at Norfolk, on the 21st inst. Midshipman Rolla Weems, of Georgetown, (D.C.) His death was caused by yellow fever taken at Thompson's
Island.

Issue of October 30, 1823

Died - The friends and acquaintances of Mr. Samuel McCleary and of Mrs.
Ann McCleary, are invited to attend the funeral of the latter from her late
residence, King Street Road, this afternoon, at 4 o'clock.

Issue of October 31, 1823

Died, on Monday last, after a short and severe illness, Mrs. Sarah
Simpson Williman, wife of Christopher Williman, and youngest daughter of
the late Dr. Alexander Baron...(Eulogy)

Issue of November 3, 1823

Died - The friends and acquaintances of Mrs. Margaret Thompson, and
her different families, are requested to attend her funeral tomorrow afternoon, at 3 o'clock, from No. 23, Guignard Street, without further invitation.

Issue of November 5, 1823

Died - The friends and acquaintances of Mr. Edward Pierce, and the
Members of the St. George's Society, are requested to attend his funeral
tomorrow morning, at 9 o'clock, from the residence of Mr. Aldich's No. 15,
Tradd Street, without further invitation.

Issue of November 7, 1823

Died, in this city, on the 2d inst. after a long and distressing illness, which was submitted to with much patience and resignation, Mrs. Emely Bellinger, in the 39th year of her age, consort of Dr. Belligner, of Barnwell District.

Died, at Montreal, on the ult. Mrs. Elizabeth, wife of Moses Myers, Esq. of Norfolk, (Virginia) aged 60.

Died, in Fairfield District, S.C. on the 14th ult. Mrs. Sarah E. Holmes, consort of Wm. Holmes, aged 37.

Died, in Fairfield District, S.C. on the 14th ult. Capt. Aaron Trapp.

(Died) In Winsborough, on the 29th ult. Mrs. Jane Crawford, consort of Andrew Crawford, aged 48.

Died - The friends and acquaintances of Mr. and Mrs. Robert Brodie, Sen. and those of Edward Newhall and Thomas W. Thayer, are invited to attend the funeral of the former from his late residence No. 112, Tradd Street, tomorrow afternoon, at 3 o'clock.

Died - The friends and acquaintances of John R. Rogers, David L. Adams, and Alexander McKinstry, are requested to attend the funeral of the latter from his late residence City hotel, East Bay, opposite Fitzsimon's Wharf, this afternoon, at four o'clock.

Issue of November 8, 1823

Married, on the 1st inst. by the Rev. Mr. Bachman, Mr. Samuel Francisco, to Miss Caroline Eckard, of this city.

Issue of November 10, 1823

Died - The friends and acquaintances of Capt. John H. Silliman, and of his brother Captain Isaac Silliman, are invited to attend the funeral of the latter, from his late residence in Mazychborough.

Issue of November 11, 1823

Died - The friends and acquaintances of Mr. John Hauck, and family and the Members of the German Friendly and Fusilier Societies, are invited to attend his funeral this afternoon at 3 o'clock, from his late residence corner of Laurens and Anson Streets.

Died - The friends and acquaintances of Captain James Thomson, and Mrs. Mary C. Thomson, and Mr. and Mrs. T. L. Smith; and likewise the members of the Methodist Episcopal Church, are invited to attend the funeral of the former from his late residence Hasell Streets, tomorrow afternoon, at three o'clock without further invitation.

Issue of November 14, 1823

Died, in Columbia, on the 9th inst. Mr. Uriah Blackman.

Died, in Columbia, on the 10th Mr. Jas. Johnson, Engineer of the Public Works of Columbia.

(Died) in Union District, on the 24th ult. Mrs. Saunders, relict of Captain John Saunders.

Issue of November 15, 1823

Died, at Philadelphia, on the 5th inst. Geo. Schaffer, of Baltimore, age 30 years, formerly proprietor of the Baltimore Feveral Republican.

Issue of November 18, 1823

Died - The friends and acquaintances of Mr. and Mrs. William Swift, are requested to attend her funeral without further invitation, from No. 336 (residence) King Street, tomorrow afternoon, at 3 o'clock.

Issue of November 22, 1823

Died - The Members of the Circular Church, and the friends and acquaintances of William S. Bennett, are invited to attend his funeral from his late residence, King Street, at 3 o'clock tomorrow afternoon.

Issue of November 22, 1823

Died - The Officers and Members of the South Carolina and Fellowship Societies, are invited to attend the funeral of their late member, William S. Bennett, from his late residence, King Street, at 3 o'clock tomorrow afternoon.

Issue of November 24, 1823

Married, in the Parish of St. James, Goose Creek, Dr. William F. Lee to Miss Ann R. daughter of the late Mr. Thomas Baker.

Died, on Friday evening last, in the 28th year of his age, Mr. William S. Bennett, of this city...(Eulogy)

Issue of November 27, 1823

Died, at Georgetown, Henry Lewin Carnes, aged 25 years.

Died, on Pee Dee River, Mrs. Agnes Fraser, consort of Dr. B. P. Fraser.

Issue of December 2, 1823

Departed this life on the 15th Nov. Mrs. Maria Rebecca Arm, in the 34th year of her age, after a short but painful illness, which she bore with Christian fortitude.

Died, at his residence in Columbia, on the 23d ult. Mr. George Wade, an old and respectable inhabitant of that place. Mr. W. we believe was the oldest native of Columbia.

Issue of December 5, 1823

Died - The friends and acquaintances of Mrs. Jane Dawson, and of the late Lawrence M. Dawson, are invited to attend her funeral this afternoon, from the residence of the late John Dawson, No. 34, Bull Street.

Issue of December 17, 1823

Died, in Georgetown, (D.C.) Benjamin Homans, Sen. late Chief of the Navy Department, in the 59th year of his age.

Issue of December 18, 1823

Married, last evening by the Rev. Mr. Howard, Mr. William A. Shepherd, to Miss Mary M. Wilcox, both of this city.

Issue of December 19, 1823

Died - The friends and acquaintances of William Stone, late of the Orchestra of the Charleston Theatre, are requested to attend his funeral tomorrow morning at 8 o'clock, from his late residence the New England Coffee House, East Bay.

Issue of December 20, 1823

Married, at Philadelphia, the 10th inst. by Mr. Levy Phillips, Mr. Joseph Jonas, Merchant of Cincinnati, Ohio, to the amiable Miss Rachael Agnes Seixas, daughter of the late Rev. Gershon Mendes Seixas, of N. York.

Issue of January 9, 1824

Died, in Newberry District, 16th ult. Mr. James Dyson, aged 59 years.
Died in Pendleton Dist. 13th ult. Mrs. Martha Davis.

Issue of January 16, 1824

Married, on Thursday 15th inst. by the Rev. Mr. Gadsden, John Champney S. Tunno, to Miss Eliza Miles, second daughter of Captain Wm. Miles, planter.

Issue of January 17, 1824

Died - The friends and acquaintances of Mrs. Margaret Blake, are requested to attend her funeral from the corner of King and Tradd Streets, tomorrow, at 12 o'clock, without further invitation.

Issue of January 19, 1824

Died - The relations, friends and acquaintances of the late Miss Elizabeth C. Bacot, and of her brothers, Thomas W. and H. H. Bacot, are invited to attend her funeral from the House of Henry H. Bacot, 49 Tradd-Street, tomorrow, at 11 o'clock, a.m. without further invitation.

Issue of January 20, 1824

Died, on the 16th inst. Mrs. Margaret Blake, relict of the late Capt. John Blake, in the 71st year of her age...(Eulogy)

Issue of January 23, 1824

Died, on the 1st inst. Mrs. Martha Johnson, of Fairfield District.
Died, on the 4th instant, Mrs. Nancy Long, of Fairfield District.

Issue of January 27, 1824

Married, at Sans Souci, near Stateburgh, on the 22d inst. by the Rev. William Barlow, Dr. Thomas Waties to Marie Huger, daughter of the late Chancellor Rutledge.

Died - The friends and acquaintances of the late Isaac Parker, Esq. as well as those of Mr. and Mrs. Edwin C. Holland, are invited to attend the funeral of the former, this afternoon at 4 o'clock.

Issue of January 28, 1824

Died, on the morning of the 22d inst. in the 89th year of his age, Capt. Robert Cochran...(Eulogy)

Died, in this city, on the morning of the 27th inst. Mr. William Lee, Printer, of Yorkshire, (Eng.) in the 35th year of his age.

Died - The friends and acquaintances of Mr. and Mrs. Alex Howard, are invited to attend the funeral of the latter, tomorrow morning at her late residence corner of Green and College Streets.

Issue of January 29, 1824

...On the evening of Sunday, the 18th inst. departed this life, in the most sudden manner, and without any previous indisposition, having attended divine service both morning and afternoon, Miss Elizabeth Catherine Bacot, in the 42d year of her age...(Eulogy)

Issue of January 30, 1824

Married, last evening by the Rev. Dr. Gadsden, Dr. Thomas G. Prioleau, to Miss Mary H. Ford, daughter of Jacob Ford, Esq.

Departed this transitory life, suddenly, on the evening of the 26th inst. in the 69th year of his age, Isaac Parker, Esq. for many years since, a respectable Planter in the Parish of St. Thomas, and a resident of this city.

Died, at Edgefield Court-House, on the 25th inst. General John S. Glascock...(Eulogy)

Issue of February 2, 1824

Married, on Wednesday evening last, by the Rev. Mr. Thomas Charleton Henry, Mr. Charles L. R. Boyd, of Chester, (S.C.), son of Dr. Charles Boyd, to Miss Mary Eliza Mathews, eldest daughter of Mr. Wm. Mathews, of St. James Santee.

Issue of February 2, 1824

Married, on Wednesday evening last, by the Rev. Mr. Hankell, Captain Thomas Budd, to Miss Caroline P. daughter of Thomas Elfe, Esq. all of this city.

Died - The friends and acquaintances of Mrs. R. Poulton, and Mr. and Mrs. C. A. Mood, are invited to attend the funeral of the latter, from the residence of the former, corner of Church and Water Streets, this afternoon at 3 o'clock precisely, without further invitation.

Issue of February 5, 1824

Died - The friends and acquaintances of Mr. George J. Lorent, deceased, are invited to attend his funeral from his late residence at Mrs. Cochran's in King-Street, at 10 o'clock tomorrow morning.

Issue of February 6, 1824

Died, at Edinburgh on the 20th of October last, Mrs. Isabella Perrie, in the 68th year of her age...(Eulogy)

Issue of February 9, 1824

Departed this life on Saturday morning, the 1st inst. in the 32 year of her age, Mrs. Mary Righton Mood...(Eulogy)

Died - The friends and acquaintances of the late Samuel Simons, are invited to attend his funeral from his residence, King Street opposite Beaufain Street, tomorrow morning at 9 o'clock.

Issue of February 10, 1824

Died, in Chester District on the 10th ult. Mr. John Knox, aged 75, a revolutionary soldier. Died in Cheraw 4th inst. Mr. Elkanah Talbot.

Issue of February 11, 1824

Married, by the Rev. Mr. McEnroe, Mr. Thomas Roger, of Rovens, (France), to Miss Euphrosine, eldest daughter of Mr. Charles Huchet, of this city.

Departed this life on the 6th February, in the 63d year of his age, Philip Gadsden, the only surviving son of the late Gen. Christopher Gadsden....(Eulogy)

Died - The friends and acquaintances of Mr. George Flagg, and of Messrs. Joseph Trescot, and Wm. H. Inglesby, are invited to attend the funeral of the former from his late residence, No. 19, Maiden Lane, this afternoon, at four o'clock, without further invitation.

Issue of February 13, 1824

Died, at Columbia, 7th inst. Miss Mary Cooper, daughter of Mr. Wm. Cooper.

Issue of February 19, 1824

Married, on Wednesday evening by the Rev. Dr. Gadsden, Ralph Izard, Esq. to Miss Eliza Lucas, daughter of General Christopher Cotesworth Pinckney.

Issue of February 20, 1824

Died - The friends and acquaintances of the late Mr. Nathaniel Lebby, are invited to attend his funeral tomorrow afternoon at 4 o'clock from his late residence No. 3, Pritchard's Lane, without further invitation.

Issue of February 23, 1824

Married, on Thursday evening last, by the Rev. T. Charlton Henry, John Stiles Bird, to Mary, eldest daughter of William McElmoyle, all of this city.

Issue of February 24, 1824

Died, on the 8th inst. in the 25th year of his age, Mr. James Thompson of Philadelphia, (Penn.) by trade a comb-maker...(Eulogy)

Died - The relatives, friends and acquaintances of Mr. Joseph B. Holmes, and the Members of the Second Independent Church, are invited to attend his funeral at 5 o'clock this afternoon, from his late residence No. 173 East Bay.

Issue of February 26, 1824

Died - The friends and acquaintances of John Henry Benson, Wm. G. Benson and George B. Locke - also of Mr. and Mrs. Taylor, are invited to attend the funeral of the former, tomorrow morning, at 9 o'clock, from No. 179, East-Bay.

Issue of February 28, 1824

...Mr. Joseph Fraser, in the very prime and vigour of life, has been suddenly called from time to eternity. After a short illness, he, on the night of the 12th inst. and in the twenty-sixth year of his age, yielded his spirit to his that gave it...(Eulogy)

Issue of March 17, 1824

Departed this life, on Tuesday the 9th of March, of a short, but painful illness, Mrs. Margaret Mercier, in the 48th year of her age, (widow of the late Capt. John Mercier,) of Georgetown, South Carolina, but for many years a respectable inhabitant of this city...(Eulogy)

Issue of March 18, 1824

Died - The friends and acquaintances of Mrs. Mary M. Brockway, are respectfully invited to attend her funeral from her late residence Beaufain-Street, (nearly opposite Archdale-Street,) tomorrow afternoon, at 4 o'clock, without further invitation.

Issue of March 20, 1824

Died - The friends and acquaintances of John and James Drummond are invited to attend the funeral of Mrs. Plant, from the residence of the latter, No. 38, Queen-Street, tomorrow afternoon, precisely at 5 o'clock, without further invitation.

Issue of March 22, 1824

Married, on the 10th inst. by the Rev. Mr. Peixotto, Mr. Jacob Moise, to Miss Rebecca, daughter of Mr. Philip Cohen, both of this city.

Issue of March 24, 1824

Died, on the 17th inst. in the 80th year of his age, Thomas Waring, Sen....(Eulogy)

Died - The friends and acquaintances of the late Theodore Gaillard, Jun. are invited to attend his funeral at 4 o'clock this afternoon, at his late residence, corner of Montague and Lynch Streets.

Issue of March 29, 1824

Died, at his residence in this city, on the 23d inst. Mr. Theodore Gaillard, Jun. in the 57th year of his age.

Issue of April 3, 1824

Died, at Beaufort, on Monday, 29th March, after much suffering, Mrs. Elizabeth Barnwell, wife of Edward Barnwell, Esq. and youngest daughter of the late Col. Osborn....(Eulogy)

Departed this life, on the 18th ult. Mrs. Mary M. Brockway, of this city, in the 49th year of her age...(Eulogy)

Issue of April 10, 1824

Died - The friends and acquaintances of Mrs. Robert Adger, Mr. James Adger, and Mr. Robert Flemming, are respectfully invited to attend the funeral of the former from her late residence, corner of King and Spring Strs. tomorrow afternoon at 5 o'clock, p.m. without furhter invitation.

Issue of April 15, 1824

Died - The friends and acquaintances of the late General William Tate, and the Members of the Cincinnati Society, are invited to attend his funeral, tomorrow morning at 8 o'clock, from his late residence, No. 249 Meeting-Street, a few doors above Boundary-Street.

Issue of April 17, 1824

...death on the 14th inst. of Frederick Rutledge, Esq....(Eulogy)

Died - The friends and acquaintances of the late Mrs. Elizabeth Howard and of Mr. and Mrs. William Purse, are invited to attend the funeral of the former tomorrow afternoon, at 5 o'clock, from her late residence No. 39 Wall-Street, without further invitation.

Died - The friends and acquaintances of Mrs. Ann B. Chitty, and of the family are requested to attend her funeral from her late residence State House Square, at 5 o'clock, tomorrow afternoon.

Issue of April 19, 1824

Departed this life on the 11th of April, after a lingering illness, which he bore with Christian fortitude, wholly resigning himself to the will of his Creator, Joseph James Glading aged 19 years and 5 months... (Eulogy)

Issue of April 20, 1824

Died, in Cheraw on the 13th inst. Mr. James Lyon, formerly editor of the Pee Dee Gazette.

Issue of April 23, 1824

Died at Mobile on the 5th inst. in the 48th year of his age, General Turner Starke, formerly of this state.

Died - The friends and acquaintances of Mr. John Langton, and of his son William, are respectfully invited to attend the funeral of the former, tomorrow evening, at 4 o'clock, from his late residence, No. 41, Market-Street, without further invitation.

Died - The members of the St. Patrick and South Carolina Societies, are respectfully invited to attend the funeral of Mr. John Langton, tomorrow evening at 4 o'clock, precisely, from his late residence No. 41 Market-Street.

Issue of April 26, 1824

Died - The friends and acquaintances of Nathaniel Heyward, Esq. and of his son Joseph M. Heyward, are requested to attend the funeral of the latter from the residence of his father, East-Bay, at 4 o'clock, this afternoon.

Died, at Low Greaves, near Ulverston lately, Mr. Wm. Sharpe, aged 46... (Eulogy)

Issue of April 29, 1824

Died - The friends and acquaintances of Mr. and Mrs. Joshua Brown and family, are respectfully invited to attend the funeral of the former, from his late residence, corner East-Bay and Vanderhorst's Wharf, at 4 o'clock this afternoon, without further invitation.

Issue of April 30, 1824

Died, in Fairfield District on 6th inst. Weston Pearson.
Died, in Winsborough, on 6th inst. William Robinson.
Died, in Winsborough, 22d ult. Capt. John Buchanan, aged 70 years - a Revolutionary officer.

Issue of May 3, 1824

Died, at the Elms, Goose Creek, on Sunday, 25th March, Joseph Manigault Heyward, Esq. third son of Nathaniel Heyward, Esq. in his 30th year.

Issue of May 4, 1824

Married, on Thursday evening last, at the Plantation of James M. Croskeys, Esq. Pon Pon, by the Rev. Dr. Delaveaux, Mr. William M'Cants, Jun. to Miss Sarah Elizabeth, daughter of Mr. Hugh Campbell.

Issue of May 6, 1824

Married, last evening, by the Rev. Mr. Henry, Martin L. Wilkins, Esq. to Miss Eliza Berkley, daughter of the late John Grimball, Esq.

Issue of May 7, 1824

Died, in St. Mathews Parish on the 26th ult. Col. Andrew Heatly, in the 64th year of his age, an officer of the Revolution...
Died, in Fairfield District, (S.C.) Mr. Hartwell Macon, aged 85 years, a soldier of the revolution.
Died, in York District on the 12th ult. Col. James Clendinen, aged 33 years.
Died, in Richaldn District on 2d ult. Sarah Caroline Rives, daughter of Green Rives.
Died, in Duplin County (N.C.) on the 20th March, Mr. Simon Wood aged 91 years, a soldier of the revolution.

Issue of May 12, 1824

Died - The friends and acquaintances of Mrs. Susan Disher, and of the late Mr. William Disher, are invited to attend the funeral of their daughter Susan, from the residence of Mrs. Suder, Society-Street (between Meeting and King Street) tomorrow morning, at 8 o'clock, without further invitation.

Issue of May 14, 1824

Married, last evening, by the Right Rev. Bishop Bowen, Robert F. Withers, Esq. of Georgetown, to Miss Caroline Wagner, daughter of the late George Wagner, Esq.
Died, at his residence in Chesterville on Sunday the 2d inst. in the 39th year of his age, after a protracted illness, George W. Coore, Esq. Commissioner in Equity for Chester District.

Issue of May 20, 1824

Died - The friends and acquaintances of John Lucas, deceased, are requested to attend his funeral from his late residence, on Gadsden's Wharf, this evening, at five o'clock precisely, without further invitation.

Issue of May 21, 1824

Died - The friends and acquaintances of Mr. and Mrs. John S. Rose, are invited to attend the funeral of the former, from his late residence No. 55, Wentworth-Street, at 7 o'clock, tomorrow morning.

Issue of May 26, 1824

Died, in Machias, Stephen Parker, Esq. in the 90th year of his age...
(Eulogy)

Issue of May 27, 1824

Died - The friends and acquaintances of Mrs. H. Crosby, and Nathaniel Cooper, are invited to attend the funeral of the former, (without a more particular invitation,) tomorrow afternoon at half past 3 o'clock, from her late residence No. 64 Anson-Street.

Issue of May 28, 1824

Died - The friends and acquaintances of William Brown, and the Members of the 3d Presbyterian and Methodist Churches, are requested to attend the funeral of Mrs. Brown, this afternoon, at 5 o'clock, from 306, King-Street.

Issue of May 31, 1824

Died, at Baltimore on the 24th inst. very deeply regretted by the community, General William H. Winder, a distinguished member of the bar, and of the Senate of Maryland.

Issue of June 2, 1824

Married, on the evening of the 1st inst. by the Right Rev. Bishop Bowen, Charles C. P. Alston, Esq. to Emma Clara, daughter of John J. Pringle, Esq.

Issue of June 3, 1824

Married, in Pineville, on the 28th inst. the Rev. Mr. David J. Campbell, Wm. Washington Couturier, Esq. to Sarah M. daughter of the late John Palmer, Esq.

Issue of June 4, 1824

Died, on the 26th ult. at Philadelphia, after a short illness, Charles Mulvey, Esq. His Catholic Majesty's Consul for the state of Georgia.

Married, on the 6th ult. at St. Stephen's Parish, by the Rev. Mr. Campbell, Stephen G. DeVeaux, Esq. to Miss Ann Blair, daughter of the late Charles Snowden, Esq.

Died, on the 1st inst. at Marietta, General Rufus Putnam, aged 86 years. In this instance of mortality, we recognize the departure of another Revolutionary Patriot

Issue of June 8, 1824

Married - In Danube, N.Y. Mr. Daniel Roff, 3 feet 3 inches high to Miss Mary Potten, 3 feet 6 inches high...

Issue of June 9, 1824

Died - The friends and acquaintances of Mr. and Mrs. Robert Shand, and Peter J. Shand, are requested to attend the funeral of the former, from his late residence No. 10 Orange-Street, this afternoon, at 4 o'clock, without further invitation.

Issue of June 10, 1824

Died, suddenly, on the 2d inst. at about half past 12 o'clock, Captain Samuel Evans, commanding U. S. Navy Yard, at Brooklyn, (New York)...(Eulogy)

Issue of June 12, 1824

Departed this life very suddenly, on the evening of the 8th inst. in the 68th year of his age, Mr. Robert Shand, a native of Scotland, but for thirty years a respectable inhabitant of this city...(Eulogy)

Issue of June 15, 1824

Died - The friends and acquaintances of Mrs. Abigail Budd, and of her son William Budd, are invited to attend the funeral of the former, from her late residence No. 52, Tradd Street, at eight o'clock tomorrow morning.

Issue of June 16, 1824

Died, at Perth Amboy, (N.J.) on the 6th inst. Commodore Jacob Lewis, in his 60th year.

Issue of June 17, 1824

Died - The friends and acquaintances of Mr. and Mrs. William H. Inglesby are invited to attend the funeral of the latter from her late residence in West-Street, tomorrow morning, at 8 o'clock.

Issue of June 19, 1824

Died, on the 7th ult. after an illness of 14 days, in the 17th year of his age, Midshipman William K. Muir, only son of the late Wm. Muir, Esq. of this city...(Eulogy)

Died, on the 9th inst. at New York of a constipation of the bowels, Normand M'Leod, Esq. late of Edisto Island, S. C. aged 70 years. He arrived in New York on the 3d inst. on the way to his family in Boston.

Died, in Litchfield, May 21, Mr. John Cotton, aged 108 years...(Eulogy)

Died - The friends and acquaintances of Mr. and Mrs. Trenholm, are invited to attend the funeral of the latter, from her late residence, No. 10 Friend-Street, tomorrow morning, (Sunday) at 8 o'clock.

Issue of June 22, 1824

Married, on the 13th inst. at New York, by the Rev. Mr. Stafford, Mr. G. F. Hyatt, of the Charleston Theatre, to Mrs. E. M. Perry of New-York.

Died - The friends and acquaintances of Mr. and Mrs. James Black are invited to attend the funeral of the latter from her late residence, No. 36, Broad-Street, this afternoon at 5 o'clock.

Issue of June 23, 1824

Died, on the 8th ult. on board the schooner Louisiana, (of New-Orleans,) Miles, Master, on her passage...

Died, on Sunday last, in Hampstead...Robert Dixon...

Died - The friends and acquaintances of Mr. and Mrs. James Galloway, and the members of the St. Patrick Benevolent Society, are requested to attend the funeral of the former from his late residence, Henrietta-Street, this afternoon, at 4 o'clock, without further invitation.

Died - The officers of the Grand Lodge of Ancient Free Masons of South Carolina, the Past Grand Officers, and Masonic Brethren generally, are requested to meet at the Grand Lodge Room (Brother Seyles') at 4 o'clock, this afternoon, to attend the funeral of our deceased Brother Jas. Galloway.

Issue of June 24, 1824

Died, in Christ Church Parish, on Sunday the 20th inst. in the 16th year of her age, Eliza Capers Jervey, the only daughter of Dr. David Jervey...(Eulogy)

Issue of June 25, 1824

...death of Mr. Norman M'Leod, of Edistor Island...(Eulogy)

Died - The members and officers of the Board of Commissioners of Streets and Lamps are requested to attend the funeral of their late Chairman E. Thayer, Esq. this afternoon, at 4 o'clock, agreeably to a resolution of the board.

Issue of June 26, 1824

Died, at the Quarantine Ground, on the 24th inst. Nathan B. Packer, Master of the Sloop Tickler, of Groton, (Con.) aged 22 years.

Issue of June 30, 1824

Died, at the residence of James Shape, Esq. in St. Bartholomew's Parish, on Friday the 25th inst. Dr. Frederick B. Tudor...(Eulogy)

Died - The friends and acquaintances of Mr. Abraham Markley, and of his son Benjamin A. Markley, and Wm. Lee, are requested to attend the funeral of the former this afternoon, at 5 o'clock, from the residence of Benjamin A. Markley, in Radcliffeborough, nearly west of St. Paul's Church.

Died - The friends and acquaintances, also the Members of the German Lutheran Church, are particularly invited to attend the funeral of the late Mr. John Paul Burn, from his late residence No. 22 Washington-Street near the Market, Gadsden's Wharf, tomorrow morning 7 o'clock.

Issue of July 2, 1824

Died - The friends and acquaintances of the late James S. Bee; of his mother, Mrs. Eliza Bee, and his brother, William Bee, are requested to attend the funeral of the former, this afternoon, at 4 o'clock, from his late residence, Moore-Street, (Horlbeck's Alley.)

Issue of July 3, 1824

Married, on Wednesday last, by the Rev. Mr. Piexotto, Mr. Fisher Moses, to Miss Rachael DePass, both of this city.

Died, suddenly, on Tuesday last, in the 34th year of his age, Mr. Benjamin Moise...(Eulogy)

Issue of July 6, 1824

Died, on the 3d inst. after an illness of some days, in the 37th year of his age, Mr. D. C. Surr, a native of Manchester, England, and resident of this place for the last 15 years.

Issue of July 7, 1824

Died - The friends and acquaintances of the late Mr. James Futerell, of Miss Futerell, and Dr. James Ramsey, and also, the members of the South-Carolina Society, are invited to attend the funeral of the former from the residence of Dr. James Ramsay, No. 74, Braod Street, this afternoon, at 6 o'clock.

Issue of July 13, 1824

⬩ Died, at Columbia 4th inst. Mr. George Herron, aged 38 years.

Died, at Columbia - Elizabeth Matilde Marshall, daughter of Dr. W. P. Marshall.

Died, on Lynch's Creek, Mr. Wm. Blair, aged 66 years, a soldier of the revolution.

Died, in Lexington, 5th inst. David Austin, Esq.

Died, in Lexington, 3d inst. Capt. John Sea, in consequence of having been struck by lightning.

Issue of July 14, 1824

Married, on Monday evening the 12th inst. by the Right Rev. Dr. England, John Benjamin Bloomfield, Esq. of London, to Miss Mary Ann Blannerhasset, eldest daughter of the late Capt. John Connolly, of this city.

Issue of July 16, 1824

Died, on the 29th June, in the 80th year of his age, Abraham Markley, a native of Pennsylvanis, from which state he removed to this city, in 1774...(Eulogy)

Issue of July 19, 1824

Departed this life, suddenly on the 29th of June last, Mrs. Hannah Moser, consort of Dr. Philip Moser, a native of Northamptonshire, Eng. and for 36 years a respectable inhabitant of this city...(Eulogy)

Died, at his residence in St. Mathews Parish on the 2d inst. John M. Caldwell, in the 54th year of his age...(Eulogy)

Departed this life, on Wednesday, the 30th of June, after a short illness of twenty-two hours, which he supported with Christian fortitude... Mr. John P. Burn, in the 73d year of his age. He was a native...in Germany ...but took up his abode in Charleston.

Issue of July 20, 1824

Departed this life on Thursday, 15th inst. after a short illness of 4 days, which he supported with Christian fortitude, Mr. Jehu Clement, aged about 32 years. He was a native of Philadelphia, and a Cabinet Maker by trade...

Died, at New York, on the morning of the 8th inst. Mrs. Lydia C. Weyman, wife of Edward B. Weyman, formerly of this city.

Issue of July 21, 1824

Died - The friends and acquaintances of Mrs. Mary Quiggins, are invited to attend her funeral from her late residence in St. Philips Street, this afternoon, at 5 o'clock.

Died - The friends and acquaintances of Mr. and Mrs. Laurent Dursse, are requested to attend the funeral of their son, from their residence in Hasell-Street, this afternoon, at 5 o'clock.

Issue of July 22, 1824

Died - The friends and acquaintances of Mr. Emanuel Durbee, are invited to attend his funeral from his late residence in King-Street, tomorrow morning, at half past 7 o'clock.

Issue of July 23, 1824

Died, lately, in Fairfield District, Charles Bradford, aged 90 years...

Issue of July 24, 1824

Died, on the 19th inst. Mrs. Sarah Hodgson, of Wexford County, (Ireland). She was the mother of Mr. William Jackson, who with his amiable wife, and two lovely children, were lost in February of last year, off Holyhead, by the wreck of brig Flora...

Issue of July 28, 1824

Departed this life on Friday morning last, after a short illness, in the 43d year of her age, Mrs. Ann J. Miles, widow and relict of the late Jeremiah Miles, Esq. of St. Paul's Parish.

Died on the 27th instant, on board the U. S. ship Hornet, lying off Old Point Comfort, Thomas N. Mann, Esq.
Diplomatic Agent from this government to Guatimala.

Died - The friends and acquaintances of Mr. Francis Thomas and Mr. Henry Bryce, are invited to attend the funeral of the former, from the house of the latter, No. 74 King Street, two doors north of Tradd STreet, this afternoon, at 5 o'clock, without further invitation.

Issue of July 31, 1824

Died, on the 20th inst. in this city, Mr. Henry Gray, in the 78th year of his age...(Eulogy)

Issue of August 9, 1824

Died - The friends and acquaintances of Mrs. Anne Fox and family are invited to attend the funeral of her son Owen Wm. Fox, without further invitation, this evening, at 6 o'clock from No. 254 East-Bay.

Issue of August 12, 1824

Died - The friends and acquaintances of Mr. Charles Scott, are invited to attend his funeral this afternoon, at 5 o'clock, from his late residence, No. 11 Tradd-Street.

Issue of August 13, 1824

Died - The friends and acquaintances of Mr. John S. Thorn, and those of Mr. Richard Fordham, are respectfully invited to attend the funeral of the former this afternoon, at half past 3 o'clock, from No. 9 Cumberland Street.

Died - The friends and acquaintances of Mr. Edward Fox, and those of his surviving relatives, are invited to attend his funeral this afternoon, at 6 o'clock, from his late residence, No. 254, East Bay.

Issue of August 16, 1824

Died, at his residence in Clarendon County, Sumter District, on the 31st ult. after an illness of five days, of bilious fever, Mr. Henry Whitney Gardner, formerly of this city, in the 30th year of his age...

Issue of August 18, 1824

Died, suddenly, on the 6th inst. at the seat of Charles Augustus Dale, Esq. Manor of Livingston, Ralph Izard, Esq. of Charleston, S. C.

Issue of August 21, 1824

Departed this life on the 7th inst. in the 31st year of her age, Mrs. Emily Ann Read, wife of John Harleston Read, Esq....(Eulogy)

Died - The friends and acquaintances of Mr. Francis Ricard, of Mrs. Mary Ricard, and of her daughter Miss Mary J. Capdeveille, are invited to attend the funeral of Mrs. Ricard: tomorrow morning, at 8 o'clock, from her late residence corner of Elliott and East-Bay Street.

Died - The friends and acquaintances of Messrs. Beckett and Davis, Mr. William Patterson, and of Mr. Charles Medford, are invited to attend the funeral of the latter, from the dwelling of the former, No. 57, East-Bay, this afternoon, at 4 o'clock.

Issue of August 23, 1824

Died - The friends and acquaintances of Mr. Levi Nash, are invited to attend his funeral this afternoon, at 4 o'clock, from No. 2 Vendue Range.

Issue of August 24, 1824

Died - Ralph Izard, Esq. of Charleston S. C. younger brother of Gen. Izard, and son of the late venerable Ralph Izard, heretofore Senator of the U. S....(Eulogy)

Issue of August 25, 1824

Died - The friends and acquaintances of James and Wm. Maynard, and of Captain Francis Brodut, are invited to attend the funeral of his nephew James Brodut, at his late residence, No. 44 Elliott-Street, this afternoon, at 4 o'clock.

Issue of August 26, 1824

Died, in Franklin County, Missouri, on the night of the 6th ult. Joseph Jones Monroe, Esq. (brother of the President of the U. States.)

Issue of August 27, 1824

Died - The friends and acquaintances of Messrs. Forbush and Green, Joseph Tyler, and T. Tupper, are requested to attend the funeral of Mr. Samuel W. Green, from his late residence, No. 105, East Bay, at 6 o'clock this afternoon.

Issue of August 28, 1824

Died, in Richmond, (Va.) on the 21st inst. in his 75th of age, Dr. William Foushee, Post Master of the above city.

Issue of August 31, 1824

Died - The friends and acquaintances of John Redfern, and his brother, are invited to attend the funeral of the latter, from No. 43 Tradd-Street, without further invitation.

Issue of September 3, 1824

Died - The friends and acquaintances of the late Mr. William Cochran, Jun. of New York, of Mr. T. W. Bacot, Jun, and Mr. Samuel Henwood, are requested to attend the funeral of the former from the residence of the latter, corner of East Bay and Craft's South Wharf, without further invitation, at 9 o'clock tomorrow morning,

Issue of September 7, 1824

Died - The friends and acquaintances of Mr. Joshua M. Coffin, late of Boston, are respectfully invited to attend his funeral this afternoon, at 5 o'clock, from Mr. Thomas Johnston's Hotel, bend of King-Street. The friends of Dr. Waring and James Smith Colburn, are also respectfully invited to attend Mr. Coffin's funeral.

Issue of September 8, 1824

Departed this life on the afternoon of Friday the 3d inst. after an illness of four days.... Mr. Peter Fiche, in the 44th year of his age. He was a native of England, but for the last eight years became a resident of our city...(Eulogy)

Issue of September 9, 1824

Departed this life on Sunday, the 29th ult. after a short and severe illness, Capt. John S. Darrell, of this city, in the 41st year of his age ...(Eulogy)

Died, at Sullivan's Island, on the 3d inst. of the prevailing fever, Mr. William Cochran, Jr. of New-York, in the 19th year of his age...(Eulogy)

Issue of September 11, 1824

Died - The friends and acquaintances of Robert B. Edwards, Jasper Carning, and Thomas Flemming, are invited to attend the funeral of the former, this afternoon, at 3 o'clock, from No. 10 State-Street.

Died - The relatives, friends and acquaintances of Miss Elizabeth Parker, those of Mr. and Mrs. Edwin C. Holland, and of Mr. and Mrs. John Holland, are requested to attend the funeral of the late Edwin C. Holland from No. 19 Legare-Street, tomorrow afternoon, at 1 o'clock.

Died - The Masonic Lodge are requested to attend the funeral of the late Edwin C. Holland, from 19 Legare-Street, tomorrow afternoon at 1 o'clock.

Died - The friends and acquaintances of Samuel Abbott, Thomas Kennedy, and Mathew O'Brien, are solicited to attend the funeral of the latter from his late residence No. 13 Market-Street, at nine o'clock tomorrow forenoon.

Died - The friends and acquaintances of Thomas and Rachel Cox, are requested to attend the funeral of their son John, tomorrow morning at eight o'clock, No. 53 Broad-Street.

Issue of September 14, 1824

Married, at Alban, (N. Y.) on the 1st inst. by the Rev. Mr. Lacey, Mr. Andrew Milne, Mrs. Martha Mair, both of this city.

Died - The friends and acquaintances of the late Mr. Loomis, are invited to attend his funeral this afternoon, at 5 o'clock, from his late residence Water-Street.

Issue of September 15, 1824

Died - The friends and acquaintances of the late Captain Peter Smith, and of Mr. Samuel Burger, and Mr. Samuel Alexander; also the members of the Mechanic's and German Friendly Societies, are respectfully invited to attend the funeral of Captain Smith, from No. 4, Mazyck-Street, tomorrow morning, at half past 9 o'clock, without further invitation.

Issue of September 16, 1824

Died, at New York, on the 7th inst. the Hon. Nicholas Ware, U. S. Senator from Georgia.

Issue of September 17, 1824

Departed this life, on the 13th instant, Mr. Hugh M'Murray, aged 28 years, a native of Ireland, but for many years an inhabitant of this city ...(Eulogy)

Died - The friends and acquaintances of Mrs. Agnes McMillan and of Richard McMillan, are invited to attend the funeral of the former, from her late residence No. 376 King-Street, tomorrow morning, at 8 o'clock without further invitation.

Issue of September 18, 1824

Died - Carey M. Keith, is no more - he fell a victim to the prevailing fever which at present rages in our city, to an alarming extent. He closed his spotless life on the 10th inst. in the 28th year of his age...(Eulogy)

Issue of September 22, 1824

Died - The friends and acquaintances of L. DeVillers, and of the late Joseph Cany, are invited to attend the funeral of the latter from No. 40 Queen-Street, this afternoon, at 5 o'clock, precisely.

Issue of September 23, 1824

Died - The friends and acquaintances of the late Augustus Smith, are invited to attend his funeral tomorrow morning, at half past 7 o'clock, from his late residence No. 27 East-Bay, without further invitation.

Issue of September 24, 1824

Died, at the Sweet Springs in Virginia, on the 1st inst. Moses Mordecai, Esq. of the vicinity of Raleigh, N.C....(Eulogy)

Died - The friends and acquaintances of John C. Barber, are particularly requested to attend his funeral this afternoon, from Mr. James McNamee's, 4 o'clock, No. 112, Church-Street.

Issue of September 25, 1824

Died, in this city on the 23d inst of the prevailing fever, in the 36th year of his age, Mr. John C. Barber, a native of Philadelphia...(Eulogy)

Died, at sea, of extreme debility, the 2d of July last, on board the U. S. brig Spark, Capt. Newton, Midshipman Gregory Purcell, in the 20th year of his age, a native of Charleston, South Carolina, son of the late Capt. Joseph Purcell...(Eulogy)

Issue of September 27, 1824

Died - The friends and acquaintances of Mr. and Mrs. David M'Dowall, and Andrew M'Dowall, are invited to attend the funeral of the former this afternoon, at 4 o'clock, from his late residence, corner of Meeting and Society Streets.

Died - The friends and acquaintances of Mr. Chaume, and Mr. A. Carivene, are invited to attend the funeral of the former, this afternoon, at 5 o'clock, from his late residence No. 124 Meeting-Street.

Died - The friends and acquaintances of Mr. and Mrs. J. C. Anthony, are invited to attend the funeral of their daughter Jane, from their residence in Hampstead, this afternoon at 4 o'clock.

Issue of September 29, 1824

Died - The friends and acquaintances, of the late Mrs. Wm. Cannon, and those of Jerry Walter and family, and Wm. M. Fraser, and family, are particularly invited to attend the funeral of the former at 4 o'clock, this afternoon, from her late residence, corner of East Bay and Laurens-Sreet, without further invitation.

Issue of September 30, 1824

Died - The friends and acquaintances of Mr. and Mrs. Bartholomew Clark, are invited to attend the funeral of their daughter Julia Ann, this afternoon, at 4 o'clock, from their residence No. 163, King Street.

Died - The friends and acquaintances of Mr. and Mrs. Joseph Tyler, are invited to attend the funeral of Mrs. Tyler, from her late residence No. 7, State-Street, this afternoon, at 4 o'clock.

Died - The friends and acquaintances of Mr. and Mrs. Emanuel Jones, and also those of Mr. and Mrs. Duryea, are requested to attend the funeral of Mrs. Jones, from the residence of Mrs. Duryea, No. 51, State-Street, at 5 o'clock, this afternoon.

Died - The friends and acquaintances of the late Mr. Wm. F. Shackelford, are requested to attend his funeral this afternoon at 4 o'clock, from No. -- Market-Street, near Archdale-Street.

Issue of October 4, 1824

Died - The friends and acquaintances of the late Mrs. Mary Fox, and of her sons William and James Fox, and of Patrick Campbell, are invited to attend her funeral this afternoon at half past 4 o'clock from No. 133, East Bay.

Died - The friends and acquaintances of Mr. and Mrs. F. Kinsey, are requested to attend the funeral of the former at 5 o'clock this afternoon, from his late residence No. 247, King Street.

Issue of October 5, 1824

Died in this city, of a fever, on the 11th inst. Robert B. Means, of Beaufort, S. C. a member of the Junior Class in Yale College aged 18 years ...(Eulogy)

Died - George Schmail, a native of the town of Reading, (Penn.) and for the last two years a resident of this city, died of the prevailing fever on the 2d inst. aged 22 years...(Eulogy)

Died - The friends and acquaintances of Mr. Henry Jenny, and Alexander England, are invited to attend the funeral of the former, from his residence in Bull-Street this afternoon, at 5 o'clock.

Issue of October 6, 1824

Departed this life on Thursday morning the 30th Sept. of the prevailing fever, Miss Ann Eliza Hillard, aged 18 years...(Eulogy)

Died, at Albany, on Saturday morning, the Hon. Philip Van Rensselaer, aged fifty eight years and five months.

Issue of October 6, 1824

Died - The friends and acquaintances of John King, Jun. are requested
to attend the funeral of his father, this afternoon, at 4 o'clock, from No.
22, Archdale-Street, opposite West-Street.

Issue of October 7, 1824

Died - The friends and acquaintances of Edward Carey, and Honore
Monpoey, are requested to attend the funeral of the former from his late
residence in King-Street, a few doors above Market-Street, this afternoon
at 4 o'clock, without further invitation.

Issue of Ocotber 11, 1824

Died...on the 5th inst. in the 27th year of his age, Mr. Henry Jenney
...(Eulogy)

Departed this life on Sunday evening the 3d inst. of the prevailing
fever, after a painful illness of eight days, which she endured with the
utmost patience and Christian fortitude Mrs. Rosanna O'Neale, a native of
Burlington, (New Jersey,) consort of John O'Neale, aged 34 years, 5 months,
and 21 days...(Eulogy)

Died - The friends and acquaintances of Mr. and Mrs. Duggan, and of
Jane Clayton, are respectfully invited to attend the funeral of Mary G.
Duggan, (daughter of the former) tomorrow morning, at 9 o'clock, without
further invitation, from the upper end St. Philips-Street.

Issue of October 12, 1824

Died - The friends and acquaintances of the late Mrs. Daniel O'Hara, of
Mr. Henry O'Hara, and Mr. A. H. O'Hara, are respectfully invited to attend
the funeral of the former from her late residence No. 20, King-Street,
tomorrow afternoon, at 4 o'clock, without further invitation.

Issue of October 14, 1824

Died, on Sunday, the 10th inst. after a protracted illness of several
months, in the 51st year of her age, Mrs. Harriet R. Cochran, wife of Charles
B. Cochran, Esq. of this city...(Eulogy)

Issue of October 21, 1824

Died, on the 15th inst. of the prevailing fever, after eight days of
severe suffering, Alexander Christie Waugh, aged 6 years, 5 months and 2
days, youngest son of Alexander B. Waugh...

Issue of October 25, 1824

Died, on Sullivan's Island, on 15th ult. of the prevailing fever,
Master William Goodman, aged 7 years, son of Mr. Benjamin Goodman.

Died, on Sullivan's Island, on 24th ult. of the prevailing fever Miss
Parmelia Goodman, aged 26 years.

Died, in this place on 17th inst. of inflamative in the brain and
paralytic stroke Mr. Benjamin Goodman, aged 44 years...(Eulogy)

Died at Walterborough, on the 18th instant, Mrs. Catharine A. L. Logan,
consort of Benjamin Logan, Esq. of Colleton District...(Eulogy)

Died - The friends and acquaintances of Mr. and Mrs. Barbot, are
invited to attend the funeral of their eldest son Louis, from their
residence the corner of Church and Tradd Streets, at 4 o'clock this afternoon, without further invitation.

Issue of October 27, 1824

Died - The friends and acquaintances of Mr. and Mrs. John S. Jones, and
Miss Jane Vermilyea, are respectfully invited to attend the funeral of the
latter, from their residence, No. 145, East Bay, without further invitation,

at half past 3 o'clock, this afternoon.

Issue of October 28, 1824

Died - The Rev. the Clergy, of different denominations, the Trustees and Officers of the College of Charleston, and the friends and acquaintances of the late Rev. J. M. Gilbert, are requested to attend his funeral from the residence of Wm. Blamyer, East-Bay continued, tomorrow morning, at 10 o'clock.

Issue of October 30, 1824

Died - The friends and acquaintances of the late Charles Pinckney, Esq. are requested to attend his funeral this afternoon, at 4 o'clock, from the house of his son, Henry L. Pinckney, in King-Street.

Died - The friends and acquaintances of Ashbel Bulkley, and of Erastus Bulkley, are invited to attend the funeral of the former from his late residence, No. 261, King-Street, at 4 o'clock, this afternoon, without further invitation.

Issue of November 2, 1824

Died, at Columbia, (S.C.) 22d ult. Mr. George Nutting, of Waltertown, (Mass.) aged 47 years.

Died, on the 23d ult. Mr. Margaret Young, aged 32 years.

Died, in Union District, Mr. Saml. Clowney, aged 82 years.

Issue of November 4, 1824

Died, on the 29th of October, died at the age of sixty-six, the Hon. Charles Pinckney.... He was born in Charleston in 1758...(Eulogy)

Died - The friends and acquaintances of the late Mr. Wm. Trenholm are invited to attend his funeral this afternoon, at 4 o'clock, from his late residence Society-Street, near Anson-Street.

Issue of November 5, 1824

Died - The friends and acquaintances of Mr. and Mrs. Nathl. Cooper, are invited to attend the funeral of their daughter this afternoon, at half-past 4 o'clock, from their residence Anson-Street.

Died - The friends and acquaintances of Christian Henry Blume, of Col. Jacob Sass, and the Congregation of the German Lutheran Church, generally, are invited tomorrow morning, at 8 o'clock, to attend the funeral of C. H. Blume, from his late residence, Anson-Street continued, near the 2d Presbyterian Church, without further invitation.

Issue of November 8, 1824

...Miss Jane Vermilyea, a native of N. York, but who had resided among us two years, when she became the regretted victim of death...on the 27th day of October, and in the nineteenth year of her age...(Eulogy)

Died - The friends of Captain Pratt are invited to attend the funeral of Miss B. Whitaker, this afternoon, at 4 o'clock, p.m. from his residence, 29 Laurens-Street.

Issue of November 9, 1824

Died, on the 12th ult. in the 76th year of her age, Mrs. Rebecca O'Hara, relict of the late Mr. Daniel O'Hara.

Died - The friends and acquaintances of Philip Muck and L. Devillers, are invited to attend the funeral of the former from his late residence, No. 90, King-Street, at 4 o'clock this afternoon, without further invitation.

Issue of November 15, 1824

Died, on Thursday, 4th November, inst., in Clarendon, Mrs. Elizabeth

Richardson, in the 51st year of her age, consort of Charles Richardson, Esq.
...(Eulogy)

Died on the 24th ult. in St. Bartholomew's Parish, Mary, the only
daughter of James Sharpe, Esq. aged three years...(Eulogy)

Issue of November 16, 1824

Died - The friends and acquaintances of Mr. Henry Hughes, Mr. and Mrs.
Edward Hughes, Dr. George A. Hughes, and Mr. C. B. Mease, are invited to
attend the funeral of the former at 5 o'clock, tomorrow afternoon, from the
residence of his father, No. 88, Tradd Street.

Issue of November 20, 1824

Married, on Thursday, the 18th inst. by the Right Rev. Bishop Bowen,
Joseph Manigault, Jun. to Miss Mary M. Huger, daughter of the Hon. Judge
Huger.

Married, on the 18th inst. by the Rev. Mr. Howard, William Kirkwood,
to Miss Susan daughter of the late George Pritchard, of Christ Church Parish.

Issue of November 23, 1824

Died, in Columbia, S.C. on the 17th inst. Samuel Farrow, Esq. of
Spartenburg, aged 60 years...

Issue of November 25, 1824

Died - The friends and acquaintances of Mr. and Mrs. Stephen West Moore,
the members of the Fellowship and Hibernian Societies, are invited to attend
the funeral of the former (without a more particular invitation) tomorrow
afternoon, at half past 2 o'clock, from his late residence in Vanderhorst
Street, opposite St. Paul's Church.

Issue of November 27, 1824

Died - The friends and acquaintances of Mr. and Mrs. John Nevill, are
invited to attend the funeral of their daughter Caroline from their
residence corner of Magazine and Mazyck Streets, at 9 o'clock tomorrow
morning, without further invitation.

Issue of November 30, 1824

Married, on the 25th inst. by the Rev. Mr. Buist, Mr. Thomas Dotterer,
formerly of Philadelphia, to Miss Mary, daughter of Mr. Robert Eason, of
this city.

Issue of December 2, 1824

Died - The friends and acquaintances of Mr. Timothy Stone, are respectfully invited to attend his funeral tomorrow morning, at 9 o'clock, from
his late residence, Clifford-Street, without invitation.

Died - The members of the Northern Volunteers, will appear at their
parade ground corner of Market and Meeting-Streets, at half past 8 o'clock,
tomorrow morning, to pay the last tribute of respect to their lamented
Brother Soldier Timothy Stone.

Issue of December 3, 1824

Married, on Tuesday evening last, the 30th ult. by the Rev. Mr. Gilman,
Thomas Heyward, Jun. to Charity, eldest daughter of Capt. Robert Wilson, all
of this city.

Died - The friends and acquaintances of Mrs. Margaret Savage, and Mr.
and Mrs. Benjamin Elliott, are requested to attend the funeral of the latter
from her late residence Legare-Street, tomorrow, at 12 o'clock.

Issue of December 4, 1824

Died, on the 2d June last, at Fair Forest, Spartanburg District, of consumption, in the 43d year of her age, Mrs. Anne Oeland...(Eulogy)

Died - The friends and acquaintances of the late Henry W. Paxton, are requested to attend his funeral tomorrow morning, at 9 o'clock precisely, from his late residence in Zigzag Court, near the Battery, without further invitation.

Issue of December 6, 1824

Died - The friends and acquaintances of the late Mr. James Flemming, are requested to attend his funeral, from No. 53, Pinckney-Street, this afternoon, at 3 o'clock.

Died - The friends and acquaintances of Mr. Robert Long, also the Officers and Members of the First Troop, are requested to attend his funeral from his late residence, in Wraggsborough, this afternoon, at half past 4 o'clock.

Issue of December 11, 1824

Died - The friends and acquaintances of the late Mr. William Bailey, and those of Mr. Daniel Cruickshanks, also his Masonic Brethren generally, and those of Washington Lodge, No. 7, in particular, are invited to attend his funeral tomorrow morning at 8 o'clock, from his late residence, No. 22 Queen-Street.

Died - The friends and acquaintances of Mrs. Jenney, are requested to attend her funeral this afternoon at half past 4 o'clock, from her late residence near the Washington Race Course.

Issue of December 13, 1824

Died - The friends and acquaintances of Archibald M. and Catharine A. P. Harvey, are requested to attend the funeral of their son, St. John Phillips Harvey, from their residence at Mrs. Langton's, Knox's Wharf, at 3 o'clock this afternoon, without further invitation.

Issue of December 15, 1824

Married, on Monday evening last, by the Rev. Mr. Bachman, Mr. John A. Jackson of this city to Miss Ann Morrison, of New York.

Issue of December 16, 1824

Died, on the 9th Dec. Mrs. Laura Dubose, wife of William Dubose, of St. Stephens Parish...(Eulogy)

Issue of December 17, 1824

Died - The friends and acquaintances of Mr. and Mrs. John Nevill, and James O'Brien, also, the members of the St. Patrick Benevolent Society, are requested to attend the funeral of the former from his late residence corner of Magazine and Mazyck-Streets, tomorrow morning, at 10 o'clock, without further invitation.

Issue of December 28, 1824

Married, last evening, by the Rev. Mr. Henry, Mr. James Mashburn, to Miss Catherine Wartenburg, both of this city.

Died, at New York, on the 18th inst. after a lingering illness, Mr. David Gillespie, in the 35th year of this age.

Issue of January 3, 1825

Married, on Thursday evening last, by the Rev. Dr. Palmer, Mr. David Bell, Jun. to Miss Elizabeth Quinby, both of this city.

Issue of January 6, 1825

Died, in Woolwich, Mass. 27th ult. Joshua Prince, son of Colonel Joshua Baker, aged 5 years...

Died, in Northwood, (N.H.) Nancy, daughter of Mr. Benjamin Morrill, aged about 10 years.

Died, at Goshen, Orange County, on the 28th November, Mr. William S. Wilkin, in the 33d year of his age...

Died, at Dundee, Mr. Sealey, teacher of dancing, aged about 90 years...

Died - The friends and acquaintances of the late N. M. Petersen, Esq. are respectfully invited to attend his funeral tomorrow morning, at 10 o'clock from Jone's Pond-Street.

Issue of January 10, 1825

Departed this life on Saturday evening last, George Edward, the infant son of Dr. Wm. Burgoyne.

Issue of January 11, 1825

Departed this life, on the 4th inst. in the 37th year of his age, Lawrence Luidens a native of Curracoa.

Issue of January 12, 1825

Died - The friends and acquaintances of the late Mrs. Elizabeth Blewer, and of Mr. J. G. Blewer, also the Members of the German Lutheran Church, are respectfully invited to attend her funeral tomorrow morning, at ten o'clock, from her late residence on Charleston Neck, corner of Meeting and Spring Streets.

Issue of January 14, 1825

Died - The friends and acquaintances of John and Margaret Dougherty are invited to attend the funeral of the latter, tomorrow morning, at 9 o'clock, from her late residence, corner of Boundary and Anson Street.

Issue of January 20, 1825

Died, at New-Haven, on the 8 inst. Eli Whitney, Esq.

Issue of January 22, 1825

Departed this life on Tuesday afternoon, the 18th inst. at 3 o'clock, Mrs. Caroline B. Broughton, the inestimable daughter of the late Tucker-Harris, M.D....(Eulogy)

Died - The friends and acquaintances of Capt. Joseph Young are requested to attend the funeral of Joseph Young, Jun. and the officers and Members of the Union Lodge of free Masons, from his residence the corner of East Bay and Haseil Street, at half past 12 o'clock.

Issue of January 24, 1825

Died - We stop the press to announce with deep heartfelt regret, the death of Major-General Robert Godloe Harper...

Married, on Tuesday evening last, by the Rev. Mr. Hanckle, Alexander Moultrie, Esq. to Miss Martha Williamson Guerrard, youngest daughter of the late Jacob Guerrrard, Esq.

Issue of January 29, 1825

Married, on Thursday evening last, by the Rev. Dr. Gadsden, Mr. Henry F. Faber to Miss Sarah, second daughter of Mr. Thomas B. Seabrook, both of this city.

Issue of February 3, 1825

Died, in this city, on the 29th of December last, Mr. Charles P.

Carpantier, teacher of the French Language...(Eulogy)

Issue of February 7, 1825

Died - The friends and acquaintances of Mr. and Mrs. Wm. Smith, Jun.
also the Members of the Second Presbyterian Church are requested to attend
(without further invitation) the funeral of the latter from her late residence in Mazyckborough, at 4 o'clock tomorrow afternoon.

Issue of February 14, 1825

Died - The friends and acquaintances of Captain John Geyer are respectfully invited to attend his funeral this afternoon, at 4 o'clock, from his
late residence No. 16, Lynch Street, without further invitation.

Issue of February 18, 1825

Married, on Wednesday evening last, by the Rev. M. Peixotto, Mr. A. C.
Labatt, to Miss Caroline Hyams, daughter of Mr. Samuel Hyams, both of this
city.

Died - The friends and acquaintances of Mrs. Ann Montgomery, and John,
James, and Washington Gebbes, are invited to attend the funeral of the former, from her late residence corner of Beaufain and Cumming Streets, tomorrow
afternoon, at half past 3 o'clock.

Issue of February 25, 1825

Died on the 24th ult. in St. Peter's Parish, Mrs. Mollett, at the patri-
archal age of ninety-eight years...(Eulogy)

Died - The friends and acquaintances of the late Mrs. Mary Burger,
also, of Samuel Alexander and Samuel Burger, are particularly requested to
attend the funeral of the former, from the residence of Mrs. E. Williamson,
No. 124, King Street, tomorrow morning, at half past 9 o'clock, without
further invitation.

Issue of February 26, 1825

Died - The friends and acquaintances of Mr. and Mrs. Barton, are invited
to attend the funeral of the latter, from her late residence No. 20 Wall-
Street, tomorrow morning, at 8 o'clock, without further invitation.

Issue of February 28, 1825

Died - The friends and acquaintances of Mrs. Sarah De St. Julien Jore,
are invited to attend the funeral service to be performer at Mr. Robert H.
Brodie's at 8 o'clock, tomorrow morning, in Wraggborough.

Issue of March 1, 1825

Departed this transitory life, on Friday morning, the 25th ult. Mrs.
Mary Burger, a native of St. Mary's, Georgia, and relict of the late Mr.
George Burger, aged 25 years...(Eulogy)

Died, on the 6th January last, after a short illness at his residence
on Pacolett, in Spartanburgh District, Bayis Earle, in the 91st year of his
age.

Issue of March 3, 1825

Died, at Lexington, (Mass.) on the 16th ult. Mr. Josiah Willington,
(father of the Editor of the Charleston Courier) aged eighty years...

Died - The relatives and friends of the late Edward Waring are requested
to attend his funeral from his late residence Mazyckborough, opposite the
second Presbyterian Church, tomorrow morning, at 8 o'clock.

Issue of March 4, 1825

Died, of spasms, on Saturday evening the 19th inst. after an illness of six days, Leekman Howard, the eldest son of Robert Howard, Esq. of this city in the 11th year of his age.

Issue of March 5, 1825

Married, on the evening of the 3d inst. by the Right Rev. Bishop England, John D. Ansley, Esq. Merchant to Miss Celina, second daughter of Charles G. A Lacoste, Esq. both of this city.

Issue of March 8, 1825

Died, in Bridgewater, Mass. Miss Olive Keith, aged 23...'

Issue of March 10, 1825

Died this morning of cramp, George Washington Prescott, aged 19 months and 12 days, only son of G. W. Prescott, Esq., Merchant of this city.

Issue of March 11, 1825

Married, on Wednesday the 9th inst. by the Rev. Mr. Piexotto, Mr. Noah J. Ellis, to Miss Esther Levin, all of this city.

Issue of March 16, 1825

Died - The friends and acquaintances of Mr. Andrew and Mrs. Mary Ann Kippenberg; also the Members of the German Friendly Society, are requested to attend the funeral of the former, from his late residence, No. 75 Queen Street, tomorrow morning, at 10 o'clock, without a more particular invitation.

Issue of March 22, 1825

Departed this life, on the 19th inst. after a protracted illness of about three months, Mr. Charles G. Mackay, aged 30 years, 11 months and 5 days...

Issue of March 23, 1825

Married, on Monday evening last, by the Right Rev. Bishop Bowen, Mr. Joseph Turpin Weyman, Merchant of this city, to Mary Elizabeth Rosaltha, daughter of Samuel Maverick, Esq. of Pendleton, (S.C.)

Issue of April 9, 1825

Died - The Reverend the Clergy of all denominations, the Commissioners of Free School for the Parishes of St. Philip, and St. Michael, the Children of Free School No. 3, the friends and acquaintances of the Reverend Robert S. Symmes, Mrs. Margaret Symmes, and Mr. Ebenezer Thayer, are requested to attend the funeral of the Rev. Robert S. Symmes, from his late residence Queen-Street, one door east of Mazyck-Street, tomorrow morning, at 8 o'clock, without further invitation.

Issue of April 11, 1825

Married, on Monday morning, by the Rev. Mr. Furman, Col. M. Irvine Keith, to Mrs. Wm. M. Heyward.

Issue of April 12, 1825

Died, in Salisbury, (N.H.) on the 24th ultimo, Mrs. Judith Bean, aged 75, on the 2d inst. Phinehas Bean, Esq., her husband, aged 74 years.

Issue of April 16, 1825

Died - The friends and acquaintances of the late Capt. John Geyer, and of Mrs. Mary Geyer, and of Miss Harriett A. Geyer, are respectfully invited to attend the funeral of the latter, from her residence No. 16 Lynches Street, tomorrow afternoon at half past 4 o'clock, without further invitation.

Died, at Marietta, on the 29th ult. Return J. Meigs, late Postmaster General of the United States.

Died, at Clarkburg, (Va.) on the 28th ult. John G. Jackson, Esq. Judge of the U. S. Court for the Western District of Virginia.

Issue of April 21, 1825

Died - The friends and acquaintances of Sebastien Aimer, and John Nouga, are invited to attend the funeral of the latter from No. 201, East-Bay, tomorrow morning, at 8 o'clock.

Issue of April 22, 1825

Married, on Tuesday evening, by the Rev. Mr. M'Dowell, William Ashley, Esq. of Telfair County, (Georgia) to Miss Mary Jane H. Morford, of Princeton, (New Jersey).

Issue of April 23, 1825

Died - The friends and acquaintances of Mrs. Mary M'Lean and of Mr. and Mrs. A. M. Burke, are invited to attend the funeral of their son William Howie, tomorrow morning, at 8 o'clock, from their residence Meeting Street.

Issue of April 25, 1825

Died, at Baltimore, on 18th inst. Lieutenant Joseph Wrange, of the U.S.N. in the 36th year of his age, after a lingering illness of a pulmonary disease.

Died - The friends and acquaintances of Mrs. Rebecca Swain, and Mrs. Hussy, are requested to attend the funeral of the former, from her late residence No. 7, Stoll's Alley, tomorrow afternoon, 26th inst. at 4 o'clock, without further invitation.

Issue of April 30, 1825

Died - The friends and acquaintances of the late Mr. William W. Fell, are invited to attend his funeral this afternoon, at 5 o'clock, from his late residence, upper end of Tradd-Street, without further invitation.

Issue of May 6, 1825

Died, at New York, on the 27th ult. Walter Hughes, late of the Charleston Theatre.

Died, at Henrietta, Monroe County, on the 11th inst. Maj. John R. Bell, a highly esteemed and meritorious officer of the United States Army, aged about 40 years...

Died, on Wadmalow Island on the 27th ult. William Micah Jenkins in the 26th year of his age...

Died - The friends and acquaintances of Mr. William and Mrs. Elizabeth Burn, and Mr. and Mrs. Hill; also, the Members of the German Lutheran Church, are invited to attend the funeral of Mrs. Elizabeth Burn, this afternoon, at 4 o'clock, from the residence of Mrs. Francis C. Hill, No. 7 Clifford-Street, without further invitation.

Issue of May 9, 1825

Died - The friends and acquaintances of William Singleton, Esq. and of Gen. Youngblood, are invited to attend the funeral of the former, from the house of the latter, in Vanderhorst-Street, Radcliffeborough, this afternoon, at 5 o'clock. The gentlemen of the bar are respectfully invited to attend.

Issue of May 12, 1825

Died - The friends and acquaintances of the late Mrs. M'Farlane, are requested to attend her funeral this afternoon, at 4 o'clock, from her late residence in State-Street.

Issue of May 13, 1825

Married, last evening, by the Rev. Mr. Henry, Mr. Wm. McCollough, of this city, to Miss Nancy, daughter of Mr. Wm. Stilley, lately of Ireland.

Issue of May 16, 1825

Departed this transitory life on Thursday, the 5th inst. in the 31st year of her age, Mrs. Elizabeth Burn, consort of Mr. William Burn...(Eulogy)

Issue of May 19, 1825

Died - The friends and acquaintances of Mr. Thomas Folker, also of Mrs. Folker, Sen. are invited to attend the funeral of the former, from his late residence corner of Elliott and Church-Streets, tomorrow afternoon, at 4 o'clock.

Issue of May 21, 1825

Married, at Boston, on the 9th inst. at St. Paul's Church, by the Right Rev. Bishop Griswold, Allen Lambard, Esq. of Charleston, S.C. to Miss Sybil Angier Farnham, of Boston.

Married, in England, the Earl of Clanricade, to Harriett, only daughter of the Right Honorable George Canning.

Died, at Baltimore, on the 13th inst. after a lingering illness, John Warner, Esq. late Commercial Agent of the United States at Havana, aged 52 years.

Issue of June 1, 1825

Died, at Philadelphia, Thomas Drayton, Esq. of Charleston.

Issue of June 11, 1825

Died - The friends and acquaintances of the late Mr. Suetonious H. Lawton, are respectfully invited to attend his funeral this afternoon, at 5 o'clock, from No. 44 Tradd-Street.

Issue of June 16, 1825

Died, on Thursday last, of the county fever, in the prime of life, Mr. Anthony Rodericks, a native of the state of New York.

Died - The relatives, friends and acquaintances of Mr. Felix Long, and Mrs. Maria Long, and also the Congregation of the Second Presbyterian Church, are invited to attend the funeral of Mrs. Long, from her late residence, King-Street Road, tomorrow morning at 8 o'clock, without further invitation.

Issue of June 20, 1825

Died - The friends and acquaintances of the late Col. John C. Prioleau, are invited to attend his funeral this afternoon, at 4 o'clock, from the residence of Dr. Philip Gendron Prioleau, corner of George and Meeting-Streets, without further invitation.

Issue of June 21, 1825

...the Reverend and truly beloved John Summerfield, breathed his last at about eleven o'clock this morning...in the 27th year of his age...(Eulogy)

Daniel D. Tompkins, late Vice-President of the United States, is no more. He expired on Saturday, after a long and painful illness, at his residence on Staten Island, in the 51st year of his age...(Eulogy)

Died - The friends and acquaintances of Mr. and Mrs. Barbant, are respectfully invited to attend the funeral of their child, at 6 o'clock, p.m. from their residence King-Street, opposite Black Bird Alley.

Issue of June 22, 1825

Died - The friends and acquaintances of Mr. John Diamond, are respectfully requested to attend his funeral this afternoon, at 5 o'clock, without further invitation, from his late residence at Johnston's Waggon Yard, King Street road.

Issue of June 27, 1825

Died, on Saturday, 25th inst. Arnoldus Vanderhost, Esq. in the 52d year of his age.

Issue of June 29, 1825

Married, on the 23d April, at the Abbey Church, Bath, England, Mr. Henry Tanton, ninety-five years of age, to Mrs. H. Galton, aged forty-seven...

Died, in this city, on the 19th inst. of county fever, Col. John Cordes Prioleau, in the 53d year of his age...

Died, in this city on Thursday 23d inst. after a painful illness of 9 days, which she bore with pious resignation to the will of her creator, Mary Lindsey, in the 14th year of her age...

Died, in Camden, S.C. Henry Dunkins, recently from Columbia County, N.Y. aged about 23.

Issue of June 30, 1825

Died, suddenly at Baltimore on the 23d inst. Gen. John Stricker, President of the Bank of Baltimore...

Issue of July 1, 1825

Married, last evening, by the Rev. Mr. Bachman, Mr. John C. Sigwald, to Miss Eliza Baker.

Issue of July 2, 1825

Died, in Paris, on the 2d May, Dr. Adam Seybert of Philadelphia, formerly a Representative in Congress and the author of the work upon the statistics of the United States, which has been so much approved.

Died, lately, in Illinois, Morris Birkbeck, Esq. of New Albion. Mr. B. drowned in crossing a brance of the Wabash on his return from a visit to Mr. Owen, at New Harmony.

Issue of July 5, 1825

Married, at Philadelphia, on the evening of the 24th ult. Mr. Barrett, late of the Charleston Theatre, to Mrs. Henry (formerly Mrs. Drummond, of the Charleston Theatre) and at present of the New York Theatre.

Died, on the 11th ult. Gen. Hugh Means, of Union District, in the 74th year of his age.

Died, on the 28th ult. near Yorkville, Mr. John H. Hayne, son of the late Col. Hayne.

Issue of July 6, 1825

Died, in Beaufort, South Carolina, on the 23d May last, after a long and painful indisposition, the Rev. Mason L. Weems, of Dumfries, Va. well known as the author of the life of Washington, and various other popular works.

Issue of July 7, 1825

Died, at Marchmont, near Quebec, 19th ult. in the 76th year of his age, the Right Rev. Jacob Mountain, D.D. Lord Bishop of Quebec. His Lordship was the first Bishop of this Diocese, to which he was consecrated in the year 1793.

Died - The friends and acquaintances of Boyce & Henry, are invited to attend the funeral of Sarah Eliza, daughter of George and Eliza Henry, from their residence King Street, at half past five o'clock.

Issue of July 13, 1825

Died - The friends and acquaintances of Mrs. Rebecca Martin, Paul S. H. Lee, and his wife Mrs. Jane E. Lee, are requested to attend the funeral of the latter from the residence of the Rev. John Bachman, in Cannonsborough, at 5 o'clock, this afternoon, without further invitation.

Issue of July 14, 1825

Died - The friends and acquaintances of John J. Mauger, Esq. and the Members of the Bar, are requested to attend his funeral this afternoon, at 5 o'clock, from his late residence at the corner of Meeting and Water Streets.

Issue of July 15, 1825

With the deepest feelings of regret, (says the Philadelphia Aurora of the 7th inst.) we have to announce, this day, the death of the revolutionary soldier and patriot, the venerable Thomas Leiper, of this city, in the 80th year of his age...(Eulogy)

Issue of July 16, 1825

(Died)...Mrs. Jane E. Lee, the amiable wife of Paul S. H. Lee, Esq. of this city, whose death occured on the 12th inst....Scarcely had she reached 32 years...(Eulogy)

Issue of July 25, 1825

Died - The friends and acquaintances of Mrs. Eliza Y. Thomson, of Mrs. Margaret Stock, and Mrs. Mary Mazyck, are invited to attend the funeral of the former from her late residence No. 12 Water Street, this afternoon, at 5 o'clock.

Issue of July 27, 1825

Died - The friends and acquaintances of Mr. and Mrs. Campbell, are invited to attend the funeral of their daughter Mary, at their residence, South Bay, tomorrow morning, at 8 o'clock.

Issue of July 28, 1825

...We have to lament the loss of Mrs. Amelia Henry...for she departed this life without a struggle, and on the morning of the 25th June, she ceased being numbered among the living...being then in the 71st year of her age...(Eulogy)

Issue of July 29, 1825

Died - The friends and acquaintances of August Danti, and particularly the Members of the French Society, are requested to attend his funeral from No. 87 Anson Street, this afternoon at 5 o'clock, without further invitation.

Issue of July 30, 1825

Died, at Andover, (Mass.) Miss Sarah Poor, aged 22....(Eulogy)

Issue of August 1, 1825

Died - The friends and acquaintances of the late Mr. Philip Crask, his Masonic Brethern, and the Members of the Charleston Mechanic Society, are invited to attend his funeral from his late residence in Pinckney Street, tomorrow morning, at 7 o'clock, without further invitation.

Issue of August 4, 1825

Died, in Cincinnati, Ohio, on Sunday week, 10th July, Mr. John Jackson, in the eighty-seventh year of his age. He was a native of Waterford, in Ireland, and came to America in 1773.

Issue of August 4, 1825

Died - The friends and acquaintances of Mr. and Mrs. John Bull, and of the family generally, are requested to attend the funeral of Mrs. Bull, from her late residence corner of Market and State Streets, this afternoon, at 5 o'clock, without further invitation.

Died - The friends and acquaintances of Mr. John M. Frazer and family, are requested to attend the funeral of Mr. D. Murray, late of Abbeville District, from the residence of the former, No. 10, Laurens Street, this afternoon, at 5 o'clock.

Issue of August 8, 1825

Died - The friends and acquaintances of Mr. and Mrs. David Alexander are invited to attend the funeral of the latter, from her late residence, No. 7, Logan Street, this afternoon, at 5 o'clock.

Issue of August 11, 1825

Died - The friends and acquaintances of the late Mrs. Ann Marr are respectfully invited to attend her funeral without further invitation tomorrow morning, at 8 o'clock, a.m. from her late residence, No. 14, Church Street continued.

Issue of August 17, 1825

Died - The friends and acquaintances of Mr. John Lewis, and the Members of the Marine Society, are invited to attend his funeral tomorrow morning at 7 o'clock, from his late residence, corner of East Bay and Market Street.

Issue of August 19, 1825

Died - On the evening of the 6th inst. in the 56th year of her age, departed this life, Theodoria, wife of James King, Planter...(Eulogy)

Died - The friends and acquaintances of Miss Virginia Pohl, and of Mr. and Mrs. Pohl, are invited to attend the funeral of the former this afternoon, at 5 o'clock, from the house of Mr. Pohl, No. 95 Market Street.

Issue of August 22, 1825

Died, on the 9th inst. John Utt, a native of N. York, and formerly of the Charleston Theatre.

Issue of August 24, 1825

(Died)...Mrs. Mary Ann Dewes, nearly 82 years....(Eulogy)
Died, in Camden on the 19th inst. Mr. Wm. Rhodes, aged 31.
Died, in Camden, on the 15th, Mr. Simon Fraser, Merchant.
Died, in Camden, on the 18th, Mr. John McDougal, aged 27.
Died, in Camden, on the 17th, Mrs. Maria Fisher, aged 115.
Died, at the Sandhills, Mr. Zachariah Cantey, eldest son of Gen. Cantey.
Died, at his residence in Fairfield, on the 19th, Mr. John Irvin, aged 30.

Issue of August 26, 1825

Died - The Reverend the Clergy, the Members of the Baptist Church and Congregation, the Members of the Bible and Tract Societies, the members of the Revolution Society, his friends and acquaintances, and the citizens generally, are invited to attend the funeral of the late Rev. Dr. Furman, from No. 100, Church Street, at 4 o'clock this afternoon.

Issue of August 27, 1825

Died - The friends and acquaintances of Mr. and Mrs. Francis Coffin, are requested to attend the funeral of the former, tomorrow morning, at 7 o'clock from the house of Mrs. Muir, in Broad Street.

Issue of August 29, 1825

(Died)...Rev. Dr. Richard Furman...(Eulogy)

Issue of August 31, 1825

Died - The friends and acquaintances of Mr. and Mrs. Francis L. Kennedy, are invited to attend the funeral of the former from his late residence, No. 125, King Street, tomorrow morning, at 7 o'clock, without further invitation.

Issue of September 1, 1825

Married, at Oyster Bay, Long Island, N. York, by the Rev. Mr. Fowler, Mr. Thomas Hilson, to Miss Eleanor Augusta Johnson, both of New York Park Theatre.

Departed this life in Upper Peru, J. B. Prevost, Esq. late Minister to South America.

Issue of September 3, 1825

Died, on the 24th inst. in Burlington, (N.J.) Robert Hazlehurst, in the 71st year of age, after a lingering illness. He was a resident in Charleston, S.C. for upwards of forty years.

Issue of September 7, 1825

Died, at Mobile, 15th August, David Sims of South Carolina aged 37 years

Issue of September 8, 1825

Died, at Grahamville, in the state of South Carolina, on the 27th of the last month, the Rev. John Carr, in the 72d year of his age.

Issue of September 12, 1825

Died - The friends and acquaintances of Mr. Benjamin Richardson Porter, those of his family, and particularly the Members and Congregation of the Baptist Church, are respectfully invited, (without further invitation) to attend his funeral at 9 o'clock, tomorrow morning, from his late residence, No. 14, Water Street.

Issue of September 13, 1825

Died, on the 19th ult. at his residence in Pendleton District, after a short and painful illness, Major Michael Dickson, in the ninety-fifth year of his age. Major D. was a revolutionary soldier.

Died, on the 31st ult. Miss Lucia, daughter of Capt. Robert Campbell, of Marlborough C.H.

Died, on the 31st ult. Mr. Wm. Bristow, Clerk of the Court of that District. (Marlborough C.H.) And on the 1st inst. his wife Stafia, both of bilious fever,

Issue of September 15, 1825

Died, on the 8th inst. Benjamin Simmons Hort, after a short illness of four days, in the 34th year of his age...(Eulogy)

Issue of September 22, 1825

Died, at New York, on the 12th inst. William Clarkson, Esq. of this city, in the 65th year of his age.

Issue of September 23, 1825

Died - The friends and acquaintances of James Rogers, Printer, are invited to attend his funeral this afternoon, from the residence of Mrs. Scott, corner of State and Ament Streets, without further invitation.

Issue of September 27, 1825

Died, on Monday, the 12th inst. at his seat of Eastern View, in the country of Rauguier, Colonel Robert Randolph, in the 65th year of his age ...(Eulogy)

Issue of September 28, 1825

Died – It is with painful emotions that we record the death of William Cummens, Esq. Counsellor at law, who departed this life at Coosawhatchie, (St. Luke's Parish) on Thursday the 22d inst. in the 29th year of his age ...(Eulogy)

Issue of September 30, 1825

(Died)...William Clarkson, Esq. Merchant of this city, who died at New York on the 12th inst. aged 65 years...(Eulogy)

Issue of October 1, 1825

Departed this life, on board the ship Sarah & Caroline, from Liverpool to this port, Samuel McNeel, Esq. many years a respectable Merchant of this city.

Departed, this life on Wednesday, the 14th September, after a painful illness of three days, in the 47th year of his age, James Swinton, Esq. of St. Paul's Parish.

Issue of October 3, 1825

Died – The friends and acquaintances of Mrs. Jane Welsh, and also of Mr. Edward Welsh, are respectfully invited to attend the funeral of the former, at half past 4 o'clock, this afternoon, from her late residence No. 2 Logan Street, without further invitation.

Issue of October 4, 1825

Died at Columbia, S.C. 26th ult. Mr. Patrick McElroy, a native of Ireland, aged 67.
Died, in Newberry District, Dr. Isreal Whippll, aged 37.
Died, in Anson County, (N.C.) Dr. John King.
Died, in Robeson County, (NC) Mr. Archibald McNeill, aged 35.

Issue of October 5, 1825

Died – The friends and acquaintances of Mrs. Sarah Johnson, and of her family, are invited to attend her funeral from her late residence No. 22, Society Street, at half past 3 o'clock, this afternoon.

Issue of October 7, 1825

Died, at Yorkville, S.C. 23d ult. Thomas McKee, Esq.
Died, at Yorkville, S.C. 25th ult. Jos. Gabbie, Sen.
Died, at Yorkville, S.C. 25th ult. Hugh Watson, aged 51 years.
Died, at Yorkville, S.C. Mr. David N. Peters, aged 23 years.
Died, at Barnstead, (N.H.) Stephen Pickering, 86...
Died, in the alms-house at Elliot, (Me.) Mrs. Hannah Smart, aged 103 years and 4 months...

Issue of October 10, 1825

Married, at Blackburn, (England) John Clegg, aged 72, who has been blind for upwards of ten years, to Jane Ainsowrth, (who is deaf as a post) aged 52 years...

Issue of October 14, 1825

Died – The friends and acquaintances of Mrs. Ann Coram (widow of the late Mr. Thomas Coram) and the Commissioners of the Orphan House, are invited to attend her funeral from her residence in Queen Street, tomorrow morning, at 8 o'clock.

Issue of October 18, 1825

Died, in Richland District, (S.C.) on the 30th inst. John Howell, Esq.
Died, in Chester District, on the 29th August, Mrs. Sophia Thompson, aged 46.
Died, at Barnwell, (C.H.) on the 2d inst. Dr. Hamilton.

Issue of October 21, 1825

Married, last evening, by the Rev. Dr. Gadsden, Mr. John Hume, Jun. to Miss Henrietta, third daughter of Mr. William Mazyck.
Died, on board the ship Galatea, of Boston, on her voyage from this port, for the Texel, Capt. John Goldthwaite, commander of said ship, a native of Boston.

Issue of October 22, 1825

Died – The friends and acquaintances of Mr. and Mrs. John Billings, are invited to attend the funeral of the former, from his late residence in Chambers Street, tomorrow afternoon, at 4 o'clock, without further invitation.

Issue of October 26, 1825

Married, on the 17th instant, at St. Paul's Church, New York, by the Rev. Mr. Schraeder, John L. Wilson, Esq. of South Carolina, to Miss Rebecca Eden, of that city.

Issue of October 29, 1825

Died – The friends and acquaintances of the late Mr. Morton Brailsford, and Mrs. Harriet Paine, are invited to attend the funeral of the former, tomorrow afternoon, at 4 o'clock, from the house of Captain Paine, No. 55, East Bay.

Issue of November 4, 1825

Died – The friends and acquaintances of Mr. Jacob Sass, also his sons Edward, George, and W.H. Sass, together with the Members of the German Friendly and Franklin Library Societies, are requested to attend the funeral of the latter, from his father's residence No. 79, Queen Street, tomorrow morning, at 9 o'clock, without further invitation.

Issue of November 5, 1825

Died – The friends and acquaintances of Mr. Francis Bevin, and Mr. Richard Smallwood, are invited to attend the funeral of the former, from the residence of the latter, on Pritchard & Knox's Wharf, tomorrow afternoon, at half-past 4 o'clock, without further invitation.

Issue of November 7, 1825

Died – The friends and acquaintances of the late Mr. Henry Conway, and the Members of the Roman Catholic Church of Charleston, are requested to attend his funeral from his late residence, at 4 o'clock this afternoon, corner of Church Street and Elliott, without further invitation.

Issue of November 8, 1825

Died, in Columbia, S.C. on the 30th ultimo, Robert L. Green, M.D. son of Dr. Samuel Green, aged 28 years.
Died, in Fairfield District, on the 12th ult. Mrs. Isabella Turner, consort of William A. Turner.
Died, in Laurens district, on the 30th ultimo, of a typhus fever,

Miss Esther B. Smith, in the beauty and bloom of life, aged about 19 years.

Died, at Pensacola, on the 23d of September, Geo. B. Brent, formerly of Virginia...(Married on the same day)...to Miss Merced A. Gonzalez, by the Rev. Mr. Maenhaut of the Catholic Church...

Died, at York, Me. Hon. David Sewall late Judge of the U.S. District Court, aged 90 years.

Issue of November 12, 1825

Died - The relatives and acquaintances of Mr. Thomas Elfe, Sen. are respectfully invited to attend his funeral, tomorrow at 12 o'clock, from his late residence No. 2, Liberty Street, without further invitation.

Issue of November 18, 1825

Died, at Boston, on the 4th inst. the Hon. William Gray, in the 75th year of his age, late Lieutenant Governor of the Commonwealth, and one of our most respected and venerable citizens...(Eulogy)

Issue of November 19, 1825

Died - The friends and acquaintances of the late Mrs. Margaret Cross, and also of her son Mr. Adam Cross, are respectfully invited to attend the funeral of his mother, from the house of Mr. A. LeBarben, No. 90, King Street, tomorrow, at twelve o'clock precisely, without any further invitation.

Issue of November 21, 1825

Died - The friends and acquaintances of Thomas and Robert Hunt are invited to attend the funeral of the latter from his late residence Meeting, near George Street, at 4 o'clock, this evening.

Issue of November 22, 1825

Died, at Northampton, Massachusetts, on the 3d inst. after a short illness, the Hon. Jonathan H. Lyman, for many years a member of the Senate and House of Representatives.

Died - The friends and acquaintances of George Platt, are invited to attend the funeral of his brother Samuel, at 4 o'clock, this afternoon, from the residence of the former, No. 16 Broad Street.

Issue of November 23, 1825

Died, suddenly, at Walterborough, on the 12th inst. General William Oswald, aged 48 years...(Eulogy)

Died - The friends and acquaintances of Capt. Saml. B. Graves, and also of Mr. Samuel Chadwick, Masters and Officers of vessels and the Members of the Charleston Marine Society, are invited to attend the funeral of the former, at 4 o'clock, this afternoon, from Mrs. Greniker's Charleston Coffee House, No. 83 East Bay.

Issue of November 24, 1825

Died - The friends and acquaintances of Mr. and Mrs. Hinson are invited to attend the funeral of their son Mitchell Hinson, from his late residence No. 11, Berresford Street, at 4 o'clock this afternoon, N.B. The Congregation of the Lutheran Church are also invited to attend.

Issue of November 26, 1825

Married, on Thursday evening last, by the Rev. Mr. Gilman, Stephen Lee, Esq. to Caroline, second daughter of William Lee, Esq. both of this city.

Issue of November 28, 1825

Died, at New York, on the 23d inst. John A. Westervelt aged 18, son of the late Aaron J. Westervelt.

Issue of November 29, 1825

(Died)...Dr. Corbett, cut off in the twenty-fifth year of his life...
(Eulogy)

Issue of December 1, 1825

Married, on Tuesday evening last, by the Rev. Mr. McEncroe, Mr. Joseph
S. Munro, (of New York) to Miss Mary Caroline, daughter of C.G.A. LaCoste,
Esq. of this city.

Issue of December 3, 1825

Departed this life on the 19th inst. Dr. William S. Stevens, in the 68th
year of his age...(Eulogy)
Died - The friends and acquaintances of Mr. C. H. Miot, and Mrs. Eleanor
P. Miot, are invited to attend the funeral of their child tomorrow morning,
at 9 o'clock, without further invitation, from the corner of King and
Society Streets.

Issue of December 16, 1825

Died, on the 4th inst. after a few days illness, Mrs. Sarah Hart,
consort of Mr. N. H. Hart, in the 20th year of her age...

Issue of December 17, 1825

Departed this transitory life on Friday 18th November, Mrs. Margaret
Crop, aged 49 years...
Died - The friends and acquaintances of Mrs. Catharine Rush, are
respectfully invited to attend her funeral tomorrow morning, at 12 o'clock,
from her late residence in Meeting Street, without further invitation.

Issue of December 20, 1825

Died, on the 16th inst. 30 years of age, after a long and painful illness,...Mrs. Rachel J. Westendorff, consort of C. P. L. Westendorff, of
this place...(Eulogy)

Issue of December 22, 1825

Died, at Philadelphia on Sunday evening, Col. S. B. Archer, Inspector
General of the Army of the United States.

Issue of December 24, 1825

Married, in N. York, on the 17th inst. by the Right Rev. Bishop Hobart,
Archibald Gracie, Jun. to Elizabeth Davidson, daughter of the late Angus
Bethune, Esq. of Charleston, S.C.

Issue of December 27, 1825

Married, on Sunday evening, by the Rev. Mr. Buist, Mr. William J.
Vincent, of Petersburg, Va. to Caroline Laura, daughter of Mr. Samuel Corrie,
of this city.

Issue of December 28, 1825

Married, on Monday evening, the 26th inst. by the Right Rev. Bishop
Bowen, Mr. Jno. Crawford, to Miss Margaret Bay, daughter of the Hon. E. H.
Bay.

Issue of December 29, 1825

Died, in St. John's Parish, Berkley, on the 17th inst. Edward Harleston, Esq. in the 65th year of his age.

Married, on Sunday evening, the 25th inst. by the Rev. Mr. Bachman, Mr. John Lloyd to Miss Ann Rebecca Brown, of this city.

Issue of January 3, 1826

Died - The friends and acquaintances of the late Henry S. Cuhun, are invited to attend his funeral tomorrow afternoon, at 3 o'clock, from the residence of Mrs. Elizabeth Wyatt, No. 173, Church-Street, without further invitation.

Issue of January 6, 1826

Married, on Thursday evening last, by the Rev. Mr. Bachman, Mr. John Oeland, of Spartanburgh, S.C. to Mrs. Catherine L. Faber, of this city.

Died - The friends of Mr. James Black and of Mr. James Adger are requested to attend the funeral of Mrs. Black, tomorrow morning, at 11 o'clock, from the residence of Mr. Black, No. 2, Hasell-Street.

Issue of January 10, 1826

Died, after a short but painful illness, on the 3d inst. Mr. Henry S. Cuhun, aged 29 years...

Issue of January 11, 1826

Died - The relations and friends of Dr. Horatio S. Waring, and Henrietta Waring, are requested to attend the funeral of their daughter Mary, from their residence in Wentworth Street, at 5 o'clock, this afternoon.

Issue of January 14, 1826

Departed this life, on the 13th Dec. the Reverend Doctor S. F. Gallagher a native of Ireland, aged 69 years...

Issue of January 16, 1826

Died, on the 6th inst. Mr. William Kershaw, late of the Firm of Messrs. Kershaw, Lewis & Co.

Issue of January 23, 1826

Died - The friends and acquaintances of Major Nathaniel Cudworth; and family, are invited to attend his funeral from Mrs. Gray's residence, No. 3, Pinckney-Street at half-past 3 o'clock, this afternoon.

Issue of January 24, 1826

Departed this life, on the 15th inst. at his plantation at Haddrell's Point, in Christ Church Parish, William Hort, Esq. at the advanced age of 77 years...(Eulogy)

Died - The friends and acquaintances of Mr. John Kennedy, and of Mrs. Kennedy, are requested to attend the funeral of the latter tomorrow morning at 9 o'clock from her late residence in Butcher's Row, Cannonborough, without further invitation.

Issue of January 26, 1826

Died - The friends and acquaintances of Capt. James M. Elford, Mrs. Elford, and Joseph Enslow; also, the Charleston Marine, Charleston Port, and St. Andrew's Societies, are requested to attend the funeral of the former tomorrow, at 3 o'clock, p.m. from his late residence on East Bay.

Issue of January 28, 1826

Died, in this city, very suddenly, on Wednesday evening last, Capt. James M. Elford, for many years past a respectable Ship Master and citizen of Charleston...(Eulogy)

Issue of January 28, 1826

Died, in Charleston on the 16th inst. after a lingering illness, full of suffering, Theodore Gourdine, Senior, in the 62d year of his age...

Issue of January 30, 1826

Married, on Wednesday evening, the 25th inst. Mr. David C. Levy, to Maria, daughter of Mr. I. C. Moses--both of this city.

Died - The friends and acquaintnaces of Mr. William Cudworth, and family; also of Mr. John Cudworth, are invited to attend the funeral of the former from his late residence, No. 39 Wall-Street, tomorrow afternoon, at half past 3 o'clock, without further invitation.

Issue of February 1, 1826

Departed this life on the 1st Dec. last, Mr. J. W. Levy, in the 27th year of his age, much lamented by his relatives and friends.

Married, at Norfolk on the 25th ult. by the Rev. Mr. Sexias, Philip I. Cohen, Esq. to Miss Augusta, daughter of Moses Myers, ESq.

Died - The friends and acquaintances of Mr. Robert Collins, are invited to attend his funeral from his late residence corner of Amen and Church Streets, tomorrow morning, at 10 o'clock, without further invitation.

Issue of February 4, 1826

Died - The relatives, friends and acquaintances of Mr. James S. Hopkins, and of Henry and Arthur H. O'Hara, are invited to attend the funeral of the former from No. 20 King Street, at 9 o'clock precisely, tomorrow morning.

Issue of February 7, 1826

Died - The friends and acquaintances of Mr. Michael Cornelios, are invited to attend his funeral tomorrow afternoon, at 3 o'clock, from his late residence No. 17 Elliot-Street, without further invitation.

Issue of February 8, 1826

Died - The friends and acquaintances of the late Francis Kinloch, Esq. are invited to attend his funeral tomorrow, at 11 o'clock, at the house of his daughter Mrs. Keating Lewis Simons, in Orange-Street, without further invitation.

Issue of February 15, 1826

Died...Francis Kinloch, was born in the year 1756, and in Charleston... (Eulogy)

Died, on the 9th inst. in Hamburg, S.C. Capt. Richard Lubock, after an illness of several weeks, which he bore with great patience and fortitude.

Issue of February 25, 1826

Died - The friends and acquaintances of the late Mrs. Margaret Denoon, of her family, and of C. Douglas, are requested to attend the funeral of the former, from the residence of the latter, this afternoon at 4 o'clock, without further invitation.

Issue of February 28, 1826

Married, on the 25th ult. in Nassau County, (East Florida) Mr. Albert F. Roux, of this city, to Miss Sarah Starret, eldest daughter of the late George Starret, Planter, deceased.

Departed this life on Sunday the 19th inst. Elizabeth Markey, infant daughter of John Markey, of this city, aged ten months and ten days... (Eulogy)

Issue of March 4, 1826

Died - The friends and acquaintances of Mr. and Mrs. Alexander Hender-son, and the Members of the American Friendly Association, are invited to attend the funeral of the former from his late residence No. 84 Queen Street, this afternoon, at 4 o'clock, without further invitation.

Issue of March 10, 1826

Departed this life on the 2d inst. Thomas Loughton Smith Ramsey, the eldest son of Dr. John Ramsey, just on the treshod of manhood, having completed his 21st year...

Issue of March 11, 1826

Married, on Thursday evening last, by the Rev. Dr. Gadsden, Frederick J. Fraser, Esq. to Isabella Elliott, daughter of Dr. Richard B. Scriven.

Issue of March 13, 1826

Married, on Wednesday evening the 8th inst. Mr. Isaac Soria, (of New York) to Miss Hetty, daughter of Mr. Moses Cohen, of this city.

Issue of March 21, 1826

Died - The friends and acquaintances of Mr. William Halsall, and the Members of the Fellowship Society are requested to attend his funeral, from his late residence in Vanderhorst's Street, tomorrow, at 4 o'clock, p.m. without further invitation.

Issue of March 29, 1826

Died, at New York on the 20th inst. in the 78th year of his age, Don. Thomas Stoughton...

Issue of March 30, 1826

Died - The friends and acquaintances of Mrs. Mary Collins, her son John Collins, and those of William Holmes, and Lady, are respectfully invited to attend the funeral of the former from her late residence Hasell-Street, tomorrow morning, at nine o'clock, without further invitation.

Died - The friends and acquaintances of Bernard Mulligan, and those of John Mulligan, Sen. and John Mulligan, Jun. are invited to attend the funeral of the former, from his late residence Black-Street, this afternoon, at 5 o'clock.

Issue of March 31, 1826

Married last evening, by the Rev. Dr. Gadsden, Ephraim Harrison, Esq. of Nassau County, in East Florida, Planter, to Miss Henrietta Ann, eldest daughter of Lewis Rouxi, Esq. of this city.

Issue of April 3, 1826

Married, on Wednesday evening last, by the Rev. Alston Gibbs, Robert Q. Pinckney, Esq. to Miss Martha S. eldest daughter of Bartholomew Gaillard, Esq. both of this city.

Married, on Wednesday evening last, by the Rev. Alston Gibbs, Henry Mazyck, Esq. to Miss Susan D. second daughter of Bartholomew Gaillard, Esq. both of this place.

Issue of April 6, 1826

Died - The friends and acquaintances of Mr. and Mrs. Hugh Smith, and his mother Mrs. John Smith and the Members of St. Andrews, South Carolina and Charleston Library Societies, are respectfully invited to attend the funeral of the former from his late residence 129 King-Street, at 4 o'clock tomorrow afternoon, without further invitation.

Issue of April 19, 1826

Married, on Tuesday evening the 18th inst. by the Rev. Dr. Dalcho, Thomas D. Condy, Esq. to Jane Washington, eldest daughter of the late James Hasell Ancrum, Esq. all of this city.

Issue of April 21, 1826

Died, in this city, on the 10th inst. Mrs. Florence Righton, in her 84th year...

Died, at Beaufort, in this state, on Thursday the 13th inst. of the prevailing influenza, Mr. James Bowman, Sen. in the 61st year of his age.

...Mr. A. Moore, who expired last night, will be intered this afternoon at 5 o'clock, from the residence of Mrs. Pierson, corner of East Bay and Tradd Street...

Issue of April 22, 1826

Died – The friends and acquaintances of Mr. Elisa Baker, are invited to attend his funeral, from his late residence No. 169 Meeting Street, this afternoon, at 4 o'clock, without further invitation.

Issue of April 25, 1826

Died, suddenly, on the 4th inst. Richard Brenan, Esq. in the 57th year of his age.

Issue of April 26, 1826

Married, in Barnwell District, on Sunday 2d inst. by the Rev. Henry Segrace, Mr. Walter G. Sikes, of Charleston, to Miss Catherine, daughter of Thomas Kennerly, Esq. Planter, of Barnwell District.

Issue of May 5, 1826

Died, in Florence, Alabama, March 26th of a pulmonary consumption, Mr. Edward S. Carey, aged 25 years...

Issue of May 8, 1826

Died – The Members of the Charleston Bible, and the St. Andrew's Societies, and the friends and acquaintances of George Macauley, Sen. deceased, are requested to attend his funeral from his late residence No. 96, Church Street, tomorrow afternoon, at four o'clock.

Issue of May 9, 1826

Died – The friends and acquaintances of Thomas A. and Susan Vardell, are requested to attend the funeral of their daughter Matilda Martha, from their residence, Vanderhorst Street, opposite St. Paul's Church, tomorrow morning, at 8 o'clock.

Issue of May 12, 1826

Married, on Tuesday the 9th inst. by the Rev. Christian Hanckel, Daniel C. Edwards, Esq. of Union District to Mary E. Ashe, of this city.

Issue of May 15, 1826

Died – The friends and acquaintances of Peter Laurans, are invited to attend his funeral from his late residence, George-Street, next to the corner of King-Street, tomorrow morning, at 8 o'clock, without further invitation.

Died – The friends and acquaintances of Mr. and Mrs. Palmer, and also of Mr. Geo. Fernandes, are requested to attend the funeral of their late sister, from her residence in Stoll's Alley, tomorrow afternoon, at four o'clock.

Issue of May 19, 1826

Married, on Tuesday evening last, by the Rev. Dr. Palmer, Mr. William Lloyd, to Miss Anna Louisa King, daughter of Mr. John King, of this city.

Issue of May 20, 1826

Married, at Black River (Sumter District) on Tuesday evening last, 16th inst. by the Rev. John Cousar, Mr. Samuel McClary, Merchant, of this city, to Miss Leonora, second daughter of Capt. Robert McFaddin, of the former place.

Died - The friends and acquaintances of Mr. and Mrs. Alexander Black, are invited to attend the funeral of their son, tomorrow afternoon, at half after five o'clock, from their residence 105 East Bay.

Issue of May 25, 1826

Died - The friends and acquaintances and Members of the Methodist Episcopal Church, are respectfully invited to attend the funeral of Mr. Joseph Baker, Senr. tomorrow afternoon, at 4 o'clock, from his late residence Boundary-Street.

Issue of May 26, 1826

Died, at Point Petre, in the Island of Guadaloupe, on the 5th of last month, Mr. Thomas Henry Buckly, in the 34th year of his age. He was a native of this city...

Issue of May 29, 1826

Married last evening, by the Rev. Mr. Bachman, Mr. Michael Shirer, to Miss Sarah Spindler, both of this city.

Issue of May 31, 1826

Died, at Newcastle, (Delaware) on the 21st inst. the Hon. Nicholas Van Dyke...

Issue of June 2, 1826

Died, at the Plantation of Mr. Alexander Broughton, St. John's, Berkley, on the 14th of May, William Dangerfield, in the 68th year of his age... (Eulogy)

Issue of June 5, 1826

Married, at Georgetown, D.C. on the 27th ult. by the Rev. Septimus Tustin, Major General Alexander Macomb, of the United States Army, to Mrs. Harriet B. Wilson, daughter of the Rev. Doctor Balch, Pastor of the Presbyterian Church in that place.

Issue of June 6, 1826

Died - The friends and acquaintances of Mrs. Elizabeth Ligtwood, are invited to attend her funeral tomorrow morning at 9 o'clock, from her late residence No. 18 Meeting Street.

Issue of June 10, 1826

Died, at Boston, Mrs. Sarah Bowdoin Dearborn, aged 64, wife of Gen. Henry Dearborn, and formerly wife of the Hon. James Bowdoin, deceased...

Issue of June 13, 1826

Married, on Saturday evening last, by the Rev. Mr. Bachman, Mr. William Gray to Miss Mary Brockaway, both of this city.

Issue of June 16, 1826

Died – The friends and acquaintances of Doctor George Logan, and of Mrs. Margaret W. Logan, are invited to attend the funeral of the latter, from her late residence corner of Meeting and Hasell-Streets, tomorrow morning, at nine o'clock.

Issue of June 19, 1826

Died – The friends and acquaintances of the late Mrs. Mary Knauff, and of Mr. and Mrs. Thomas Johnson, are requested to attend the funeral of the former this afternoon, at 5 o'clock, from her late residence, corner of Spring and King Streets, Charleston neck.

Issue of June 21, 1826

Died, at Edingsville on Tuesday the 13th inst. of a lingering and painful illness of some months standing, in the 28th year of her age, Mrs. Caroline Holmes, wife of Mr. James T. W. Holmes...

Issue of June 26, 1826

...Mrs. Margaret White Logan, who departed this life on the 16th inst. aged 45 years and 9 months... She was the daughter of Daniel Polk, Esq. of Sussex, Delaware, deceased and consort of Dr. Geo. Logan, of this city...

Issue of June 30, 1826

Died – The friends and acquaintances of John Marshal and of Mrs. E. S. Greenland, are requested to attend the funeral of Mrs. Martha Ann Marshall, this afternoon at 5 o'clock, at her late residence, Mary-Street in Wraggsborough.

Issue of July 1, 1826

Died, on Monday morning last the 26th June 1826, at his late residence in Beaufain Street D. William Henry Drayton, in the fortieth year of his life...

Died – The friends and acquaintances of the late Mr. Moses Andrews, and Mrs. Andrews, and Capt. Robt. S. Long and the Members of the Republican and Federalist Artillery Company, are respectfully invited to attend the funeral of the former from his late residence No. 35 Hasell Street, this afternoon, at 4 o'clock.

Issue of July 3, 1826

Died, at Vera Cruz, on the 15th May, of the prevailing fever, Dr. M. Phillips, of Philadelphia.

Issue of July 5, 1826

Died, on Saturday, the 25th ult. in Philadelphia Mrs. George Izard, in her 59th year.

Issue of July 6, 1826

...(Contained in the last Portsmouth Journal). About three weeks ago the public were informed of the deceased Nathaniel Haven, Esq. late editor of that paper. Since then three other members of the same family have died-Miss Augusta, daughter of John Haven, aged 21; Augustus Lord, aged 28, son-in-law of N. H. Haven; and Miss Clarissa, aged 21, daughter of the late Henry Haven...(Eulogy)

Died – The friends and acwuaintances of Mrs. Christiana Guy, of James Guy, and those of T. H. Robinson, are respectfully invited to attend the funeral of the former from the residence of the latter, at No. -- Wentworth Street, at 6 o'clock, this evening, without any further invitation.

Issue of July 6, 1826

Died - The friends and acquaintances of Wm. Stevens, are invited to attend his funeral this afternoon, at 4 o'clock, from his late residence No. --- Wall Street.

Issue of July 8, 1826

Departed this transitory life on the 26th ult. after a protracted illness, Mrs. Ann M'Cants Burch, in the 23d year of her age...(Eulogy)

Died - The relatives, friends, and acquaintances of Mrs. Sarah Heitman, and of Mrs. Petterson, are invited to the funeral of the former from the residence of the latter, No. 12 Bedon's Alley, tomorrow afternoon, at 4 o'clock without further invitation.

Issue of July 10, 1826

Died, on Sunday morning, the 2d inst. Capt. Jonathan Emery, in the 42d year of his age...(Eulogy)

Issue of July 12, 1826

(Died)...John Middleton...(Eulogy)

Died - The friends and acquaintances of Mr. Greneker and Mrs. Whitney are invited to attend the funeral of the adopted son of the former, from her residence 87 East Bay, at 4 o'clock this afternoon.

Issue of July 18, 1826

Died - The friends and acquaintances of Mr. and Mrs. Gibson, are invited to attend the funeral of the latter from No. 31, East Bay, tomorrow morning, at 9 o'clock.

Issue of July 19, 1826

Died - The friends and acquaintances of the late Optimus S. Dickson, and of Mr. G. P. Williams, are requested to attend the funeral of the former, without further invitation at five o'clock, this afternoon, from No. 69, Market Street.

Issue of July 24, 1826

Died, on the 23d inst. Nicholas Cruger, Esq. in the forty-eighth year of his age.

Issue of July 25, 1826

Died, at Cambridge, Mass. on the 13th inst. Mr. Rufus Bunnell, of the house of Beers & Bunnell, of New York, and Beers, Bunnell & Booth of this city.

Died - The friends and acquaintances of William M. and Maria Frazer, are invited to attend the funeral of their son James Robertson, tomorrow morning, at 8 o'clock, from No. 31, Broad Street, without further invitation.

Issue of July 26, 1826

Departed this life on Thursday the 23d ult. at the dwelling of Dr. McBride, the Rev. Wm. J. Wilson, Pastor of the Presbyterian Church in Salem, Sumpter District, S.C.

Issue of July 28, 1826

(Died)...Capt. James Kennedy, of the First Continental Regiment of the State, died on the 15th inst. after a long and painful submission to a severe and agonizing disease. He was a native of Pennsylvania, born on the 31st October, 1756...(Eulogy)

Issue of July 31, 1826

Died - The friends and acquaintances of Captain George and Mrs. Easterby, are requested to attend the funeral of their daughter Mary, this afternoon, at 5 o'clock, from their residence 87 East Bay, without further invitation.

Issue of August 9, 1826

Departed this life on Monday morning 31st ult. Mary Watson, eldest daughter of Capt. George and Mrs. Easterby, of this city, aged 6 years, 11 months and 23 days...(Eulogy)

Issue of August 11, 1826

Died on the 21st June, at Bobsavannah Plantation...Mrs. Jane Peake... and in this city on the 18th July, her sister, Mrs. Elizabeth Gibson...
Died, at his residence at Sligo, on Monday evening the 3d July Col. Henry Hampton in the 74th year of his age...(Eulogy)
Died, at Barboursville, Virginia, on Monday last, the 31st day of July, in the 76th year of her age, Mrs. Mary Barbour, mother of the Secretary of War.

Issue of August 15, 1826

Died, at Weybridge, Vermont, on the morning of the 2d inst. Mrs. Zulma Caroline Ripley, consort of Mr. William Y. Ripley, Merchant of this city.
Died - The friends and acquaintances of Mr. and Mrs. Stephen C. Wheeler, are requested to attend the funeral of their son, Samuel Holmes, from their residence No. 54, Society Street, this afternoon, at 5 o'clock, without further invitation.

Issue of August 16, 1826

Died - The friends and acquaintances of Mr. and Mrs. Crovat, are invited to attend the funeral of the latter, this afternoon, at 4 o'clock, from No. 296 King Street.
Died - The friends and acquaintances of Mr. Philip Breen, are respectfully invited to attend his funeral this afternoon, from his late residence, corner of Chalmers and Church Street, at 5 o'clock.

Issue of August 18, 1826

Died - The friends and acquaintances of Mr. and Mrs. Course, of Mr. and Mrs. Willington, and of Mr. and Mrs. Starr, are invited to attend the funeral of Mrs. Course, from her late residence, East Bay, tomorrow morning at 9 o'clock.

Issue of August 19, 1826

Died - The friends and acquaintances of Doctor and Mrs. Thomas Legare, are invited to attend the funeral of Mrs. Legare from her late residence, St. Phillip Street, tomorrow morning, at 7 o'clock.

Issue of August 22, 1826

Died in this city, on Sunday, 20th inst. Mr. Wm. Smith, (Comb maker), a native of Philadelphia...

Issue of August 24, 1826

Died on Saturday, August 19th, Mrs. Susan Legare, wife of Dr. Thomas Legare of this city...(Eulogy)

Issue of August 29, 1826

Died, at New York, on the 19th inst. of consumption, Mr. William Longley, a native of Nassau, N.P. for several years a residence of N. York, and the last three of Charleston, S.C.

Issue of August 30, 1826

Died - The friends and acquaintances of Mr. C. H. and Mrs. Mood, and also of Mrs. Knust, are requested to attend the funeral of Mrs. Mood, from the residence of Mr. Poyas, in Coming Street, tomorrow morning, at 8 o'clock without further invitation.

Issue of August 31, 1826

Married in Wayne County, N.C. on the 8th inst. by the Rev. John Howell, Mr. Hoehead Speight, of Greene County, aged 77½ years, weight 99 3/4 lbs. to Mrs. Sally Peacock, of the former county, aged 44 years, weight 333 3/4 lbs.

Issue of September 1, 1826

Died, on the 19th inst. Sampson Mordecai, Esq. in the forty-fourth year of his age...(Eulogy)

Died - The friends and acquaintances of Mr. and Mrs. James Stillman, are respectfully invited to attend the funeral of their infant son, this afternoon, at half past 4 o'clock, from No. 173, East Bay, without further invitation.

Issue of September 11, 1826

Died, at Germantown, on the 31st ult. Mrs. Mary Deas, widow of the late David Deas, Esq. of this city.

Died, on the 1st inst. at Philadelphia, Mrs. Anna Maria Walsh, aged 37 years, wife of Robert Walsh, Esq. Editor of the National Gazette.

Died on the 3d inst. the Hon. Joseph B. M'Kean, president of the District Court, for the city and county of Philadelphia, in the 63d year of his age.

Died - The friends and acquaintances of the late Capt. John Wilkie and of his brothers, Wm. B. George and Joseph and the officers and members of the Marine Society, are invited to attend his funeral this afternoon, precisely at 5 o'clock, from the residence of Wm. B. Wilkie No. 32, Church Street.

Issue of September 13, 1826

Died, on Tuesday the 15th September, 1826, at Beaufort, South Carolina, the Rev. Benjamin S. Screven, aged 43 years, 7 months, and 17 days... (Eulogy)

Departed this life on the night of the 1st inst. a few minutes before 10, Mrs. Elizabeth Ancrum, consort of William Ancrum of this town, aged 44 years and some months.

Died - The friends and acquaintances of Mr. and Mrs. Petigru, are invited to attend the funeral of their son, this afternoon, at 5 o'clock.

Issue of September 15, 1826

Died, at Cathagena, on the 9th of July, in the 25th year of his age, William Berrien, ESq. vice consul of the United States at that port, formerly of Philadelphia.

Died - The friends and acquaintances of Mr. David and Mrs. Ann Bailey, are invited to attend the funeral of the latter at 4 o'clock this afternoon, from her late residence, No. 2, Green Street, near the College, without further invitation.

Issue of September 16, 1826

Died, in Georgetown, S.C. 12th inst. Mr. William F. Brown, a native of this city.

Died - The friends and acquaintances of the late Mr. Arthur H. O'Hara, of Mrs. Henry O'Hara and of Mrs. Mary Mazyck, are requested to attend his funeral this afternoon, at 4 o'clock, from his late residence No. 20 King Street, without further invitation.

Issue of September 21, 1826

Departed this life on the 10th inst. in the 4th year of his age, George Burch, eldest son of Edward C. Burch, of this city...(Eulogy)

Issue of September 22, 1826

Departed this life at Yorkville, on the 1st inst. in the prime of life, Samuel M'Creary, Jun. Post Master at Beckhamville, aged thirty-five years and three months.

Issue of September 23, 1826

(Died) This morning after a severe illness of seven days, Col. Robert Andrew Taylor, in the 35th year of his age...
(Died) On Tuesday last, Mr. John Waldo, aged 64.
(Died) In Kingstree, on the 24th day of August last, Capt. Samuel Malcomone, aged about 55 years.
(Died) On Pee Dee, the 16th of Sept. Mrs. Margaret Hales, consort of Mr. Alexander Hales.

Issue of September 25, 1826

(Died) In Darlington District, 8th inst. Mrs. Lydia Wilson, aged 40 years.
(Died) At Darlington, C. H. 12th inst. Col. Elisha Rogers, aged 39.

Issue of September 26, 1826

(Died) In Columbia, S.C. 17th inst. Mr. James Stark, son of Robert Stark, Esq. in the 19th year of his age.
(Died) In Greenville, S.C. 14th inst. Mr. Alexander Sloan, aged 40 years.

Issue of October 3, 1826

(Died) At his seat near Baltimore, on the 26th ult. Capt. Robert Trail Spence...
(Died) In Columbia, S.C. 27th ult. Stephen W. Doane, aged 25, a native of Tennessee,
(Died) In Columbia, S.C. 27th ult. Tho. G. Reynolds, aged 26, a native of Connecticut.
(Died) In Marlborough District, S.C. Elias Jones, Jun. a native of Maine.
(Died) In Harlborough, S.C. John McFarland, aged about 65.

Issue of October 4, 1826

(Died) At Lebanon Springs, on the 22d ult. William Crafts, Esq. late of Charleston, S.C.
(Died) At Norfolk of the prevailing fever, Mr. Daniel Lyon, aged 30, of the firm of D. Lyon & Co.
(Died) At Norfolk, Capt. Eppes Spain, aged 51.

Issue of October 6, 1826

Died, at Lebanon Springs, (N.Y.) on the 22d ult....the Hon. William Crafts, of this city, in the 40th year of his age...(Eulogy)
Died, in this city, on the 2d instant in the 35th year of his age, Mr. John Goodwin, a native of Charleston, (Mass.)...(Eulogy)
Died at Norfolk, of the prevailing fever, Thos. B. Price, aged 25.
Died at Norfolk, John C. Smith, aged 22.
Died in Hampton Roads, Capt. John Winkley, of ship Eliza, of Portsmouth, N.H.
Died - The friends and acquaintances of John W. Payne, and of William Payne & Sons, are requested to attend the funeral of the former from No. 28 Broad Street, this afternoon at half past 5 o'clock, without further

invitation.

Died – Charleston Riflemen———You are ordered to assemble at the Circular Church this afternoon, at 4 o'clock properly armed and accoutred, to pay the last tribute of respect to your former Captain J. W. Payne.

Issue of October 9, 1826

Died – The friends and acquaintances of Mr. John Fitzgerald, and Mrs. Fitzgerald, are invited to attend the funeral of the former from his late residence on South Bay, tomorrow morning, at 8 o'clock. The officers and members of the Irish Volunteers, are also respectfully invited.

Issue of October 11, 1826

(Died) At Philadelphia, 3d inst. in the 64th year of his age, Mr. Wm. Purvis, of South Carolina.

(Died) On the 3d inst. at Baltimore, Miss Philadelphia Levy, aged 85 years.

Issue of October 13, 1826

Married, on Wednesday evening last, by the Rev. Gabriel Capers, Captain Samuel Wragg Capers, of Sumter District, to Miss Sarah Margaret Brandt, of this city.

Departed this life on the 5th inst. in the 33d year of his age, John William Payne, of the firm of William Payne & Sons, greatly beloved and lamented by all who knew him,

Died at his residence, near Cannellsville, Fayette County, Pa. on Thursday, 21st ult. Major Uriah Springer, in the 73d year of his age.

Died, at Morristown, N.J. on the 10th ult. in the 74th year of his age, General John Doughty...

(Died) In East Greenwich, RI on the 26th ult. William Greene, Esq. aged 83, the eldest surviving brother of Gen. Nathaniel Greene, of the Revolutionary army.

Issue of October 16, 1826

Departed this life on Tuesday last the 10th inst. Mrs. Charlotte M. Ravenel, wife of Dr. Edmund Ravenel, and eldest daughter of T. Ford, Esq. aged 30 years.

Issue of October 17, 1826

(Died) Near Darlington Court House, Mrs. Abigail Law, wife of Mr. Elias D. Law, on the 28th of September last, aged 30 years.

(Died) At Darlington Court House, on the 9th inst. Major George Bruce, aged about 58 years.

(Died) On the 9th inst. at St. Barth Parish, Colleton District, Agnes, daughter of James Sharpe, aged two years.

Issue of October 18, 1826

Married, on the evening of the 14th inst. by the Rev. Dr. Palmer, Mr. William S. King to Miss Letitia, eldest daughter of the late Capt. William Laidler, of this city.

Issue of October 19, 1826

Married, on the evening of the 17th instant by the Rev. Dr. Dalcho, Mr. Robert D. Lawrence, to Miss Hannah Ainscie, eldest daughter of Dr. Edward Brailsford, all of this city.

Issue of October 21, 1826

Married, on Thursday evening the 19th inst. by the Rev. Dr. Frederick Dalcho, Edward Frost, Esq. to Miss Harriet V. Horry, eldest daughter of Mr. Elias Horry.

Issue of October 23, 1826

Married, on Tuesday evening, the 17th inst. by the Rev. Mr. Phillips, Mr. Benj. S. Smith, Merchant, to Miss Martha Hasell, daughter of Capt. R. S. Long, all of this city.

Died - The friends and acquaintances of Mr. and Mrs. Thomas Airs, and those of John M. Frazer's family, are requested to attend the funeral of Mrs. Airs, this afternoon, at 4 o'clock, from her late residence Lauren's Street, without further invitation.

Issue of November 3, 1826

Married, at New York, on the 25th ult. by the Rev. Mr. Knox, Mr. John Clark, merchant of Rushville, New York, to Miss Olive Jackson, daughter of the late Col. Giles Jackson of Burkshire, Mass. and his twenty sixth child...

Issue of November 4, 1826

Married, on Thursday evening, the 2d inst. by the Rev. Dr. Dalcho, Colonel Nathaniel Greena Cleary to Colleton Graves daughter of the late General M'Pherson.

Issue of November 8, 1826

(Died) At New York on the 28th ult. Joshua Canter, ESq. for many years a respectable inhabitant of this city.

(Died) At New York on the 30th ult. Mr. Seth L. Cowing, of Providence, R.I. and formerly an eminent merchant of this city.

Issue of November 9, 1826

Died, in this city, on Sunday, the 22d ult. of a highly bilious fever, after a short and severe illness, Maria Haig, second daughter of Mr. David Haig, in the 22d year of her age.

Issue of November 10, 1826

Married, yesterday morning, at St. Philip's Church, by the Rev. Mr. Gibbes, Dr. John Bellinger, to Miss Mary Geraldine Northrop, only daughter of A. B. Northrop, ESq. deceased.

Died in London, on the 12th of July, in the 60th year of his age,... Robert Bell, Esq. the proprietor and Editor of Bell's Weekly Despatch...

Died - The friends and acquaintances of Mr. and Mrs. Ansley, are respectfully invited to attend the funeral of their son, tomorrow morning, at 10 o'clock, a.m. from their residence No. 19 Horlbeck's Alley.

Issue of November 11, 1826

Died - The friends and acquaintances of Mrs. Margaret Slade, and of Mr. and Mrs. Murden, are respectfully invited to attend the funeral of the former, from the residence of the latter, 110 Tradd Street, tomorrow at 12 o'clock.

Issue of November 13, 1826

Died, in this city, on Sunday, the 22d ult. of a highly bilious fever, after a short and severe illness, Maria Haig, second daughter of Mr. David Haig, in the 22d year of her age...(Eulogy)

Departed this life on the 28th day of October last, at New York, Mr. Joshua Canter, in his sixtieth year...(Eulogy)

Died - The friends and acquaintances of Mr. Christopher and Christian D. Happoldt, together with the members of the German Lutheran Church, and German Friendly Society, are requested to attend the funeral of the former, from his late residence in Cannonsborough tomorrow afternoon, at 3 o'clock.

Died - The friends and acquaintances of Mr. and Mrs. S. Chisolme, are invited to attend the funeral of their daughter, Eliza, tomorrow morning, at 9 o'clock, from the corner of King and George Streets.

Died in Eastport, on Saturday, October 21, very suddenly Mr. Henry Waide, a Revolutionary Patriot, aged 60 years...

Departed this life on the 16th ult. in the 54th year of her age, Miss Harriet Bacot, daughter of Peter Bacot, Esq. formerly of this city, merchant, deceased

Died - The friends and acquaintances of Mr. Thomas T. Purse, and of Mrs. Jennett Purse are requested to attend the funeral of the latter, from their residence No. 19, Pincknev Street, tomorrow morning, at 9 o'clock.

Died, on the 4th inst. of the country fever, Mr. John Bassnett Legare, in the 33d year of his age...

Died, of yellow fever, on the 10th of July last, in the Island of Jamiaca, Thomas Corbett Irving, in the 29th year of his age, a native of this place.

(Died)...Arthus Simpkins, on Friday the 29th Sept. 1826, at his residence, full of years.... This venerable man had nearly reached his 84th year...(Eulogy)

Died, in Greenville district, on Tuesday last, Capt. William Young, in the 67th year of his age...

Died - The friends and acquaintances of Mr. George Dalgleish, also the members of the St. Andrew's and Mechanics Societies, are respectfully invited to attend his funeral from his late residence, corner of Queen and Mazyck Streets tomorrow afternoon at half past 3 o'clock.

Married on Thursday evening 16th inst. by the Rev. Mr. Buist, Mr. Joseph B. Rivers, of James Island, to Miss Sarah Bill of this city.

Died - The friends and acquaintances of Mrs. Monefeldt, and of J. B. A. Monefeldt, are invited to attend the funeral of the latter tomorrow morning, at half past 8 o'clock, from his late residence No. 30 Hasell Street, without further invitation.

Died - The friends and acquaintances of Mr. and Mrs. Henry Wheeler, and the Baptist Congregation generally, are requested to attend the funeral of the former from his late residence, corner East Bay and William's Wharf, tomorrow afternoon, at 3 o'clock, without further invitation.

Died - The friends and acquaintances of Mr. and Mrs. Daniel Cruikshanks, and of Mr. John Ferguson, are respectfully invited to attend the funeral of W. B. Cruikshanks, from his father's residence No. 22 Queen Street tomorrow morning at 9 o'clock.

Died - The friends and acquaintances of Mr. Charles Stone and those of Mrs. Sarah Stone, also those of the Methodist Episcopal Church, are invited to attend the funeral of the latter from her late residence in King Street opposite Whim's Court, tomorrow morning at 8 o'clock precisely.

Died - The Faculty of Charleston College, and the Instructors in its Grammar School, and such members of the upper classes of the Grammar School, as may be in the city are respectfully invited to attend the funeral of Master John Blake Bowen, from the house of his father in Cannonsborough, tomorrow, at 10 o'clock a.m.

Issue of December 4, 1826

Died - The friends and acquaintances of the late Capt. Grenon, of the French ship Egle and of Pitray and Veil are invited to attend the funeral of the former precisely at 4 o'clock this afternoon, from Mrs. Picault's Queen Street.

Issue of December 13, 1826

Died - The friends and acquaintances of Wm. Dewees, his sons, and of the late Col. Phillip S. Postell, are particularly invited to attend the funeral of the latter tomorrow morning, the 14th inst. at half past 8 o'clock, from the residence of Wm. Dewees, Mazyckborough, without further invitation.

Issue of December 15, 1826

Died - The friends and acquaintances of Mrs. Eliza M'Cormick, and of Mrs. Eleanor Halliday, are invited to attend the funeral of the former from her late residence corner of East Bay and Tradd Streets, without a more particular invitation tomorrow afternoon, at half past 3 o'clock.

Issue of December 18, 1826

Died, on the 2d inst. at Milton, (Va.) Andrew Monroe, the last remaining brother of the late President of the U. States. He was a Naval officer in the Revolutionary War.

Issue of December 20, 1826

Married, on Tuesday evening, the 19th inst. by the Rev. Mr. Sheenan, Mr. Augustus Paul Trouche, to Miss Mary Caroline Poincignon, all of this city.

Died - The friends and acquaintances of Capt. Edward Johnson and of David B. Lafar, are invited to attend the funeral of the former without further invitation this afternoon, at half past 3 o'clock, from his late residence, corner of Guignard Street and Maiden Lane, No. 13.

Issue of December 21, 1826

Married, on Tuesday evening last, by the Rev. Samuel Gilman, Mr. Henry S. Tew to Miss Caroline Jane Courtenay, both of this city.

Died, at Savannah, 19th inst. Col. John L. Seabrook, of South Carolina.

Issue of December 27, 1826

Died at North Haven, (Conn.) on the 1st inst. Mrs. Amy Hull, widow of the late Benjamin Hull, aged 100 years, 5 months and 25 days...(Eulogy)

Died on the 23d Nov. Mr. Eli Sackett, aged 84.

Died at Philadelphia on 13th inst. Hannah Archer, aged upwards of 105 years...

Issue of December 28, 1826

Died, on the 2d November last, near St. George (Delaware) of a malignent fever which prevailed in that neighborhood, John Edward Eason, of this city, aged 20 years...(Eulogy)

Died - The relatives and acquaintances of Mr. William Smith, of his father, the late Capt. Peter Smith, and of his mother, Mrs. Mary M. Smith, are invited to attend the funeral of the former, from the residence of the latter, No. 4, Mazyck Street, tomorrow morning, at 9 o'clock.

Issue of December 29, 1826

Died at his Plantation on James Island on the morning of the 15th inst. Mr. Henry S. Rivers, in the 49th year of his age...

Issue of December 30, 1826

Died - The friends of the late Henry Izard, are invited to attend his funeral at his residence South Bay, tomorrow morning, at half past 8 o'clock.

Issue of January 2, 1827

Married on Wednesday evening last, 27th Dec., by the Rev. Mr. Hanckle, at Beaufort Island, Lawrence Edwin Dawson, Esq. of this city, to Miss Mary W. Rhodes, eldest daughter of the late Dr. Nath. H. Rhodes, of the former place.

Issue of January 3, 1827

Died, in Camden, S.C. on the 21st. Mr. Benjamin Harper, of Waxbaw, Lancaster District.

Died on the 24th inst. Eleanora L., eldest daughter of Lovick Young, Esq. aged 12 years and two months.

Issue of January 4, 1827

Died - The friends and acquaintances of the late Mr. P. R. Lachichotte, and of his family, are invited to attend his funeral tomorrow morning, 5th inst. at 10 a.m., without further invitation, in Wall Street, No. 11.

Issue of January 6, 1827

Died, on board the U. S. schr. Grampus, on her passage from Pensacola to Havana, on the morning of the 30th Nov., Lieut. Comd't Joseph Cassin, of the U. S. Navy...(Eulogy)

Issue of January 10, 1827

Died, in Rehoboth, 23d ult. Rev. Thomas Simmons, aged 104 years and 6 months...

Issue of January 11, 1827

Died - The friends and acquaintances of Mr. and Mrs. Louis Boudo, and of Mrs. Jane Dile, also the Masonic Brethren, of the former are invited to attend his funeral from his late residence No. 160 King Street at 4 o'clock tomorrow morning without further invitation.

Issue of January 12, 1827

Died - The friends and acquaintances of Mrs. Mary Spears, and sons, Mr. David Haig, and Mr. Thomas Price are invited to attend the funeral of the former from her late residence tomorrow morning at 9 o'clock.

Issue of January 13, 1827

Died, in this city, on Tuesday afternoon the 19th December last, Capt. Edward Johnston, aged 60. A native of England, and upwards of forty years, a resident of this place.

Died - The friends and acquaintances of Mr. Plowden Weston and the members of St. George's Society are invited to attend his funeral at his late residence Queen Street tomorrow at 12 o'clock.

Issue of January 16, 1827

Married, on Tuesday evening the 9th inst. in the village of Barnwell, by the Rev. Darling Peeples, Dr. James O. Hagood, to Miss Indiana Margaretta, daughter of the late John C. Allen, Esq. deceased, all of Barnwell District.

Issue of January 20, 1827

Died, at Springfield, (Mass.) on the 5th inst. while sitting in his chair, Harrison Gray Otis, Jr. Esq. of Boston.

Issue of January 26, 1827

Departed this life, on Sunday evening, the 31st ult. Mr. John Colhoun, aged 70 years, a native of Fort Scholosser, State of N. York, and for upwards of twenty years keeper of the Charleston Light House...(Eulogy)

Issue of January 30, 1827

On Tuesday, the 16th inst. departed this life in the 78th year of her age, Mrs. Mary Morris, relict of Robert Morris, Esq....(Eulogy)

Issue of February 2, 1827

Married, last evening, by the Right Rev. Bishop Bowen, Edward Rutledge Laurens, Esq. to Miss Margaret Horry, daughter of Elias L. Horry, Esq. all of this city.

Married, on Wednesday evening last by the Rev. Alston Gibbes, Julius G. Huguenin, Esq. of St. Luke's Parish, to Theodora Octavia, youngest daughter of the late Theodore Gaillard, Jun. Esquire of this city.

Issue of February 3, 1827

Married, on Thursday evening last, by the Rev. E. Sinclair, Mr. P. G. Bessent, of St. Mary's (Georgia), to Miss Mary Ann, second daughter of Capt. William Fair, of this city.

Died, near Stateborgh, on the 22d ult. Mrs. Sarah James, late the wife of Judge James...(Eulogy)

Issue of February 6, 1827

Died - The relatives, friends and acquaintances, of Mr. and Mrs. Wm. Bell, are invited to attend the funeral of the latter, tomorrow afternoon, at 4 o'clock, from her late residence, Society-Street, without further invitation.

Issue of February 7, 1827

Died - The friends and acquaintances of Mr. and Mrs. A. E. Miller and Mr. Richard Hart, and of Mr. John James Fowler, are respectfully requested to attend the funeral of the latter from his late residence No. 4 Broad Street, tomorrow afternoon, precisely at 4 o'clock, without further invitation.

Issue of February 14, 1827

Died, in Augusta, William Hogan, Attorney at Law, late from Charleston and formerly from Philadelphia.

Issue of February 15, 1827

Married, on Tuesday evening last by the Rev. Dr. Palmer, Charles L. Dezel, Esq. to Caroline, youngest daughter of the late Stephen Mazyck, Esq. of this city.

Issue of February 17, 1827

Died - The friends and acquaintances of Robt. Jackson, Sen. of Mr. M. A. Jackson, of Robt. Jackson, Jun. and of Wm. T. and J. B. M'Cready, are requested to attend the funeral of the former, from his late residence, King Street, near Boundary...at half past 4 o'clock, tomorrow afternoon.

Issue of February 21, 1827

Married, on the 18th inst. by the Rev. Mr. Manly, Mr. Edward Roach, to Miss Esther Ann Conyers, both of this city.

Issue of February 23, 1827

Married, last evening by the Right Rev. Bishop England, Mr. Charles Harper, of Baltimore, to Miss Charlotte H. Chiffelle, eldest daughter of Thomas P. Chiffell, Esq. of this city.

Issue of March 2, 1827

Married, on Wednesday evening last, by the Rev. Mr. A. Buist, Mr. John Denoon, to Miss Lillias Douglas.
Died - The friends and acquaintances of Mr. Martin Moult are requested to attend his funeral tomorrow morning at 10 o'clock from the Planters Hotel, Church Street.

Issue of March 6, 1827

Died, on Wednesday, 14th February, at his dwelling in Wagon Alley (Baltimore), Jacob Nurser, in his 114th year...(Eulogy)

Issue of March 12, 1827

Died - At Boston, Hon. Christopher Gore, formerly Governor of the Commonwealth of Massachusetts.
Died, at Savannah 9th inst. Alex. Hunter, Surveyor of the port.

Issue of March 14, 1827

Died - The friends and acquaintances of Mr. and Mrs. Schirer, the members of the German Friendly and Mechanic Societies, and members of Lodge No. 16, are invited to attend the funeral of John Schirer, tomorrow morning at 8 o'clock, from his late residence in Queen Street, without further invitation.

Issue of March 16, 1827

Died - The friends and acquaintances of the late Dr. Samuel Wilson, and the members of the several societies to which he was attached, are invited to attend his funeral tomorrow morning at 9 o'clock from his late residence in Archdale Street.

Issue of March 22, 1827

Departed this life, on Thursday, the 15th inst. at his residence, in Archdale Street, Dr. Samuel Wilson, after a severe and protracted illness. Dr. Wilson was born in Charleston, on the 26th January, 1763...(Eulogy)

Issue of March 23, 1827

Died, at his residence, in Washington City, on the 19th instant, Richard Bland Lee, Esq. aged 65 years.

Issue of March 24, 1827

Departed this life on the 18th instant, Mr. John Boyle, a respectable planter in St. Paul's Parish...(Eulogy)
Died in New York, 14th inst. Anthony Bleecker, Esq.

Issue of March 27, 1827

Died - The Captains of vessels now in port, the members of the Charleston Marine Society, and the friends and acquaintances of Captain Clark Tinkham, are respectfully invited to attend his funeral this afternoon, at 5 o'clock, from his late residence in Ann-Street, Mazyckborough.

Issue of March 30, 1827

Died - The friends and acquaintances of William Allan, and the members of the St. Andrews and South Carolina Societies, are invited to attend his funeral from his late residence No. 46 Tradd-Street at 4 o'clock, tomorrow afternoon, without further invitation.

Issue of April 2, 1827

Died - The friends and acquaintances of Mr. and Mrs. Peter D. Foot, also of John J. and David B. Lafar, are requested to attend the funeral of the former, from his late residence on the Bay, back of the Post Office, tomorrow afternoon, at half past 3 o'clock.

Issue of April 3, 1827

Died - The friends and acquaintances of Mr. and Mrs. James Mulligan, Mr. and Mrs. Bizeul are requested to attend the funeral of the former, from his late residence No. 26 State Street, tomorrow morning, at 9 o'clock.

Issue of April 4, 1827

Departed this life on the 2d inst. Mrs. Rachel Harby, consort of Mr. Isaac Harby, aged 45 years and 9 months...(Eulogy)
Died, at New York, 28th ult. Dr. Chever Felch...

Issue of April 6, 1827

Married, on Tuesday evening last, by the Rev. Mr. Hanckell, Mr. Benjamin S. Gibbes, to Miss Elenora, daughter of James Shoolbred, Esq. all of this city.

Issue of April 9, 1827

Died, at St. Thomas on the 20th October, 1826, of Yellow Fever...Mr. Isaac Mender Seixas, a native of this city, aged 48 years and 2 months...

Issue of April 10, 1827

Died - The friends and acquaintances of Mr. Francis Carmand, and of the late Dr. J. B. Martin, are requested to attend the funeral of the latter this evening, at four o'clock, without further invitation from his late residence, corner of Anson and Society Streets.

Issue of April 11, 1827

Married, at New York 30th ult. by the Rev. F. C. Schaeffer, Mr. H. Schultz, formerly of Hamburg, to Miss Fanny Edee, of that city.

Issue of April 18, 1827

Married, on Thursday, the 5th April, by the Rev. Mr. Buist, Oliver H. Middleton, Esq. to Susan H. daughter of the late Dr. Robert T. Chisolm, Esq. of Edisto Island.
Departed this life on the 15th ult. Mrs. Ann Collins, in the 65th year of her age...(Eulogy)

Issue of April 19, 1827

Died on the 16th of January, at St. Petersburgh, Eleanor Isabella, second daughter of Henry Middleton, Esq....(Eulogy)

Issue of April 20, 1827

Married in this city, on Thursday evening last, by the Rev. Dr. Gadsden, Peter J. Mallett, Esq. of Fayetteville, N.C. to Miss Ellenor M. DeBerriere, daughter of the late Col. DeBerriere.

Issue of April 20, 1827

Died at Liverpool on the 8th ultimo, William Molyneux, Esq. father of
A. L. Molyneux, Esq....(Eulogy)

Issue of April 25, 1827

Died at New York on the 15th inst. in the thirty fourth year of his age,
James Freeman Dana, M.D. Professor of Chemistry in the College of Physicians
and Surgeons of the University of the state of New York.

Issue of April 26, 1827

Died - The friends and acquaintances of the late Mrs. Beswicke, and of
Mr. and Mrs. John N. Thomas, are requested to attend the funeral of the
former, from the residence of the latter, No. 13, Cumberland Street, at 10
o'clock, tomorrow morning, without further invitation.

Issue of April 28, 1827

Died - The friends and acquaintances of Mr. and Mrs. Wm. Pritchard, and
of Mr. George Pritchard, are requested to attend the funeral of the latter,
from the residence of his father on Mey's Wharf, tomorrow morning, at 12
o'clock, a.m. without further invitation.

Issue of May 2, 1827

Died at New York on the 24th ult. Henry Cruger, Esq. in the 88th year
of his age.

Issue of May 8, 1827

Died at his residence, No. 518 Broadway, last evening in the 73d year
of his age, the Hon. Rufus King...(Eulogy)
Died at Philadelphia, 29th of April, the Honorable William Tilghman,
Esq. chief justice of the Supreme Court of Pennsylvania, in ths seventy first
year of his age.

Issue of May 9, 1827

Married, on Wednesday 9th inst. in Michael's Church, by the Rev. Dr.
Dalcho, Benjamin Jenkins, Esq. of St. Helena, to Miss Isabella, youngest
daughter of Thomas Chaplin, Esq. of Ladies Island.

Issue of May 10, 1827

Departed this life at Beaufort S. C. on the morning of the 4th inst.
Capt. Paul A. Cartwright, in the 75th year of his age, a native of Newport,
R. I....(Eulogy)

Issue of May 11, 1827

Died - The friends and acquaintances of the late Thomas W. Price, and
also those of his sisters and sons, are invited to attend his funeral tomorrow morning, at 9 o'clock, from the residence of Mrs. B. Skirving, corner of
Bull and Coming St. without further invitation.

Issue of May 12, 1827

Died - The friends and acquaintances of Mr. Francis and Mrs. Mary Mott,
and family, and the members of the South Carolina Society, are invited to
attend the funeral of the former from his late residence No. 34, Church
Street, tomorrow morning, at 8 o'clock precisely, without further notice.

Issue of May 19, 1827

Died...Mrs. Denorah, wife of Mr. Benjamin Gannett, died at her
residence in Sharon, Mass. on the 29th ult. aged 67...(Eulogy)

Issue of May 19, 1827

Died - The friends and acquaintances of Mr. and Mrs. George Trescot, and of Mr. and Mrs. Charles Carrere, and family, are requested to attend the funeral of Mr. George Trescot, from the residence of Mr. George Carrere, corner of Broad and Friend Streets tomorrow afternoon, at 5 o'clock.

Issue of May 21, 1827

Died - The friends and acquaintances of Mr. Godfrey C. and Mrs. Mary W. Schutt, as also the friends of Mrs. Frances Motte, are invited to attend the funeral of Mrs. Schutt, tomorrow morning, 10 o'clock, at No. 2 Meeting Street.

Died - The friends and acquaintances of Mr. James Taws, and of Robert Childs, are requested to attend the funeral of the former from the residence of the latter, no. 143 Meeting Street, this afternoon, at 5 o'clock without further invitation.

Issue of May 22, 1827

Died at Providence, R. I. on the 11th inst. Lieut. Pardon M. Wipple, of the U. S. Navy, in the 37th year of his age.

Died on the 23d ult. at his residence on Beaver Creek, in Kershaw District, Col. Adam M'Willie, in the 60th year of his age.

Issue of May 23, 1827

Died in Montreal, on Monday evening, 7th May 1827, Mr. Wm. Spiller, a native of England. Comedian and lately manager of the Montreal Theatre.

Issue of May 25, 1827

Died on the 7th inst. at Rowley, (Mass.) Robert Coffin, Esq. the "Boston Board."

Issue of May 26, 1827

Died - The friends and acquaintances of the late Godfrey C. Schutt, and of his brother John G. Schutt, and the members of the South Carolina Society, are invited to attend the funeral of the former, from his late residence, No. 2, Meeting Street, this afternoon, at 3 o'clock precisely.

Issue of May 28, 1827

Died - The friends and acquaintances of John Maynard Davis, and Mrs. Mary E. Davis, are invited to attend the funeral of the former, from the residence of the Rev. John Bachman, Cannonsborough at 5 o'clock, this afternoon.

Issue of May 30, 1827

Departed this life on the 26th inst. Capt. William Henry Bentham, aged 42 years and 7 months.

Issue of June 2, 1827

Died at Mataneas on the 23d April, where he had gone for the benefit of his health, Isreal Pickens, late Governor of Alabama.

Died - The relatives, friends and acquaintnaces of the late Mr. George Eager, are requested to attend his funeral from Philadelphia Street, this evening, at 5 o'clock, without further invitation.

Issue of June 5, 1827

Died - The friends and acquaintances of Mr. and Mrs. Thomas Duggan, are invited to attend the funeral of their son, Thomas, this afternoon, at 4 o'clock, from his late residence St. Phillips Street, without further invitation.

Issue of June 6, 1827

Died at Boston, Mass. 26th ult. the Hon. William Phillips, late Lieut. Governor of the Commonwealth of Massachusetts.

Issue of June 20, 1827

Died - The relatives, friends and acquaintances of Robert J. Turnbull and Mrs. Turnbull, are requested to attend the funeral of Mrs. Turnbull, at 8 o'clock, tomorrow morning, from her late residence in Logan Street, without further invitation.

Issue of June 22, 1827

Died - The friends and acquaintances of Mr. and Mrs. Bradshaw, are invited to attend the funeral of their infant daughter, this afternoon, at 6 o'clock.

Issue of June 25, 1827

Died in consequence of a most distressing accident in St. Bartholomews Parish, on the 8th ult. Barkley Ferguson, in the 52d year of his age... (Eulogy)

Issue of June 27, 1827

Died at Greenville, Tenn. in May last, Alexander Sevier.
Died on the 6th March last, in Vera Cruz, Mr. John Tofel, in the 57th year of his age, a native of Genoa, and for many years a resident of Charleston.

Issue of June 28, 1827

Died - It is with regret we learn, by a letter of the 19th ult. from the Post-master at Greenville, Tennessee, to the Editor, that Major Alexander Sevier, is no more....(Eulogy)

Issue of July 5, 1827

Died - The friends and acquaintances of Joseph B. Paine, and his father Thos. Paine, are invited to attend the funeral of the former, from the house of the latter, No. 55 East Bay, this afternoon at 4 o'clock.

Issue of July 6, 1827

Died - The friends and acquaintances of Mr. Frederick A. Geyer, are invited to attend his funeral from his late residence No. 18 Lynch's Street, this afternoon, at 5 o'clock.

Issue of July 10, 1827

Died - The friends and acquaintances of Mrs. Barbara Wilson, and of Mrs. Thomas Chrietzburg, are respectfully invited to attend the funeral of the former from her late residence in Warren Street, opposite St. Paul's Church, Radcliffboro', tomorrow morning, at 7 o'clock, a.m.

Issue of July 11, 1827

Died, on board the ship Othello on her passage from this port for New York, Margaret B. Bowen, third daughter of the Rt. Rev. Dr. Bowen, aged six years and sever months.

Issue of July 12, 1827

Departed this life on the 4th inst. Mrs. Mary A. E. Cogdell, aged 67 years...(Eulogy)
Departed this life on the 4th inst. in the 24th year of his age, William Henry Capers, Esq. of Daniel's Island....

Issue of July 12, 1827

...departed this transitory life, Mr. Fredrick Augustus Geyer, in the 25th year of his age...(Eulogy)

Died, in Columbia on the 24th June, of a short and painful illness, Mrs. Jane Marks, wife of Dr. Elias Marks, aged 39...(Eulogy)

Died - The friends and acquaintances of the late John T. Cowan, are respectfully invited to attend his funeral this afternoon at 5 o'clock, from the residence of Mr. W. L. Porter, No. 47, East Bay.

Issue of July 14, 1827

Married, at New York, on the 5th inst. by the Rev. Benjamin T. Onderdonk, Dr. P. Moser, of this city, to Miss Charlotte Sophia Wilcox, eldest daughter of Samuel Wilcox, deceased of New York.

Issue of July 18, 1827

Died - The friends and acquaintances of the Rev. J. Brown, and Mrs. M. H. Brown, are requested to attend the funeral of the latter, this afternoon, at 4 o'clock, from No. 89 East Bay.

Died - The friends and acquaintances of Mrs. Ann Hutchinson, are requested to attend her funeral, this afternoon, at 5 o'clock precisely, from her late residence, No. 8 Champney's Street, without further invitation.

Issue of July 19, 1827

Died - The friends and acquaintances of Mrs. Sarah Tucker, of Mrs. Mary T. Jeannerett, and of Mr. Charles S. Tucker, and in particular his Masonic friends, are invited to attend his funeral from his late residence No. 68 Church-Street, this afternoon, at 5 o'clock.

Issue of July 20, 1827

Departed this life on Monday last, in the 6th year of her age, Florida P. daughter of His Excellency Richard J. Manning, late Governor of this state.

Issue of July 23, 1827

Died - The friends and acquaintances of Miss Mary Ann Morgan, are respectfully invited to attend her funeral from her late residence, 36 George-Street, tomorrow afternoon, at 4 o'clock.

Issue of July 25, 1827

Died, on board the U. S. Frigate Constellation, in this harbor, on Wednesday night, at 10 o'clock, after an illness of 8 days, of bilious remittent fever, Midshipman Edward Worthington, of the U. S. Navy, a native of Kentucky.

Issue of July 28, 1827

Died, on the 18th inst. Mrs. Ann Hutchinson, aged 63 years...(Eulogy)

Died - The friends and acquaintances of Mrs. Mary Taggart, and of Mr. and Mrs. Bloomfield, are invited to attend the funeral of the former from her late residence, No. 7 Orange-Street, at 5 o'clock this afternoon, without further invitation.

Issue of July 31, 1827

Departed this life on Sunday night, of ulcerated sore-throat, Thomas Moser Green, aged eighteen months and eleven days; second son and only child of Thomas P. Green...

Issue of August 7, 1827

Died on Wednesday evening last, after a protracted and painful illness,

Mrs. Hannah Roper, in the seventy fifth year of her age--relict of William Roper, Esq. deceased.

Issue of August 9, 1827

Died - The friends and acquaintances of Mr. Thomas Johnston, and his wife Elizabeth Johnston, (particularly the members of the Second Presbyterian Church) are requested without further invitation, to attend the funeral of the latter, this afternoon, at 5 o'clock, from her late residence No. 226 King Street.

Issue of August 9, 1827

Died - The friends and acquaintances of Mr. and Mrs. Robert Little, are invited to attend the funeral of the latter, from her late residence, Charlotte-Street, Mazyckborough, this afternoon, at 5 o'clock.

Issue of August 11, 1827

Died - On the last 4th of July, in the county of Warren, (Georgia) John Torrance, Esq....(Eulogy)

Died - The friends and acquaintances of Mr. Flauel Loomis, and the members of Lodge No. 14, are respectfully invited to attend his funeral this afternoon, at 5 o'clock, from his late residence at the NE corner of Church and Tradd Streets.

Issue of August 13, 1827

Died in this city, on the 9th inst. suddenly, Mrs. Mary Little, consort of Robert Little, Esq. aged 61 years and 5 months...(Eulogy)

Issue of August 14, 1827

Died - The friends and acquaintances of Mr. James Black, and of his son James Campbell Black, are respectfully invited to attend the funeral of the latter, from his late residence in Spring-Street,(between Meeting and King Streets) this afternoon, at 4 o'clock.

Died - The friends and acquaintances of Mr. Wm. Frazer and family and those of Mrs. Margaret Passman, late of New York, are particularly invited to attend the funeral of the latter, from the residence of the former, No. 31 Broad Street, tomorrow morning at 8 o'clock without further invitation.

Issue of August 17, 1827

Died - The friends and acquaintances of the late John Andrew Leibbrandt, and of Mr. and Mrs. Bensse, are requested to attend the funeral of the former from the residence of the latter on East Bay, between Pinckney and Guignard-Streets, this afternoon at half-past 4 o'clock.

Issue of August 18, 1827

Died - The relatives and friends of St. Lo Mellichamp. Sen. and of his sons, are invited to attend the funeral of the former from the residence of Mr. Stiles Mellichamp, four doors above the Tobacco Inspection, tomorrow morning, at 8 o'clock.

Issue of August 20, 1827

Died - The friends and acquaintances of James B. Blackmore, and of Messrs. De Villers and Poirier, are invited to attend the funeral of the former this afternoon at half past four o'clock, without further invitation from No. 40 Queen-Street.

Issue of August 23, 1827

Died, in this city, at the residence of Mr. J. C. Hanahan, on the 13th inst. after a short, but painful illness, of 5 days, Mr. Elias C. Roberts, aged 40 years and 5 months...

Died - The relatives, friends and acquaintances of John Strobel, Dr. B.
B. Strobel, Frederick Beard, and Frederick L. Strobel, are respectfully
invited to attend the funeral of the latter, tomorrow morning, at 8 o'clock,
from his late residence, No. 13 Mazyck-Street, without further invitation.

Issue of August 25, 1827

Died - The friends and acquaintances of Mr. and Mrs. Henry F. Faber,
also those of Mr. Thomas B. Seabrook, are invited to attend the funeral of
Mr. Faber, tomorrow afternoon, at half-past 5 o'clock, from her late residence corner Pitt and Montague Streets.

Issue of August 26, 1827

Died, on the 1st instant, at the Sweet Springs, in Virginia, Mr. Solomon
Marks, Jr....

Died - The friends and acquaintances of Mr. Thomas G. Buswell and of
Manning Belcher, are requested to attend the funeral of the former from his
late residence 298 King-Street, this afternoon at 4 o'clock.

Died - The friends and acquaintances of the Rev. John Honour, and of Mr.
and Mrs. John Honour, are invited to attend the funeral of the latter's
child, from No. 24 Mazyck-Street, this afternoon, at 4 o'clock.

Issue of August 28, 1827

Died, at his residence near Totruss, in St. Matthew's Parish, on Friday
last, 17th instant, Dr. Jno. Louis Raoul...

Issue of August 29, 1827

Died on Sullivan's Island on the 20th inst. after a short but distressing illness of three days, Mary Ann, eldest daughter of Mr. Daniel Macaulay,
of this city...(Eulogy)

Died - The friends and acquaintances of Mr. George P. Ham, and of Mr.
John M. Vanrhyn, are requested to attend the funeral of the former from the
residence of the latter, No. 71 East Bay, this afternoon at 4 o'clock.

Issue of August 31, 1827

Died on the 28th inst. of the prevalent fever, Mr. George P. Ham, aged
27, a native of Portsmouth, N. H....

Died - The members of the Medical Society of South Carolina, are
requested to attend the funeral of their deceased President, Dr. M. Irvine,
from his late residence in Lamboll-Street, this afternoon, at 4 o'clock.

Issue of September 1, 1827

Died...Dr. Matthew Irvine...(Eulogy)

Departed this life on Monday the 27th ult. in the 56th year of her age,
Mrs. Judith De La Motta...(Eulogy)

Died in Winchester,(Vir.) on the 6th ult. Mrs. Margaret Windle, in the
96th year of her age...

Issue of September 5, 1827

Died on Monday evening, 2d inst. in the 73d year of his age, Mr. Levi
Salomons, a native of Germany, but a citizen of Carolina, and a resident
at Georgetown.

Died - The friends and acquaintances of Thomas and John Blackwood are
requested to attend the funeral of their nephew Samuel Blackwood Singer,
from the residence of Thomas Blackwood No. 18 Pitt-Street, this afternoon
at 4 o'clock.

Issue of September 6, 1827

Died...Mr. Thomas Broughton, who died at the residence of his mother, in this city on Thursday, the 30th of August, aged 19 years...(Eulogy)

Departed this life very suddenly on the evening of the 5th September, in the 68th year of his age, Mr. John Bee Holmes. He was the eldest son of Mrs. Rebecca Edwards...(Eulogy)

Died - The friends and acquaintances of Mr. and Mrs. Samuel Wragg Capers, also of Mr. J. W. Brandt, are requested to attend the funeral of Mrs. Capers, this afternoon, at 5 o'clock, from the South Carolina Society Hall, Meeting Street.

Died - The friends and acquaintances of Mr. and Mrs. Peter M. Ehney, are invited to attend the funeral of their son Theodore H. Ehney, from their residence in Pinkney Street, this afternoon, at 4 o'clock, without further invitation.

Departed this life, on the 10th inst. at Edingsville, in the 64th year of her age, Mrs. Mary Hamilton, widow of the Hon. Paul Hamilton...

Died, at Flushing, Long Island, on the evening of the 5th inst. Joseph Howland, Esq. formerly a merchant of this city...

Departed this life on the 10th inst. Mrs. Sarah Rivers, consort of Mr. Joseph B. Rivers, of James' Island, in the 31st year of her age...

Died - The friends and acquaintances of the late Captain John P. Chazal, and of Mrs. E. C. Chazal, are invited to attend the funeral of their youngest son Stephen Alfred, tomorrow morning, at 8 o'clock, from his late residence No. 46, Anson Street.

Died - The friends and acquaintances of J. R. Valk, are invited to attend the funeral of his daughter Maria A. Valk, from his residence No. 65 Meeting Street, tomorrow at 1 o'clock.

Died - The friends and acquaintances of Mr. and Mrs. Henry Sifly, and those of James C. Norris, and Jacob F. Mintzing, are respectfully invited to attend the funeral of Master Henry Jacob Sifly, from the residence of his father, No. 24 Friend-Street, tomorrow morning, at half past 8 o'clock.

Died - The friends and acquaintances of Colonel William Paine, late U.S. Military Store-keeper, and the officers, Civil and Military, of the U.S., are respectfully invited to attend his funeral, precisely at 4 o'clock, this afternoon, from the Carolina Coffee House.

Died, at Mobile on the 9th inst. Mr. John Cline, a native of Virginia.

Died, at New Orleans, Mr. Isaac Thom, a native of New Hampshire.

Died, Mathew H. Jovett, Esq. an artist of rare genuis, at New Orleans.

Died, at New Orelans, Dr. Richard Dorsey, of Maryland, aged 24.

Died, Col. John M'Farland, editor of the Aleghany Democrat.

Died - Charles V. Potier, Esq. aged 60, a native of Havre de Grace, and for the last 40 years a resident of Louisiana.

Died, at Baton Rouge, on the 3d inst. Mr. Alexander Thomas.

Died, at Baton Rouge, on the 4th inst., Walter H. Mears, Esq....

Died, at Pensacola, on 10th, John Home Purves, Esq....

Died, at the Cherokee Ponds, S.C. on the 13th inst. Major Charles Goodwin, in the 71st year of his age...

Died - The friends and acquaintances and the members of the Fellowship and Mechanic's Societies, are invited to attend the funeral of John Whiting deceased from his late residence Meeting (near Wentworth) street, tomorrow morning at 8 o'clock.

Issue of October 4, 1827

Died, at Fort Moultrie, on Sunday last, Doctor Charles Luce, of the U. S. Army, aged 28 years...

Died, at Georgetown, on the 1st Mr. Robert M'Teer, in the 58th year of his age...

Issue of October 5, 1827

Died in this city, on Wednesday, the 15th August last, of a dropsy in the chest, Miss Eunice Fury, aged 23, native of New York.

Died, at the residence of John O. Heriot, Esq., Sumpter District, on the 23d ult. in the 69th year of her age, Mrs. Agnes Kirkpatrick...

Died, at Newberry on the 27th ult....Mr. Daniel Hawley, in the 26th year of his age...

Died, in Trenton, N.C. on the 18th ult. Christopher Bryan, Esq. in the 43d year of his age.

Died, in Trenton, N.C., at the same place on the 21st ult. Mr. Joseph Green.

Died, on the 22d ult. at little Saluda, in Edgefield District, Mrs. Sabra J. Rudolph, wife of Mr. Zebulon Rudolph, Jr. in the 21st year of her age.

Died, on the 23d, at Edgefield C. House, Mr. John B. Price, a native of Baltimore, Md. in the 27th year of his age.

Died, on the 20th, at Longstreets Mills, Edgefield District, Mr. James D. Brown a native of Ireland.

Died - The Revd. the Clergy, the Members of the several religious denominations, and the friends and acquaintances of the late Rev. J. C. Henry, D.D. and Pastor of the 2d Presbyterian Church, are requested to attend his funeral from the late residence of Mr. John Robinson, Wraggborough, tomorrow morning, at 8 o'clock, without further invitation.

Issue of October 6, 1827

Died in this city on the 25th ult. Col. Wm. Paine...aged 84 years and 2 months...

Issue of October 9, 1827

Departed this life on the 25th ult. at the residence of Dr. Thomas A. Elliott, Orageburgh District, Mrs. Elizabeth Badger, of this city, aged 61 years.

Issue of October 10, 1827

Died - The friends and acquaintances of John Geddes, and of his daughter Harriet Anne Geddes, and the members of the First Presbyterian Church, are invited to attend the funeral of the latter, tomorrow afternoon at 4 o'clock, from her father's residence opposite the Circular Church.

Issue of October 12, 1827

Died, at Georgetown, on Saturday last, Miss Jane Brown.

Died, at New York, suddenly, Mr. John Cockle, of that city, formerly merchant of Charleston, S.C.

Died - Mr. Samuel Dusenberry, in the 33d year of his age...

Died, at Wilmington, N.C. on the 29th ult. Mr. T. W. Hedrick, in the 27th year of his age, a native of Washington, D.C....

Issue of October 16, 1827

Died - ...the sister of our beloved Pastor, Miss Joanna M. England...

Died at Platt Springs, in this state, Henry Hane, aged 26, a native of Germany.

Issue of October 16, 1827

Died, in Edgefield District, Capt. John Ryan, aged 82.

Died, in Abbeville District, Maj. John Bowie, aged 88, a partizan officer of the Revolution.

Died, on the 4th inst. at the residence of Dr. Mayhew, (Beaver Creek) in Kershaw District, Mr. Thos. B. Durell...

Died, in Camden, 6th inst. in the 37th year of his age, Rev. Raynolds Bascom...

Died, at Savannah, on the 18th inst., 41st year of her age, Mrs. Ann J. Durkee, of Wilmington Island.

Died, on Sunday morning 30th ult. Daniel Humphreys, Esq. aged 88...

Died - The relatives, friends and acquaintances of Mr. and Mrs. LeBleux, are invited to attend the funeral of the latter, from the residence, of the former, No. 250 King Street, at 4 o'clock, this afternoon, without further invitation.

Issue of October 22, 1827

Died, on the 11th ult. at Cape Haytien, James E. Brice, Esq. American Commercial Agent at that place...

Issue of October 29, 1827

Died, at Providence, on the 18th inst. Mr. Thomas Simmons, of this city, and formerly a resident of that town, aged 62 years.

Died - The relatives, friends and acquaintances of Wm. Beard, John Strobel, Dr. B. B. Strobel, and Frederick Beard, are invited to attend the funeral of the latter, from his late residence No. 13 Mazyck Street at half past 3 o'clock, tomorrow afternoon.

Died - The friends and acquaintances of James H. Spears are requested to attend his funeral from his late residence in Church Street, opposite the Baptist Church, tomorrow morning, at 11 o'clock.

Issue of October 30, 1827

Died at New York 21st inst. in the 14th year of her age, Mary Ann De Jongh, daughter of the late Joseph De Jongh, of Charleston, S.C.

Died, near Summerville, (Alabama) on the 28th ult. William A. Jones, in the 51st year of his age, a native of Virginia.

Died, at Chelatchir Heights, in Dallas County, on the 25th ult. in the 87th year, Col. Alex. Outlaw, formerly of Jefferson County, Texas.

Issue of November 13, 1827

Died, on the 1st inst., at his residence near Coosawhatchie, Patrick Walch, Esq. in the 37th year of his age...(Eulogy)

Issue of November 16, 1827

Died - The relations, friends and acquaintances of Mr. and Mrs. Francis Y. Legare, Mr. Jas. Legare, and Mrs. Francis Motte, are invited to attend the funeral of Mrs. Martha Legare, from her mother's residence, No. 34 Church Street, this afternoon at 4 o'clock.

Issue of November 17, 1827

Married, on Thursday evening last, by the Rev. Dr. Dalcho, George B. Reid, Esq. to Miss Eliza Smith, third daughter of Dr. John Ramsay,--all of this city.

Issue of November 19, 1827

Married, on Wednesday evening last, 14th inst. by the Rev. Allston Gibbes, George Hall Ingraham, Esq. to Mary Rachel, third daughter of B. Gaillard, Esq. all of this city.

Issue of November 27, 1827

Died - The friends and acquaintances of Mrs. Susan Dey, and of Mr.
Benjamin Dey, are invited to attend the funeral of the former, from the
residence of Mr. John C. Hoff, No. 84 Queen Street, without further invitation, tomorrow morning, at 8 o'clock.

Issue of November 29, 1827

Married, on the 16th inst. by the Rev. Dr. Bass, Mr. Edward Jones, to
Miss Ann Elizabeth eldest daughter of Jacob and Elizabeth STroub, both of
Charleston.
Died - The friends and acquaintances of the Rev. S. Gilman and wife,
the clergy of Charleston, and the members of the Second Independent Congregation, are invited to attend the funeral of Mrs. Abigail H. Gilman, from
the residence of her son in Cannonborough, tomorrow morning, at 9 o'clock.

Issue of November 30, 1827

Died - The friends and acquaintances of Capt. John String, are invited
to attend his funeral from his late residence in Wraggsborough, tomorrow
morning at 9 o'clock.

Issue of December 7, 1827

Married, at New York on the evening of the 28th ult. by the Rev. Mr.
Hart, Mr. M. M. Noah, to Miss Rebecca, only daughter of Mr. Daniel Jackson,
all of that city.
Died, at New York on the night of the 28th ult. Isabella Pyne, eldest
daughter of the John Pyne, Esq. of South Carolina.

Issue of December 8, 1827

Died at his residence on Blackswamps, S.C. on 14th Nov. William H.
Lawton, Esq. in the fifty-third year of his age...

Issue of December 11, 1827

Married, this morning at St. Michael's Church by the Rev. Bishop Bowen,
John Butler, of Philadelphia, to Gabriella M. Morris, eldest daughter of
Colonel Lewis Morris, of South-Carolina.

Issue of December 13, 1827

Died - The friends and acquaintances of F. and C. Winthrop and of Capt.
Edmund Gardner, late of the brig Mina, are particularly invited to attend
the funeral of the latter, from Mrs. Hilman's residence, 69 East Bay, at a
quarter after 3 o'clock, this afternoon.

Issue of December 15, 1827

Married on Wednesday last, Abraham Moise, Esq. of this city, to Caroline
Agnes, third daughter of Isaac C. Moses, Esq. of St. Paul's Parish.
Died, at Norfolk, on the 8th inst. at half past five o'clock, in the
87th year of his age, Mr. Martin Oster...

Issue of December 20, 1827

Died, on the 16th ult. in St. Johns, Berkley, at the residence of
Thomas Broughton, Esq. Mr. James Birchard...

Issue of December 26, 1827

Married, at Columbia, on 20th inst. by the Rev. Mr. Folker, Robert
Wilson Gibbs, Esq. of this city, to Miss Caroline Guignard, daughter of James
J. Guignard, Esq. of Columbia.

Issue of December 27, 1827

Died – The friends and acquaintances of Mr. and Mrs. Charles H. Tunis and of Mr. and Mrs. James Mitchell are respectfully invited to attend the funeral of Mrs. Tunis from her father's residence No. 50, Meeting-Street, tomorrow afternoon, at half past 3 o'clock.

Issue of January 11, 1828

Died – The friends and acquaintances of the late Miss A. E. Van Rhyn are invited to attend her funeral tomorrow morning at 10 o'clock from her residence in Broad-Street without further invitation.

Issue of January 18, 1828

Died, on 7th inst. at his father's residence in this city...Mr. Archibald Gibson, aged 28 years and 4 months.

Issue of January 19, 1828

Married, on Tuesday evening, 15th inst. by the Rev. Mr. Buist, Alexander Gordon, Esq., to Miss Jane, second daughter of Daniel Cruikshanks, Esq., all of this city.

Died, in Charleston, on Tuesday the 15th inst. Wm. J. Collins, aged thirty-two years--he has left behind him to regret his loss an affectionate wife and sister...

Died – The friends and acquaintances of Mrs. Payenville, widow, are requested to attend her funeral this afternoon, at 4 o'clock, from her late residence in Ellery-Street.

Issue of January 22, 1828

Died – The friends and acquaintances of the late Mr. Paul Hill, his Masonic Brethren, the members of the German Friendly Society and those of the Lutheran Church, are respectfully invited to attend his funeral tomorrow afternoon at 3 o'clock, from his late residence No. 7, Clifford-Street, without further invitation.

Issue of January 29, 1828

Died, on the 23d inst. at the residence of Chas. Baring, Jr. Esq. Combahee,...Henry T. Farmer, M.D. in the 42d year of his age.

Issue of February 7, 1828

Married, on yesterday evening the 6th inst. in St. Philips Church, by the Rev. Dr. Gadsden, James Robertson, Esq. to Miss Ellen Atkins both of this city.

Issue of February 8, 1828

Died – The friends and acquaintances of Mrs. Sarah Legare are invited to attend her funeral from her late residence in Anson-St., directly opposite Lauren's Street, on tomorrow morning at ½ past 9 o'clock.

Issue of February 16, 1828

Died – The friends and acquaintances of the late Mrs. Mary Irvine, and of Mrs. Keith, are requested to attend the funeral of the former, at 5 o'clock, tomorrow afternoon, the 17th inst. at the corner of King and Lamboll Streets.

Issue of February 19, 1828

Died, on the 15th ult. in Fairfield District, aged 66, John W. Starke...

Died on board the steam boat Marion, on her passage from Savannah to Purysburgh, on Friday 15th inst. Capt. Gamaliel Darling...

Issue of February 22, 1828

Married, on Thursday, the 7th instant, by the Rev. F. Rutledge, Henry Ravenel, to Elizabeth P. daughter of the late E. Coffin of St. Helena.

Issue of February 26, 1828

Died - The friends and acquaintances of Mr. and Mrs. N. T. Goodrich, are invited to attend the funeral of the former from his late residence, Cannon-Street, tomorrow afternoon at 4 o'clock.

Issue of March 1, 1828

Died - The friends and acquaintances of the late Wm. Broadfoot, and Wm. Davidson, Jun. are invited to attend the funeral of the former, from No. 294 East Bay, tomorrow afternoon, at half-past 3 o'clock.

Issue of March 3, 1828

Departed this life on the 1st inst. Mrs. Sarah A. Moise, in the 37th year of her age...(Eulogy)
Departed this life on the 22d day of January, Mr. Paul Hill, in the 85th year of his age...

Issue of March 5, 1828

Died - The friends and acquaintances of late Gen. John Geddes and of his son, John Geddes, the Revd. the Clergy, the Judges and members of the Bar, the respective Societies to which they belonged, and the citizens generally, are invited to attend their funeral, from their late residence No. 122 Meeting-Street, at 10 o'clock tomorrow morning.

Issue of March 7, 1828

Departed this life on the 1st inst. in his 50th year, William Broadfoot, Esq....

Issue of March 12, 1828

Married on Tuesday the 4th inst. by the Rev. Dr. Palmer, Wm. E. Haskell, to Susan, second daughter of the late John Ball, Esq. Planter.

Issue of March 14, 1828

Married, on Tuesday last at the German Lutheran Church by the Rev. Mr. Bachman, Paul S. Hl Lee, Esq. to Miss Lynch Helen Vanrhyn, all of this city.

Issue of March 19, 1828

Died - The friends and acquaintances of Mr. Daniel Hazard, and of Capt. Dan. Brown, are invited to attend the funeral of the former from the residence of the latter in Zigzag Alley, at 3 o'clock, this afternoon, without further invitation.

Issue of March 21, 1828

Died - The friends and acquaintances of Mr. and Mrs. Robert Downie, are requested to attend the funeral of the latter from her late residence Broad-Street, this afternoon, at 4 o'clock.

Issue of March 22, 1828

Departed this life on the 13th inst. Mrs. Harriet Russell Cassin, a native of London, and from infancy an inhabitant of this city, in the 26th year of her age...(Eulogy)

Issue of April 1, 1828

Died - The relatives and friends and acquaintances of Mr. John Cox, and of Mrs. Eleanor Cox, and of Mr. Thomas Sereven, and particularly the members of the Baptist Church, are invited to attend the funeral of Mr. John Cox, from the residence of Mr. Thos. Johnson, No. 226 King-Street, this afternoon, at half past 3 o'clock, without further invitation.

Issue of April 3, 1828

Married, last evening, by the Rt. Rev. Bishop Bowen, Bentley Hasell, Esq. to Catharine DeNully, daughter of the late Nicholas Cruger, Esq.

Issue of April 7, 1828

Died...departed this life on the 27th ultimo, Mr. Robert H. Mills, in the 27th year of his age...(Eulogy)

Issue of April 8, 1828

Married, on Thursday evening last, by the Rev. Dr. Dalcho, George A. Trenholm to Ann Helen, eldest daughter of the late John Holmes, all of this city.

Married, on Thursday the 3d inst. by the Rev. Dr. Leland, Mr. J. Jenkins Mikell, of Edisto Island, to Miss Emily Price, daughter of the late Rev. Dr. Price of James Island.

Issue of April 9, 1828

Married, on Tuesday evening last, by the Rev. Bishop England, Mr. Lawrence Ryan to Mrs. Ann Ball Waring, all of this city.

Issue of April 10, 1828

Died - The friends and acquaintances of the late Capt. Wm. Long and of William Patton are invited to attend the funeral of the former, from on board the Schr. Temple at Edmondston's Wharf, at 4 o'clock, this afternoon.

Issue of April 12, 1828

Married, on Wednesday evening the 9th inst. by the Rev. John Bachman, Mr. Andrew C. Dibble, formerly of Danbury, Conn. to Miss Henrietta M. H. daughter of S. J. Wagner, Esq. of this city.

Issue of April 16, 1828

Died, in Jamaica, L. I. (New York) on the 8th inst. Gen. John Thomas Jones, aged 39.

Issue of April 21, 1828

Died, on the eleventh inst. Edward C. Pinkney, Esq. of the Bar of Baltimore.

Issue of April 25, 1828

Died - The friends and acquaintances of Mr. and Mrs. Richard Shea, are invited to attend the funeral of Mr. Thomas S. Lanquest, tomorrow morning at 10 o'clock from the residence of Mr. Richard Shea in Henrietta-Street, without further invitation.

Issue of April 26, 1828

Died at St. Augustine on the instant, Mrs. Maria B. Habersham, of Charleston, (So. Car.) aged 31 years.

Issue of May 6, 1828

Died, in Manchester, Vt. Joseph Burr, Esq. aged 54...

Issue of May 9, 1828

Died, in Washington on the 2d inst. the Honorable Thomas Tudor Tucker, Treasurer of the U. S., in the 84th year of his age...(Eulogy)

Issue of May 14, 1828

Married, on Thursday evening last, by the Rev. Dr. Leland, Mr. Edw. C. Burch, to Miss Georgianna Rivers, eldest daughter of William Rivers, Esq. of James Island.

Died - The friends and acquaintances of Louis Dubois, Mrs. E. Dubois, J. Chartrand, D. LeBleux, and F. Carmand, are invited to attend the funeral of the former from his late residence in Queen-Street, at 5 o'clock, tomorrow afternoon, 15th inst.

Issue of May 16, 1828

Died - The friends and acquaintances of Mr. William H. Lewis, are invited to attend his funeral tomorrow morning, at 8 o'clock, from the residence of his mother, George-Street, near King.

Issue of May 20, 1828

Died of consumption on the 16th inst. Mr. William H. Lewis, in the 26th year of his age...(Eulogy)

Issue of May 29, 1828

Died - The friends and acquaintances of Henry Stocker and family, also the members of the Fire Company of Axemen are invited to attend his funeral tomorrow afternoon at 4 o'clock from his late residence No. 14 East end of Laurens-Street.

Issue of June 7, 1828

Married, on Wednesday evening last, the 4th inst. by the Rev. Wm. A. M'Cowall, D.D., James Ross, to Ann, second daughter of Alex. Henry; all of this city.

Issue of June 9, 1828

Died - The relatives, friends and acquaintances of Miss Elizabeth P. Righton, and the Congregation of the Baptist Church, are invited to attend her funeral tomorrow morning, at 9 o'clock, from her late residence in Water-Street, without further invitation.

Died - The friends and acquaintances of Mr. and Mrs. Suav, are requested to attend the funeral of the latter from her late residence George-Street, No. 3, at 5 o'clock, this afternoon, without further invitation.

Issue of June 10, 1828

Died - The friends of Miss Caroline Crafts, of Miss Margaret Crafts, and of the late Hon. William Crafts, are invited to attend the funeral of the former, at No. 19 Bull-Street, tomorrow afternoon at 4 o'clock, without a more particular invitation.

Issue of June 21, 1828

Died - The friends and acquaintances of Mr. and Mrs. W. P. Dove, of his mother Mrs. Wing, and Mrs. Flint, are invited to attend the funeral of Mr. Dove, without further invitation, from his late residence on Pritchard's Wharf, this afternoon, at 4 o'clock.

Died - The friends and acquaintances of Mr. and Mrs. John Bennett, Jun. and of Mr. and Mrs. James Eyland, are invited to attend the funeral of the former from the residence of Mr. James Eyland, 172 King Street, tomorrow afternoon at 5 o'clock, without further invitation.

Issue of June 23, 1828

Departed this life on Sunday morning, the 15th inst. at the residence of his father, on Chehaw, Mr. David Sarzedas, Jun. a native of this city, in the 43d year of his age...(Eulogy)

Issue of June 28, 1828

Married, on Thursday the 26th inst. by the Rev. Dr. Gadsden, the Rev. Thomas House Taylor to Miss Ann Manigault, daughter of Joseph Manigault.

Issue of July 10, 1828

Died at Sullivan's Island on the 6th instant, after a long and painful illness, Mrs. Ann Cruger, widow of the late Nicholas Cruger, Esq. in the fifty-third year of her age.

Died - The male friends and acquaintances of Mrs. Charlotte Waller, and of her son Joseph Whilden are invited to attend the funeral of the former, tomorrow morning, at half past 8 o'clock, from her late residence in Magazine Street, without further invitation.

Issue of July 14, 1828

Died - The friends and acquaintances of Mrs. Jean Poincignon and of her brother Eteine, are respectfully invited to attend the funeral of Francis Poincignon, at 5 o'clock, this afternoon, from his residence in Queen-Street, No. 19, without further invitation.

Issue of July 19, 1828

Died - The friends and acquaintances of the late Mrs. Isaac M. Wilson, are invited to attend her funeral, at 6 o'clock this afternoon, from the residence of her brother Mr. Robt. W. Mazyck, No.-- Wall Street.

Died - The friends and acquaintances of Mr. and Mrs. James Adger, are invited to attend the funeral of their neice Miss Margaret Ellison Adger, from their residence in King Street tomorrow morning at half past 8 o'clock, without further invitation.

Issue of July 26, 1828

Died - The friends and acquaintances of Mrs. C. Readhimer, Mr. P. Readhimer and also of Mr. and Mrs. Simons, are requested to attend the funeral of the former at 7 o'clock tomorrow morning, from her late residence in Columbus Street.

Issue of July 29, 1828

Died - The friends and acquaintances of Mr. John Wallis, and of Mr. John Dunn, are invited to attend the funeral of the latter from his late residence No. 132 Meeting Street, tomorrow morning, at 9 o'clock, without further invitation.

Issue of July 31, 1828

Died - The friends and acquaintances of Captain Lubbock and Curry, (of the steam boat Washington,) are invited to attend the funeral of Mr. H. D. Greene, of Savannah, from Capt. Lubbock's, No. 1 South Bay, at 4 o'clock, p.m. tomorrow evening.

Issue of August 8, 1828

Died - The relatives, friends, and acquaintances of William H. Gibson and of John Bergstadt, are respectfully invited to attend the funeral of the latter, from the residence of the former No. 89 East Bay, this afternoon at four o'clock without further invitation.

Issue of August 13, 1828

Married at Paris, on Saturday, the 7th June, at the house of his Excellency Mr. Brown, Envoy Extraordinary and Minister Plenipotentiary of the United States to the Court of France, by the Rt. Rev. Bishop Luscombe, Daniel Glover, Esq. of New York, to Miss Ann Mary Cruger, daughter of B. P. Cruger, Esq. of the same place.

Departed this life on the 10th ultimo, in the 60th year of his age, Dr. John Ramsay, of St. Paul's Parish...(Eulogy)

Died - The relatives and friends of Mrs. Susanna Tonge, are invited to attend her funeral, from her late residence, Church Street continued, tomorrow morning, at 6 o'clock.

Issue of August 18, 1828

Died - The friends and acquaintances of the late James Bradshaw, are invited to his funeral tomorrow morning, at 9 o'clock from his late residence No.--Broad Street.

Died - The friends and acquaintances of Mr. and Mrs. Connolly, of John M. Murray, and the members of St. Michael's Church, are invited to attend the funeral of the former, from her late residence, No. 14 South Bay, at 10 o'clock tomorrow morning,

Issue of August 21, 1828

Died on Sunday the 17th inst. Drake Villepontoux, of St. Johns Berkley.. (Eulogy)

Issue of August 22, 1828

Died - The friends and acquaintances of George G. Elford, of the late Captain James Elford, Joseph L. Enslow, and Highan & Fife, are requested to attend the funeral of the former, from his late residence, No. 119 East Bay, this afternoon, at half past 4 o'clock.

Issue of August 26, 1828

Died on the 13th inst. in Anderson District, very suddenly, Hon. John Wilson, formerly member of Congress from Greenville and Pendleton.

Died a few days since, Capt. Wm. Mason, Post Master at Masonville, York District, (S.C.)

Issue of August 27, 1828

Died - The friends and acquaintances of A. E. Miller are requested to attend the funeral of Mr. Joseph Cammeron from his late residence at Mrs. Bruen's, George Street, this afternoon, at 4 o'clock precisely.

Issue of August 28, 1828

Died - The friends and acquaintances of Mr. and Mrs. John Robinson, and Mr. and Mrs. John T. Robinson, are invited to attend the funeral of John T. Robinson, from his late residence Charlotte Street, Mazyckborough at 5 o'clock this afternoon.

Issue of August 29, 1828

Died - The friends and acquaintances of W. H. Miller, and Frederick Miller, are invited to attend the funeral of the latter, from his mothers residence No. 52 Anson Street, this afternoon at 5 o'clock.

Issue of September 2, 1828

Died on the 29th August in the 20th year of his age, Frederick James, second son of the late James Miller, Merchant of this city.

Issue of September 5, 1828

Died, at Baltimore on the 30th ult. the Reverend Enoch George, one of the Bishops of the Methodist Episcopal Church, aged about 60 years.

Issue of September 8, 1828

Died on the 30th ult. near Milton, (N.C.) Bartlett Yancey, Esq. formerly a member of Congress, and for many years Speaker of the Senate of the state of North Carolina.

Died - The friends and acquaintances of Mr. Peter Desportes, are invited to attend his funeral tomorrow morning, at half past 6 o'clock, from the residence of Mr. J. Lafon, East Bay.

Issue of September 9, 1828

Died on Beaver Creek, in Sumter District, at a very advanced age, Mr. Arthur Cunningham...

Died, on Saturday, the 30th ult. at Galddens Grover, Fairfield District, in this state, John M'Watters, a soldier of the Revolution, in the 84th year of his age.

Issue of September 10, 1828

Died on Sunday evening the 7th inst. at Sullivans Island, William E. Morris, late Captain in the Army of the United States...(Eulogy)

Died - The friends and acquaintances of Dr. J. H. B. Malcomson and of Dr. Dickson, are invited to attend the funeral of the former from his late residences No. 54 St. Philip's Street, at eight o'clock tomorrow morning.

Died - The friends and acquaintances of James and Edward S. Courtenay and of their grandfather, the late Samuel Smith, Senor, are respectfully invited to attend the funeral of the latter, from the residence of the former No. 35 St. Philip's Street, at 4 o'clock, this afternoon at half past 4 o'clock.

Died - The friends and acquaintances of Hamilton Crawford and of James Adger, are invited to attend the funeral of the former from the residence of the latter this afternoon at half past 4 o'clock.

Issue of September 13, 1828

Departed this transitory life, on the 24th ultimo, David Adams, Esq. in the 75th year of his age...(Eulogy)

Issue of September 15, 1828

Died - The friends and acquaintances of Mr. C. Edmondston, and Mr. A. E. Miller, and of Mr. Nicholas Gray, are requested to attend the funeral of the latter, from the house of Capt. Watson, No. 7 Tradd Street, this afternoon, at 5 o'clock.

Died - The friends and acquaintances of Mr. and Mrs. R. B. Lawton, and Mr. Chas. H. Reilly are respectfully invited to attend the funeral of the child of the former, at 8 o'clock tomorrow morning from their residence, No. 133 Church Street.

Issue of September 17, 1828

(Died)...Mrs. Mitchell King...(Eulogy)

Died - The friends and acquaintances of Miss Hannah Ford, and of Mr. Henry Nevle, are invited to attend the funeral of the former, from her late residence corner of Broad and Logan Streets, tomorrow morning, at 11 o'clock a.m.

Issue of September 25, 1828

Died - The friends and acquaintances, the members of the Methodist Episcopal Church, and the Rev. Clergy of the city, are invited to attend the funeral of the Rev. Asbury Morgan, tomorrow morning, at 10 o'clock, from his late residence, corner of Pitt and Boundary Streets.

Issue of September 27, 1828

Died - The relatives, friends and acquaintances of Mr. Thomas Sigwald, members of the German Friendly and German Fusilers Societies, and Lutheran Church, are respectfully invited to attend his funeral tomorrow afternoon, at 4 o'clock, from his late residence No. -- Queen Street between Friend and Mazyck Streets.

Issue of September 29, 1828

Died - The relatives, friends and acquaintances of Mrs. Mary S. Blum and of John A. Blum and Wm. D. Blum, are requested to attend the funeral of Wm. D. Blum, from the residence of his mother, King Street, tomorrow morning, at 8 o'clock without furhter invitation.

Issue of October 7, 1828

Died last evening at Sullivans' Island, Capt. Robert Henley, of the U. S. Navy.
--The friends and acquaintances of the deceased, and officers of the Navy, Army, and Militia, are respectfully invited to join the funeral procession which will be formed tomorrow morning at 9 o'clock, on Crafts South Wharf.

Issue of October 8, 1828

Died at Greenbush, N.Y. Rensslaer County, General John J. Van Rensselaer

Issue of October 11, 1828

Died - The friends and acquaintances of William Simpson, and those of Joseph A. Winthrop, are invited to attend the funeral of the former from his late residence in Minority Street, tomorrow morning, at 8 o'clock, without further invitation.

Issue of October 17, 1828

Married on Wednesday evening, 15th inst. by the Rev. Mr. M'Encroe, Mr. A Benoist, to Miss F. Aveilhe, both of this city.

Issue of October 23, 1828

Died, at his residence in Richland District, on the morning of the 29th ult. Jacob Deleon, Esq. in the 64th year of his age.

Issue of November 7, 1828

Died - The relatives, friends and acquaintances of the late Henry Laurens, are invited to attend the funeral of the former tomorrow morning, - at 8 o'clock from the residence of his mother, No. 290 East Bay.

Issue of November 17, 1828

Married on Thursday evening, 13th inst. by the Rev. Dr. Dalcho, Francis M. Weston, Esq. of All Saints, to Mary, second daughter of Charles Weston, Esq. of London.

Issue of November 21, 1828

Died - The friends and acquaintances of Mr. and Mrs. Joseph Clarke, and of Miss Pringles, are invited to attend the funeral of Mrs. Clarke, tomorrow morning, at 11 o'clock from the residence of Miss Pringles, No. 48 Meeting Street.

Issue of November 24, 1828

Married on Thursday evening last, by the Revd. Dr. Dalcho, Isaac W.

Girardeau, Esq. of James Island to Miss Margaret Thomasine, daughter of the late Capt. Thos. Campbell Cox, of this city.

Issue of November 27, 1828

Married on Wednesday evening the 26th instant, by the Rev. Mr. Gildersleeve, Doctor Robert Durant, to Miss Mary M'Faddin, youngest daughter of Capt. M'Faddin, all of Sumter District.

Died at his house on East Bay, on the night of the 22d inst. after a painful and lingering illness William Roper, Senior, Esq.

Issue of November 28, 1828

Died - The friends and acquaintances of Mr. Isaac Motte, and Miss Charlotte Broughton, are invited to attend the funeral of the latter, without further invitation, at 10 o'clock tomorrow morning, from the residence of Mrs. Motte, No. 54 Meeting Street.

Issue of December 4, 1828

Died - The friends and acquaintances of the late Mrs. Elizabeth Bee, are invited to attend her funeral tomorrow afternoon, at half past 3 o'clock, from her late residence, Meeting Street, without further invitation.

Issue of December 6, 1828

Died - The friends and acquaintances of Mr. James Nelson, are invited to attend his funeral tomorrow afternoon, at 4 o'clock from his late residence on Hampstead.

Issue of December 8, 1828

Died - The friends and acquaintances of Mr. and Mrs. Robert A. Pringle, are invited to attend the funeral of the former, from the residence of Mrs. Maxwell, No. 91 Meeting Street, at eight o'clock tomorrow morning.

Issue of December 9, 1828

Died at Philadelphia, on the 30th ult. after a long and painful illness, Joseph Allen Smith, Esq. of South Carolina.

Issue of December 13, 1828

Married on Tuesday evening last, by the Rev. Dr. Leland, Mr. William M. Lawton, to Miss Martha, daughter of Josiah Taylor, Esq.

Married on Thursday evening last, the 11th inst. by the Rev. Mr. Buist, Kinsey L. Burden, Jr. Esq. to Mary Eugenia, eldest daughter of the late Dr. James Air, all of this place.

Issue of December 15, 1828

Died of a lingering illness, Mrs. Margaret Smith, late of Savannah, Geo. 48 years.

Issue of December 24, 1828

Departed this transitory life on Thursday the 4th December, Mrs. Eliza Bee, aged 76 years...(Eulogy)

Issue of December 26, 1828

Married on Tuesday evening last, by the Rev. Mr. Hanckel, Mr. Jonah M. Atkinson, of Santee, to Miss Susannah Ann, second daughter of Col. C. J. Steedman of this city.

Died in this city, on Tuesday the 23d inst. after a short illness, Mrs. Sarah Goldsmith, aged 43 years...

Issue of December 30, 1828

Married on the 24th inst. at Orangeburgh, by the Rev. John Murrowe, Sermon Bonsall, Esq. (formerly of Philadelphia) to Miss Mary C. P. Jennings.

Issue of December 31, 1828

Died - The friends and acquaintances of Mr. and Mrs. John Falls Walker and of Mrs. Flint, are invited to attend the funeral of Jane Flint, daughter of the former, from their residence No. 23 State Street, on Friday morning, 2d January 1829, at 8 o'clock, without further invitation.

Issue of January 3, 1829

Died, on the 28th ultimo at Amelia Island, E. F. after a long illness... Mrs. Henrietta A. Harrison, wife of Ephraim Harrison, Esq. and daughter of Lewis Roux, Esq. of this city.

Issue of January 6, 1829

Died...Authur Vardell, a promising and only son of John J. and Sarah Frazer, who departed this life on the 3d inst. aged 2 years and 7 months.
Died, in Columbia, on the 25th ult. Mr. Turner Bynum...
Died, near Columbia, on the 30th Oct. Wm. Marvin, in the 40th year of his age.

Issue of January 10, 1829

Died - The relatives, friends and acquaintances of Mrs. Susanna Guissin-daniel, also the members of the Methodist Episcopal Church, are invited to attend her funeral from her late residence No.--- Beaufain-Street tomorrow morning, the 11th inst. at 12 o'clock without further invitation.

Issue of January 17, 1829

Married, at Baltimore, the Hon. John H. Eaton, of the U. S. Senate, to Mrs. Margaret Timberlake, widow of the late J. Timberlake, of the U. S. Navy.

Issue of January 19, 1829

Died - The friends and acquaintances of Mr. C. J. Graeser and those of Mr. C. A. Graeser, also the members of St. Andrew's Society, are respectfully invited to attend the funeral of Mr. C. J. Graeser, tomorrow afternoon at half past 3 o'clock, from his late residence No. 58 East Bay.

Issue of January 28, 1829

Died - The friends and acquaintances of Mr. Brockholst Livingston Carroll, of his brother Gabriel H. Carroll, and J. L. Norton, are invited to attend the funeral of the former, from his late residence, corner of Middle and Minority-Streets, tomorrow afternoon, at half past 3 o'clock, without further invitation.

Issue of January 30, 1829

Died - The friends and acquaintances of the late Mrs. Catherine Stoll, are respectfully invited to attend her funeral, from her late residence, No. 31 Beaufain Street, tomorrow afternoon at half past 3 o'clock precisely.

Issue of February 6, 1829

Died, in St. Paul's Parish on the 29th January last Mr. Wm. Boineau, in the 54th year of his age.

Issue of February 9, 1829

Died, in Salem, on the 29th January, the honorable and venerable Timothy PIckering, aged 84 years...

Issue of February 12, 1829

Died, at Louisville, (Ky.) on the 19th ult., Col. Richard Taylor, aged 84...

Issue of February 18, 1829

Died, at Savannah on the 16th last, Mrs Rebecca D'Lyon, consort of Levy S. D'Lyon, attorney at law, of that place.

Died - The friends and acquaintances, the members of the Artillery Society, and his Masonic Brethren are invited to attend the funeral of the late Samuel Richards, Esq. from the residence of M. M. Frazer, No. 7 Queen-Street, tomorrow afternoon, at 4 p.m. without further invitation.

Issue of February 19, 1829

Died, at Pon Pon on the 13th inst. of the prevailing typhus fever J. E. M'Pherson Lockwood, son of Capt. T. P. Lockwood.

Died - The friends and acquaintances of the late Col. Thomas Morris, are requested to attend his funeral from his late residence, corner of East Bay and Wentworth Streets, tomorrow morning, at 10 o'clock without further invitation.

Issue of February 21, 1829

Married, on Monday evening last, by the Rev. Mr. Neufuille, John C. Vaughn, attorney at law of Camden, S. C. to Miss Sarah C. D. Clark, of this city.

Died - The friends and acquaintances of Mr. and Mrs. John Falls Walker, and of Mrs. Flint, are invited to attend the funeral of Mrs. Walker, from her late residence, No. 23, State-Street, tomorrow at 1 o'clock, p.m. without further invitation.

Issue of February 24, 1829

Died, on the 12th inst., Mrs. Margaret Waugh, consort of A. B. Waugh, of this city...(Eulogy)

Issue of February 25, 1829

Died, at Montpelier, Va. the residence of James Madison, departed this life on the 11th inst. Mrs. Eleanor Madison...

Died - The friends and acquaintances of the late Florian Charles Mey, Esq. and of his sons Charles S. and John H. Mey...are respectfully invited to attend his funeral tomorrow afternoon at 3 o'clock, from his late residence in Pinckney-Street.

Died - The Cincinnati Society, the Revolution Society, the St. Andrew's Society...of Major Alexander Garden are invited to attend his funeral tomorrow morning at 9 o'clock from his late residence in Short Street.

Issue of March 7, 1829

Married, last evening by the Rev. Mr. Munds, Mr. Wm. C. Tharin, of this city, to Miss Margaret L. Symers, of Norfolk, Va.

Died - The friends and acquaintances of Captain John S. H. Cox and of Mrs. Arabella Cox, are respectfully invited to attend the funeral of the former from his late residence East Bay No. 245, tomorrow at 12 o'clock.

Issue of March 12, 1829

Married, on Thursday morning last, by the Rev. Dr. Bowen, Mr. John T. Robertson, of this city, to Mrs. Elizabeth R. Jenkins, eldest daughter of the late William Reynolds, Esq. of Wadmalaw Island.

Issue of March 26, 1829

Died, on 22d inst. at his residence in Prince Williams Parish, (S.C.)

James McPherson, Esq. in the 36th year of his age.

Died - The friends and acquaintances of Mr. anc Mrs. John H. Dawson, are requested to attend the funeral of the latter from her late residence in Meeting Street, tomorrow morning at 11 o'clock.

Issue of March 30, 1829

Died, at Princeton, N. J. 15th inst. after a lingering illness, the Rev. Robert Gibson, formerly of Charleston.

Issue of March 31, 1829

Departed this life, on Tuesday the 24th day of March, inst. at Darlington Court House, in the midst of the circuit..., the Honorable Theodore Gaillard...aged 62 years...(Eulogy)

Issue of April 2, 1829

Married, at Liverpool, England, on the 2d Feb. Mr. Wm. Barry, to Miss Margaret, daughter of the late Mr. James Johnston, merchant, late Charleston, U. S.

Died, on the 23d February last, out venerable fellow citizen, Florian Charles Mey, Esq. departed this life, in the 83d year of his age...(Eulogy)

Issue of April 10, 1829

Died, on the 2d inst. Solomon Nathan, a native of England: The deceased was 53 years of age...

Issue of April 16, 1829

Married, on Monday evening last, by the Rev. Mr. Manley, Mr. John Randolph to Miss Ann Claudio, daughter of Mr. Charles H. Mist, all of this city.

Issue of April 22, 1829

Died, at Concord, N. H. very suddenly, whilst engaged in arguing a cause before the Supreme Court of that state, the Hon. Ezekiel Webster, of Boscawen, N. H. brother of the Hon. Daniel Webster, of Boston, aged about 52.

Issue of April 24, 1829

Died, at her late residence, in Orangeburgh District on the 15th inst. Mrs. Ann Rowe, wife of Donald Rowe, in the forty-fourth year of her age... (Eulogy)

Died - The friends and acquaintances of Mrs. Melliscent Colcock, the Hon. Judge Colcock, and Mrs. Eliza Ferguson are invited to attend the funeral of the former from her late residence No. 11, Lamboll-Street, at 9 o'clock, tomorrow morning.

Issue of April 30, 1829

Married, on the 22d inst. by the Rev. W. States Lee, Benj. S. Logan, Esq. of Bartholomews, to Miss Dorothea L., eldest daughter of Joshua Lockwood, Jr. Esq.

Issue of May 15, 1829

Married, on Monday evening the 11th inst. by the Rev. Mr. Walsh, of Georgia, Mr. John B. Heriot, to Miss Emmeline S. Yates, both of this city.

Issue of May 28, 1829

Died - In this city, on the 21st May, 1829, Mr. James Wiley, a native of the county of Antrim (Ireland).

Issue of June 2, 1829

Died - Capt. Allen M'Lane...on Friday, the 22d May, in the 83d year of his age.

Issue of June 3, 1829

Died, on the 6th ult. at White Hall, St. Lukes Parish, Thomas Heyward, Esq.

Issue of June 4, 1829

Died - The friends and acquaintances of Mr. Charles Freer, and of Miss Stanyarne, are invited to attend the funeral of the former from the residence of Mrs. Waring, Wentowrth-Street, this afternoon, at half past 4 o'clock.

Issue of June 5, 1829

Died - General Daniel Stewart, a patriot of 1776, died at his residence in Liberty County, Georgia, on the 27th ult. aged 69 years.

Issue of June 9, 1829

Married, on the 27th ult. by the Rev. Mr. Converse, the Hon. George M'Duffie, to Miss Mary Rebecca Singleton, daughter of Richard Singleton, Esq. of Sumpter District, S. C.

Issue of June 15, 1829

Died - The friends and acquaintances of Col. Wm. Rouse, and the members of the Bible and Mechanic Society are invited to attend his funeral tomorrow morning, at 9 o'clock, from his late residence No. 83 Market-Street.

Issue of June 16, 1829

Died - on the 6th inst. in Chathan County, Geo., Mrs. Mary E., wife of James Sharpe, Esq.

Died - The friends and acquaintances of John M. Green, and of his mother Mrs. Edmund Green, and of Thomas P. Green, and Wm. H. Holmes, are requested to attend the funeral of the former, from his mothers residence, Washington-Street, Mazyckborough at 5 o'clock, tomorrow afternoon.

Issue of June 26, 1829

Married - last evening were united in the bands of wedlock, by the Right Rev. Bishop Bowen, Thomas How, Esq., of Waccamaw, All Saints Parish, with Miss Ann Isabel Gibbes, second daughter of Wm. Hasel Gibbes, Esq. of this city.

Issue of June 29, 1829

Died - The relatives, friends and acquaintances of the late Mrs. John Lining, of Edward B. Lining, and of Henry O'Hara, are invited to attend the funeral of the former, from the residence of the latter, No. 2, New Street at 6 o'clock this afternoon.

Issue of July 2, 1829

Died - The friends and acquaintances of Mr. and Mrs. Joseph B. Bennett, Mrs. Pilsbury, also Mr. and Mrs. Robert Giles, and the members of the Washington Light Infantry, are requested to attend the funeral of the former, from the residence of Mrs. Chonte's at the corner of Market and Anson Streets, at 6 o'clock precisely tomorrow morning.

Issue of July 6, 1829

Married - at New York, on Tuesday last, by the Rev. Mr. Knowles, Mr. James Shaff, victualler, of Fulton Market, weighting sixty-three pounds, to

Miss Matilda Castine, of the same weight, both of that city.

Issue of July 8, 1829

Died - The friends, relatives and acquaintances of Col. Francis Cobia, and of his mother Mrs. Cobia, are respectfully invited to attend the funeral of the latter from her late residence No.--- Montague Street at half past four o'clock this afternoon.

Issue of July 9, 1829

Died - The friends and acquaintances of Mrs. Esther Folker, and of the late Thomas Folker, and of Mrs. Esther Lloyd are invited to attend the funeral of the former from her late residence corner of Church and Elliott Streets, this afternoon, at 4 o'clock.

Issue of July 10, 1829

Married last evening by the Rev. Doctor McDowall, Mr. Joel W. Fenn, to Miss Mary, daughter of Thomas Legare, Esq.

Issue of July 11, 1829

Died on the 19th June, at his residence in Sumpter District, of a bilious inflammatory fever, Capt. Robert McFadden, in the 66th year of his age...(Eulogy)

Issue of July 13, 1829

Died - The friends and acquaintances of the late Mrs. Elizabeth Stoll, and of her sons William and Justinus Stoll, are respectfully invited to attend the funeral of the former, tomorrow morning at 8 o'clock from the residence of William Stoll, No. 331 King Street.

Issue of July 16, 1829

Died on the 17th April last, in the 99th year of her age, Mrs. Mary Cochran, relict of the late Captain Robert Cochran of this city...(Eulogy)

Issue of July 21, 1829

Died in Limington, (Me.) Mrs. Rowe, wife of Lazarus Rowe, aged 104 years...(Eulogy)

Issue of July 22, 1829

Died in this city, on the 29th ult. in the 80th year of her age, Mrs. Mary Lining, relict of Captain John Lining...(Eulogy)

(From the N. York Evening Post July 14) Died yesterday, at his house in Hudson Street, William Coleman Esq. late Senior Editor of this paper, in the 64th year of his age...(Eulogy)

Issue of July 25. 1829

Died - The friends and acquaintances of Mr. and Mrs. A. Manson, the members of the St. Andrew's and Union Light Infantry Societies, are invited to attend the funeral of the former from his late residence Tradd Street, tomorrow afternoon at 5 o'clock.

Issue of August 6, 1829

Died this morning, after a short and destressing illness, Mr. Charles Gilfert, aged 42 years, late manager of the Bowery Theatre...(Eulogy)

Issue of August 8, 1829

Died - The friends and acquaintances of Mrs. Frances Rugge, and of Mr. and Mrs. Carrere and family, are invited to attend the funeral of the former from the residence of the latter, corner of Broad and Friend Street, tomorrow morning, at 12 o'clock.

Issue of August 12, 1829

Departed this life on Saturday, the 8th instant, in the 70th year of her age, after a severe and protracted illness, Mrs. Mary Morris, relict of the late Colonel Thomas Morris, and daughter of Gen. Christopher Gadsden, deceased.

Died at Key West on the 9th ult. Capt. Manuel Foentes, of that town.

Died on the 18th, Col. Philip L. Hoffman, a native of New York.

Died on the 6th, Mr. James Weed, son of Mr. Amos Weed, of Darien, (Conn) in the 24th year of his age.

Issue of August 13, 1829

Died at New-Haven, Con. on the 27th ult. Jane L. Floyd, adopted daughter of Dr. Benj. M. Palmer, of Charleston, S. C. aged 16.

Died in London, on the 15th June, Mr. Thomas Wilson, an eminent merchant and banker, of the house of Thomas Wilson & Son.

Issue of August 14, 1829

Died - The friends and acquaintances of Mr. and Mrs. Horatio G. Street, and of their son M. H. Street, are respectfully invited to attend the funeral of the latter, from the residence of the former without further invitation this afternoon at 5 o'clock.

Issue of August 17, 1829

Died - The relatives, friends and acquaintances of Mr. and Mrs. States Rutledge and of Mrs. Laurens are invited to attend the funeral of the former tomorrow morning at 10 o'clock from the residence of the latter 290 East Bay, without further invitation.

Died - The friends and acquaintances of Major Paul S. H. and Mrs. Lynch H. Lee, are invited to attend the funeral of their son, John Van Rhyn Lee, from their residence in Cannonsborough tomorrow morning at eight o'clock.

Issue of August 19, 1829

Died on the 14th inst. Lydia Lucas, daughter of Doctor Wm. Hume; aged 1 year and 4 months.

Issue of August 24, 1829

Died on the 22d of June, at sea on board the Lady Rowena, from this port to Liverpool, Miss Louisa Martha Gourdin, of this city...(Eulogy)

Issue of August 25, 1829

Died - The relatives, friends and acquaintances of Mr. and Mrs. R. J. Turnbull, are invited to attend the funeral of Mrs. Turnbull, tomorrow morning at 9 o'clock, at the residence of Mr. Turnbull in Logan Street, without further invitation.

Issue of August 27, 1829

Died - The friends and acquaintances of Mrs. Frances Mease, Charles B. Mease, and of Mr. Edward Hughes, are invited to attend the funeral of the former, from the residence of Mr. Thomas J. Horsy, No. 231 in the bend of King Street, tomorrow morning at half past 8 o'clock.

Issue of August 28, 1829

Died at St. Augustine, lately, after a few days' illness, Mr. Lewis Hughuen, a native of France.

Died at St. Augustine on the 17th instant, Mrs. Solana, an old inhabitant of that city.

Issue of August 28, 1829

Died - The friends and acquaintances of Miss Mary Haly, and of Mr. and Mrs. Bloomfield are invited to attend the funeral of the former, from the residence of the latter, No. 118 King Street at 9 o'clock tomorrow morning without further invitation.

Issue of August 29, 1829

Died this morning, in the Marine Hospital, Elias Bradford, Jr. of Kingston, (Mass.) aged 30 years, mate of the brig Magnolia, of Boston, from Havana.

Issue of September 1, 1829

Died of epilepsy, at Edingsville, on the morning of the 28th instant, Francis Marion, eldest son of Sandiford Holmes, in the 19th year of his age.
Died at Havre, in July last, Mr. Eugene Be. Fayolle, late of this city.
Died at Columbia, on the 25th ult. Thomas E. Taylor, second son of Thomas Taylor, Jr. of that place, and a member of the Junior Class of the South Carolina College.
Died on the 27th ult. Mr. John G. Walsh, son of Dr. John Walsh, formerly of Columbia.
Died in Laurens District, on the 14th ult. Miss Lucy B. Herndon, youngest daughter of Col. Berry Herndon, of Newberry District.

Issue of September 3, 1829

Married on Montreal (Canada) on the 12th ult. Mr. Esdail E. Cohen, of this city, to Miss Frances Hays, of the former place.
Died on the 27th ultimo, at Sullivan's Island, in the 53d year of his age, Major John L. Hall, late of the U. S. Marine Corps.
Died in Abbeville District a short time since, Major John M'Comb.
Died, at Sand Hills, Augusta, on the 29th ult. Mrs. Rebecca Lamar, relict of the late Basil Lamar, Sen. aged 53.
Died, in Augusta, 29th ult. Mr. Philip Crane, merchant, a native of Canton, (Mass.)
Died, in Milledgeville, 22d ult. the Rev. George Hill, Stationed Minister of the Methodist Episcopal Church in that place.
Died, at New Orleans, 11th ult. of yellow fever, Mr. George H. Adams, a native of Pennsylvania.
Died at New Orelans, 13th, Mr. Frederick Degen, aged 26, a native of Leghorn, (Italy)
Died, at New Orleans, Mr. Paul Wolfe, aged 42, a native of Northumberland county, (Penn.)
Died at New Orleans, 14th, Mr. Jas. E. B. Austin, aged 25, a native of Missouri.
Died at Baltimore on the 25th ult. Colonel Richard Waters, aged 75, a soldier of the Revolution.
Died on the 23d ult. John Beale Davidge, A.M.M.D. Professor of Anatomy in the University of Maryland.
Died in Schoharie, (N. Y.) Mr. Lemuel Cuthbert, editor and proprietor of the Schoharie Republican, aged 27.

Issue of September 9, 1829

Died at Charlotte, (N. C.) on the 27th ult. Joseph Wilson, Esq. an eminent lawyer of that state.

Issue of September 12, 1829

Died at Baltimore, on the 6th inst. after a short illness, William Gilmor, Esq.
Died on Edisto Island, on the 27th ult. Moses Smith, in the 34th year of his age, of the country fever, leaving a wife and child to bemoan his loss.

Died at Savannah, on the 4th inst. Mr. Clark Jenkinson, aged 24, a native of England, but for several years a resident of New York, and latterly of Savannah.

Died in Lumberton, (N. C.) on the 8th inst. after an illness of several weeks, Dr. Willis Pope.

Died at his residence on Rockfish, Cumberland Co., N. C. on the 28th ult. after an illness of 14 hours, John M'Pherson, aged 70 years.

Died at Magnolia, Florida, on the 24th ult. Mr. Samuel Collins, of a bilious fever taken at Apalchicola.

Died in Quincy, Floria, on the 23d ult. Mr. Caleb Snell, a native of Warren, R. I. but for many years a respectable merchant of Newbern, N.C.

Died at Key West, on the 11th ult. Mr. Samuel R. Phillips, aged 24, a native of Newport, R. I.

Issue of September 15, 1829

Died on the 1st inst. Mr. James M'Clain, of York district. He was a soldier of the late war, in which he lost one arm.

Died at Church Hill, Alabama, on the 22d ult. Mr. Eugene Williams, formerly of Camden, aged 21.

Died at his residence, near Greensborough, Alabama, on the 3d ult. of bilious cholie, Mr. Richard M. Harrison, in the 44th year of his age...

Died at Montgomergy, Alabama, on the 30th ult. Otho Belt, in the 40th year of his age, a native of Washington City.

Died - The friends and acquaintances of Mrs. Jane B. Prioleau are invited to attend her funeral from her late residence 22 Guignard Street tomorrow afternoon at 5 o'clock, without further invitation.

Issue of September 17, 1829

Died at Plane Hill near Camden, on the 2d instant, the infant son of Gov. Miller, aged 4 weeks.

Died near Columbia, on the 9th instant, of consumption, at the house of Mr. Davis, Mrs. Mary Catharine Ann Moore, in the 20th year of her age, wife of Mr. John D. Moore, of this city, and only daughter of M. M'Elroy of that place.

Died near Augusta, (Geo.) on the 11th inst. at their Sand Hill residence Mrs. Jane W. Musgrove, wife of Robt. H. Musgrove, Esq. in her 31st year.

Died at Appling, Columbia County, (Geo.) on the 4th inst. Joseph Woodbridge Lee, of Butternut, Otsego country N. York, teacher in the Academy at Appling.

Issue of September 21, 1829

Died at Princeton, N. J. on the 8th inst. Mr. William Alston, eldest son of John Ashe-Alston, Esq. of S. Carolina.

Issue of September 23, 1829

Died in this city in the 13th instant, in the 86th year of her age, Mrs. Mary Mazyck, widow of Wm. Mazyck.

Died at Washington, 17th inst. Edward Jones, Esq. late Chief Clerk in the Treasury Department, aged 74 years and 9 months.

Issue of September 24, 1829

Died at Paris, (France) on the 3d of August last, Dr. Joseph H. Ramsay, of this city.

Issue of September 25, 1829

Died at Georgetown, on Friday night last, after a painful and protracted illness, Mr. William Sherrell.

Died at North Island, on Monday morning last, Mr. John Hall, aged about

36 years.

Died in Anderson District, Rev. Moses Holland, in the 71st year of his age, and in the 47th or 48th year of his ministry.

Died at Trenton, (N.J.) on the 7th instant, Dr. Francis Adrian Van Der Kemmp, D.D. after an illness of three days.

Died - The friends and acquaintances of Vernal Cart, Esq. are invited to attend his funeral from his fathers residence No. 28, Bull Street, this afternoon at 4 o'clock.

Issue of September 28, 1829

Died in this city, on the 22d instant, in the 22d year of his age, Augustus Clements, a native of Dunkirk, France.

Died, in Augusta, on the 21st inst. Mr. Samuel Rae, merchant a native of Ireland.

Died in Columbus, (Geo.) on the 5th inst. Mr. Pleasant Robinson, a native of Guilford County, N. C.

Died at Fredericksburg, (Va.) 22d instant, at a advanced age, Mr. Joseph Verone, a soldier of the Revolution.

Died in Adams, (Mass.) on the 18th inst. Israel Jones, Esq. aged 91 years.

Issue of September 29, 1829

Died on Thursday, 10th instant, James Hunter, one of the contractors on section 114 of the Juniata Canal, and a resident of Derry township, in that county.

Died on Friday 11th inst. Henry R. Seymour, contractor on section 108 of the Juniata Canal, and formerly of the state of New York.

Died at Richmond, (Vir.) 12th inst. Mr. John Ewing, in the 46th year of his age.

Died on Tuesday, the 8th instant, at St. Clairville, Ohio, Mr. David Irwin, and a young man, his apprentice, named Elijah Johnson...

Died at Washington City, on the 21st instant, after a sudden and painful illness, Edward S. Lewis, Esq. of that city...

Issue of September 30, 1829

Died at Washington City, 22d instant, Mr. John S. Bell, aged 23 years and six months, a native of Sackett's Harbor, in the state of New York.

Died in New York, on the 4th instant, the Rev. John Riddell, Pastor of the Associate Reform Congregation of Robinson's Run, Pa. aged 71 years.

Died on the 22d inst. in the 31st year of his age, Mr. G. Baird, a Ministering Brother of the Baptist denomination...

Issue of October 1, 1829

.Died at New Orleans, on the 1st ult. of the prevailing fever, Mr. Myer J. Ellis, in the 36th year of his age, a native of New York, and for several years a resident of this city.

Died, in New York on the 23d ult. after a short illness, Mrs. Ellen Wilkie, wife of William Wilkie, Esq. of Charleston, S.C.

Died at Norfolk, 23d ult. Mr. Peter Fevrier, in the 71st year of his age...

Died in Baltimore, on the 22d ult. Mr. Thomas Powers, formerly of Washington City, in the 23d year of his age.

Died in Edgefield District, on Saturday evening the 19th ult., Capt. Benjamin Harrison, in the 61st year of his age.

Died at Church Hill, Montgomery county, Alabama, on the 16th ult. Mr. Eugene Williams, Printer, in the 22d year of his age, a native of Camden, S. C.

Died in Warrenton, (Geo.) on the 12th inst. George A. Dawson, Esq. Attorney at Law, in the 63d year of his age.

Died in New Orleans, on the 3d ult. James Jenkins, formerly of Richmond, Va. aged about 45 years.

Issue of October 1, 1829

Died in New Orleans, of the prevailing fever, on the 6th ult. Daniel Southard, a native of New York, aged about 25 years.

Died in New Orleans, on the 6th ult. Mrs. Dupuy, aged 57 years, mother of Mr. Dupuy, late Postmaster of that city.

Died in New Orleans, Mr. Thomas F. Townsley, of the firm of Townsley & Prieur.

Died in New Orleans on the 7th ult. in the 43d year of his age, Mr. J. M. Ernest Pottier, a native of Paris.

Died in New Orleans, Mr. Benjamin Tucker, aged 28 years, a native of Bloomfield, New Jersey.

Died in New Orleans on the 11th ult. Stephen Vail, a well known and highly respected citizen.

Issue of October 2, 1829

Departed this life on the 19th inst. Mrs. Mary Jenkins, consort of Mr. John Jenkins, of Johns Island, Planter, in the 27th year of her age... (Eulogy)

Issue of October 3, 1829

Died in Orangeburg District, on the 22d ult. Mrs. Anne E. Felder, daughter of the late Washington Potter, of this city.

Died, on the 7th ult. at the residence of her father in Abbeville District, Elizabeth M. Parker, daughter of Thomas Parker, in the 8th year of her age.

Died in Columbus, (Geo.) on the 5th ult. Mr. Pleasant Robinson, a native of Guilford county, N. Carolina.

Died at Philadelphia on the 25th ult. in the 66th year of his age, Samuel Wetherhill, Esq.

Died on the 23d ult. at Fredericktown, Md. the Reverend Jonathan Hellfenstein, late Pastor of the German Reformed Congregation of that place, in the 86th year of his age.

Died in Limington, (Maine) on the 14th ult. Mr. Lazarus Rowe, aged 104 years...

Issue of October 5, 1829

Died in Barnwell District (S.C.) on the 27th ult. Mr. Daniel Gordon, aged about 38 years.

Died in Augusta (Geo.) on the 27th ult. Mr. Allan Dreghorn, a native of Long-Govan, Scotland, aged 25.

Died at Savannah during the week, Robert Kerr, Pennsylvania, aged 65 years.

Died at Savannah during the week, Thomas Stone, New York, 23 years.

Died at Wilmington, (N.C.) 24th ult. in the 61st year of his age, George Hutchinson.

Died at Wilmington, (N.C.) on the 25th ult. in the 54th year of his age, Mr. Joseph Jacobs.

Died in Franklin county, (N.C.) on the 25th ult. after a lingering illness of nearly five months, the Rev. Bartholomew Fuller, in the 61st year of his age.

Died at his residence in Scotland Neck, Halifax county, 29th ult. after a short illness, David Clark, Esq. a highly respectable and influential planter.

Died at the sound near Wilmington, on the 18th ult. Mr. Patrick Kirk, formerly of Fayetteeville.

Died on the 22d ult. at "Traveller's Rest," King and Queen county, (Vir.) Philip Gatewood, Esq.

Died on the 21st ult. in Rutherford County, after a short illness the Rev. and venerable Joseph D. Kilpatrick, Pastor of the Third Creek and Back Creek Congregations.

Issue of October 5, 1829

Died, in New York, on the 19th ult. in the 26th year of his age Doctor John Denny, of the United States Navy.

Died on Long Island, New York, 25th ult. Gardner Thomas, Purser in the U. S. Navy, in the 52d year of his age.

Died at Nashville, (Tenn.) on the 7th ult. the Rev. Hubbard Saunders, having just completed the 63d year of his life.

Died at Belfontaine (Missouri) on the 2d ult. Major John Whistler of the U. S. Army.

Issue of October 10, 1829

Died in Wilmington, N. C. on the 5th inst. Mr. Augustus Remoussin, formerly of Charleston, S. C. aged 45 years, after an illness of 8 days.

Died - The relatives, friends and acquaintances of Edwin Alonzo Swinton, Mrs. Ann J. B. Swinton, and Wm. H. Swinton, are invited to attend the funeral of the first named, from the residence of Mr. Swinton, in Wall-Street, near Laurens, tomorrow at 12 o'clock, a.m.

Issue of October 13, 1829

Died - The friends and acquaintances of Mr. and Mrs. Evan D. Jones, are invited to attend the funeral of the former from his late residence, No. 33, Laurens Street, at 4 o'clock this afternoon.

Died in Georgetown on Thursday last Miss Sarah Pawley, an old and much respected inhabitant of that place.

Died on the 8th inst. Mrs. Sarah P. Tarbox, age 60 years, a native of Middletown, Connecticut. For the last 40 years of her life she has been a resident of Georgetown.

Died at his residence in Lexington district on the evening of the 6th inst. Col. John W. Lee, after a painful and lingering illness of many months.

Died at her residence in Sumter District, on the 24th ult. in the 21st year of her age Mrs. Eliza L. Spann, wife of Richard R. Spann, and only daughter of Robert Weston, Jun. of Richland District.

Died at his seat in Bladen county (N.C.) on Monday, the 28th ult. at the age of 55, David Gillespie, Esq.

Died in King William county (Va.) on the 21st ult. in the 73d year of his age, Mr. Ralph Horne...

Died at Philadelphia 4th inst. after a short but severe illness, aged 65 years, Mr. George Hobson, merchant, of that city.

Died on the 5th inst. in Philadelphia, in the 61st year of her age, after a lingering illness, Mrs. M. B. Carey, wife of Mr. M. Carey.

Died in Salem, Mass. Mr. Thomas Thornton, a native of England.

Died at Brooklyn, on the 5th inst. of a disease of the heart, Capt. Henry W. Kennedy, in the 33d year of his age, a native of Buck's county, Pennsylvania...

Issue of October 15, 1829

Died on the 5th inst. at her residence in Tatness, Mrs. Margaret A. Thompson, youngest daughter of the late James Sinkler, Esq.

Died in Mazyckborough, on the evening of the 10th inst. in the 23d year of her age, Miss Elizabeth Myers, only daughter of Capt. David Myers, of this city.

Died at New Orleans, on the 9th ult. Dr. E. Audler, late of this city.

Died in Forsyth, (Geo.) on the 1st inst. John Richardson, in the twentieth year of his age...

Died in Forsyth, (Geo.) on the 2d inst. in Norfolk County, (Va.) Major James Tatem, in the 52d year of his age.

Died in the city of Baltimore, on the 5th inst. of the yellow fever, after a short illness, Mrs. Ruhamah Pindall, widow of the late Col. James Pindall, of Clarkesborg, Harrison county, Virginia.

Died at Kingston, R. I. on the 30th ultimo, Major Jeremiah Niles, aged 80 years, a partior of the Revolution.

Issue of October 15, 1829

Died at Mobile, on the 27th ult. of the prevailing fever, Miss Mary Southworth, aged 15 years.

Died at Mobile, on the 30th ult. Dr. F. W. H. Osborne, a native of North Carolina, and aged 28 years.

Died on the 1st inst. of the prevailing fever, Mr. Samuel Knapp, a native of New York, aged 35.

Issue of October 20, 1829

Died in Newberry District, S.C. Mr. Tho. Oadel, aged 38.

Died in Newberry District, S. C. Sarah, daughter of Captain Duckett, aged 19.

Died in York District, 11th inst. Mrs. Mary Bailey, wife of Thomas Bailey.

Died in Columbia, Mr. Augustus Burdett.

Died in Monticello, S.C. Mrs. Mary Smith Paul, aged 23.

Died in Camden, Glorvina Eliza eldest daughter of M. M. and Cynthia, L. MuCulloak, aged 11.

Died at his residence on Little Lynchs Creek, S.C. Finley M. Siveen, native of Invernesshire, aged 83.

Died in Columbia, on the 11th inst. Mr. John Bow, a native of Connecticut, aged about 33 years.

Died at Darien, (Geo.) on the 9th inst. Mr. William Butler, a native of England, but for the last 15 years, a resident of M'Intosh county, aged 45 years.

Died at Hartford, Ga. on the 1st inst. Dr. Austin Janes, a native of Massachusetts, aged about 27.

Died on Haymount, (N.C.) 11th inst. of a puerperal fever, Mrs. Marion Winslow, consort of Mr. Edward L. Winslow in the 22d year of her age.

Died in Fayetteville, on the 12th inst. of a paralysis, Mrs. Ann Bebee, consort of Mr. Asia Bebee, in the 56th year of her age...

Died in Granville county, N.C. Wm. Bullock, Sen. Esq. a gentleman of great piety and hospitality.

Died in Granville county...Miss Eliza Cobb, daughter of the Rev. Jesse Cobb, in her 17th year.

Died in Iredell county, on the 16th ult. Mr. John M'Lean, Sen. in the 70th year of his age.

Died in Mecklenburgh county, on the 20th ultimo, Mrs. Celia Hood, consort of John H. Hood, and only daughter of Mr. Thomas Black, late of S. Carolina, aged 43 years.

Issue of October 21, 1829

Died - The friends and acquaintances of Mrs. Anne Davis, Capt. Thomas Davis, and Mrs. Mary E. Wilson, and likewise the members of the 3d Presbyterian Church, are particularly invited to attend the funeral of the former from her late residence No. 75, Church Street at 3 o'clock tomorrow afternoon

Issue of October 23, 1829

Died on the 10th inst. at Newbern, (N.C.) in the 30th year of his age, Capt. George L. Hart, formerly a resident of Derby Connecticut.

Died at Tomoko, in the beginning of October, of bilious fever, James Ormond, Esq. a planter, a native of Scotland, but long a resident of Florida.

Died at Tomoko, Mr. Kenneth M'Rae, Planter, a native of Scotland.

Died at Quarantine, New York, on the 11th inst. Mr. Ebenezer Pettingell, mate of Schr. Henry Waring.

Died at Pleasant Valley, Ulster county, on the 13th inst. Capt. Andrew R. Miller,...in the 73d year of his age.

Died in Duxbury, Vermont, on the 23d ult. Widow Remembrance Heaton, aged 83...

Issue of October 24, 1829

Died - The friends and acquaintances of Mr. George Gibbs are requested to attend his funeral, this afternoon, at 4 o'clock, from his late residence No. 4 State Street.

Issue of October 27, 1829

Died on the 15th inst. in Fairfield District, Mrs. Nancy Free, in the 57th year of her age.

Died in Louisville Jefferson county, Geo. on the 17th inst. Mr. John Jacob Schley, in the 77th year of his age.

Died in Lexington, Davidson county, (N.C.) on the 10th inst. Samuel Dusenbery, Esq. aged about 70 years...

Died in Augusta, (Geo.) on the 21st inst. Mrs. Margaret wife of Welcome Allen, in the 33d year of her age.

Died at Middletown, Conn. in the 90th year of her age, Mrs. Mary Alsop, relict of Richard Alsop, and mother-in-law of the Editor of the New York Dailey Advertiser.

Died at Mobile, on the 7th inst. Mrs. M'Leod, of North Carolina, aged 25, of fever.

Died at Mobile, on the 8th, Nancy M'Leod, North Carolina, aged 8, fever.

Died at Mobile, David Finley, aged 40, fever.

Died at Mobile, on the 9th, N. M'Neil, Ireland, aged 40, debility.

Died at Mobile, John Hawley, England, 44, consumption.

Died at Mobile, David Ware, North Carolina, aged 40, fever.

Died at Mobile, on the 12th Moses Gooding, Maryland, aged 45, fever.

Died at his plantation in West Baton Rouge, on the 24th ult. John M. Wilson, Esq. formerly of Worcester, Mass., but for many years a resident of Pinckneyville, Miss.

Issue of October 30, 1829

Died in York District, on the 15th instant, Miss Eliza Lucinda M'Call, of the village of Yorkville.

Died in York District on the 30th ult. on board the sloop Splendid, lying off Caesar's Creek, (Florida), Gregory Weems, M.D....

Died at Key West, on the 27th ult. Miss Jane, daughter of Mr. Joseph Ximenes, in the 13th year of her age...

Died at Key West, on the 2d instant Mr. John M. Wilson, a native of Philadelphia.

Died on the 14th inst. at the house of Joseph Carroll, in York District, Thos. Carroll, in the 93d year of his age...

Died at Louisville, (Geo.) 17th inst. Mr. John Jacob Schley, aged 77.

Died - The friends and acquaintances of James R. Baird, of Mrs. Eliza Baird and of John B. Baird, are invited to attend the funeral of the former, from his late residence, Wolf Street, Hampstead, tomorrow morning, at 10 o'clock, without further invitation.

Issue of October 31, 1829

Died - The friends and acquaintances of the late Mr. Thomas Rivers, are invited to attend his funeral from his residence in Anson Street tomorrow at half past 12 o'clock.

Issue of November 2, 1829

Died at Georgetown, on Wednesday, 28th ult. Mrs. Eleanor Wragg, an old and respectable inhabitant of that town.

Died at Georgetown on the 29th ult. in the 22d year of his age, Mr. John Potter.

Died at Georgetown on the 29th ult., Mrs. Mary Marsh, relict of the late Captain Robert Marsh.

Issue of November 3, 1829

Died, in this city, on the 17th inst. Charles S. Mey, a respectable and successful merchant of this city, aged 42 years and 7 months...(Eulogy)

Issue of November 4, 1829

Died - The friends and acquaintances of Captain and Mrs. Wilson, are requested to attend the funeral of their daughter Mrs. Thos. Heyward, from the house of Mrs. Forrest, in Hasel Street, at nine o'clock, tomorrow morning.

Issue of November 6, 1829

Died in York District, on the 24th Mr. John Forbis, aged about 90 years...
Died in York District, on the 26th ult. Mr. Andrew M'Collouch, between 50 and 60 years of age...
Died in Anson County, (N.C.) on the 20th ult. Joseph Tanner, Esq.
Died in Rowan county, on the 16th ult. Mr. Thomas Oakes, aged about 60.
Died in Stokes county, on the 18th ult. Mrs. Elis Barbara Reed, aged 88 years...
Died in St. Augustine, on the 14th ult. Mr. W. E. Allen, a native of England.
Died in St. Augustine, on the 14th ult. Mrs. Ann Keogh, a native of Ireland.
Died in St. Augustine on the 15th ult. Mr. Andrew Keogh,...
Died at his plantation, Tomoka, E. F. on the 7th ult. after an illness of a few days, Kenneth Macrae, Esq. in the 24th year of his age.
Died - The friends and acquaintances of the late Mr. Charles Carrere and Mrs. E. Carrere and family are invited to attend the funeral of the former from his late residence Broad Street tomorrow afternoon at 4 o'clock, without further invitation.

Issue of November 9, 1829

Died at Beaufort, on the 28th ult. Joseph Guerard, Esq. a native of this city, aged 68 years.

Issue of November 14, 1829

Departed this life, in Greenville, So. Ca. on the 15th ult. in the 30th year of her age, Mrs. Eliza Ferugson Bacot, wife of Daniel D. Bacot, Esq....(Eulogy)
Died - The friends and acquaintances of William Burn, Henry Burn and George A. Burn, are respectfully invited to attend the funeral of the latter from the residence of Henry Burn, Cannon Street, this afternoon at 4 o'clock without further invitation.

Issue of November 16, 1829

Died in New York, Captain David Canter, formerly of this city, aged 53 years.

Issue of November 18, 1829

Married on the 14th inst. by the Rev. Francis H. Rutledge, Edward McCrady, Esq. to Miss Louisa Rebecca Lane, only daughter of the late Robert Lane, Esq.
Died, suddenly, on the afternoon of the 23d ult. Mr. George Gibbs, in the 65th year of his age, a native of Newport (R.I.) but for more than 40 years a highly respected resident of this city...(Eulogy)
Died - The friends and acquaintances of Daniel McKeegan, and Neil and John McKeegan, are invited to attend the funeral of the former, from No. 61 Market Street tomorrow morning at 9 o'clock, without further invitation.

Died in this city, on the 13th inst. Mrs. Antonia Emilia D'Almeda, a native of Funchal, Madeira Island, in the 33d year of her age.

Died at Savannah, on the 15th inst. of consumption, Mr. Alonzo W. Kinsley, of the house of A. W. Kinsley & Co. of Albany, New York.

Died very suddenly, on the 23d ult. at Mrs. Liggons, on his way to Augusta, Shadrach Flewellin, Esq. of Warren County.

Died at Mobile Point, on the 4th inst. after a short illness, Thomas Brownjohn, Esq. formerly of Poughkeepsie, in the state of New York.

Died at the Navy Yard, (Pensacola) on the 17th ult. Mr. Jno. Speiden, foreman to the Naval Constructor.

Died in New London, on the 30th ult. Mr. John Shepard, aged 82...

Issue of November 20, 1829

Died at Cheraw, on the 15th instant, Dr. John G. Lance, aged 33 years.

Died in Savannah, on the 16th instant, Mrs. Eleanor Belcher, wife of William Belcher, aged 60 years.

Died in Danville, (Va.) on the 9th instant, Gen. Thomas H. Clark, Editor of the Telegraph.

Died at Milton, (N.C.) on the 10th instant after a short illness, produced by a kick from a horse, Mr. John Elmore, of that county.

Died at Newbern, (N.C.) on the 12th instant, after a protracted indisposition, Minor Huntington, Esq. formerly editor of the Hornet's Nest,...

Issue of November 21, 1829

Died - The friends and acquaintances of Mrs. Harriett A. Holmes, of Francis S. Yates and Kinsey Borden, Jr. are invited to attend the funeral of the former from the residence of Mr. Yates, Ladson's Court, tomorrow morning, at 12 o'clock without further invitation.

Married on the 19th instant, by the Rev. Mr. Hanckel, Lieut. Petigru, to Miss Mary Ann LaBruce, daughter of the late John LaBruce, Esq. of All Saints Parish.

Died - The friends and acquaintances of the late Mrs. Jane Gates, and of Mr. and Mrs. W. G. Simms, Jun. are requested to attend the funeral of the former from the residence of the latter, King Street Road, tomorrow morning at 9 o'clock, without further invitation.

Issue of November 25, 1829

Died in Abbeville District 4th inst. the Rev. James Crowther, aged 65.

Died in Columbus County, (N.C.) on the 19th ult. Luke Yates, Esq. aged 63.

Died in Raleigh, (N.C.) on the 9th inst. Wm. H. Hunter, M.D. in the 29th year of his age.

Died at Knoxville, (Tenn.) on the 27th ult. Dr. Joseph C. Strong, aged 24, a citizen of that place, and a graduate of the Medical College of Philadelphia.

Died at Paris, on the 7th of October, Mr. Seligman Michael, Grand Rabbi of the Israelite persuasion, at the aged of 95 years...

Issue of December 4, 1829

Married last evening by the Rev. Mr. Buist, Mr. William Birnie, to Mrs. Mary Bryce, both of this city.

Issue of December 8, 1829

Died in this city, on the 29th ult. Mrs. Mary Elizabeth Vanroeves, a native of Rotterdam, Holland, in the 54th year of her age.

Died in Columbia, on the 27th ult. Mr. James Hunt, a native of Fifeshire, Scotland, for many years a resident of Columbia.

Died at his residence near Caswell Court House, (N.C.) on the 28th ult. Capt. John H. Graves, in the 83d year of his age.

Died in Spottsylvania County (Vir.) Philip Thornton, Esq. in the 53d
year of his age.

Issue of December 15, 1829

Died on the 30th at the Quarter House on Charleston Neck, Mr. Daniel
Richard Besselieu.

Died at Wilmington, (N.C.) on the 22d ult. Dr. John Louis Wright, son of
the late Judge Wright, aged 24 years.

Died in Wilmington, (N.C.) on the 2d inst. Miss Susannah Jacobs, eldest
daughter of the late Mr. Joseph Jacobs, aged 24 years.

Died in Newbern, (N.C.) on the 11th ult. Mr. Minor Huntington...

Died at Frederick, (Md.) Colonel John M'Pherson, aged 69 years...

Died at Philadelphia, 5th inst. Mr. John E. Molineux.

Died at Philadelphia, 5th inst. Charles Miller, Jr. in the 30th year of
his age.

Died at Koepenich, on the 10th Oct. the eldest son of General Blucher...

Died at Lausanne, on the 23d Oct....Thomas, Marquis of Headford,
Knight of St. Patrick,...in the 72d year of his age...

Died - The friends and acquaintances of Mr. and Mrs. Robt. Bright, and
of Mr. and Mrs. McWhinnie, and of Dr. Joseph Johnson, are invited to attend
the funeral of Mrs. Robert Bright, from her late residence No. 11 Broad
Street, tomorrow afternoon at half past 4 o'clock, without further invitation

Issue of December 19, 1829

Married on the evening of the 10th by the Rev. Dr. Buist, Mr. B. F.
Moore, to Miss Maria M. Dorrill, eldest daughter of Mr. Robert Dorrill, of
this city.

Issue of December 23, 1829

Died in Lancaster, S.C. on the 4th inst. Mr. James Neeson, (for some
time a resident of Salisbury) a native of the county of Tyrone, Ireland, aged
about 22 years.

Died in Savannah, on the 9th inst. Dr. John B. Barthelot, aged 68
years...

Died in Chesterfield county, Virginia, on the 29th ult. Jeremiah
Minter, in the 64th year of his age...

Died in Portsmouth, (N.H.) on the 5th inst. Hon. James Sheafe, aged
70...

Died in New Orleans, on the 3d inst. Charles Ewing, a native of
Philadelphia, aged 31 years.

Issue of December 26, 1829

Married on Tuesday morning, the 22d inst. in St. Paul's Church, by the
Rev. Mr. Hanckel, Dr. Andrew Hasell, to Joanna, eldest daughter of Dr. Paul
Weston.

Died - The friends and acquaintances of Mr. and Mrs. A. Y. Walton are
invited to attend the funeral of Mrs. Walton, this afternoon at 3 o'clock,
from No. 116 Wentworth Street.

Issue of December 29, 1829

Died in Savannah on the 8th inst. after a lingering illness, Miss
Eliza White, a native of New York, in the 21st year of her age.

Died in Fayetteville, (N.C.) Catharine Massey, daughter of Mr. Thomas
H. Massey, aged 11 years.

Died in Cumberland County, (N.C.) on the 2d inst. of paralysis, Mr.
Cornelius Autry, aged 75 years.

Died in Sampson county, (N.C.) on the 6th inst. of a bilious fever, Mr.
Samuel Birdsey, of Middletown, (Conn.)

Issue of December 29, 1829

Died at Philadelphia, on the 8th inst. Wm. Seal, M.D. Assistant Surgeon
U. S. Navy, in the 34th year of his age, of consumption.
Died at New York on the 17th inst. after an illness of several weeks,
Midshipman Helmuth I. Gaedike, of the U. S. Navy, aged 23 years and four
months.
Died at Kinderhook, of pulmonary consumption, James Adger Whiting, son
of General Charles Whiting, in the 18th year of his age.
Died in Woodford County, Kentucky, at an advanced age, Mrs. Elizabeth
Watkins, the consort of Henry Watkins, Esq. (whose death was announced last
week) and the mother of the Hon. H. Clay.

Issue of December 31, 1829

Died - The friends and acquaintances of the late Captina Thomas Logan,
are requested to attend his funeral tomorrow morning, at 9 o'clock precisely,
from Mr. S. Aimars, No. 199, East Bay.

Issue of January 2, 1830

Married, at Mount Pleasant, on the 23d ult. by the Rev. Mr. Campbell,
Richard Yeadon, Junr. Esqr. of this city, to Miss Mary Videau, daughter of
Francis Marion, Esq. of St. John's Berkeley.

Issue of January 5, 1830

Died, at Columbia, 29th ult. Benjamin Courson, in the 43d year of his
age.
Died, at Lexington Court House, on the 11th ult. William Jones, Esq....
Died, 27th ult, Lexington District, Mr. James Hunt, a native of Fifeshire, Scotland, for many years a resident of Columbia.

Issue of January 6, 1830

Died, at Columbia, on the morning of the 30th ult. at the residenct of
his father, Joshua James, son of Mr. John James, in the 20th year of his age.
Died, in Columbus, (Geo.) 18th ult. Mr. Benj. Jepson, Sr. in the 63d
year of his age, a native of Boston, Mass., but for the last 30 years a
resident of Green County.
Died - on the night of the 26th ult. at his residence in Waynesborough,
Burke County, Dr. Benjamin Franklin Green, in the 28th year of his age.
Died, in Baltimore, on the 27th ult. in the 59th year of his age, Nicho-
las G. Ridgely, Esq....
Died...in Baltimore on the 29th ult. after a protracted illness Mr.
William Munday, bookseller, in the 76th year of his age.

Issue of January 8, 1830

Died - The friends and acquaintances of Mr. and Mrs. John C. Jones, and
the members of the German Friendly Society, are invited to attend the
funeral of the former from his residence corner of Wentworth and Cumin-
Streets at 3 o'clock tomorrow afternoon.

Issue of January 9, 1830

Died, at Philadelphia, on the 30th ult. Isaac Jones, Esq. in the 78th
year of his age...
Died, at Philadelphia, Captain William Hawkes, a native of Marblehead...
Died, at Philadelphia on the 1st instant, Turner Camac, Esq. in the 85th
year of his age.
Died, at Philadelphia, Mrs. Maria B. Johnson, in the 80th year of her
age.

Issue of January 19, 1830

Departed this transitory life on the 8th of January, in the 54th year of his age, John C. Jones...

Died, at his residence in York District, on the 3d inst. Mr. Robert Pilcher, about 75 years of age.

Died at York District, on the 2d inst. Doctor William Miskeley, in the 70th year of his age.

Died, near Augusta, (Geo.) on the 27th ult. Howell Rowell Marshall, aged 33.

Died, on the 12th instant, at Fayetteville, N.C. Mr. Isaac Newberry, aged 29.

Died, at Fayetteville, N.C., on the 13th Mr. Wm. Tillinghast.

Died, at Richmond, (Va.) 11th inst. Mr. Benjamin Hemingway, aged 45,...

Died, in Washington, Mr. John Connell,...

Died, in Chester county, Penn., George Hoffman, aged 95...

Died, at Philadelphia, 8th inst. Jonathan Carmalt, aged 71.

Died, at Philadelphia on the 7th, Isaac Thomas, 67.

Died, at Philadelphia, on the 2d inst. in the 50th year of his age, Jacob Sperry, Esq....

Died, at Montgomery, (Ala.) 27th ult. Mrs. Mary Gause, 61, relict of the late John Gause of North Carolina.

Issue of January 29, 1830

Died, in Savannah, on the 27th inst. Mrs. Sheftall, consort of Dr. Moses Sheftall, of that place.

Died, on board the ship Samuel Robertson, on her passage from Liverpool to this port, Wm. KcKenney,...

Died, in Suffolk, (Vir.) on the 14th inst. suddenly, Dr. John Murdaugh, aged 52.

Died, in Ontauga county (Ala.) Rev. Samuel Newton...

Died, in Montreal, U. C. Sir John Johnson, Bart. aged 83...

Died, on board brig Motion, on her passage from New Orlenas to Havre, Peter H. Coffin, a native of Nantucket, and John Cheswill, a native of Marseilles; and on her return passage Wm. Coltin, a native of Philadelphia.

Died, at his house in Chinchester, (Eng.) Dec. 3, Gen. Oliver Nichos, Colonel of the 66th regiment, aged 88...

Died, at New Church in Rossendale, in his 88th year Henry Hargreaves, Esq.

Died, in London, 11th Dec. Benj. Tucker, Esq. of Trematon Castle, Cornwall...

Died, on the 13th Dec. at his seat, Oulton Park, Cheshire, aged 63, Rev. Sir Philip Gray Egerton, Bart.

Died - The friends and acquaintances of Mrs. Lydia Lucas Cantwell, and of P. Cantwell, are respectfully invited to attend her funeral from her late residence Gadsden's Wharf, North, without further invitation, at 9 o'clock, tomorrow morning.

Issue of February 2, 1830

Married on Wednesday evening last, by the Rev. Mr. Bachman, Jacob F. Mintzing, Esq. to Miss Louisa, daughter of Edward Thwing, Esq. all of this city.

Issue of February 3, 1830

Died, at New York, on the 25th ult. Ann Elliott, aged 15 years daughter of Robert W. Rutherford, and granddaughter of the late Col. Lewis Morris of S. Carolina.

Issue of February 4, 1830

Died - The friends and acquaintances of Mr. Henry Boisbon, are respectfully invited to attend his funeral this afternoon, at 4 o'clock, from his late residence, East Bay, between Elliott and Tradd-Streets, without any further invitation.

Issue of February 5, 1830

Married, on Thursday evening, the 21st ult. in St. David's Church Cheraw by the Rev. John W. Chanler, the Rev. Alexander W. Marshall, to Miss Elizabeth Ann, daughter of Dr. Richard Maynard, all of Cheraw.

Issue of February 8, 1830

Died suddenly, at his planatation on Santee, on the morning of the 26th December, Daniel Flud, Esq. aged 56 years and a few days...(Eulogy)

Issue of February 11, 1830

Died, on the morning of 20th ult. at her residence on North Santee, in the 22d year of her age, Mrs. Henrietta Hume, the wife of Mr. John Hume, Jr. and third daughter of Wm. Hazyck, of this city.

Issue of February 15, 1830

Died, on the 2d day of October, aged 60, at his place of residence in Prince William's Parish, S. C., Capt. William Deloach...

Died, at his farm, near Freedom, Baltimore County on the 5th inst. after a severe illness of 12 days, Col. Peter Little, in the 54th year of his age.

Issue of February 16, 1830

Died, on the 3d inst. after a long and lingering illness, Henry Ingraham Esq. in the 42d year of his age.

Died, in York District on the 25th ult. Mrs. Nancy Winston, consort of Mr. George Winston, and daughter of the Rev. Bartholomew Fuller, aged 34 years.

Died, at Beaufort, on the 5th instant, Mrs. Jane Graham, aged 22 years, 1 month and 22 days, consort of Mr. James Graham...

Died, at his residence in Alexandria, on the 12th of January last, Mr. Allen Kellog, aged 25, a native of Litchfield, Connecticut...

Issue of February 17, 1830

Died, at Savannah, on Sunday last Captain Henry W. Lubbock, formerly of this city.

Issue of February 18, 1830

Died, in Abbeville District, on the 4th instant, Mr. Ira Griffin, aged about 50.

Died, at St. Augustine, on the 7th inst. of consumption, Mrs. Susan Fleischman, of that city.

Died, at St. Augustine on the 8th, Mr. Sheafe, of Portsmouth, N.H.

Issue of February 22, 1830

Died - The relatives, friends, and acquaintances of Mrs. H. Bennett and Miss Martha Wells, also the members of the Methodist Church are invited to attend the funeral of the latter from the residence of the former in Hampstead at 8 o'clock tomorrow morning without further invitation.

Issue of February 24, 1830

Died, in the city of New York on the 17th Feb. the venerable Revolutionary character Col. Henry Rutgers.

Issue of March 1, 1830

Married, on the 17th instant, David D. Cohen, Esq. to Mary, eldest daughter of Mr. Nathan Hart, all of this city.

Issue of March 4, 1830

Died, at John's Island, 18th ult. Micah Jenkins, Sen. Esq., aged 78.
Died, near Eatonton, Geo. on the 16th ult. Jesse Bledsoe, Esq.
Died, in Edenton, N. C. on 24th ult. John Cheshire, Esq.
Died, at Cincinnati, Mr. Alexander Drake, the celebrated comedian.
Died, at New Orleans, 14th ult. Mr. Leblanc, the French comedian.
Died, at Cahawba, Ala. on the 14th ult. Walter Crenshaw, a member of the
Bar, formerly of South Carolina.

Issue of March 9, 1830

Died - The friends and acquaintances of Beekman M'Call, of James Heil-
bron, and John Woddrop, are requested to attend the funeral of the former
from his residence corner of East Bay and Hasell Streets, tomorrow morning
at 9 o'clock, without further invitation.

Issue of March 12, 1830

Married, in St. Michael's Church on Wednesday morning last, by the Right
Rev. Bishop Bowen, John Berkley Grimball, Esq. to Miss Meta A. Morris, second
daughter of Col. Lewis Morris.
Died, in Raleigh, (N.C.) at the residence of Gavin Hogg, Esq. the Rt.
Rev. John Stark Ravenscroft, D.D. Bishop of the Protestant Episcopal Church
in N. C., in the 58th year of his age.
Died, at Smithfield, (N.C.) on the 23d ult. after a short illness, Dr.
R. H. Helme...
Died, on Saturday evening last in the 45th year of his age, after a
short but severe illness, William Washington, Esq. only son of the late
General William Washington...(Eulogy)

Issue of March 13, 1830

Died, in Philadelphia on the 5th inst. Mr. Samuel Shinn, in the 60th
year of his age.
Died, in Philadelphia on the 23d ult. Mrs. Mary Howell, widow of the
late Arthur Howell, aged 82.
Died, at Newport, R.I. on the 2d inst. Mr. Benjamin Brenton, at the
advanced age of 93 years.
Died, in Autauga county, (Ala.) on the 20th ult. Mr. Thomas Townsend,
aged 40.
Died, at New Orleans on 23d ult. Major Elijah Clarke, a native of
Georgia...

Issue of March 15, 1830

Died - The friends and acquaintances of Mrs. Mary R. Belcher, and of
her daughter Mary P. Belcher, are invited to attend the funeral of the
latter from her late residence Meeting-Street tomorrow morning at 9 o'clock.

Issue of March 17, 1830

Died, at York, (Pa.) on the 6th instant, Frederick Manning Wadsworth,
Esq....
Died, Lord Reddesdale, January 16, in the 82d year of his age...

Issue of March 19, 1830

Married, on Tuesday evening 16th inst. by the Rev. Mr. Phillips, Mr.
Justinus Stoll, to Miss Elizabeth Sarah Smith, all of this city.

Issue of March 27, 1830

Married, on Thursday evening 18th inst. at Mount Pleasant, by the Rev.
Mr. Fowler, Dr. Robt. L. Bailey, to Eliza Lydia, eldest daughter of the late
Thos. Pearce, Esq.

Issue of March 29, 1830

Died - The friends and acquaintances of the late Stephen Elliott,...., are invited to attend his funeral tomorrow, at 10 o'clock, a.m. from his late residence in Short-Street.

Issue of April 1, 1830

Died, at Liverpool, (England) on the 27th January, Mrs. Maury, consort of James Maury, Esq. late Consul of the United States for that port.

Issue of April 6, 1830

Died - The relatives and friends of the late Mr. Henry S. Scott, are invited to attend his funeral tomorrow morning at 8 o'clock from the residence of Mr. R. F. Howard, Mazyckborough.

Issue of April 10, 1830

Married, last evening, by the Rev. Mr. Gibbs, Mr. Robert W. Wright, to Miss Caroline F. Deveaux, of this city.

Died - The friends and acquaintances of Mr. L. J. Abrahams, are requested to attend his funeral tomorrow morning at 10 o'clock, from his late residence No. 9 Market-St., without further invitation.

Issue of April 14, 1830

Died, at Wilmington, Abbeville District, S.C. on the 4th inst. Mrs. Eliza Woodson, consort of the Rev. Moses Waddell, D.D. in the 60th year of her age.

Died, at Georgetown, Delaware, on the 1st inst. the Hon. Nicholas Ridgely, in his 72d year...

Died, at Troy on the 4th inst. Hon. Samuel M'Coun, Mayor of that city, in his 57th year.

Died, at Boston, on the 5th inst. George W. Clay, aged 30.

Died, at Boston, on the 5th inst., Michael Boland, aged 81.

Died, at Medford, on the 1st inst. Mrs. Mary Kidder, aged 78.

Died, near Prince Frederickstown, Calvert County, Md. on the 20th ult. a colored man named Bazil, aged 114...

Died, at New Milford, Conn., 28th ult. Josiah C. Booth, aged 37 years...

Died, at Philadelphia, 5th inst. after a short but severe indisposition, Capt. Hiram Fox, in the 55th year of his age.

Died, in New Orleans, 23d ult. Mr. Joseph Quays.

Issue of April 15, 1830

Died, in Louisville, Ga. on the 31st ult. Mrs. Mary Triggs, wife of the Rev. John Triggs, in her 31st year.

‣ Died, at his residence, in Jones County, on the 2d inst. James D. Wilson in his 34th year.

Died, at his residence in Edgefield District, in this state, Charles Bussy.

Died, lately, in Lincoln County, Ga. Noah Walton.

Died, at Philadelphia, on the 8th inst. Daniel Brantergam, in his 76th year.

Died, at Philadelphia, on the 7th inst. Miss Eliza Kurtz, in her 22d year.

Died, at New York, on the 6th inst. John Brogan, aged 89.

Died, at Cazenoria, N.Y., Robert Smith, aged 96.

Issue of April 17, 1830

Died, at Fayetteville, N.C. on the 31st ult. Mr. Neill M'Neill, aged 67.

Died, at Fayetteville on the 4th inst. Archibald F'Fadyan, aged 74.

Died, at Brooklyn, 5th inst. Mr. David Taber, formerly of Norwich, Con., aged 85.

Issue of April 17, 1830

Died, at Orwigsburg, Pa., Samuel D. Franks, Esq....

Died, at Marianna, Florida, on the 24th ult. in the twenty fifth year of her age, Mrs. Ann Maria Blebridge.

Died, in Monroe county, (Geo.) on the 27th ult. after a long and afflicting illness, Mrs. Anna Teresa Macarthy, wife of Roger Macarthy, Esq.

Died, at Sodua, (East Ridge) Wayne county (N.Y.) on the 27th ultimo, in the 24th year of his age, Stephen Stone, youngest son of the Rev. William Stone....

Issue of April 19, 1830

Died, at Georgetown, on the 21st, the Rev. Thomas Avant, of the Methodist Church, aged 64 years.--and on the 30th ult. his son, Mr. Eli Avant, in the 25th year of his age.

Issue of April 21, 1830

Died, near Columbia, 31st ult. Mrs. Mary M. Tidwell, relict of the late Gnuman Tidwell, in the 35th year of her age.

Died, on the 4th inst. in the Indian Land, Thomas M'Canee, an old and respectable citizen of York district...

Died, Mrs. Posthuma D. Colcough, wife of John A. Colcough, of Santee.⁺

Died, at Richmond, Va. 14th, Mr. George M. Guy, innkeeper.

Died, on board the U. S. ship Guerrere at Valparaiso, on the 3d of January last, Midshipman Lucius Miller, youngest son of Major Thomas R. Miller of Washington city.

Died, in Dighton Mass. 7th inst. John Hathaway, Esq....in his 73d year.

Issue of April 23, 1830

Died, at Columbia, S.C. on the 16th inst. James T. Goodwin, aged 43....

Died, at his residence in York district, on the 15th inst. James Baxter, aged 60.

Died, at New York, on the 13th inst. Mrs. Maria M'Rae Drummond, aged 23.

Died, at Albany, on the 13th inst. Daniel M'Glashan, printer in the 39th year of his age.

Died, at Middletown, R.I. on the 4th inst. Walliam Bailey, Esq. aged 62...

Departed this life, at Walterborough, on the 11th instant...Felix Broneau Warley, in the 43d year of his age.

Died - The relatives, friends and acquaintances of Mrs. Ann H. and Mr. Robert Aldrich are requested to attend the funeral of the former, from her late residence No. 15 Tradd Street, tomorrow afternoon at 4 o'clock, without further invitation.

Issue of April 24, 1830

Died - The friends and acquaintances and particularly the congregation of the Third Presbyterian Church are invited to attend the funeral of Samuel Bigelow from his late residence West-Street tomorrow afternoon at ½ past 3 o'clock.

Died - The friends and acquaintances of Mr. and Mrs. Robert Walker, are requested to attend the funeral of their daughter Jane, from their residence Church Street, at half past 12 o'clock p.m. tomorrow, without further invitation.

Issue of April 26, 1830

Died, in this city, on the 20th instant, David Myers, in the 19th year of his age, a native of this place.

Issue of April 27, 1830

Died - The friends and acquaintances of Mr. Richard Smallwood, are invited to attend his funeral tomorrow afternoon, at 4 o'clock from his late residence No. 22 Market-Street.

Issue of April 28, 1830

Died, on the 17th inst. at Philadelphia, J. D. Godman, M.D., Professor of Anatomy, Natural History, aged 32 years.

Died, in New-York, on the 21st instant, Col. Thomas Barcley,...

Issue of April 30, 1830

Died, at Wilmington, N.C. on the 29th ult. Thos. Beatty, aged 24.

Died, in Towan County, N.C., Mrs. Unity Ford, wife of Frederick Ford.

Died, in Rowan County, N.C., John Andrews, aged 58 years and 9 months.

Died, in Rowan County, David Stewart, aged 62.

Died, at Milton, Indiana, on the 25th ult. Temple Ballinger.

Died, in the County of Cape Cirardeau, Missouri, on the 1st ult. John Harris, in his 65th year.

Died, at New York, on the 21st inst. William Crolins, in his 78th year.

Died, at Athol, Mass. on the 18th inst. the Rev. Joseph Estabrook, aged about 70.

Died, at Nantucket, on the 10th inst. Thos. Gardner, in his 94th year...

Died - Drowned near Barnstable, Benjamin Sandford...

Issue of May 3, 1830

Died, in this city, on the 27th ult. Mary Jeannerett Ryan, daughter of Laurence Ryan, Esq., aged 14 months and 27 days.

Died, in Beaufort, on the 24th ult. Thomas Fuller, Sen. in the 71st year of his age.

Died, in Columbia, on the 9th ult. Mr. William Thompson...

Died, in Cheraw, on the 21st ult. Mrs. Rebecca Ann, consort of Joseph H. Towns, Esq. in the 35th year of her age.

Died, in Augusta, on the 24th ult. Mr. James Moore...

Died, in Fayetteville, (N.C.) on the 26th ult. in the 35th year of his age, Peter James Mallett, Esq. of the firm of C. & P. Mallett.

Died, on Upper Sound, N.C. on the 18th ult....Mr. John Averitt, aged about 65 years.

Died, in Rockingham county, N.C. on the 23d ult. Joseph M'Cain, Esq. a highly respected citizen.

Died, in Culpepper county (Vir.) on the 16th ult., Rev. James Garnett, Sen. in the 87th year of his age....

Died, in Hanover, (Vir.) on 25th ult. Dr. James Lyons.

Died, in Richmond County, (Vir.) on the 19th ult. Dominic Bennehan, Esq. in the 32d year of his age.

Died, on the 25th ult. Mr. Robert Brown, an old and respectable inhabitant of the Navy Yard Hill, Washington City, D.C.

Died, at Mount Meigs (Ala.) on the 11th ult. Mr. Albert Borde, age 37.

Died, in Hartford, (Con.) George Peaslee, Esq., Attorney at Law, of Burlington, Vermont, aged 29.

Issue of May 5, 1830

Died, at Richmond, on the 29th ult. James H. Corwin, formerly of New York.

Died, at Philadelphia, on the 27th ult. Isaac Patterson, in his 58th year.

Died, at New York, on the 27th ult. Mrs. Deborah Gage, aged 42.

Died, at New York, on the 26th ult. Simeon F. Randolph, in his 38th year.

Died, at New York, on the 26th ult., Henry Lloyd, in his 39th year.

Died, at Hartford, Conn. on the 22d ult. George Peastee, Esq. Attorney at Law, of Burlington, Vt. aged 39.

Issue of May 6, 1830

Died, at Augusta, Ga. on the 28th ult. Charles Granville...

Died, at Augusta, Ga., James Moore...

Died, in Tuscaloosa County, Alabama, on the 16th ult. Elizabeth Foster, in the 63rd year of her age.

Died, at Philadelphia, on the 28th ult. John M. Hess, in the 65th year of his age.

Died, at Philadelphia, on the 26th John S. Hanley, Printer, in his 30th year.

Died, at Philadelphia, on the 28th, Christian Roch, aged 72.

Died, at Philadelphia, on the 26th Jacob Winand, formerly of Baltimore, in his 67th year.

Died, at New York, on the 27th ult. Andrew Heron, a native of Ireland, in his 88th year.

Issue of May 7, 1830

Married, on the evening of the 4th by the Rev. Mr. Buist, Mr. L. Arnold of Boston, to Miss Susan Smith, eldest daughter of Wm. Smith, Esq. of this place.

Died, on Monday the 29th ultimo, at Lower Providence Montgomery county, Pa. the Rev. William Strawbridge, Pastor of the Baptist Church...in the 74th year of his age...

Died, at Sauguoit, Oneida county, New York, on the 9th ult. in the 78th year of his age, Kirtland Griffin, Esq.

Died, in New York, 28th ult. Mrs. Sybil Coats, in the 78d year of her age.

Died, in New York, on the 16th ult....Capt. J. Jones, aged 46 years....

Died, in Lyndeborough, N.H. Mr. Nathan Green, aged about 75.

Died, on the 25th of March last, at Nassau, N.P. Mrs. Harriet W. Hawkins, after an illness of five weeks.

Issue of May 8, 1830

Married, on Wednesday evening last, by the Rev. Dr. Palmer, Mr. I. S. Bailey, to Miss Hannah Jane, daughter of Mr. Wm. McElmoyle, all of this city.

Died - The relatives, friends and acquaintances of Mr. Samuel Parker, are invited to attend his funeral from his late residence No. 6 George Street tomorrow at half past 12 o'clock, p.m. without further invitation.

Issue of May 10, 1830

Died, at Old Fort, Beaufort, S.C. on the 3d instant, Archibald Smith, of Savannah, aged 75.

Died, at New Orleans, on the 24th ult. Stephen Deranto, a native of Bordeaux, in his 73d year.

Died, at Alexandria, D.C. on the 30th ult. Miss Rebecca King, aged 35.

Died, at Norfolk, (Va.) on the 2d inst. Mrs. Sarah Nivisan, relict of the late Colonel Nivisan, of that place.

Died, at Portsmouth, Va. on the 1st instant, Edward Allen, aged 23.

Died, at Philadelphia, on the 29th ult. Mrs. Catharine Miller, in her 57th year.

Died, at New York, on the 30th ult. Thomas Franklin, Register of that city, in his 67th year.

Died, at Montreal, lately, aged 86, Mr. Wm. Langhorn, a native of Westmoreland, (Eng.)...

Issue of May 11, 1830

Died, at Norfolk on the 5th inst. Miss Elizabeth Ann, youngest daughter of Thomas Dickson, Esq.

Died, at Portsmouth, Va. on the 2d inst. Mrs. Elizabeth Toukin, consort fo Charles Toukin, in her 37th year.

Issue of May 11, 1830

Died, at the Washington Navy Yard, on the 2d inst. in the 60th year of his age, Capt. Edward Barry...

Died, at Baltimore, on the 2d inst. in his 64th year, Rossitter Scott...

Died, at Philadelphia, on the 2d inst. Mary B. wife of Wm. Tams, in her 26th year.

Died, in New York on the 2d inst. Wm. H. Cook, in his 23d year.

Died, in New York on the 2d inst. Thomas E. Smith, in his 53d year.

Died, in New York on the 2d inst. Mrs. Ann Dutcher, in her 53d year.

Died, in New York on the 2d inst. George H. Scott, in his 48th year.

Died, in New York on the 2d inst. Thomas Franklin, late Chief Engineer of the Fire Department of that city.

Issue of May 12, 1830

Died, at Germantown, on the 30th ult. Michael Lippard, in his 86th year...

Died, at York Borough, Md. lately, Wm. Hazlet, aged about 45, from Baltimore.

Died, in New York on the 4th inst. Amos Belslen, in his 66th year.

Died, in New York on the 1st inst. Robert Ashmore Cooper, aged 48, a native of East Jersey.

Died, in New York on the 3d Capt. John Campbell, late of the 13th Regiment, U.S.A., in his 43d year.

Died, at New York, on the 4th, Enoch Dodgshnan, in his 51st year.

Died, in New York on the 4th, James Smith, aged 63.

Died, in New York, on the 4th, Mrs. Hannah Ash, relict of Wm. Ash, aged 70.

Died, at Carlisle, Baudes Challeun, Lower Canada, Thomas Sherrer, Esq. aged 60 years...

Died, at Washington, on the 1st inst. Mr. Simon Cantwell, a native of the county of Limerick, Ireland, aged 68 years.

Issue of May 13, 1830

Died, at Savannah, on the 7th inst. Capt. Thomas Clark...

Died, in Southampton County, on the 28th ult. Mrs. Sarah Harris, aged 27.

Died, at Baltimore, on the 29th ult. Col. John Bouldin, in his 70th year.

Died, at Baltimore on the 16th inst. Stephen Winingder, aged 50.

Died, at Washington, D.C. on the 29th ult. Capt. Samuel Carter, of Prince Edward County, Va....

Died, on the 10th ult. on Beach Island, S.C., Rev. Thomas Polhill...

Died, at his residence, near Madison, Morgan County, on the 29th ult. William West, Sen. in his 68th year.

Issue of May 15, 1830

Died - The friends and acquaintances of Alexander Hannah, are requested to attend his funeral from his late residence, corner of Boundary and St. Philip Streets, tomorrow morning at 8 o'clock.

Issue of May 17, 1830

Died, at the Sand Hills, near Augusta, at the house of his mother-in-law (Mrs. Walker), on Sunday morning, 9th inst. aged 35 years, Mr. L. A. Rigail, a native of New York...

Issue of May 18, 1830

Died, on the 13th inst. George, son of Doctor Wm. Hume, aged 1 year and 2 days.

Died, at the Navy Yard, Gosport, at the residence of Com. Barron, George S. Hope, aged near 3 years.

Issue of May 18, 1830

Died, at Richmond, on the 11th inst. Mrs. Hannah Fleisher.
Died, at Philadelphia, on the 11th inst. Mrs. Elizabeth Keen.
Died, at New York, on the 10th inst. Silas Butler, Jr. aged 29;
Died, at New York on the same day, Daniel Merritt, late of Troy, aged 66
Died, on the 8th inst. Wm. C. Shankland, son of Robert Shankland, aged 24.
Died, at Lancasterville, S.C. on the 9th inst. Smith L. Lewis,...

Issue of May 19, 1830

Died - at Richmond, Va. on the 13th instant, Armistead S. Hopkins.
Died, at Richmond, Va. on the 5th instant, Mrs. Martha Harrison, wife of Captain Wm. Harrison, of Caroline county.
Died, at Baltimore on the 12th instant, Captain William R. Patton....
Died, at New York, on the 10th inst. Peter Wessells, Printer, in his 28th year.
Died, at New York on the 6th, Ebenezer K. Kirkham, formerly of Fishkill, Dutchess county, aged 25 years.
Died, at Albany, N.Y. on the 9th instant, Mrs. Maria A. Winne, in her 29th year, wife of Dr. Barent P. Stoats.
Died, at Albany, N.Y. on the 9th instant, Frederick W. Farnam, Cashier of the bank of Newburgh.

Issue of May 20, 1830

Died, at Cincinnati, on the 5th inst. James B. Merrio, aged 21.
Died, on the 29th ult. at Louisville, Ky., Miss Elizabeth G. Reilly, only daughter of Mr. Boyd Reilly, formerly of Cincinnati.
Died, at Eaton, Ga. on the 10th instant, Moses B. Hamilton, Rector of the Academy of that place, and a native of Massachusetts.
Died, at his residence, near Watkinsville, on the 2d inst. Geo. W. Lumpkin, in the 29th year of his age.
Died, at his residence, near Lawrensville, Ga. on the 9th instant, Major John Alexander, in his 75th year.
Died, at Philadelphia on the 12th inst. John Allister, Sen. in his 78th year.
Died, at Philadelphia on the 12th inst. Sarah M'Kinley, in her 67th year.
Died, at Philadelphia on the 12th inst. James H. Smith, in his 26th year.
Died, at New York, on the 11th instant, Anne Bolton, wife of C. W. Faber, in her 23d year.
Died, at Philaddelphia, on the 11th, Mrs. Esther Neilson, aged 78.
Died, at York, U.C. on the 3d instant, Isabel Metcalf, wife of the Rev. Franklin Metcalf, aged 27.

Issue of May 21, 1830

Died - The friends and acquaintances of Mr. John Moore, are respectfully invited to attend his funeral this afternoon, at 5 o'clock, from his late residence, corner of Bull and Smith Streets.

Issue of May 22, 1830

Died - The friends and acquaintances of Mr. and Mrs. B. J. Evans, of Mrs. Massey Graves, and of Mr. and Mrs. Sebring, are respectfully invited to attend the funeral of Mrs. B. J. Evans, from her late residence No. 31 Broad St. tomorrow afternoon at 5 o'clock.

Issue of May 24, 1830

Died, at Wilmington, N.C. on the 11th inst. Capt. Samuel Russell, aged 42.

Issue of May 24, 1830

Died, in Cumberland County, N.C. on the 7th inst. the Rev. James Vann...

Died, in Orange County, N.C. on the 6th, Thomas Hart, in the 94th year of his age.

Died, at Philadelphia, on the 16th inst. S. H. Chapman, of the Walnut Street Theatre, aged 29.

Died, at Philadelphia on the 16th inst., Capt. Samuel Evans, aged 51.

Died, at Philadelphia, on the 15th inst. Edwin Thomas.

Died, at Philadelphia, on the 14th inst. C. Allen, in his 21st year.

Died, at New York, on the 14th inst. Noyas S. Packer, in his 21st year.

Died, at New York, on the 14th inst. William Bookstare, in his 21st year.

Died, at New York on the 14th inst., James Grant, aged 53.

Died, at New York, on the 13th inst. Mrs. Ann Decker, in the 39th year of her age.

Died, at Providence, R.I. on the 13th inst. Miss Hannah Vial, aged 66.

Died, at Providence, R.I. on the 13th inst., Nathaniel Wilbour, aged 42.

Issue of May 25, 1830

Died, at Washington, D.C. on the 18th inst. Jonas Keller...in the 62d year of his age.

Died, at his residence in Symmes Township, Hamilton county, Ohio: on the 9th inst. Peter Bell, Esq....

Died, at Baltimore on the 17th inst. Mrs. E. Ganteagme, in her 55th year

Died, at Philadelphia on the 16th inst. Samuel Hause, in his 59th year.

Died, at Philadelphia, on the 17th inst. Charles Callaghan, in his 67th year.

Died, at Philadelphia, on the 15th inst. Mrs. Lydia Clark of Providence, R.I., aged 77.

Died, at New York, on the 17th inst. Mrs. Jane Moore, in her 67th year.

Died, at New York, on the 16th inst. Wm. M. M'Queen, in his 31st year.

Died, at West Newbury, Capt. Caleb Kimball, 86.

Died, at Beverly, John Baker, aged 75.

Died, at Braintree, Col. Wm. Allen, aged 84...

Died, at Lexington, on the 1st ult. W. Corley, a native of Edgefield district, S.C. aged 24 or 25 years.

Issue of May 27, 1830

Died, at Baltimore, on the 18th inst. Mrs. Elizabeth Harwood, wife of Thomas Harwood, aged 34.

Died, at Philadelphia, on the 19th instant, George Cousland, aged 33.

Died, at Philadelphia on the 16th instant, Joseph Parke, of East Bradford Township, Chester County, in the 99th year of his age.

Died, at New York, on the 19th inst. James Lyon, aged 53.

* Died, at New York, on the 19th inst. Walter R. Wood, in his 35th year.

Died, in New York on the 20th Mrs. Julia Maria, wife of Caleb S. Fiske, aged 33.

Died, in New York, on the 20th, Michael Garney, aged 40.

Died, at New York, on the 20th, at the American Hotel, Thomas W. Miller aged 25, a native of Washington City, D.C.

Died, at Boston, on the 16th inst. William Jennings, aged 70.

Died, at Boston, on the 17th, Joseph Ham, aged 36, formerly of Portsmouth, N.H.

Died, at Cedar Fields, the residence of her father, (Col. E. Simpkins) near Edgeifled C. H., Mrs. Susan Ann Butler, at the close of her 19th year.

Died, at Augusta, on the 24th instant, Reuben Kent.

Died, in Edgefield District, on the 15th inst. Mrs. Hannah Spencer, in her 59th year.

Issue of May 28, 1830

Died, in Cumberland County, N.C. on the 16th inst. James M'Neil, in his

55th year.

Died, at his residence, near Wilkesboro', N.C. on the 26th ult., George Jones, in his 87th year.

Died, at Baltimore, on the 10th inst. Arthur Upshur, a native of Northampton County, Va.

Died, at Philadelphia, on the 19th inst. Miss Antoinette C. daughter of Joseph Kenton, in her 18th year.

Died, at Philadelphia on the 19th inst., Geo. Wiltberger, in his 60th year.

Died, at Philadelphia on the 20th instant, Mrs. Jane Wilson wife of Samuel Wilson.

Died, in the borough of Easton, Pa. on the 16th instant, Mrs. Anna Maria Erb, aged about 72.

Died, in Hubartown, Vt. on the 30th March last, Mrs. Elizabeth Carpenter in her 94th year.

Died, at Portland, Thos. Smith, of Baltimore, aged 30. He fell down a flight of stairs and broke his neck!

Issue of May 29, 1830

Died, at CAmbridge, Md. 21st inst. Wm. H. Fitzhugh, Esq. of Ravensworth, Fairfax, Co.(Va.)

- Married, by the Rev. Mr. Manly on Tuesday evening 25th inst. Mr. Francis C. Blank,...to Miss Eleanor, daughter of the lat Mr. Thomas Chapman, of Georgetown, S.C.

Issue of June 1, 1830

Died on the 28th ult. deeply regretted by a numerous acquaintance, at the residence of his father in this state, Mr. William Bones, Merchant of Augusta, Geo. in the 30th year of his age.

Died, at Norfolk, on the 25th ult. in his 49th year, Mr. Elisha C. White.

Died, in Richmond on the 25th ult. Mr. Robert Graeme, a native of Scotland, in the 23d year of his age.

Died, in Philadelphia, on the 4th ult. Dr. Joseph Stouse, in the 57th year of his age.

Died, in Providence, (R.I.) on the 21st ult., Mr. George Read, aged 44 years, a worthy and much respected citizen.

Died, in East Cambridge, (Mass.) Eleazer Hooper, Postmaster in that town, aged 47, formerly of Portsmouth.

Died...on the 8th of November...Mr. Andrew M. Fanning, of Norwich, aged 26 years, son of the late Thomas Fanning, Esq.

Issue of June 3, 1830

Died - The friends and acquaintances of Mrs. S. D. Gunther, and of her son F. G. H. Gunther, with his Masonic Brethren, are invited to attend the funeral of the latter, this evening, at 5 o'clock from 218 King-Street.

Issue of June 4, 1830

Married, last evening, by the Rev. Mr. Bachman, Dr. William Wilkins, of Purisburg, (S.C.) to Miss Martha C. Broer, of this city.

Died, at Georgetown, S.C. on the 2d inst. Mr. Daniel Cumbee.

Died, at St. Augustine, on the 23d ult. by drowning, Henry A. Hampden, of New York aged 15.

Died, at St. Augustine, on the 28th ult., Joseph Pegroon, of Massachusetts.

Died, at St. Augustine, on the 2d inst. Mrs. Martha Brailsford.

Died, in Runcombe County, Mr. John Burns, a native of Ireland, aged 110.

Died, at Baltimore on the 28th ult. Dr. John Archer, of Ind.

Died, at Philadelphia, on the 28th ult. James Sheadaker, aged 49.

Died, at Philadelphia, on the 26th, Peter Murto, aged 31.

Issue of June 4, 1830

    Died, at Philadelphia, on the 26th, James Wright, aged 26.
    Died, at Philadelphia, on the 27th, Gottlieb Gross.
    Died, on the 24th, near Bainbridge, Ohio, Mr. Wm. Bainbridge, aged 86...

Issue of June 7, 1830

    Died, at the Female Academy in Sparta, Hancock County, Miss Sophronin
J. Magrauder, in her 15th year.
    Died, at the residence of his mother-in-law in Easton, New Jersey, on
the 22d ult. Edward P. Banks, late editor of the Belvidere Apollo, in his
35th year.
    Died, at Philadelphia, on the 28th ult. James Weaver, in his 23d year.
    Died, at Philadelphia, on the 28th ult. Mrs. M. A. Harriott Plumer, in
her 20th year.
    Died, at Elkton Md. on the 18th ult. Dr. John Groome, in 62d year.
    Died, at New York, on the 27th ult. William Bryce, in his 48th year.
    Died, at New York, on the 26th Mrs. Maria G. wife of David Morris, aged
25.

Issue of June 8, 1830

    Died, at Philadelphia on the 29th ult. Mrs. Elizabeth Fox, widow of
Edward Fox, Esq.
    Died, at Moreland Pa. on the 29th ult. Mrs. Hannah Breck, in her 83d
year, relict of the late Samuel Breck, Esq.
    Died, at New York, on the 30th ult. William Bryar, in his 75th year.
    Died, at New York, on the 30th ult. Sarah M'Tur, in her 56th year.
    Died, at New York, on the 30th ult. Miss Jannet Dominick, aged 18.
    Died, at New York, on the 28th, John Ledgefield, aged 52.
    Died, at the family residence, Brooklyn, on the 30th ult. Mrs. Elizabeth
Mercein, aged 68, wife of Andrew Mercein.
    Died, at Rochester, on the 27th ult. Mrs. Harriet, wife of Mr. Levi A.
Ward, aged 19.
    Died, at Scituate, on the 26th ult. Mr. Gideon Jenkins, aged 77, a
soldier of the Revolution.
    Died, at his residence in Fairfield District, on the 17th ult. George
Free, in his 58th year.
    Died, in Greenville, S.C. on the 21st ultimo, Thomas Munday, in his 37th
year, he was a native of England, but for a number of years past, a resident
of this city.

Issue of June 9, 1830

    Died, in Mississippi, at the residence of her son, the Hon. Peter
Randolph, Mrs. Sally Randolph, aged 69.
    Died, at Philadelphia, on the 1st inst. Elizabeth Luvier, daughter of
John Eyler.
    Died, at New York on the 31st ult. Phebe, wife of Samuel Picketh, aged
50.
    Died, at New York, on the 30th Thos. Jefferson Winship, son of Daniel
Winship, in his 27th year.
    Died, at Newark, N.J. Mr. Jesse B. Johnson, aged 40 years.
    Died, at Newark, N.J., on the 27th ult. Mrs. Sarah, wife of Charles
Hedenburg, deceased, in her 64th year.
    Died, at Newark, N.J., on the 30th Mr. David Beach, in the 54th year of
his age.
    Died, on the 29th ult. at Middleville, Dr. Isaac A. Baldwin, a
respectable Practitioner, and useful citizen.
    Died, at the Cove, Stamford, Conn., at the residence of her father, Jno.
Wm. Holly, on the 28th ult. Elizabeth A. wife of Lieutenant M'Kenny, of the
U.S.S.Brandywine, in the 34th year of her age.
    Died, at an advanced age, on the 23d ult. at his residence in Adolphus-
town, U.C., Alexander Fisher, Esq....

Issue of June 10, 1830

Died, at Cincinnati, on the 22d ult. Wm. Tucker, Printer, aged 50, a native of Worcester Co. Massachusetts.

Died, in Williamsburg, (Va.) on the 28th ult. Mrs. Elizabeth M'Candlish, in her 74th year.

Died, at Fortress Munro, (Va.) on the 3d inst. Mrs. Harriet Wodsworth Larned Kirby, wife of Maj. Reynold M. Kirby, of the U. S. Army.

Died, at Baltimore, on the 3d inst. Charles Guildener.

Died, at his residence in Anne Arundul County, on the 26th May, Rezin Estep, Esq. in his 67th year.

Died, at Philadelphia, on the 1st inst. James Power, Printer, in the 27th year.

Died, at New York, on the 1st inst. Thomas Armstrong, aged 32.

Died, at New York, on the 1st inst. Dr. Robert Hogg, in his 35th year.

Issue of June 11, 1830

Died, in this city, on the 20th ult. Mr. John Moore, aged 32 years, a native of Belfast, Ireland, for many years an inhabitant of this city.

Died, at Baltimore, on the 3d inst. Charles Buildener.

Died, at Baltimore, on the 17th ult. Mrs. Jennings, wife of Thomas Jennings, of that city.

Died, at Philadelphia, on the 3d inst. Capt. Robert H. Campbell, in his 38th year.

Died, at New York, on the 3d inst. Mrs. Effe Stout, in her 79th year.

Died, at New York, on the 3d inst. John Adamson, stone cutter, aged 44.

Died, in the village of Madison, Green County, on the 23d ult. Selish Dan, aged about 56.

Died, at Middletown, Conn. on the 28th ult. Daniel Walworth, aged 70.

Died, at Boston on the 31st ult. Mrs. Mary Pike, aged 61.

Died, at Boston, James Lee, aged 30.

Died, at Columbia, S.C. on the 1st inst. Mr. James T. Munds, in the 22d year of his age.

Issue of June 12, 1830

Died, at Philadelphia, on the 4th inst. Thos. M'Kay, aged 70.

Died, at Philadelphia, on the 4th inst., Rebecca A. Corbin.

Died, at Philadelphia, on the 3d inst. Luke W. Morris.

Died, at Philadelphia, on the 3d inst. Captain Robert H. Campbell, in his 38th year.

Died, at Philadelphia, on the 4th inst. Mary M. Hall, wife of John Hall, Esq. in her 26th year.

Died, near Euphrata, Lancaster County, on the 30th ult. John Spread, in his 67th year.

Died, at New York, on the 3d inst. Joseph Lewis, aged 40.

Died, in Milford, Mass. on the 26th Maroh, John Van Vinkle, in his 96th year...

Died, in Livingston, Essex county, N.J., Stephen Edwards, aged 61.

Died, at New Orleans, on the 26th ult. Lewis Chaveau.

Died, in Ray County, Tennessee, on the 29th April, Jonathon Golley, in his 30th year.

Died, on the 10th ult. in the vicinity of Tallahassee, Florida, of a pulmonary affection, Mrs. Marianne Prioleau, widow of the late Col. John Cordes Prioleau, of this city.

Issue of June 14, 1830

Departed this life on the 30th ultimo, in the 45th year of her age, Mrs. Sarah W. Logan, wife of Mr. C. M. Logan, and youngest daughter of the late Isaac Chanler, M.D. of this city...(Eulogy)

Issue of June 9, 1830

Died, at Washington County, Ga on the 5th ult. Mrs. Mary S. Lane, aged 18.

Issue of June 17, 1830

Died, at Cincinnati, Benjamin Hayden, formerly of Boston, aged 35.

Died, at Pendleton, S.C. on the 24th ult. Stephen Chastain, Sr. in his 68th year.

Died, at Baltimore on the 10th inst. Frederick Timmerman, in his 30th year.

Died, at his residence in Morgantownship, on the 29th ult.at an advanced age, Isaac Weaver, Esq.

Died, in Germantown, Pa. on the 2d inst. Henry Gravenstine, Sr.

Died, at New York, on the 8th inst. Mrs. Mary Macelway in her 25th year.

Died, at Mount Pleasant, N.Y., Dennis Darling, aged 57.

Died, at Southold, Wm. S. Beebe, aged 16.

Died, at Portsmouth, N.H. Saml. Fernald, Esq. aged 74.

Died, at Plymouth, Beza Hayward, Esq., aged 78.

Died, in London, March 29, James Rennell, Esq....in the 88th year of his age.

Died - The friends and acquaintances of Mr. Thomas Bridgwood, and Mr. Thomas Johnston, are requested to attend the funeral of the former from the residence of Mr. Johnston, at the bend in King-Street, tomorrow morning at 8 o'clock.

Died, at Maiden Creek, Burkes Countyr, Pa. on the 2d inst. Dr. Thos. Mathias, in his 23d year.

Died, in Reidminstertownship, Bocks County, on the 25th ult. Wm. M'Neely in his 71st year.

Issue of June 18, 1830

Died, at Alexandria, D.C. on the 11th inst. Thomas Steel, in his 66th year.

Died, at Philadelphia on the 8th inst. John Cox, Sen. late Watchman of the Northern Liberties of Philadelphia.

Died, in Nashville, Tennessee, on the 25th ult. Miss Martha Norvell, in her 19th year.

Died, at New York on the 9th inst. John Hawkins, in his 80th year.

Died, at Bloomingdale, Henry STolenburgh, aged 55.

Died, at Fort Niagara, on the 25th ult. Capt. Young, of the U. S. Army.

Issue of June 19, 1830

Died, at Savannah, Ga. on the 15th inst. Captain Thomas Davis.

Died, in Scriven County, Ga. on the 13th inst. Miss Mary Abb Freemen, in her 18th year.

Died, at Baltimore, on the 28th ult. Samuel Krebs, in his 46th year.

Died, at his residence in Redford County, Md. on the 8th inst. Col. John Watts, a gallant and distinguished Revolutionary Officer.

Died, at Philadelphia, on the 11th inst. Mrs. Mary M. Brand, in her 45th year.

Died, at Philadelphia, on the 11th inst., Mrs. Juliana Porrier, aged 93.

Died, at New York, on the 11th inst. Theodore Fowler, aged 41.

Died, at Philadelphia, on the 10th, Mrs. Mary Eghert, in her 38th year.

Died, at Philadelphia, on the 10th, Mrs. Hannah C. Shepherd, aged 26.

Died, in Norwich, Chenengo County, on the 18th ult. Col. William Brush, aged 80, a soldier of the Revolution.

Died, at Boston, Joseph Lamb, aged 63.

Died, at Boston, Mrs. Mary, wife of Samuel Dillaway, and eldest daughter of Josiah Knapp, Esq.

Died, at Tallahassee, Florida, on the 30th ult. Mr. George Buchanan, a native of Scotland, an old and higly respectable resident of Savannah.

Died, at New Orleans, 12th ult. Dr. Isaac De Costa.

Issue of June 21, 1830

Died, at his residence, Milford, Bryon County, Ga. on the 13th inst. Mrs. Eliza Footman, wife of Edward Footman, and daughter of the late Benjamin Ward.

Died, at Wilmington, N.C. on the 12th inst. Mrs. Mary Sampson, in her 85th year.

Died, at Wilmington, on the 11th, Josiah Martin, aged 30.

Died, at Norfolk, Va. on the 14th inst. Col. William Anderson, of the U.S. Marine Corps.

Died, at Staunton, Va. on the 11th inst. Mrs. Elizabeth W., consort of John C. Pulliam, in her 24th year.

Died, at Baltimore on the 10th inst. Joseph Wall, in his 23d year.

Died, at Baltimore, on the 14th, Mrs. Elizabeth, consort of William W. Keyser.

Died, at Baltimore, on the 13th, Miss Lydia A. Thump, in her 26th year.

Died, at Baltimore, on the 12th, Miss Elizabeth Gittings, in her 26th year.

Died, at his residence, in Manchester, Md. on the 15th inst. John Potts.

Died, at New York, on the 11th inst. Nathaniel Bradford, in his 55th year.

Died, at New York, on the 10th inst. John Tingue, aged about 27.

Died, at Carmel, N.Y., John son of Joseph Craft, aged 25.

Died, at Carmel, N.Y., suddenly, Hannah Cronk, aged 76.

Died, in Courtland, Stephen Curry, aged 88.

Died, at Augusta, Ga. on the 15th inst. Mrs. Kezia Arnold, in the 67th year of her age.

Issue of June 23, 1830

Died, in New York, 15 instant,..., Thomas Watson, aged 46 years, a native of Richmond, (Va.) but of late years a resident of Charleston, (S.C.)

Died, in Union District, on the 5th of May, Mrs. Louisa Gist, late consort of Wm. Gist, aged 18 years.

Died, at Norristown, (Pa.) on Monday morning, Edwin L. Carrell, Attorney at Law, aged 24.

Died, at New York, on the 6th inst. Mr. Edmund Post, of Westbury, L.I. aged 68.

Died, at New York, Capt. Charles Webber, of schr. Delta, of Augusta, (Me.) aged 40 years.

Died, at the Theological Seminary, in Auburn, on the 2d inst. after an illness of six days, John L. Howard, aged 27.

Died, at Newark, suddenly, Edward E. Woodruff, aged 27.

Died, at Bellville, on the 8th inst. Mr. Wm. Batchaler, aged 71, a native of Great Britain...

Died, at Augusta, Sussex County, N.J., a few days since, Col. John Gustin, at an advanced age, a prominent citizen of that country.

Died, in New Haven, Rev. Isaac Kimball, pastor of the Baptist Church in Wallingford, aged 46.

Issue of June 26, 1830

Died - The friends and acquaintances of Captain John Williamson, John Stoney and John Magrath,..., are invited to attend the funeral of the former, from his late residence at Mr. John Evringhams, No. 240 East Bay, tomorrow afternoon at 5 o'clock.

Issue of June 28, 1830

Died, in Savannah, Ga. on the 19th inst. Mrs. Isabella Chadbourn, wife of Jacob Chadbourn, aged 21 years and 6 months.

Died, at Philadelphia, on the 19th inst. Mrs. Hannah Gill, wife of Captain Robert Gill, in her 81st year.

Died, at New York, on the 18th inst. Peter Crawbuck, in his 67th year.

Died, at New York, on the 18th inst. Mrs. Hannah Burns, aged 76.

Issue of June 28, 1830

Died, at Bench Island, S.C. on the 19th inst., Casper Nail, Jr. aged about 36.

Issue of June 29, 1830

Died, at Columbia, S.C. on the 12th inst. Gabriel Friday, in his 74th year,...

Died, at Baltimore, on the 21st inst. William Duff, in his 51st year.

Died, at Philadelphia, on the 21st inst. Mrs. Mary Hughes, wife of James Hughes, in her 43d year.

Died, at New York, on the 31st inst. John Culbert, aged 45.

Died, at Whitestone, L.I. on the 18th inst. Mrs. Elizabeth Johnson, relict of J. Johnson...

Died, at Molden, on the 16th inst. Mrs. Sally Oakes, aged 75.

Died, in Needham, Miss Mary Steedman, aged forty.

Died, on board brig Scron, on her passage from Matanzas to Boston, Miss Louisa Shepherd, of Bath, Me. aged 21.

Issue of June 30, 1830

Departed this life on Saturday, the 27th instant, in the 82d year of his age,..., Capt. John Williamson, Merchant of this city...

Died, at Wilmington, D.C. on the 3d instant, Mrs. Leith Irving, in her 73d year, relict of Dr. Lerin Irvin, late of Somerset County, Md.

Died, in Cape May County, Md. near Dennis' Creek, on the 15th inst. Mrs. Elizabeth Rumpley.

Died, at Norristown, Pa. on the 14th inst. Edwin S. Carrell, Attorney at Law.

Died, at New York, on the 21st inst. Thomas Crighton, in his 38th year.

Died, at New York, on the 21st inst. Captain Hezekiah Atwood, of Boston, aged 42.

Died, at Norwalk, Con. on the 17th inst., Esther, wife of Henry Belden, Esq. in her 57th year.

Died, in Berkley, Mass. on the 8th inst. Capt. Thomas Briggs, aged 98 years...

Issue of July 1, 1830

Died, at his seat, in Stokes county, N.C. on the 9th ult. Joseph Kerner, Esq., Post Master at Dobson's Cross Roads, in his 62d year.

Died, at Norfolk, on the 25th ult. Mrs. Sarah Tebo, in her 22d year.

Died, at Petersburg, Old Dominion, on the 23d ult. Mrs. Mary Warner, of Upper Darby, Chester County, in her 77th year.

Died, at Petersburg, on the 23 ult. Joseph Gossuer.

Died, at New York, on the 23d ult. Martha, widow of the late Captain John Ferrier, in her 66th year.

Died, at Sag Harbour, Long Island, N.Y. on the 20th ult. Mrs. Sarah Crowell, daughter of Samuel L'Hommedieu, Esq. in her 42d year.

Died, at the residence of her mother in Edgefield district, on the 19th inst. Lucretia Crain, in the 21st year of her age.

Issue of July 2, 1830

Died, on the 23d ult. at her residence in Johnsonville, James Island,... Mrs. Margaret M. Lawton, consort of Winborn Lawton, in the 43d year of her age.

Died, near Yorkville, S.C. on the 26th ult. George Washington Ward, in his 25th year.

Died, at New York, on the 26th ult. Mrs. Catharine Leister, wife of John Low, Jr. in the 34th year of her age.

Died, at New York, on the 25th, after a lingering illness, Alex. Dillon.

Died, at New York, on the 25th, Mrs. Elizabeth Poss, in her 47th year.

Died, in poughkeepsie, on the 19th ult. Mrs. Tabitha Tice, consort of

Captain Isaac Tice, in her 46th year.

Died - The friends and acquaintances of Mr. and Mrs. James H. Ladson are invited to attend the funeral of their daughter Eliza, from the residence of Mrs. Fraser, Tradd-Street, this afternoon at half past 5 o'clock.

Issue of July 3, 1830

Died, at his residence at Gravelly Hill, in the county of Bedford, Va. on the 8th inst. Col. John Watts, in the 75th year of his age.

Died, at Philadelphia, on the 24th ult. John How, in his 65th year.

Died, at New York on the 25th ult. Mr. Horatio Grim, son of the late Philip Grim.

Died, at New York, on the 25th ult., Thomas Benton, in the 51st year of his age.

Died, at Cambridge, N.Y. Ann Small, aged 88.

Died, at Providence, R.I. on the 13th ult. Capt. Wm. Arnold, aged 38.

Died, in Smithfield on the 17th ult., Augustus Aldrick, aged 70.

Died, at Columbia county, Ala. on the 9th ult. Col. Thos. D. Carr, aged 27.

Died, at the plantation of Mr. George Hill, in Columbia county on the 24th ult. Mrs. Ann B. Hill, in her 27th year.

Died, in Savannah, during the week ending the 29th ult. a Mrs. Charitv Wade, of South Carolina, aged 32.

Issue of July 6, 1830

Died - The friends and acquaintances of Mr. and Mrs. W. Meeker, are invited to attend the funeral of the latter, from her late residence No. 57 Wentworth St., this afternoon at 4 o'clock, without any further invitation.

Issue of July 7, 1830

Died, at Baltimore, on the 28th ult. Job Merryman, aged 60.

Died, at Baltimore, on the 29th, Beal Israel, in his 71st year.

Died, at Baltimore, on the 29th, Capt. Daniel Clayton, in his 45th year.

Died, at Conewingo, (M.D.) on the 30th ult., Joseph Day, late of the state of New York, aged 35.

Died, at Philadelphia, on the 27th ult. Samuel Platt, aged 29.

Died, at Philadelphia, on the 18th, Derusha Curtis, an approved Minister of the Monthly Meeting of Friends of Philadelphia, for the Northern District, aged 51.

Died, at New York, on the 29th ult. George Jeny, Merchant of Rochester, and formerly of Hartford, (Conn.) aged 36.

Died, at New York, on the 28th ult. Augustus Lafayette Speight, aged 45.

Issue of July 8, 1830

Died, at Pendleton, S.C. on the 23d ult. Colonel John G. Hunter, aged 26

Died, in Morgan County, Ga. on the 23d ultimo, Faulkner Heard, aged about 43.

Died, in Madison County, Ga. on the 17th ult. Mrs. Mary Sayes, in her 87th year.

Died, at Norfolk, Va. on the 1st inst. Edwin Stark, aged 62.

Died, at his residence, in Westmoreland County, Va. on the 23d ult. William Augustine Washington, in his 26th year.

Died, at Baltimore, on the 30th ultimo, Thomas Harban, a native of Coventry, (Eng.) aged 44.

Died, at Philadelphia, on the 30th ultimo, Miss Carolina, wife of Andrew Moore, aged 28.

Died, at Philadelphia, on the 29th, Richard Dorff, aged 36.

Died, at Philadelphia, on the 29th, Jacob Bricker, in his 64th year.

Died, at New York on the 29th ult. Mrs. Sarah, wife of Elijah Pearson, and daughter of the Rev. John Sanford, D.D.

Died, at Portsmouth, N.H., Hon. Elijah Hall, aged 87...

Died, at Medefield, Mass. Deacon Jonathan Wright, aged nearly 96...

Issue of July 8, 1830

Died, on the 9th inst. at Marie, near Quebec, Nouvelle Beauce Jecques Gaque, and Magdaline Morin, his wife, both 77 years old...

Issue of July 9, 1830

Died, on the 5th inst. Jacob Read, Esq., eldest son of the late Gen. Read, of South Carolina.

Died, at Georgetown, S.C. on the 20th inst., Andrew Patterson, aged 28, a native of Ireland.

Died, at Georgetown, S.C. on the 3d inst. George Potter in his 17th year son of the late Obadiah Potter, Esq.

Died, at New York, on the 1st inst. Samuel Hull, of Hertfordshire, Eng. aged 23 years.

Died, at New York, on the 1st inst., Mrs. Sarah, wife of Peter Cameron, aged 39.

Died, at New York, on the 30th ult. Ebenezer Lang, aged 59.

Died, at New York on the 30th ult., David S. Mirchell, in his 19th year.

Issue of July 12, 1830

Died, on the 6th inst., Reginald Herber, son of Rev. Wm. H. Mitchell, aged 10 months...

Died, at Savannah, on the 30th ult. Thomas S. Luther, aged 38, a native of Massachusetts.

Died, in Richmond, Va. on the 28th ult. Major Wm. Price, at an advanced age, he was a soldier of the Revolution.

Died, on the 17th ult., in Sewisky, Allegany county, Pa. Major Daniel Fleet, aged 82.

Died, on the 1st inst. at his farm in Baltimore county, James Madison in the 76th year of his age.

Died, at Philadelphia on the 3d instant, Ann, wife of Isaac Bonsall, Steward of the Pennsylvannia Hospital.

Died, at Philadelphia, on the 3d, Mrs. Susan Kelly, aged 32.

Died, at Philadelphia, on the 4th Aaron H. Corwine, in his 27th year, formerly of Cincinnati, Ohio.

Died, at Philadelphia, on the 4th, Matthew Bujac, in his 48th year.

Died, at New York, on the 3d inst. Margaret W. Shaffer, in her 67th year.

Died, at New York, on the 2d inst. Mary, wife of Isaac Wood, M.D.

Died, at New York, on the 2d inst. Miss Elenor Leech, in her 24th year.

Died, at Fernandina de Zaqua, Island of Cuba on the 27th ult. Thomas Davy, aged 41, son of the lat Wm. Davy, Esq., American Consul at Leeds.

Died, at Edgefield Court House, on the 5th instant, Mrs. Sabra Jeter, wife of John S. Jeter, aged 39.

Died, at New Orleans, on the 28th ult. Mrs. Alcase Lavarty.

Died, in Norfolk, Col. Wm. Anderson, of the U. S. Marine Corps...

Issue of July 13, 1830

Died, at Smiths Ford, in Yorkville District, on the 26th ult., Henry Smith, aged 52.

Died, at Philadelphia, on the 4th inst., Matthew Bryan, aged 43.

Died, at Philadelphia, on the 5th, Martin L. Cassey, in his 38th year.

Died, at New York, on the 3d inst., Henrietta Esther, only daughter of Calvin Bolis.

Died, at Unadilla, Otsego county, on the 26th ult. of pulmonary consumption, Boswell Wright, Esq.

Died, at Canewingo, Md. on the 30th June, Joseph Day. late resident of the state of New York, aged about 35 years.

Died, at Quebec, Dr. F. Blanchet, who some time since, took his medical degree in New York...

Issue of July 14, 1830

Died, on the 23d ult. at Haywood, his seat in Westmoreland County, Va., Wm. Augustine Washington, in his 26th year.

Died, at Alexandria, D.C. on the 26th ult. Daniel Wright, in his 56th year.

Died, at Harrisburg, Pa. on the 29th ult. Mrs. Ann Reynolds, consort of the Rev. John Reynolds, Rector of St. Stephen's Church.

Died, at Philadelphia, on the 6th inst. Martin L. Cassey, in his 38th year.

Died, at Philadelphia, on the 6th inst., Benoit Ferre, of consumption.

Died, in Philadelphia, on the 6th inst., Mrs. Margaret M., wife of Ambrose White, in her 47th year.

Died, at his residence, in Schuyler, N. Y. on the 26th ultimo, Robert Burch, Esq. aged 68.

Died — The friends, relatives and acquaintances, and the members of the American Friendly Association, the Union Harmonic Society, and the Masonic Fraternity, are respectfully invited to attend the funeral of the late Mr. Charles Holmes, from the corner of East Bay and Ellery Street, tomorrow morning at 8 o'clock, without further invitation.

Issue of July 16, 1830

Died, in Madison County, Tennessee, Capt. Joseph Love, aged 23, son of Gen. Thomas Love, of Macon County, N.C.

Died, in Spartanburg District in this state, on the 18th ult. the Rev. Thomas Bomar, aged 60.

Died, at Baltimore, on the 7th inst., Joseph M'Donough, in his 48th year.

Died, at Baltimore, on the 5th inst. Samuel Houston, aged 31.

Died, at Anapolis, Va. on the 3d inst. Edward R. Ridgely, Esq. in his 32d year.

Died, at Philadelphia, on the 8th inst. Wm. Pickering Smith, in his 53d year.

Died, at Philadelphia, on the 29th ult., Andrew Hall, in his 91st year.

Died, at New York, on the 7th inst. Phoebe Hicks, aged 51.

Died, at Flatbush, L.I. on the 7th inst. John Clarkson, son of the late Charles Clarkson.

Issue of July 17, 1830

Died, at Philadelphia, on the 9th inst. Mrs. Ann Hutchinson, consort of James Hutchinson.

Died, at Philadelphia, on the 8th inst. Mary, daughter of W. Sutton, of Kensington.

Died, at New York, on the 8th inst., Isaac Rhodes, in his 49th year.

Died, at New York, on the 7th, Mrs. Mary, wife of Mathew Nelis, in her 38th year.

Issue of July 18, 1830

Died, at New York, on the 6th inst., James W. Anderson, aged 45.

Issue of July 20, 1830

Died, at Darlington, C.H. in this state, James H. Henry, in his 28th year.

Died, at Norfolk, Va. on the 15th ult. Miss Martha Saunders.

Died, at Baltimore, on the 10th inst., Frederick German, in his 41st year.

Died, at Hilsborough, London county, Va. on the 4th inst. Solomon Parsons, in the 53d year.

Died, at Philadelphia on the 11th inst. Mrs. Harriet H., wife of Geo. W. Gill, aged about 23.

Issue of July 20, 1830

Died, at New York, on the 12th inst., John C. Krenmel, aged 78.

Died, at New York, on the 10th inst., Edward Delanoy, aged 25.

Died, on Governors Island, on the 10th inst. William Cherrington, of Baltimore, aged 52, he has been blind 18 years.

Died - The friends and acquaintances of the Rev. Gabriel W. Wayne, of Georgetown, (S.C.) are invited to attend his funeral from the residence of Francis D. Poyas, No. 63 Queen-Street, at 4 o'clock this afternoon.

Issue of July 23, 1830

Died, at Norfolk, Va. on the 17th inst., James Rudder.

Died, at Hartford, Co. on the 4th inst., Mr. John Hall, aged 77.

Died, at New Haven, Ct., Mrs. Delia Chidsey, aged 31.

Died, at Philadelphia, on the 15th inst., the Rev. Noah Davis, in the 28th year of his age. Agent of the Baptist General Tract Society.

Died, suddenly, at New York, on the 14th instant, John Dickie, aged 47.

Died, at Charlestown, Mr. Joseph Gossom, aged 100, a Revolutionary Pensioner.

Died, at Newburyport, Mrs. Eunice Knight, aged 73.

Died, at Portsmouth, Mrs. Margaret Manning, aged 56.

Died, at Salem, Mr. Simeon Peters, aged 49.

Issue of July 27, 1830

Died, at Philadelphia, on the 20th inst., Mr. Charles Boyle, aged 25.

Died, at Philadelphia, on the 20th inst., Joseph Canover, Senr. aged 54.

Died, at Baltimore, on the 19th inst. Mrs. Mary Hoffman.

Died, at Baltimore, on the 20th Mrs. Mester Taylor, aged 73, a native of Bristol, England, after a protracted illness, in the 101st year of her age.

Died, at Baltimore, Mrs. Mary Wood, suddenly.

Died, at New York, on the 18th inst., Mr. Rutgur Vanderbelt, in his 28th year.

Died, at Worcester, Buiah Clark, aged 19...

Died, at Lancaster, Mr. John Carter, aged 41.

Died, at Shutesbury, Mr. Samuel Wood, formerly of New Salem, aged 81, a revolutionary pensioner.

Issue of July 28, 1830

Died, at Philadelphia, on the 19th inst., Miss Henrietta Morrison, aged 24.

Died, at New York, on the 19th, James Langley, aged 57.

Died, at Peacham, Vt. Wm. Chamberlain, Esq. Professor of Languages, and Treasurer of Dartmouth College, aged 39.

★ Died, at Warren, R.I. Capt. Nimmo, aged 76.

Died, at Bristol, Samuel Allen, aged 23.

Issue of July 31, 1830

Died, at New York, 22d inst. after a few days illness, Mr. Wm. F. Macon, of Richmond, Va.

Died, at Amsterdam, Montgomery county, on Friday morning last, John Jay Danforth, Esq., counsellor at law, in the 33d year of his age.

Died, at Norwich, Conn. on the 15th, suddenly, Dr. Nathan Tisdale, aged 58 years.

Died, at New Orleans, on the 24th inst. Captain Henry G. Strong, of Bristol, R. I. late master of brig Mordecai, aged 24 years.

Died, at Jackson, Louisiana, on the 9th July, Mrs. Clara Ingalls, wife Dr. Thomas R. Ingalls, Professor of Natural History in the College of Louisiana.

Issue of August 3, 1830

Died, in Yorkville, on the 19th ult., Mrs. Sarah Woodward, consort of Thos. Woodward, Esq. and daughter of Col. David Myers, of Richland.

Died, in Yorkville, on the 17th ult., Mrs. Elizabeth Chambers, aged 88.

Died, in Yorkville, on the 23d ult., Mr. Jas. Saddler, an aged and respectable citizen.

Died, at Middletown, Conn. on Wednesday, the Hon. Saml. W. Dana, formerly a Senator of the U.S....

Died, at Milton, N.H. widow, Patience Clements, aged 101 years and 6 months.

Died, at Philadelphia, on the 24th ult. George Knou, Sen., aged 65.

Died, at Philadelphia, on the 24th ult., Emeline Harder, aged 14.

Died, at Philadelphia, on the 26th ult. Wm. Hanley.

Died, at Philadelphia, on the 26th ult., John Stevenson, aged 56.

Died, at Philadelphia, on the 26th ult., Miss Sarah Ann Browne, aged 24.

Died, at New York, Jacob Townsend, Esq. aged 38.

Died, at New York, Martin Quingley, aged 49.

Issue of August 5, 1830

Died - The friends and acquaintances of Mrs. Celia Cohen, of Mr. and Mrs. Groning, also the members of the Methodist Episcopal Church, are requested to attend the funeral of the former, tomorrow morning at half past 8 o'clock, from the residence of the latter, corner of Tradd and Greenhill Streets.

Issue of August 6, 1830

Died, in Cuba, on the 28th June, Dr. Theodore Essweine, formerly of this city.

Died, at Augusta, on the 25th ult. in the 76th year of his age, Philip St. Maria, a native of Madrid, but for the last 50 years a resident of the United States.

Died, at Newbern, N.C. on the 26th ult., Mrs. Margaret Ann Freshwater, consort of Mr. James Freshwater.

Died, at Raleigh, on the 25th ult., the Rev. Josiah James Kirkpatrick, Pastor of the Presbyterian Congregation of Fayetteville.

Died, at Raleigh, on the 30th ult. very suddenly, Mrs. Eliza Childs.

Died, on the 30th ult., Mrs. Esther Cameron, of Wilmington.

Died, in Robeson County, on the 24th ult. Lewis Barge, Esq. aged 60 years.

Issue of August 7, 1830

Died, in New YOrk on the 15th Monsieur Claudius Lubasse, the celebrated dancer and ballet master at the Bowery Theatre, aged 50 years.

Died, in Charlestown, (Mass.) on the 24th ult., Capt. Daniel Low, late master of the ship Clematis.

Died, at New Lotts, L. Island, on the 28th ult. Mr. Christian Duryee, aged 80 years, an old and respectable inhabitant of that place.

Issue of August 13, 1830

Died, at Fort Macon, near Beaufort, N.C. on the 28th ult., Mary M'Intire daughter of Lt. Wm. A. Eliason, of the U. S. Engineer Corps.

Died, at Lincolnton, N.C. on the 26th ult. Beverly J. Thompson, Esq. Attorney at Law.

Died, in Lexington, on the 23d ult., Mr. Jesse Hargrave.

Died, in New York on the 4th inst. Isaac Blackburn, Esq., D.A. Com'ry General in his B. M. Service, aged 31.

Died, at New York, on the 2d inst., Mrs. Phebe Summers, aged 41.

Died, in Providence, R.I. on the 30th ult., John Lippitt, Esq. aged 68.

Died, in Warren, R.I., Capt. Shubel Burr, aged 43.

Issue of August 13, 1830

Died, in Portland, Miss Elizabeth, daughter of Captain P. Pierce, aged 15...

Issue of August 14, 1830

Died, newr Washington City, on the 9th inst., George Graham, Esq. late Commissioner of the General Land Office.

Issue of August 16, 1830

Died, at Charlotte Hall, St. Mary's county, Md. on the 6th inst., Joshua Hutchins, Merchant of Baltimore.

Died, in the county of Spottsylvania, Pa. on the 17th ult. the Rev. William E. Waller, aged 85...

Died, in Portsmouth, N.H., Hon. J. Sherburne...He died in the mansion of his father...

Issue of August 17, 1830

Died, in Georgetown, on the 10th inst., Margaret Hall, relict of the late Mr. John Hall.

Died, in Georgetown, on the 9th inst., Mr. Israel Solomons.

Died, at St. Augustine, on the 27th ult. by lightning, David, son of Andrew Storrs, aged 14.

Died, at St. Augustine, on the 25th Arthur O'Keafe, by bruises from a rice tierce.

Died, at St. Augustine, on the 21st of consumption, Mrs. Jane D. Brush, of New York.

Died, in New York, on the 5th inst., Joseph Antiguenave, merchant, in the 49th year of his age.

Died, at Mexico, Oswego Co., N.Y. on the 22d ult. after a short illness, Mrs. Emily Dundas, wife of Burnet Dundas, Esq.

Issue of August 19, 1830

Died - The relatives, friends, and acquaintances of the late Miss Eliza S. Simons, are invited to attend her funeral from the residence of Edward Simons, in Maiden Lane tomorrow morning at 9 o'clock, without further invitation.

Issue of August 20, 1830

Died, in Philadelphia, 12th inst., Mrs. Sarah Rhea, aged 32 years.

Departed this life on Wednesday evening, at a quarter past eleven o'clock, at his residence in the Northern Liberties, Philip M. Russell, Esquire, at the advanced age of ninety years...

Issue of August 24, 1830

Married, in Bumcombe Co., North Carolina on the 14th instant, Mitchell King, Esq. of this city, to Margaret, daughter of the late McMillan Campbell, Esquire.

Died, on the 8th inst. Orange County, Dr. William Rafferty, Principal of St. John's College, Annapolis...

Died, at West Chester on Saturday, 14th inst., Gracia Rubine, aged 6 months, daughter of Robert J. Turnbull, M.D. of Charleston, S.C.

Issue of August 25, 1830

Died - The relatives, friends and acquaintances of Mr. and Mrs. William Parker, are requested to attend the funeral of the former, from his late residence near the west end of Tradd St. this afternoon at 6 o'clock without further invitation.

Issue of August 27, 1830

Died, in Union District, on the 18th inst. Mr. Edward Henly, aged about 21 or 22 years.

Died, on the 9th inst. near Greensborough, Geo., Mrs. Elizabeth Randall, daughter of Mr. Vincent Sanford, aged 20 years.

Died, at St. Augustine, the 17th inst. of a consumption, Mr. Andrew Little, a native of Ireland, and lately a resident of Charleston.

Died, on the 18th, in New York, Mrs. Margaret Graham, wife of Samuel Graham, aged 35 years.

Died, at Bridgehampton, L.I. on Thursday, the 5th inst. Mr. Joseph Edwards, aged 32 years.

Issue of August 28, 1830

Died, on Tuesday night, the 24th ult. after a few days illness, of country fever, in the 31st year of his age, Wm. M'Kenzie Parker...(Eulogy)

Died, in Richborough, Geo. 21st inst. Samuel Walker, aged about 25 years, a native of New England...

Died, in Philadelphia, on the 20th inst. Mr. James M'Colloch, in the 66th year of his age.

Died, in Philadelphia, on the 20th inst., Joseph A. Wigmore, aged 64 years.

Died, at Monticello, Sullivan county, N.Y. on Monday evening last, after a short illness, Julius O. Thorn, of New York, merchant, son of Wm. Thorn.

Died, at Cardwell, N.J. on the 16th inst. in the 18th year of her age, Adeline, daughter of Stephen Gonover, Esq. of New York.

Died, in New Orleans, on the 7th inst. in the 20th year of her age, Caroline M. Saul, wife of Jas. Saul, of that city, and youngest daughter of the late Daniel Jaudon, of Philadelphia.

Issue of August 30, 1830

Died, in New York, on the 23d inst. Col. Marinus Willett, at the advanced age of upwards of 90 years.

Issue of August 31, 1830

Died, at New York, on the 3d inst. John M. Cannon, Esq. Attorney at Law.

Issue of August 24, 1830

Died, in Sumpter District, 13th inst., Mrs. Elizabeth W. Wilson, aged about 25 years, and consort of James H. Wilson, of Middle Salem, Sumter District.

Died, in New York, on the 15th instant, Mr. John H. Archer, aged 38 years.

Issue of September 4, 1830

Died - The friends and acquaintances of John H. Knauff, and of his sister Mrs. Johnston are invited to attend his funeral tomorrow morning, at 7 o'clock, from his late residence Hampstead, without further invitation.

Issue of September 7, 1830

Died in Columbia, on the 18th ult. John Flinn, aged 26, a native of Dublin, Ireland, and for some time past a merchant of that place.

Died, near Sumterville, on the 19th ult., Miss Mary Ann Chandler, aged 22.

Died, in Hamburg, S.C. on the 31st Ult., Rossetter Robbins, aged 31.

Died, in Augusta on the 1st inst. Mrs. Margaret Dent, wife of Major James T. Dent.

Died, in Norfolk, Dr. George Balfour, in his 68th year.

Died, near Tallahassee, Florida, on the 18th Aug., Charles Black, Esq. aged 52.

Issue of September 7, 1830

Died, on Thursday, the 13th ult. at her father's house in Centre township, Va., Miss Jane Wallace, in the 20th year of her age...

Died, at Covington, on the 13th ultimo, John Pritchard, aged 31, a native of Liverpool, England, formerly of Savannah, Ga. but late resident of New Orleans.

Died, in New Orleans, on the 21st ult. Thomas Johnston, a native of Charlestown, Mass., aged 21.

Died, in New Orleans, on the 22d ult., Mrs. Mary Ann Gladding, aged 37.

Died - The friends and acquaintances of Mrs. Jane R. and Mr. Peter Mood, and of Mrs. Poulton, are requested to attend the funeral of Mrs. Jane R. Mood, from her late residence corner of Water and Church-Streets, this afternoon, at 4 o'clock, without further invitation.

Issue of September 11, 1830

Died - The friends and acquaintances of the late Alfred S. Gaillard, are invited to attend his funeral this afternoon at 4 o'clock, from the residence of his brother, S. T. Gaillard, King-Street.

Issue of September 13, 1830

Departed this life, on the 10th inst. in the 54th year of his age, Nathaniel B. Mazyck, Esq. late merchant of this city...(Eulogy)

Issue of September 14, 1830

Died - The friends and acquaintances of Lieutenant Solomon Harby, of the United States' Revenue Cutter South Carolina, of his father, Isaac Harby, deceased, and of Henry J. Harby, are requested to attend the funeral of the former, from his lresidence No. 253 East Bay, tomorrow morning, at 9 o'clock, without further invitation.

Issue of September 16, 1830

Departed this life, on Tuesday last, in the 19th year of his age, Lieutenant Solomon Harby, eldest son of the late Isaac Harby, Esq....(Eulogy)

Died, in Savannah, on the 6th inst. Mr. Wm. H. Coe, aged 36 years, a native of Springfield, N.J. and for the last 11 years a native of Savannah.

Died, on the 30th of August, at Lewisburg, Va., the Rev. John E. Annan, A. M. Pastor of the Presbyterian Church, in Petersburg, Va.

Died, in New Orleans, on the 31st ult. of prevailing fever, Mr. Constant Vernier, of Paris, aged 22 years, employed at the office of French Consul.

Died, on the 31st ult. of prevailing fever, Mr. Henry D. Newman, Printer of New York, aged 17.

Died, on the 31st ult. of consumption, Miss Ann Onyet, sister of Mrs. Diamond.

* Died, on the 31st ult., Jas. Gardner, a native of Scotland.

Died, at New Orleans on the 1st inst., Chester Holmes, Esq. aged 62, formerly of Middletown, Con.

Died, at New Orleans, on the 2d inst. of prevailing fever, Charles Milhau, of Baltimore.

Issue of September 20, 1830

Died, at the residence of her father, near Manchester, on the 14th inst. Mrs. Mary Rebecca M'Duffie, consort of the Hon. George M'Duffie, and daughter of Richard Singleton, Esq.

Died - The Rev. the Clergy, the members of the Masonic Fraternity, and the friends and acquaintances of the late Rev. Dr. Thomas Mills, are respectfully invited to attend his funeral, this afternoon, at 4 o'clock, from the residence of his daughter, Mrs. Honoria Query, No. 279 King Street.

Issue of September 22, 1830

Departed this life, in this city, on the 31st ult. John Jacob Schnell, aged 59 years and 7 months...(Eulogy)

Issue of September 28, 1830

Died, in Sumpterville, S.C. on the 7th inst., Holloway James, aged about 60.

Died, in Hancock County, Va. on the 1st inst. the Rev. Edmund Shackleford, in his 50th year.

Died, at Springfield, Hanover County, Va., Mrs. Lucy Nelson, in her 88th year.

Died, at New York, on the 17th inst., John P. Geraerdt, M.D. aged 28.

Died, at New York on the 16th Gurdon Gallup, Groton, Conn. aged 33.

Died - The friends and acquaintances of Mr. and Mrs. Handsberry, and of James Handsberry, are invited to attend the funeral of the latter from his late residence No. 65 Queen-Street, this afternoon at half past 4 o'clock.

Issue of September 29, 1830

Died - Yesterday was committed to its earthly house the body of Thomas Smith, Jun. of St. Paul's Parish, Stono, who died on Saturday last of apoplexy...(Eulogy)

Died, in Richland District, S.C. on the 2d instant, Uriah J. Goodwyn, aged 46.

Died, in New York, on the 19th inst., Mrs. Zelia D. Henderson, wife of Stephen Henderson, Esq. of New Orleans, and daughter of the late J. N. Drestrehan, Esq....

Died, in New York, on the 20th, Robert Gillespie, of the firm of R. Gillespie & W. M'Leod, of that city.

Died, in New York, on the 20th, John Newell, aged 43, formerly a merchant of Philadelphia, but late a merchant of that city.

Died, at New York, on the 20th, Mr. Robert Graham, aged 76.

Died, in New Orleans, on the 12th inst. Eliza Bell Sterrett, wife of James R. Sterrett, Esq. Attorney at Law of that city.

Died, in New Orleans on the 12th inst. of Yellow fever, Mr. Benjamin Reid, of New York, aged 23.

Died, of consumption, Mr. Cyrus Turner, Printer, aged 40, a native of Massachusetts.

Died, in Cadiz, July 27th, Mr. Horatio Sweet, of Boston, Mass....

Died - The friends and acquaintances of Mrs. Martha F. Washington, are invited to attend her funeral this afternoon, at half past 4 o'clock, from her late residence Lamboll-Street, without further invitation.

Issue of September 30, 1830

Died, on Friday last, at Mrs. Clark's, about eight miles from Charlottesville,..., George Hay, Esq. a Judge of the Federal Court, for the District of Virginia, and son-in-law of Ex-President Monroe...

Issue of October 1, 1830

Died, Thursday evening, the 9th inst. Mrs. Margaret Drummond, consort of John Drummond, aged 31 years and 10 months, a native of this city...

Died, at Albany, 18th ult. Mr. John C. Johnson, Printer, and editor of the Northern Watchman, of Troy, in the 28th year of his age.

Died, at Smith's Creek, in the Parish of Sussez, King's County, N.B. on the 12th of August, Mrs. Jane M'Cowan, in the 104th year of her age...

Issue of October 6, 1830

Died, in Washington City, on the 28th ult. Mrs. Mary Orr, wife of the Rev. Isaac Orr, Secretary of the African Education Society.

Died, in Washington City, on the 25th ult., Joseph Thomas Mitchell, aged 55.

Issue of October 6, 1830

Died, in Halifax County, N.C. on the 27th ult. Mrs. Rispah Griswold, of New Jersey, aged 64.

Died, in Iredell County, N.C. Alex. M'Coy, aged 76, a native of Scotland, and emigrated to America, in 1772.

Died - at Valparaiso, on the 8th April last, Mr. John Homans, second son of the late Benjamin Homans, of the Navy Department, Washington.

Issue of October 7, 1830

Died, near Milledgeville, on the 20th ult. Mrs. Sarah A. Cheney, of this state.

Died, in Macon, Ga. on the 24th ult. Albert C. Clifton, a native of Henrico County, Va. aged 32.

Died, at his residence in Hancock County, Ga. on the 1st inst. Rev. Edmond Shackelford, aged 49.

Died, near Zanesville, Ohio, on the 14th Aug. last, Major Jonathan Cass in his 77th year, he was in several battles during the Revolutionary War.

Died, at Norfolk, Va. on the 1st inst., Mrs. Sarah Hatton, in her 49th year.

Died, at New York, on the 29th ult. Samuel Young, in his 22d year.

Issue of October 8, 1830

Died, on the 4th inst., Julia Augusta, second daughter of Dr. Thomas Y. Simons, aged 7 years and 4 days.

Died, at his residence, in Georgetown, on the 27th ult. Isaac Carr, Esq. in the 40th year of his age.

Died, at Stony Point, at the residence of his son, near Yorktown, Va. on the 22d ultimo, in his 72d year, David Meade Randolph, Esq. formerly Marshall of Virginia.

Died, at Washington on the 1st, John Francis Orne, in his 23d year.

Died, at Philadelphia, on the 27th ult. Mrs. Barbara Metts, aged 75.

Died, at Philadelphia, on the 26th, Michael Concord, in his 78th year.

Died, at Philadelphia, on the 20th ult., John Read, in his 48th year.

Died, at Philadelphia, on the 29th ult., Mrs. Margaret M. Farland.

Died, at New York, on the 29th ultimo, Miss Rhoda R. Ayers, of consumption.

Died, at New York, on the 29th ultimo, Mrs. Elizabeth Randalls, aged 57.

Died, at Providence, on the 28th ult., John J. Smith, aged 52.

Died, at Nantucket, on the 19th ult., Latham Gardner, Esq. aged 70.

Died, in Fairfield, S.C. on the 21st ult. at the house of Wm. Adger, Esq. the Rev. James Rogers, in his 62d year.

Died, at Riceborough, Ga. on the 27th ult., Dr. Ezra Gildersleeve, aged about 21, son of the Rev. Mr. Gildersleeve, of Wilksbarre, Pa.

Died, at St. Augustine, on the 28th ult., Mrs. Lydia Boyce, formerly a resident of this city.

Issue of October 11, 1830

Died, at sea on the 19th September, on board the ship Majectic, Thaddeus Pickens, a native of New Bedford, Mas., chief mate of said ship, aged 30 years.

Died, at Savannah on the 29th ult., Mrs. Mary M. Gromet, aged 64.

Died, at New Orleans, on the 26th ult., Lloyd D. Cooper, aged 20, a native of Middletown, Con.

Died, at New Orleans, on the 30th ult. at his plantation, All Saints Parish, So. Carolina, Samuel Wilson, in his 53d year.

Died, at Washington, D.C. on the 3d inst., Mrs. Margaret Carfy, aged about 72.

Died, at Philadelphia, on the 2d inst. Mary Smith.

Died, at Philadelphia, on the 2d inst., Mary, widow of the late Capt. Jacob Hinders, in the 34th year of her age.

Died, at Philadelphia, on the 1st, Henry Baker, aged 41.

Issue of October 12, 1830

Died, at Sumpter District, on the 18th ult. Samuel E. Conyers, aged 24.

Died, at Sumpter District, on the 26th William Plowden, in his 43d year.

Died, at Sumpter District, on the 3d inst., Samuel J. Nelson, aged 37.

Died, at his residence in Matthews County, Va. on the 1st inst. Capt. William Thomas, aged 30.

Died, on the 6th inst. in the county Hanover, Va., Fleming B. Cross, in his 39th year.

Died, at Baltimore, Md. on the 4th inst., Capt. Henry Dashiel, aged 62.

Died, at Philadelphia, on the 3d inst. Margaret Ross, wife of Samuel Ross, Esq.

Died, at Philadelphia, on the 4th inst. Miss Mary R. Robinson, of pulmonary complaint.

Died, at Millham, near Trenton, N.J. on the 3d inst., James E. Moore, formerly of Philadelphia.

Died, at Nassau, N.P. on the 1st inst., Mrs. Elizabeth Butler, widow of the late George Butler, Esq.

Issue of October 13, 1830

Died - The friends and acquaintances of Miss Emeline Bignon, of Miss Datty and Mesers. Devillers and Poirier are respectfully invited to attend the funeral of the former at Miss Datty's residence, Legare-Street, this afternoon at 4 o'clock, without further invitation.

Issue of October 14, 1830

Married, at St. Andrews, N.B. on the 25th ult. Capt. William Allen, of the ship Hogarth of New York, to Eliza, eldest daughter of Henry Hutchins, Esq. of the former place.

Issue of October 15, 1830

Died, in New York, on the 6th inst. in the 60th year of his age, Lawrence Finn, formerly a British officer, and only a few months in this country

Died, at Westchester, N.Y. on the 5th inst., Robert Givan, Esq. in his 81st year.

Died, at New York, Va. on the 7th inst., Samuel Allen, after a long and painful illness.

Died, at Philadelphia, on the 3d inst., Mrs. Christian Miller, in the 73d year of her age.

Died, at Philadelphia, on the 3d inst., David H. Vanie, in the 31st year of his age.

Died, at Philadelphia, on the 5th inst. Mrs. Eliza Francis.

Died, at Philadelphia, on the 6th inst. Jacob Epley, late of Penn Township, in the 56th year of his age.

Died, at Lewis, Del., Miss Elizabeth Howard, aged 19 years.

Died, on the 6th inst., at New York, Francis Hutton, aged 29.

Died, at New York, on the 4th, Mrs. Mary Kahn, in the 69th year of her age.

Died, at Boston, on the 3d inst., John P. Boyd, Naval Officer, for the port of Boston and Charlestown,...

Died, at Milton, Pa. on the 2d inst., Josiah Spurr, Editor of the Boston Commentator, aged about 35....

Died, at New Orleans, on the 29th ult., Capt. Daniel E. Tucker, of the Steamboat Natches.

Died, at New Orleans, on the 23d ult., Joseph C. Smith, aged 31, formerly of Boston, Mass.

Died, at Augusta, Ga. on the 11th inst., James R. Gould, Esq.

Issue of October 16, 1830

Married, on Wednesday evening last, by the Rev. Mr. Gibbes, Mr. Charles D. Carr to Miss Margaret Emma Prevost, both of this city.

Issue of October 16, 1830

Died, at New York, on the 7th inst., Rachel Pearsall, widow of the late Edmund Pearsall.

Died, at New York, on the 6th, Mortimer L. Snow, aged 25.

Died, at New York, on the 7th, Capt. Clement Fisher, on Nantucket, aged 26.

Died, at the Alms-House, in Lynn, Mass., Mr. Donald M'Donald, aged 108. He was born in Scotland in 1722.

Died, in Savannah, on the 11th inst., Mary Ann, wife of Geo. Lott Phillips, aged 43, daughter of Major Wm. Seale...

Died, at Havana, 1st inst. of the Yellow Fever, after an illness of seven days, Capt. N. T. Smith, of the brig William, of Savannah.

Issue of October 19, 1830

Departed this life, on the 26th Sept., Miss Elizabeth Mary Parker, aged 27 years, 1 month.

Died, in Savannah, on the 7th inst. in the 42d year of his age, Mr. John G. Fordham, a native of this city...

Died, in Fairfield District, on the 4th inst., John T. Wrenchy, aged 38...

Died, in Columbia, on the 14th inst. John B. Brown, a native of Richmond (Va.) and for several years a resident of Columbia.

Died, in Sumterville, (S.C.) on the 11th inst., Mrs. Elizabeth Bradford, aged 79.

Died, in Augusta, (Geo.) on the 11th inst., Jas. R. Gould, of Litchfield, (Conn.)

Died, in Washington City, on the 10th inst., Capt. Peter Mills, a native of New York, and an officer of the Revolution, aged 104 years.

Died, in New Haven, (Con.) on the 24th ult., Henry Daggett, Esq. aged 90.

Died, at Port Gibson, (Mis.) on the 12th ult., Darney Carr Cozby, Esq. Counsellor at Law.

Died, at Jefferson Barracks, near St. Louis, on the 20th ult., Lieut. James H. Wright, a native of South Carolina, and graduate of the Military Academy in 1829.

Died, in Mercer County, (Ky.) on the 19th ult., Col. Gabriel Slaughter, formerly Lieut. Governor, and for many years acting Governor of Kentucky.

Died - The relatives, friends, and acquaintances of Mrs. Mary Ann Gabian, of her daughter Miss Fabian and of Miss Broughton, are requested to attend the funeral of the former from her late residence No. 49, Anson Street tomorrow morning at 10 o'clock.

Issue of October 20, 1830

Died, at Fort Dearborn, Chicago, on the 29th August last, Lieut. John G. Furman, U. S. 5th Infantry, son of the late Rev. Dr. Furman of this city, in the 25th year of his age, after a short but violent bilious attack.

Died, on the 25th ult. in Williamsborough District, in the 30th year of her age, Mrs. Mary Martha Sabb, wife of Major Morgan Sabb, of said District.

Died, at Darien, (Geo.), Capt. Pearce, of the brig President Manning, of New York.

Died, in New York, on the 9th inst. Mr. Edward Buckley, aged 39, formerly of Wethersfield, (Con.)

Died, at New York, on the 10th inst., Major James Fairlie, aged 37.

Died, at New York, on the 11th inst., Mrs. Sarah Riker, aged 40.

Died, in Brooklyn, (N.Y.) on the 10th inst., Dr. Freeman Wheeler, aged 27.

Died, in Albany, on the 8th inst., Captain Richard Dunsenberry, aged 71.

Died, at sea, on the 27th ult. on his passage from Berbice to Halifax, H.B. Inglis, Esq., a native of South Carolina.

Died, at Philadelphia, on the 12th inst., Mrs. Mary Thorton.

Died, on the 12th inst., at his residence in Blackley Township, Gavin Hamilton, long a respectable inhabitant of Philadelphia.

Died, in Germantown, on the 9th instant, George Heft, in his 42d year.

Died, at New York, on the 11th inst., William Sherwood, aged 18.

Died, at Utica, on the 28th ult., Jason Parker, aged 67.

Issue of October 22, 1830

Died, at St. Augustine, on the 6th inst., John Lambias.

Died, at Salisbury, N.C. on the 6th inst., Mrs. Maria Beard, wife of Major John Beard, Jr.

Died, in Rowan Co., N.C., on the 7th inst., Mrs. Tabitha Pinkston.

Died, in Rowan Co., N.C., on the 8th, Mr. Michael Smith, aged 23.

Died, in Rowan Co., N.C., on the 13th, Mrs. Margaret Crosby, aged 52.

Died, at Rowan Co., N.C., on the 19th, Tirza, daughter of Wm. Crosby, aged 24.

Died, at Philadelphia, on the 9th inst., Mary Knight, wife of Dr. Alexander Knight, aged 37.

Died, at New York, on the 13th inst., Mrs. Ann Bunce, aged 55.

Died, at New York, on the 13th inst., Wm. W. Kingsland, aged 20.

Died, at Oswego, N. York, Col. Eli Parsons, aged 82.

Died, at Nantucket, Mass., Lathan Gardner, Esq., aged 75.

Died, at Rio Grande, Brazil, Walter F. Pleasants, aged 28, late of Philadelphia.

Issue of October 25, 1830

Died, at Beaufort, S.C. on the 14th inst., John A. Joyner, Esq. in the 29th year of his age.

Died, at Washington, D.C. on the 15th inst., the Rev. Daniel Southwell, of Murfeesborough, N.C.

Died, at Washington, D.C. on the 9th, Wm. Blair, a clerk in the general post office, and brother-in-law of Judge M'Lean.

Died, at Richmond, Va. on the 7th inst., Thomas Adkins.

Died, at Richmond, Va., on the 16th, Mrs. Elizabeth Robinson, in her 48th year.

Died, at Philadelphia, on the 16th inst., Charles Gravenstinf, aged 35.

Died, at Philadelphia, on the 16th inst., Thomas Wilson, aged 37.

Died, at New York, on the 5th inst., Mrs. Rose, wife of Arthur G. Rose of Charleston, S.C.

Died, at New York, on the 5th inst., James Kelton, aged 47.

Died, at New York, on the 5th inst., John T. Ferris, aged 22.

Died, at Providence, R.I. on the 9th inst., Oliver Carpenter, aged 85.

Died, in Bath, Mrs. Rachel Lambard, in her one hundredth year.

Died, at Edgefield, Court House, S.C., on the 18th inst., Mrs. Rebekah Frazier, consort of Col. Benj. Frazier, aged 36.

Died, at Augusta, Ga. on the 22d inst., Capt. Dabney Berry.

Died, at Augusta, Ga. on the 22d inst., James M. Thompson.

Issue of October 26, 1830

Died, at Philadelphia, on the 18th inst., Miss Ann Rawlings, in the 38th year of her age.

Died, at Philadelphia, on the 18th inst., Mr. David Thacher, formerly of Yarmouth, Mass., in the 64th year of his age.

Died, at Bridgetown, (N.J.) Mrs. Sarah Bates, consort of Mr. Benjamin Bates, Jr.

Died, at Bridgetown, (N.J.), on the 18th inst., Mr. Henry Meyers, Sen. in the 78th year of his age.

Died, at New York, on the 17th instant, Mrs. Eliza H. Van Boskerck, in the 33d year of her age.

Died, at New YOrk, on the 17th inst., Mr. John Johnson, aged 67 years.

Issue of October 26, 1830

Died, at New York, on the 17th instant, Mrs. Mary Walker.

Died, at New York, on the 16th inst., Thomas Richards, of a paralytic affection, in the 50th year of his age.

Died, at Middletown Point, (N.J.) on the 11th instant, Susannah, wife of Garret Heirs, in the 21st year of her age.

Died, at Freehold Monmouth county, (N.J.) on the 13th, Dr. Gilbert S. Woodhull.

Died, at Burlington, Vt. on the 12th inst., Francis Child, Esq. aged 67 years.

Died, at Fairfield District on the 5th instant of bilious fever, John T. Wrenchy, in the 28th year of his age.

Died, in Camden on the 9th instant, the Rev. Thomas L. Wynn, aged 32, minister of the Methodist Episcopal Church...

Issue of October 27, 1830

Died, at St. Lewis (Missouri) on the 21st July last, Mr. Eugene Brenan, formerly of Columbia, (S.C.) aged 83.

Died, at Alexandria, (D.C.) on the 26th inst., Mrs. Alice L. Waterhouse.

Died, at Baltimore on the 19th inst., William Heal, in the 64th year of his age...

Died, at Philadelphia on the 19th instant, Jacob Augustus, son of William Fisher, in the 17th year of his age.

Died, at Philadelphia on the 18th inst. in the 48th year of her age, Mrs. Mary Black, wife of Mr. Thomas Black.

Died, at Philadelphia on the 11th of October 1830, Mrs. Eliza Mason, consort of Dr. William K. Mason, in her 37th year.

Died, at Philadelphia on the 15th inst., Mathew Hand, in the 77th year of his age.

Died, at Philadelphia on the 17th, Mrs. Elizabeth Castor, relict of Frederick Castor, in the 80th year of her age.

Died, at Rochester, N.Y., on the 14th inst., Lieutenant Henry Clark, of the 5th Regiment of the U. S. Infantry.

Issue of October 28, 1830

Died, at Walterboro, on the 8th inst., Thomas Boone, Esq. aged 45.

Died, at Cincinnati, Ohio, on the 9th inst., David Kilgowe, Esq. aged 63

Died, at North Providence, R.I. on the 18th inst., Daniel Lyman, an officer of the Revolutionary Army.

Died, in Pawtuxet, on the 17th inst., Capt. James Whitney, aged 85.

Died, in New Orleans, on the 9th inst., of prevailing fever, Mr. William Nutter Young, a native of Lexington, (Ky.)

Died, on the 10th, Mr. Wilson Cook, printer, a native of Chilicothe, (Ohio).

* Died, on the 12th, Mr. Dashwood, printer, aged about 30, a native of England, and late from New York.

Died, on the 14th, Mr. Thomas Lee, of the firm of T. &. G. Lee.

Died, at New Carthage, (La.) on the 3d inst., Mr. Hampden Haile, aged 30, a native of Union District, (S.C.)

Died, in Jefferson County, (Miss.) on the 6th inst. Mr. Gabriel Scott.

Died, on the 30th ult. at the Hotel of Wm. P. Gadsbury, Esq. (Miss.), John H. Fernandis, Esq. A. M. L. D., aged 32.

Died, at his residence, at Edmond's Hill, Norfolk Co., James Hall Sloan, aged 35.

Died, at Baltimore, on the 13th inst., Samuel Stinchcomb, aged 28.

Died, at Philadelphia, on the 20th inst., Wm. Priestman, aged 83.

Died, at Philadelphia, on the 20th inst., Thomas Lewis, aged 27, of the firm of Horner & Lewis.

Died, at New York, on the 20th inst., Chas. B. Falconi, aged 37.

Died, at New York, on the 19th, Wm. A. Halstead, aged 22.

Died, at New York on the 19th, Jacob Hunter, aged 21.

Issue of October 28, 1830

Died, at New York, on the 18th, John Butler, aged 38.
Died, at Fishkill, Dutchess County, on the 11th inst., Jeromus Rapalhe, aged 74.

Issue of October 29, 1830

Died, in Union District, on the 15th inst., Mrs. Nancy Collins, consort of Gen. Joseph Collins, and mother of the Hon. Wm. T. Nuckells.
Died, in Philadelphia, on the 19th inst., Mrs. Ann Brown, wife of James Brown, Esq. late Minister Plenipotentiary of the U. S., in France.
Died, in Lower Mackefield, Bucks County, (Penn.) on the 25th ult., Daniel Wharton, in the 85th year of his age.
Died, at Noxtown Farm, in the state of Delaware, on the 8th inst., John Saul, aged 61, for many years a minister of the Society of Friends.
Died, at New York, 20th inst., Mr. Peter Mabie, late Merchant of that city, aged 60.
Died, at New York, Mr. Patrick Cady.
Died, at White Plains, Westchester Co. the 16th inst., Mr. Adam Mabee, in the 52d year of his age.
Died, at St. David, (N.B.), Stephen Sharman, Jun. aged 19 years.
Died, in Salem, (Mass.) Mrs. Sarah Putman, widow of the late Bartholomew Putman, Esq. aged 90.
Died, at her residence in Nanjemoy, Md. on the 16th inst., Mrs. Elizabeth Shepherd.
Died, on the 10th, Robert Stern, in the 21st year of his age.
Died, at Hamilton, Upper Canada, on the 29th ult., Valentine Efner, Printer, aged 40.
Died, at Quebec, on the 12th inst., Mary S. Mead Forrance, aged 23, wife of Benj. Forrance, Esq.

Issue of October 30, 1830

Died, in this city on the 26th instant, in the 30th year of his age, Mr. A. C. Cruickshank, a native of Aberdeen, Scotland.
Died, at Edisto, on the 23d inst. in the bloom of youth and meridan beauty, Miss Susan Mathewes, third daughter of John R. Mathewes, Esq... (Eulogy)

Issue of November 1, 1830

Died, at Northampton Co., N.C. on the 14th ult., John W. Harrison, Esq. clerk of the Court of Pleas and Quarter Session of that county.
Died, at Norfolk, Va. on the 21st ult. Martha H. Batt, aged 64.
Died, at Washington, D.C. on the 22d ult., Mrs. Emmeline M. Reynolds, aged 40.
Died, in the county of Brunswick, Va. on the 24th Sept., Rev. Wm. Thomas Pennington, aged 80.
Died, at Philadelphia on the 24th ult., Rebecca, wife of Thomas Philipps aged 54.
Died, at Philadelphia, on the 24th ult., Charles H. Rohr, M.D.
Died, at New York, on the 23d ult., Jane M. Michael.
Died, at New York, on the 23d ult., James V. Smith, aged 52.
Died, at New York on the 22d, Mrs. Ruth Porter, aged 67.
Died, at New York on the 22d, Mrs. Mary Holmes, aged 67.
Died, at New Rochelle on the 21st ult., Henry Starton, formerly of Brooklyn, L.I., in the 70th year of his age.
Died, in Barnwell District, on the 25th ult. after an illness of 18 days, Mr. Robert Dunbar aged about 53 years.
Died, at Athens, (Geo.) on the 24th ult., Cicero Holt, after a protracted illness of more than a year.
Died, in Lincoln County, (Geo.) 25th ult., Mrs. Elizabeth Creswell Jones, consort of Col. Wm. Jones, and daughter of Thomas Talbot, Esq. of Wilkes county, in 33d year of her age.

Issue of November 1, 1830

Died, at his residence near Warrenton, (Miss.) on the 30th Sept., Dr. Solomon C. Phillips.

Died - The friends and acquaintances of David and Susannah Ross, are respectfully invited to attend the funeral of their daughter Susannah Eliza, from their residence No. 4, Mott's Lane, tomorrow afternoon at 3 o'clock.

Issue of November 2, 1830

Died, in Rutherfordton, N.C. on the 19th ult., Owen Forman, from Onondaga County, N.Y., in the thirty third year of his age.

Died, in Northampton County, N.C. on the 14th ult., John W. Harrison, Esq. Clerk of the Court of Pleas...

Died, in the hospital at Cincinnati, on the 18th ult. of pulmonary consumption, Mr. Benjamin G. Benjamin, Printer, aged 37 years, supposed to have relations in North Carolina.

Died, in New Orleans, on the 17th ult., of the prevailing fever, Mr. Samuel Reed, aged 31 years, a native of Ireland, and late from New York.

Died, in Charlotte County, N.C. on the 8th ult., Mrs. Iby Jamison.

Died, in Charlotte County, N.C. on the 22d ult., Miss Margaret M'Kelvey.

Died, in Salem, Stokes, Co., N.C. on the 14th ult., Mrs. Bagge, aged 52.

Died, in Richmond Va. on the 26th ult., Miss Margaretta E. Digges, aged 26.

Died, at Baltimore, Md. on the 22d ult., Matthew Swan, of the firm of M. & W. Swan.

Died, at Philadelphia on the 23d ult., Samuel Brauner, aged 23.

Died, at New York, on the 23 ult., Wm. Hulley.

Died, at Baltimore on the 26th ult., Mrs. Mary Williams, wife of John Williams, aged 77.

Issue of November 3, 1830

Died, at New York, on the 25th ult., Mr. John P. Plain of consumption, aged 30.

Died, at Cross Keys, Vt., Dr. Joshua C. Cummings, a native of New Preston, Conn., aged 27.

Died, in Philadelphia, 25th ult., after a protracted illness Mrs. Rebecca Sims, aged 62, wife of Joseph Sims, Esq.

Died, in Philadelphia, 25th ult., Mrs. Mary Goodman, aged 75.

Died, at Philadelphia, on the 26th ult., after a protracted illness, Mrs. Charlotte M. B. Davison, aged 56.

Died, in Portsmouth, R.I., widow Mary Lawton, aged 99 years, a member of the Society of Friends...

Died, at his plantation, in the parish of Ascension, Lov., on the 1st ult. after a short illness, Mr. Wm. Smith Stanbury, son of Gen. Tobias E. Stanbury, of Maryland.

⋆ Died, in New Orleans, 15th ult., after a long and painful disease, Mr. Zenon Roman, a brother of the Governor elect of Louisiana...

Died, at St. Louis, on the 8th ult., after a short but painful illness, Oliver N. Bostwick, Esq. merchant of that place, and formerly a resident of New York.

Issue of November 5, 1830

Died, on Sunday morning, the 31st of October, after a protracted illness Miss Susan Hall, in the 79th year of her age...(Eulogy)

Issue of November 12, 1830

Died...In making these solemn reflections, we record the death of our deceased friend, John Allen Miles, who expired on the 5th inst. aged 18 years and 4 months...(Eulogy)

Issue of November 16, 1830

Died, at St. Augustine, on the 3d instant, Mrs. Mary Ferguson, consort of Mr. John Ferguson, and daughter of Mr. Daniel Cruikshanks, of this city... (Eulogy)

Issue of November 18, 1830

Died - The friends and acquaintances of Mr. James M. Eagar, Robert Eagar and A. Y. Walton, are invited to attend the funeral of the former, from the residence of the latter, in George Street, this afternoon, at 4 o'clock.

Issue of November 20, 1830

Died - The friends and acquaintances of Mr. and Mrs. Le Bleux, are invited to the funeral of their son, this afternoon at 4 o'clock, without further invitation.

Issue of November 23, 1830

Died - The friends and acquaintances of William H. Miller, and of Charles E. Miller, are requested to attend the funeral of the former, from the residence of his mother, No. 52, Anson Street, tomorrow morning, at 9 o'clock, without further invitation.

Issue of November 29, 1830

Died - The friends and acquaintances of Mrs. Margaret Gidiere and of Mr. J. J., J. M., and Philip N. Gidere, are invited to attend the funeral of the latter from his late residence No. 358 King-Street, tomorrow afternoon at 4 o'clock, without furhter invitation.

Issue of December 3, 1830

Married, on Wednesday evening, the 1st instant, at the Unitarian Church, by the Rev. Mr. Gilman, Mr. Richard W. Hutcherson, to Miss Mary H. Chamberlain, both of this city.

Issue of December 7, 1830

Died - The friends and acquaintances of Mr. and Mrs. William McWhinnie, and the members of the St. Andrews' Society, are respectfully invited to attend the funeral of the former from his residence, No. 71 East Bay, at 9 o'clock, tomorrow morning.

Issue of December 14, 1830

Died - The relatives, friends and acquaintances of the late Mrs. Gen. William Washington, of late William Washington, Esq. and of Mrs. Jane Ancrum, are invited to attend the funeral of the former, tomorrow afternoon, at half past 4 o'clock, at her late residence, without a more particular invitation.

Issue of December 20, 1830

Married, at Barnwell Court House on the 16th inst. by the Rev. Mr. Duncan, Edmund Bellinger, Jun. to Columbia W. Allen, daughter of John C. Allen, Esq. deceased.

Issue of December 21, 1830

Departed this life, on Tuesday, the 7th inst Timothy Ford, Esq., aged 68 years...(Eulogy)

Issue of December 22, 1830

Died - The friends and acquaintances of Mr. William H. Brown are invited to attend his funeral at 4 o'clock this afternoon, from Mr. Gouldsmith's, at the corner of Swinton's Lane and King-Street.

Died - The friends and acquaintances of Mary Madelaine Bicais, and of her son Peter Paul Bicais, are invited to attend the funeral of the former from her late residence in Market-St. opposite Mr. Ling's Coach Maker Shop, tomorrow afternoon, at 3 o'clock.

Died - The friends and acquaintances of Mr. and Mrs. John Cessford Ker, and of the late Mrs. Isabella D. Perry, are invited to attend the funeral of Mrs. Ker, from her late residence, Meeting Street, tomorrow morning, at half past 9 o'clock.

www.ingramcontent.com/pod-product-compliance
Lightning Source LLC
Chambersburg PA
CBHW021857020426
42334CB00013B/375